THE DARK SIDE OF NATION-STATES

War and Genocide

General Editors: Omer Bartov, Brown University; A. Dirk Moses, European University Institute, Florence/University of Sydney

In recent years there has been a growing interest in the study of war and genocide, not from a traditional military history perspective, but within the framework of social and cultural history. This series offers a forum for scholarly works that reflect these new approaches.

"The Berghahn series Studies on War and Genocide has immeasurably enriched the English-language scholarship available to scholars and students of genocide and, in particular, the Holocaust."—**Totalitarian Movements and Political Religions**

THE DARK SIDE OF NATION-STATES

Ethnic Cleansing in Modern Europe

Philipp Ther

Translated from the German by Charlotte Kreutzmüller

berghahn
NEW YORK · OXFORD
www.berghahnbooks.com

Published by
Berghahn Books
www.berghahnbooks.com

English-language edition
© 2014, 2016 Berghahn Books
First paperback edition published in 2016

German-language edition
© 2011 Vandenhoeck & Ruprecht GmbH & Co. KG
Die dunkle Seite der Nationalstaaten. Ethnische Säuberungen im modernen Europa

Polish-language edition
@ 2012 Wydawnictwo Poznańskie
Ciemna strona państw narodowych. Czystki etniczne w nowoczesnej Europe

The translation of this work was funded by Geisteswissenschaften International
– Translation Funding for Humanities and Social Sciences from Germany, a joint
initiative of the Fritz Thyssen Foundation, the German Federal Foreign Office, the
collecting society VG WORT and the Börsenverein des Deutschen Buchhandels
(German Publishers & Booksellers Association)

Library of Congress Cataloging-in-Publication Data

Ther, Philipp.
[Dunkle Seite der Nationalstaaten. English]
The dark side of nation states : ethnic cleansing in modern Europe / Philipp Ther ;
translated from German by Charlotte Kreutzmüller.
    pages cm. — (Studies on war and genocide ; volume 19)
    Includes bibliographical references.
    ISBN 978-1-78238-302-4 (hardback) — ISBN 978-1-78533-195-4 (paperback) —
ISBN 978-1-78238-303-1 (ebook)
    1. Genocide—Europe—History—20th century. 2. Nationalism—Europe—
History—20th century. 3. Europe—Ethnic relations—History—20th century.
4. Europe—Politics and government—20th century. 5. Europe—History, Military—
20th century. I. Title.
    D445.T42713 2014
    304.6'630940904—dc23

                                                                2013033635

British Library Cataloguing in Publication Data

A catalogue record for this book is available from the British Library.

ISBN: 978-1-78238-302-4 hardback
ISBN: 978-1-78533-195-4 paperback
ISBN: 978-1-78238-303-1 ebook

CONTENTS

Introduction

❧

The twentieth century, more than any other era in history, was shaped by organized terror. It was the century of concentration camps, gulags, and ideologically motivated mass murder. "Ethnic cleansing" was not at the extreme end of the scale of terror, partly because of the motivations behind it. The primary goal of ethnic cleansing was not to murder and destroy a population group but to forcibly remove one from a given area. Unlike the Nazis' death camps and the Bolsheviks' gulags, ethnic cleansing was not invented by a totalitarian dictatorship and did not signify a breach of civilization. Ethnic cleansing is a product of the nation-state and hence one of the basic components of modern Europe. This explains in part why it occurred on such an extensive scale, affecting at least thirty million people in Europe in the twentieth century and laying waste to a large part of the continent. This book seeks to record, analyze, compare, and elucidate every large-scale removal of a population group in modern Europe.

In keeping with the United Nations (UN) and the International Court of Justice (ICJ) in The Hague, ethnic cleansing is defined here as the systematically organized, enforced removal, by violent means and usually permanently, of a group defined by ethnicity or nationality.[1] The negative utopia of ethnic purity condemned not only people but also their culture. The organizations and individuals engaged in ethnic cleansing burned books, desecrated cemeteries, blew up mosques and churches, and sometimes leveled whole villages.

Four closely related phenomena fall into the category of ethnic cleansing. "Flight" takes place mostly in the context of armed conflicts or war and is not perceived as final by those affected. It becomes ethnic cleansing when refugees are prevented from returning to their former home on account of their ethnicity or nationality. "Expulsions," in contrast, aim toward permanent removal and sometimes occur in retaliation. They are based on a higher level of planning but not on international agreements. "Deportations" are similarly unilateral but enforced within a state and not across borders. The fourth and by far most frequent subcategory is that of contractually arranged, forced resettlements (*wysiedlenie* or *przesiedlenie* in Polish and similar terms in all other Slavic languages; *Zwangsaussiedlung* in German). The technical terms "population exchange," "transfer," and "repatriation" are favored by proponents of ethnic cleansing and are euphemistic.

Because of the atrocities committed in the former Yugoslavia in the 1990s, ethnic cleansing has been outlawed and is prosecuted by the ICJ in The Hague. But in the first half of the twentieth century, the international community arranged or participated in removing populations on a massive scale. One of the major questions this book seeks to address is why Western democracies supported an international order based on radically homogenized nation-states. While ethnic cleansing has become an internationally current scholarly term, it is harder to find a name for the people who were violently removed from their homes. Where possible, this book distinguishes between expellees, deportees, and resettlers, or refers to refugees in general, as was the norm in aid organizations and among contemporary observers.

Ethnic cleansing is often bracketed together with genocide, or seen as a precursor of the "crime of all crimes." But using a broad definition of the term genocide based on Raphael Lemkin's original concept or the "UN Convention on the Prevention and Punishment of the Crime of Genocide" of 1948 has certain drawbacks for historical analysis. Ethnic cleansing and genocide differ in several respects—in objectives, outcomes, and spatial dimensions. According to the Genocide Convention, genocide aims for the "destruction" of a certain population group. The term destruction, however, can be interpreted in a number of ways that need to be differentiated. It makes a difference whether a group and its individual members were physically destroyed or removed to another territory, although the latter could claim a high toll as well. According to international law, genocide is based on a "specific intent" (*dolus specialis*), making it comparable to first degree murder.[2] The main goal of ethnic cleansing, however, is the systematic removal of a population group from a given area, not mass, on-the-spot killing.

The difference between the two phenomena is evident not least in the impact on the targeted group: the proportion of fatalities rarely exceeds 10 percent in instances of ethnic cleansing, but can amount to almost

100 percent in the case of genocide. Czech historian Jan Havránek has summarized the difference between genocide and ethnic cleansing by comparing the fate of Prague's Jews and the German minority in Bohemia: "The path of the latter, after crossing the Bavarian or Saxon border, ended in poverty, left with only their hands and their heads to rely on. The path of the former almost always led via Theresienstadt to the gas chambers of Auschwitz."[3] It is, then, important to distinguish between different kinds of terror and suffering. Doing so does not reduce the seriousness of the crime of "ethnic cleansing". As a result of the war in Bosnia and Herzegovina, the International Criminal Tribunal for the former Yugoslavia (ICTY) imposed long prison sentences on the perpetrators of various crimes against humanity related to ethnic cleansing (*etničko čišćenje* in Serbian). But the judges in The Hague distinguished these crimes from genocide.[4] The mass murder at Srebrenica, planned in cold blood and claiming more than 7,000 lives, was the only act to be condemned as genocide.

Spatial dimensions are another important factor distinguishing ethnic cleansing from genocide. The proponents of population removals always had a place of destination and reception in mind for the refugees, usually a coethnic state. Consequently, most instances of ethnic cleansing connected distant places and involved crossing international borders. Deportations within a state, such as took place in the Soviet Union under Stalin, were the exception. While Stalin's victims were not deported to a supposed external homeland, they were nevertheless moved across huge distances. Genocide, by contrast, is often carried out on the spot, in the place of settlement of the nation affected. Examples are the countless mass shootings of Jews in Nazi-occupied Eastern Europe and the massacres of Armenians in Eastern Anatolia (although many Jews and Armenians were also deported over large distances), the recent genocide in Rwanda, and other cases in Eastern Europe that will be dealt with in chapter 3 of this book.

On account of these differences and in view of the extensive literature on the subject, this book will not engage with the Nazi genocide of the Jews in depth. From the outset, the Nazi hatred and persecution of Jews was accompanied by racist fantasies of destruction, which were not echoed to such a radical degree in any case of ethnic cleansing. It would be questionable, then, to interpret Auschwitz as the continuation or escalation of the ethnic cleansing of the Jews in the 1930s. Genocides operate as deportation to oblivion, as the rail tracks ending in Auschwitz-Birkenau eerily symbolize. However, as Götz Aly has shown, there were connections on an organizational level between the destruction of the Jews and the deportation and expulsion of other population groups during World War II.[5] The Nazis often used the same trains for routes of deportation, expulsion, and settlement, and they brought new settlers to places where the Jews had been killed or deported.

The term "ethnic cleansing" has been used so often that it is high time to define it properly. Gaining currency among scholars about twenty years ago, it was borrowed from the language of the perpetrators and their mentors. It was not, as is often presumed, invented by the media covering the Yugoslav conflict. The concept of "cleansing" appears throughout the twentieth century and occasionally even in the nineteenth century in documents, newspaper articles, and political writings concerned with the ideal of homogenous nations and nation-states and the minorities supposedly obstructing it. It originates from military references to territories being "cleansed" of the enemy in war. Communists and advocates of other ideologies harnessed the purification rituals invented by various world religions for the purpose of political cleansing. In the age of modern nationalism, these roots germinated in the idea that entire nations and their territories could be cleansed. The word "cleansing" often appears in German sources (*Säuberung*) from the late nineteenth century, but also exists as *Očysta* in Czech, *Oczyszczenie* in Polish, *Chistka* (Чистка) in Russian, and *Čišćenje* in the now defunct Serbo-Croat.[6] Correspondingly, nearly all the standard literature on problems with minorities in Europe, ethnic conflicts, expulsions, and ethnic cleansing focuses on the eastern part of the continent. But there is also the French term *épuration* and the English equivalent, "purification." This was, then, a pan-European concept that should be portrayed as such and not merely as a problem of Eastern European history. Indeed, the global dimensions of ethnic cleansing should be considered, since ultimately the practice and the ideas it was based on were exported from Europe to other parts of the world.

To explain the causes of ethnic cleansing, one must also consider all of Europe, since prominent Western European politicians and scholars were among the key supporters of ethnic homogeneity and mass population movements. These should be distinguished from "ethnic migration," which is pursued by specific ethnic groups but does not involve any clear element of force.

Sources show that the prefix "ethnic" was added only in the last three decades. It was superfluous up to the mid-twentieth century, since it went without saying that, in the context of discourses on nation, the term "cleansing" referred to national minorities. These were not regarded as a valuable addition to the nation-state but as a problem and a danger, as foreign bodies in the flesh of the nation. Eric Hobsbawm sees a direct connection between the founding of nation-states and ethnic cleansing:

"The logical implication of trying to create a continent neatly divided into coherent territorial states each inhabited by a separate ethnically and linguistically homogenous population, was the mass expulsion or extermination of minorities."[7] Norman Naimark and Michael Mann have criticized the model of the democratic nation-state along similar lines.[8] Why did common concepts of nation, and the idea and practice of the nation-state, cause minorities to be viewed as personae non gratae? This is one of the questions considered in chapter 1 of this book.

The first point analyzed is "population policy," which was predicated on the introduction of statistics. In the late nineteenth century, the population of Europe was classified according to mutually exclusive and apparently objective national categories. Zygmunt Bauman has identified this pseudoscientific, bureaucratic practice as a building block of modern Europe. The German Empire and subsequently other European states tried to manipulate the ethnic composition of their populations in disputed regions by purposeful colonizing measures. As a rule, nationalist-motivated settling was followed by attempts at forced removals in later years.

The goal of ethnic cleansing—the homogenization of nationally defined states—could equally be achieved by the assimilation and settling of coethnic groups. This book makes a departure from previous studies on ethnic cleansing by also considering these methods of striving for national homogeneity. In this way, the narrative can avoid breaking off at the point where victims lose their homeland. The history of ethnically cleansed regions and countries did not come to an end there. They continued to be inhabited by people who had to come to terms with the traumatic events they had experienced; often settlers had been refugees, too. This state of affairs has been largely disregarded by recent literature, which tends to dwell on the violence, bloodletting, and deaths, and afterward leave the "bloodlands" of Eastern Europe as if their history had ceased to exist along with the dead. Other methods of ethnic homogenization, the largely failed attempts at forced assimilation and additive population policy, are explored here.

Recent, constructivist literature emphasizes the mutability and subjectivity of concepts of ethnicity. While people did not necessarily think of themselves in national or ethnic terms,[9] states did, using these pseudo-objective criteria. Contemporary documents in English frequently utilize the term "race," indicating a rigid, starkly delineated understanding of nation. Nationality was rarely determined by individuals' self-perception or sense of belonging but by how bureaucratic institutions classified them. Millions of people were persecuted because they did not have a concrete or exclusive sense of nationality.

According to Foucault's concept of power, the very classification of nationalities may contain an element of violence. Yet one should not equate cultural repression with physical violence. Social sciences, especially, tend to speak of "ethnic cleansing" in reference to cases that have more in common with forced assimilation and do not involve any change of location. But being forced to outwardly conform, perhaps in denial of one's true identity, is not the same as being forced to leave one's homeland at gunpoint or to escape acute physical danger. The late Polish historian Krystyna Kersten made the useful distinction between "direct force," which emerges from an act or threat of violence, and "situative force," which develops when those affected see no alternative but to leave their homeland because they expect their "social death."[10] Ethnic cleansing was based on a growing asymmetry in the modern age between the perpetrators—individuals and groups—and the victims of violence. Violence in the context of ethnic cleansing was often open and demonstrative, intended to humiliate and inspire terror in the targeted group. The perpetrators of this violence transgressed religious and moral codes, attacking victims' sexuality and dignity. Due to the pointedly public and often ritual character of these actions, they can be defined as "symbolic violence."

Another characteristic of ethnic cleansing is the total and systematic nature of its execution. In this regard, a critical turning point was reached as early as the 1920s. This is shown by diachronic comparison with the early modern era. From the fifteenth to the eighteenth century, population groups that did not conform to the ideal of religious homogeneity were driven out of parts of Europe. However, these expulsions were not as well organized as in modern times and were mostly confined to specific regions or towns. Violence and terror was usually sudden and short-lived while migration, such as that of the Huguenots, continued for several decades. Many people simply converted, and this was often welcomed. Aside from a few notable exceptions, like Spain in the sixteenth and seventeenth centuries, this distinguished the religious persecution of the early modern era from modern ethnic cleansing.

A distinction should also be made between ethnic cleansing and the actions of the European settlers in North and South America and Australia. In terms of death tolls, what happened to the Amerindians and indigenous Australians had more in common with genocide. Yet as a comparative study on "forced removal" has shown, the primary objective of these deportations was to acquire land as cheaply as possible. Often enough this resulted in a logic of elimination, but there were no ideologically charged, outspoken ethnonational claims to certain territories or plans to exterminate minorities as in the twentieth century.[11]

Even though the "white" settlers treated Africans and Amerindians with colonialist contempt, the high death toll among the native populations was due less to willful murder or genocide than to the diseases and epidemics the colonists brought with them.

Yet these distinctions should not mask certain lines of continuity between early modern and modern history. There is a connection in European history between Christian and nationally defined ideals of homogeneity. Various national movements in Europe were grounded in religious or denominational motives. The Balkan nations' wars of liberation against the Ottoman Empire were also legitimized by religious causes. In the early twentieth century, the violence against "the Turks" mutated into ethnic cleansing. These connections are considered in chapter 1, on the preconditions of ethnic cleansing, under the subheading "Christian Intolerance." The title is not intended to imply that other religions were necessarily more tolerant than Christianity in all its phases and variations. The Sunnite Ottomans, for example, committed repeated massacres of the Shiites of Mesopotamia. Nevertheless, far more Muslims than Christians were targeted for mass persecution and expulsion in Southeastern Europe. This applies especially to converts and their descendants, who often held privileged positions in the Ottoman Empire but were viewed with suspicion in Habsburg-ruled Spain and Austria. The policy of jus sanguinis, defining nationality by parentage, which led to the persecution and expulsion of religious and, later, national minorities, was a European invention, as was the homogenous nation-state.

But it took a modern state apparatus and population policy to put these principles into practice on a broad scale. Statistics on nationality, which were standardized at the International Statistical Congresses of the latter nineteenth century, provided a key. Censuses recorded populations in terms of supposedly objective national criteria, down to the remotest villages. These statistics counted down to the last digit of seven- or eight-figure numbers, indicating that the state assigned nationality or ethnicity to all at birth. The compulsion to be clear on the issue grew, making life difficult for anyone with a multinational or protonational identity. There was little scope for changing nationality, which became even more difficult than changing religion in the age of religious wars. Chapter 1, on the preconditions of ethnic cleansing, and the chronologically ordered chapters 2–5, trace the process by which anonymous bureaucracies classified and ultimately segregated populations according to national criteria. From 1918, a consensus prevailed on the norms governing this classification and on the homogenization of nation-states. As is evidenced in the Paris Peace Treaties and the first period of ethnic cleansing (see chapter 2), the goal of homogenization took priority over the protection of minorities. But modern Europe was also built upon a categorization of the population according to social criteria, especially in the Soviet Union. Most literature fails to differentiate between ethnic cleansing and the social cleansing directed against noblemen, kulaks, and many other groups during the Stalinist era. Again, the difference between the two phenomena is best determined by exploring the motivations of the perpetrators.

This book focuses on the perpetrators for several reasons: a two-hundred-page survey cannot cover all aspects of a subject in depth. Furthermore, in the last ten to twenty years, much has been said and written about the victims of ethnic cleansing. The specialist literature has followed the universal trend toward victimology, which can also be observed in other fields, such as scholarship on Native Americans. By empathizing so intensely with the victims, authors risk reducing persecuted individuals and groups to mere objects of history. To analyze ethnic cleansing, it is important to bear in mind that refugees had often taken one side in an ethnic conflict; some had been perpetrators before they became victims. True, this often occurred in reaction to trauma, flight, or expulsion. But assuming victims' collective innocence would not correct previous constructions of collective guilt. This book therefore avoids polarizing victims and perpetrators but seeks to maintain an overview of the different periods and causes of ethnic cleansing. Most victim-centered literature, moreover, concentrates on one, usually nationally defined group, one example being German literature on the postwar German expellees (*Vertriebenen*). Studies in this field received strong political support in the 1950s and 1960s and were used to underpin legal, financial, and territorial demands during the Cold War. These ethnocentric victim narratives lost relevance in the era of détente, when international reconciliation was sought. In the last decade, however, narratives centered on one nation have become fashionable again, especially in Germany.[12] It is therefore false, but in line with traditional and postmodern victimologies, to claim that German suffering has been a taboo subject.[13]

A comparative approach is the best method for dealing with all these analytical and normative problems. My own dissertation of 1998 was, to my knowledge, the first comparative analysis of the flight, expulsion, and forced resettlement of the members of two nations. In the last fifteen years, a number of comparative publications have appeared on Poland, Ukraine, Hungary, Turkey, Greece, and other nations that were affected by ethnic cleansing. Due credit must go to the *Lexikon der Vertreibungen* (Encyclopedia of Expulsions), edited by Stefan Troebst, Holm Sundhaussen, and Detlef Brandes, for documenting all known cases of ethnic cleansing from A to Z.[14] Likewise, this book is based not only on Western literature, but also on current research in all the major countries affected by ethnic cleansing. The state of research in more than fifteen European and extra-European countries is outlined in the annotated bibliography and will hopefully inspire and assist further investigation.[15]

The first, pioneering book dealing with the most important cases of ethnic cleansing in Europe over the entire twentieth century was Norman Naimark's *Fires of Hatred*. The task of subsequent authors has been greatly simplified thanks to the example Naimark provides in terms of material and methodology. The title chosen by the publisher is somewhat misleading, since hatred or vengeance at most influenced the manner in which population removals were carried out. Practically all cases of ethnic cleansing were very well organized, as Naimark himself writes. Ethnic cleansing did not break out spontaneously but was planned in an exceedingly rational way. It arose from specifically European and modern ideas of nation and nation-states. But Naimark's choice of cases for comparison, in particular his consideration of the Nazi persecution of Jews in the Third Reich, does not entirely convince. To understand the flight, expulsion, and forced resettlement of Germans from East Central Europe after World War II, it is essential to consider the ethnic cleansing that took place under German occupation and German hegemony during World War II as well as Poland's shift west. Similarly, a long chain of events preceded the genocide of the Armenians in the Ottoman Empire and the expulsion of the Greeks from nascent Turkey. In this respect, Benjamin Lieberman's overview, beginning in the nineteenth century, is commendable.[16] While Lieberman's broader temporal focus is elucidating, his tendency to equate any case of communal violence with ethnic cleansing overstretches and dilutes the latter concept. But his consideration of individual victims, hatred, and suffering brings the reader closer to the events and makes them tangible.

As the many examples in this book show, only a fraction of all cases of ethnic cleansing were caused by the irrational hatred and violent conduct of "ordinary citizens." Most were the result of processes engineered by international politics and steered by nation-states. Their portrayal and analysis should then begin on these two levels.

Various forms of historical comparison can be applied to this end. This book seeks to identify the most significant similarities and differences and formulate a typology of ethnic cleansing by comparing national and regional case studies. Comparison is made both synchronously, that is, between countries, regions, towns, and villages within one epoch, and diachronically, between different times. Groups targeted by ethnic cleansing often experienced a sequence of distinct phases of flight and contractual removal. This distinction is not merely academic, as a new phase could have dramatic consequences, tipping the balance toward either life or death.

Diachronic comparison between different epochs can be illuminating, and is sometimes imperative. The ethnic cleansing that took place in Croatia and Bosnia in 1991–95 cannot be grasped without knowledge of events between 1941 and 1944, for example. Thus, the comparisons in this book also seek to show the correlations between individual cases of ethnic cleansing. The comparative method is sometimes criticized for focusing too much on structures and causal chains and for de-personalizing history. In response to such criticisms, chapters 2–5 present the masterminds of ethnic cleansing in each period. Some readers might miss more detailed information about medium-level or local agents of ethnic cleansing (many of whom have been convicted at the IJC since 1995), but their radius of action often changed dramatically depending on their orders from above. This also had a major impact on *how* ethnic cleansing was carried out, which is an equally important and elucidating topic as the "why" question.

When considering and comparing different epochs, the question of when ethnic cleansing actually began inevitably arises. According to Lieberman and Sundhaussen, it was first practiced in the nineteenth century.[17] Certainly, the flight and expulsion of about two million Muslims from Southeastern Europe following the war of 1876–78 had much in common with modern cases of ethnic cleansing. Yet the migrations triggered then were hardly organized and took place over several decades. Furthermore, the governments concerned did not yet pursue population policies or the systematic settlement of members of the respective titular nations. Ultimately, these wars and the continuing violence they sparked were triggered more by religious than by ethnic differences. This is reflected in the use of the term "Turks," which originally denoted all Southeastern European Muslims and did not primarily signify nationality until the early twentieth century. Hundreds of thousands of Muslims from the Balkans and the Caucasus followed the sultan-caliph's call to devout Muslims to return home to what remained of the Ottoman Empire. His policy shows that religious motivations still predominated over national considerations. There were, then, not only "push" but also "pull" factors at play. For these reasons, the mass flight of Muslims from Southeastern Europe and the Caucasus in the nineteenth century is analyzed in chapter 1, on the preconditions of ethnic cleansing.

The actual starting point is taken here to be the two Balkan Wars of 1912 and 1913. The population shifts that took place during and following these wars were mainly ethnopolitical and were state-planned and organized. The nation-states involved were struggling for dominance over disputed areas by means of ethnic homogenization and pursued purposeful, large-scale settlement policies to this end. The Balkan Wars also marked a watershed in another respect: they prompted the first international agreements on the "exchange" of minorities. Rather than being rooted in a supposedly unique tradition of violence and intolerance in the Balkans, they were the outcome of an international consensus and negotiations with the major Western powers. For this reason, chapter 2, on the first phase of ethnic cleansing, gives special consideration to international diplomacy and the rationality characterizing it. When I started to write this book, I did not intend to devote so much attention to diplomatic history; I was primarily interested in the motives and mechanisms of violence at the sites of ethnic cleansing. But as my research progressed, I was so astounded by the Western consensus on ethnic cleansing and its long-term continuities that these aspects became two guiding themes of the book.

The Treaty of Lausanne, which provided for the first instance of large-scale ethnic cleansing in two states, Turkey and Greece, marked the end of this period in the mid-1920s. Contrary to the opinion of many scholars, ethnically defined population shifts were not confined to the Balkans. France pursued a policy of *épuration* in Alsace, setting a precedent among democratic nation-states in Central Europe. This case shows that, with regard to the history of ethnic cleansing, Europe's "dark side" covered more than just the eastern part of the continent. To paraphrase Mark Mazower, Europe was a "dark continent," overshadowed not only by its ideologies, but also by the way its nation-states implemented them.[18] Even if this book does not intend to engage in victimology, those who suffered as a result of ethnic cleansing nevertheless deserve the empathy of today's authors and readers. The lack of any such sensitivity following the Treaties of Neuilly and Lausanne had dire consequences: the new round of "population exchanges," which began in 1937–38, was broadly accepted as a way to "solve" domestic and international conflicts.

The Munich Agreement is most often linked with the failed policy of "appeasement" toward Hitler. But it also marked a further turning point in the history of ethnic cleansing. With this agreement, the European great powers abandoned the half-hearted protection of minorities written into the Paris Peace Treaties and redrew the borders of Central Europe along ethnic lines. The new order outlined in Munich affected not only the border regions of the Czech lands but also southern Slovakia. In the ensuing years, a series of contracts were drawn up concerning the resettlement, exchange, or one-sided "transfer" of minorities in the parts of Europe occupied by Nazi Germany or ruled by its allies. Chapter 3 considers and compares instances of ethnic cleansing in the Soviet Union and asks to what extent the phenomenon is characteristic of totalitarian dictatorships. In *Bloodlands,* Timothy Snyder concentrates on the Nazis and the Soviets in his chapter on ethnic cleansing as he does throughout the book.[19] But as is shown in detail below, apportioning the blame above all to Hitler and Stalin is misleading. These dictators utilized ethnic cleansing, but tended to favor other, even more evil measures to achieve their goals. Ethnic cleansing was more characteristic of democratic or authoritarian regimes.

During the second phase of ethnic cleansing, 1938–44, "wars within the war" broke out in several parts of Europe, once again triggering large-scale flight and expulsion. This is explored in a comparative section in chapter 3 on the Ukrainian-Polish and Serbo-Croatian conflicts. These wars were inflamed by the negative example set by the Nazis, such as in their treatment of Jews and their cooperation with the radical wings of the respective nationalist movements. By the time the German army withdrew from the occupied territories in Central and Eastern Europe, a large part of the continent had been permanently scarred by ethnic cleansing. After the war, the population shifts performed under German occupation and hegemony were not treated by the West as crimes to be rectified, but as a point of departure for a new postwar order.

Chapter 4, on the third phase of ethnic cleansing, 1944–48, opens with a survey of Allied negotiations. The first point on the postwar agenda arranged by Great Britain, the Soviet Union, and the United States in the fall of 1943 was Poland, then occupied by the German Reich. The Allies decided to shift Poland westward by about two hundred kilometers, benefiting the Soviet Union at Germany's expense. The new Poland was supposed to be a homogenous nation-state without Germans or other minorities. In fall 1944, in a speech in Parliament on the future of Poland, Winston Churchill announced a "clean sweep" to finally take care of the "mixture of populations" causing "endless trouble."[20] He had in mind the ethnic reshuffling of entire East Central Europe from the western border of the Soviet Union to Germany's new eastern border. It is a striking fact that here, as in earlier cases, ethnic cleansings were planned and borders drawn by experts who had little or no specialist knowledge of the regions in question or of the logistical difficulties involved in forcibly resettling millions of people. They followed an imperial tradition of mapping that began in colonial India in the early twentieth century.

Reverberations from events in the British colonies were pivotal for the postwar order created after the Balkan Wars and after World War I. For this reason, the book in hand also takes postcolonial approaches into account and extends the scope of its investigation beyond the geographical boundaries of Europe. Another reason for going beyond Europe was the fact that the ideology and practice of ethnic cleansing were adopted in two former British colonies, India and Palestine. As the comparative case study in chapter 4 shows, at least 13 million people were affected here by ethnic cleansing in 1947–50. Highlighting the impact of European ideologies and political practices in the Near East and southern Asia might provoke accusations of "Eurocentrism," but it should be stressed once more that the utopia of homogenous nation-states originated in Europe.

After Great Britain, it was chiefly the Soviet Union that supported ethnic cleansing at the conferences in Tehran, Yalta, and Potsdam. This is as well researched as the extensive deportations within the Soviet Union. Nevertheless, the literature on "Soviet ethnic cleansing" should be approached with caution, because it tends to make little distinction between ethnic and social cleansing. With regard to Soviet history between 1938 and 1953, then, the key question to ask is when and why the state's brutal social cleansing gained an ethnic thrust.

By the 1990s, there was no longer an international consensus on mass population removals. After the long period of peace in Europe since 1945, the ethnic cleansing that took place in the former Yugoslavia seemed like a return to the bad old days of World War II. Indeed, Milošević and the Serbian nationalists in Croatia and Bosnia harnessed such associations for their own ends, deliberately evoking memories of genocidal violence under the Ustasha (*Ustaša* in Croatian) regime in order to mobilize their supporters and legitimize renewed violence. The "ghosts of the past" in the title of chapter 5, on the 1990s, were also among the causes of the violent conflicts in the Caucasus. In each case, the war shaped the course of ethnic cleansing, as is considered in special depth in the case study on Bosnia and Herzegovina. This war claimed many victims on all sides, not only among Bosniaks. As the more recent, substantially moderated statistics on casualties—and a veritable *Historikerstreit* in Bosnia and Herzegovina—have shown, Serbs did not make up a significantly smaller proportion of the victims. They constituted about one-third of the population at the outbreak of the war and about a quarter of its casualties by the end of it. It is important to note, however, that the Bosnian Serbs, unlike the Bosniaks, counted members of the

military and relatively few civilians among their victims. The highest
number of civilian Serbs in any Bosnian town died in Sarajevo, killed by
fire from the Bosnian Serb Army. It was, then, also a war among Serbs,
and not simply an ethnic war to be blamed ex post facto on one specific
nationality. Correspondingly, chapter 5 looks for political explanations
and analyzes the motives of those involved.

All four empirical chapters (chapters 2–5) refer to significant publications from the countries in question as well as Western secondary
literature. These were read in the original, as far as my knowledge of the
respective languages allowed, or via specially commissioned synopses or
translations. In addition, this book relies on various archival materials.
Back in the 1990s, I collected German, Polish, Czech and Soviet documents from the late wartime and early postwar period for my dissertation and a cowritten volume published in the US about ethnic cleansing
in Central Europe.[21] The evidence collected by the International Court
in The Hague is an excellent source for research into ethnic cleansing in
the former Yugoslavia in the 1990s. The Open Society Archive (OSA) in
Budapest has gathered many reports from the various bodies and representatives of the United Nations (some of these are also available on the
webpage of the UN), international and local NGOs, eyewitness reports
and other ego-documents.[22] For all the periods here it was also worth
re-reading diplomatic documents such as the protocols of the Lausanne
Conference in 1922–23. Last but not least, some great source collections
have been published in recent years.[23] All these materials have been
consulted to ensure an equal source basis, in terms of quantity and qual-
ity, for the entire span of the investigation. In this respect, too, this is a
book trying to write a history covering all, or at least most of Europe.

Notes

1. On the use of this term by the UN and the ICJ, see Cathie Carmichael, *Ethnic Cleansing in the Balkans: Nationalism and the Destruction of Tradition* (London, 2002), 2.
2. On the definition of "genocide" under international law, see William A. Schabas,
   Genocide in International Law: The Crime of Crimes (Cambridge, 2009).
3. Jan Havránek, "Das tragische Jahrzehnt in Mitteleuropa," in *Nationale Frage und
   Vertreibung in der Tschechoslowakei und Ungarn 1938–1948*, ed. Richard G. Plaschka,
   Horst Haselsteiner, Arnold Suppan and Anna M. Drabek (Vienna, 1997), 17.
4. See the two key trials dealing with events in northern Bosnia, where there were
   mounting violations of human rights in 1992. Despite high sentences for the accused,
   all charges of genocide were dropped in appeal proceedings. See the ICTY website
   at http://www.icty.org/x/cases/stakic/cis/en/cis_stakic.pdf and http://www.icty.org/x/
   cases/jelistic/cis/en/cis_jelistic.pdf (accessed 18 October 2010).

5. See Götz Aly, *Final Solution: Nazi Population Policy and the Murder of the European Jews* (London, 1999).
6. Cyrillic script is transcribed phonetically here, except in the case of imported names and terms, e.g., Kiev.
7. Eric Hobsbawm, *Nations and Nationalisms since 1780* (Cambridge, 1990), 133.
8. See Norman M. Naimark, *Fires of Hatred: Ethnic Cleansing in Twentieth-Century Europe* (Cambridge, 2001); Michael Mann, *The Dark Side of Democracy: Explaining Ethnic Cleansing* (Cambridge, 2005).
9. On the Habsburg Empire, see Pieter Judson, *Guardians of the Nation: Activists on the Language Frontiers of Imperial Austria* (Cambridge, 2006). See also various articles in Omer Bartov and Eric D. Weitz, eds., *Shatterzones of Empires: Coexistence and Violence in the German, Habsburg, Russian and Ottoman Borderlands* (Bloomington, IN, 2013).
10. See Krystyna Kersten, "Przymusowe przemieszczenia ludności: Próba typologii," in *Utracona Ojczyzna: Przymusowe wysiedlenie, deportacje i przesiedlenia jako wspólne doświatczenia*, ed. Hubert Orłowski, Andrzej Sakson (Poznań, 1996), 13–31.
11. See Richard Bessel and Claudia B. Haake, eds., *Removing Peoples: Forced Removal in the Modern World* (Oxford, 2009). See also Dirk Moses, ed., *Empire, Colony, Genocide: Conquest, Occupation and Subaltern Resistance in World History* (Providence, RI, 2008). On the racist elements of land grabbing, see *Patrick Wolfe, "Land, Labor, and Difference*: Elementary Structures of Race," *American Historical Review* 106 (2001): 866–905.
12. Perhaps this is why Ray Douglas's book was immediately translated and enthusiastically received in Germany. In terms of framework and scope, it is strikingly similar to much of the literature published in the early Cold War period of the 1950s and 1960s (when another American scholar, Maurice de Zayas, gained popularity among German expellee organizations). See Ray M. Douglas, *Orderly and Humane: The Expulsion of the Germans after the Second World War* (New Haven, CT, 2012).
13. On the comprehensive research in postwar Germany, see Gertrud Krallert-Sattler, *Kommentierte Bibliographie zum Flüchtlings- und Vertriebenenproblem in der Bundesrepublik Deutschland, in Österreich und in der Schweiz* (Vienna, 1989).
14. See Detlef Brandes, Holm Sundhaussen, and Stefan Troebst, eds., *Lexikon der Vertreibungen: Deportation, Zwangsaussiedlung und ethnische Säuberung im Europa des 20. Jahrhunderts* (Vienna, 2010).
15. The annotated bibliography contains full citations for all books and articles listed.
16. Benjamin Lieberman, *Terrible Fate: Ethnic Cleansing in the Making of Modern Europe* (Chicago, 2006).
17. See Holm Sundhaussen, "Bevölkerungsverschiebungen in Südosteuropa seit der Nationalstaatswerdung (19./20. Jahrhundert)," *Comparativ* 6 (1996): 25–40.
18. Mark Mazower used the metaphor of darkness in his 1998 book that provides succinct analyses of the major European ideologies. The book in hand is concerned above all with the realization and destructive consequences of these ideologies.
19. Timothy Snyder, *Bloodlands: Europe between Hitler and Stalin* (New York, 2010).
20. Winston S. Churchill, *His Complete Speeches 1897–1963,* vol. 7, *1943–49* (New York, 1974), 7069.
21. See Philipp Ther, *Deutsche und polnische Vertriebene: Gesellschaft und Vertriebenenpolitik in der SBZ/DDR und in Polen, 1945–1956* (Göttingen, 1998); Philipp Ther and Ana Siljak, eds., *Redrawing Nations: Ethnic Cleansing in East-Central Europe, 1944-1948* (Boulder, CO: Rowman & Littlefield, 2001)
22. See the holdings HU OSA, 304-0-2 (International Human Rights Law Institute, Interim and Supplementary Reports of the UN Special Rapporteur); HU OSA 304-0-6 (International Human Rights Law Institute, Materials on Ethnic Cleansing); HU

OSA 304-0-4 (International Human Rights Law Institute, United Nations, International Red Cross Committee, International Court of Justice). The OSA has also collected a great amount of press clippings.

23. Among those published in the last ten years are Hans Lemberg and Włodzimierz Borodziej, eds., *Die Deutschen östlich von Oder und Neiße 1945–1950: Dokumente aus polnischen Archiven,* 4 vols. (Marburg, 2000–2003); Stanislaw Ciesielski, ed., *Umsiedlung der Polen aus den ehemaligen polnischen Ostgebieten nach Polen in den Jahren 1944–1947* (Marburg, 2006). A similar documentation based on Czech sources (see the annotated bibliography) is in process. The files of the ICJ are an important source for the 1990s.

CHAPTER 1

PRECONDITIONS OF ETHNIC CLEANSING

$\mathcal{C\!\!\mathscr{S\!\!S}}$

Major developments in the nineteenth century paved the way for ethnic cleansing: the emergence of modern nationalism, the theory and practice of the nation-state, and the "minority problems" they gave rise to. This short list hints at the fact that contemporary analyses of the nineteenth century are inevitably done in the light of the catastrophes of the twentieth century. But the danger of arriving at teleological and sweeping causal explanations can be avoided if each period is studied in its own right. Hence, this chapter is dedicated to preconditions of ethnic cleansing and thus mostly the nineteenth century, while the main and empirical chapters of the book (chapters 2–5) focus on the agents, or initiators, of ethnic cleansing.

It is almost a truism to identify nationalism as the main cause of ethnic cleansing. Following Benedict Anderson, nationalism is defined here as an ideology of national movements, and the nation as a construct. The key question to ask, then, is why concepts of nation became so narrow over the course of the nineteenth century in Europe that ethnic cleansing became feasible in later years.

A second, closely related issue explored in this chapter is the theory and practice of the nation-state. While radical nationalists fantasized about ethnic cleansing as early as 1848, it took modern states to carry it out. In this context, it is important to consider not only nation-states in the narrow sense but also "nationalizing empires." The Prusso-German and Russian empires both pursued centrally controlled population policies with a nationalizing goal, sparking conflicts that had fatal repercussions well into the twentieth century.

National minorities emerged when nations consolidated and modern, centralist nation-states were built. Though not recognized as subjects under international law until the Paris Peace Treaties of 1919–20, minorities had been the subject of a mostly negative discourse prior to that. They came to be perceived as a problem and a danger in the second half of the nineteenth century. The third section of this chapter traces these changing attitudes toward minorities in national and international policy.

Subsequently, this chapter reflects on "European modernity," in reference to Zygmunt Bauman. Why was the population of Europe counted and categorized so rigidly and—in most countries—in terms of national majorities and minorities? How did the stark and seemingly objective distinctions drawn between ethnically defined population groups facilitate later population removals?[1] Finally, chapter 1 shows the impact of Christian intolerance on violent nationalism and ethnic cleansing.

The Ideology of Modern Nationalism

Specialists in the history of nation building and nationalism have frequently distinguished between state-engineered nationalism and cultural nationalism. This distinction was already inherent in Friedrich Meinicke's dual concept of the civic nation and the cultural nation (*Staatsnation* and *Kulturnation*). Certainly, most Western European national movements—the Norwegian, Irish, and Catalan being notable exceptions—operated in the context of already existent nation-states,[2] whereas the nations east of the Rhine were defined chiefly by culture and above all by language. "Which is the German's fatherland?" asked Ernst Moritz Arndt, one of the leading German nationalist activists of the early nineteenth century: "As far's the German accent rings / And hymns to God in heaven sings."[3] This fixation on cultural expression and institutions arose from the political context of Central and Eastern Europe. Here, national movements operated within empires where state and linguistic borders did not match. Language, literature, music, or culture was often the best and sometimes only instrument available for marking out and mobilizing the prospective members of a specific nation. In this sense, nation building took place on a horizontal, or spatial, and a vertical, or societal, level.

Cultural or linguistic nationalism is often portrayed as more exclusive than the state-led nationalism of Western Europe. But a closer look at France at the time of the French Revolution refutes this. Bertrand Barère, a member of the revolutionary Committee of Public Safety, declared in a speech in 1794:

> Federalism and superstition speak Breton; emigration and hatred of the Republic speak German; the counter-revolution speaks Italian and fanaticism speaks Basque. Let us smash these instruments of harm and error. ... To leave the citizens in the ignorance of their vernacular is to betray the fatherland. ... Citizens, the language of a free people must be one and the same for all.[4]

Barère's words reveal the centralist and leveling aspect of early nationalism. Linguistic nationalism was a crucial instrument for mobilizing society in France's defense in the Revolutionary Wars.

Rigidly differentiating between nationalism based on existing states and nationalism based on culture is problematic in view of the fact that national movements were prone to adapt their principles according to the political and social context. A case in point is the modern Polish national movement, which was initially oriented toward the state in the late eighteenth century but found itself relying on cultural factors following the country's partition. Conversely, in some nation-states, culture played a crucial role in promoting identification with the titular nation. Some examples are the German Empire, Czechoslovakia, and interwar Poland. These cases contradict the view, propounded by the older tradition of nationalism studies, that modern nationalism spread from Western to Eastern Europe, becoming increasingly narrow and aggressive along the way.[5]

Furthermore, the distinction between civic nations and cultural nations has given rise to a normative bias often articulated as an East-West conflict. Hans Kohn, and Ernest Gellner a generation after him, contrasted an inclusive nationalism specific to Western Europe with an exclusive nationalism found in Central and Eastern Europe. The same normative contrast has inspired other dualities, such as a subjective versus objective or political versus ethnic nationalism. Ernest Renan is widely regarded as symbolizing a civil and open definition of the nation. It is worth bearing in mind, though, that he published his concept of nation as the "plebiscite du jour"[6] in a period when the inhabitants of the disputed region of Alsace would probably have voted in favor of France and against the German Empire, had there been a referendum. After 1918, France applied criteria of extraction going back two or three generations to determine who was French and who was not in Alsace. In England, too, the nation was increasingly viewed as a fixed unit, defined by objective criteria. The term "race" was commonly interchanged with "nation" from the late nineteenth century in English as well as in other

European languages. Equated with race in this way, the nation came to be seen as objectively definable by immutable characteristics. Contrasting the supposedly subjective, open, civic—in short, good—Western European brand of nationalism with the "bad" nationalism of Central or Eastern Europe, then, makes little sense.

To gain a European perspective, it is necessary to ask why the prevailing understanding of nation in Western and Eastern Europe grew so narrow by World War I that it subsequently legitimized mass population removals. A look at the history of nationalism will help to answer this question. In the brief outline here, particular attention is paid to how nationalism changed over the course of the "long" nineteenth century and how an "ethnic" nationalism emerged, based mainly on origin.

Most historians agree that nation building in Europe gained crucial impetus from the French Revolution and the Revolutionary Wars. Being able to mobilize soldiers by appealing to their national sentiments gave the *Grande Nation* a considerable advantage over the armies of the anciens régimes. The sense of belonging to the nation even overrode social distinctions. Napoleon's campaigns prompted nationalist mass mobilization in many other countries of Europe. The Spanish, Russians, Germans, and other peoples fought for their rulers against Napoleon or simply against "the French" in the Wars of Liberation.

The animosity that had meanwhile built up was vented when Napoleon was finally defeated and it came to establishing a framework for peace. Prussian reformer Freiherr vom Stein wrote in 1814 to the governor of the Duchy of Berg: "Any people that wishes to be truly national does not place such trust in foreigners as to mix with them in civil community ... It is our duty to the German fatherland to cleanse the Rhineland of everything that made it un-German and holds it in such a state."[7] While Stein's primary concern in the letter was the dispatch of civil servants from France to the Rhineland, his discriminating, generalizing, and vitriolic tone is striking, and especially his use of the word "cleanse" (*säubern*).

Similar attitudes were displayed in later anti-imperial liberation movements. In 1830 and 1863, Polish insurgents rose up not only against the autocratic rule of the Romanov dynasty but also against "the Russians" in general. In the German Empire, the Polish national movement rebelled against "the Germans" and not just against the Hohenzollerns, the Irish rallied against "the English"—and so on. Crucially, these cases of national mobilization were all fuelled by concepts of opposing national collectives, of "us" and "them." This antagonistic tenet of nationalism does not require further elucidation here. It is important to note, however, that the principle of liberty—one of the supreme values of the

Western world—was often asserted against the background of ethno-national antagonism.

The heritage of feudalism in the continental empires caused further friction. These states were not unmodern or backward in general, as even the multinational empires had mass movements and mass media, two basic components of modern nationalism. But specific nationalities often dominated certain social spheres, causing ethnic and social boundaries to intersect. For example, in many areas of Poland a large part of the urban middle class was not ethnically Polish, but German or Jewish. In regions and cities where two or more nationalities coexisted, parallel societies emerged as a result. In the early modern era, peace could be maintained thanks to the established social hierarchies regulating political organization and the course of daily life. In the early, romantic phase of national movements, moreover, concepts of national territory had not yet concretized, leaving this level of conflict initially dormant.

With their twofold demand of equality for all nations and all their members, however, modern national movements challenged the very foundations of the old order. Not surprisingly, the empires resisted and sought to repress their various aspiring subject nations for many years. But by the time of the 1848 revolutions, even the most tenacious regimes were forced to yield. While the Habsburgs tried to mediate between different national movements via a consolidated state and the new constitution of 1867, other multinational empires allied with their titular nation to become "nationalizing empires." Cases in point are the Prusso-German Empire, which fell somewhere between nation-state and empire,[8] the Russian Empire, the Hungarian half of Austro-Hungary, and the Ottoman Empire in the early twentieth century.

The rulers of these empires encouraged their majority nations to collaborate in repressing the minority nationalities. In the German and Russian empires, the Polish were the main targets; in the Ottoman Empire, the persecution of Armenians and other Christian groups assumed popular dimensions long before the genocide of 1915. The nationalism of these empires was, then, just as exclusive as that of the anti-imperial liberation movements. In the case of the German Empire, it was even based on racist notions of superiority. In summary, nationalism was brought under state control, with the effect of restricting but also intensifying it.

In practice, nationalism became increasingly exclusive, especially after the 1848 revolutions. While the prerevolutionary national movements of the *Vormärz* period still frequently cooperated and coagitated, they now went separate ways. This is best illustrated by the case of Bohemia.

When the national German assembly was convened in Frankfurt, the emergent Czech national movement was compelled to take a side. Czech national leader František Palacký decided against joining the national assembly for fear that the Czechs would become just a small minority in a German nation-state. Instead, he aligned his nation with Vienna, hoping that the Austrian Empire would become a federal state with a place for a Czech-ruled Bohemia. In turn, this move had the inadvertent effect of mobilizing the German-speaking population of Bohemia. They, too, intended to fight against becoming a minority, ruled by the Czechs.

Thus, nations clashed over regional dominance as early as 1848 and in the period immediately afterward.[9] Such conflicts continued to determine the course of events in the major countries of the Habsburg monarchy and other multinational empires. The national movements' demands for political dominion were so absolute that they left little scope for compromise. In Hungary, for example, the Magyar revolutionaries' claim to power provoked resistance from resident Serbs, Croatians, and Romanians. In Transylvania, Romanian peasants rallied together and raided Hungarian-owned estates.

The failure of the revolutions in the Habsburg Empire, not least due to these burgeoning national conflicts, left all sides embittered. In a polemic written by Czech Democrat Karel Havliček, the author expressed his hope for the "extinction" not only of the Germans in Bohemia but also of the "Germanized," meaning those of Czech descent who had conformed to German ways. Romanian revolutionary and later historian Nicolae Bălcescu gloated that Transylvania had been completely "cleansed" of Hungarians.[10] Too much importance should not be attached to these and similar writings, since they constituted no more than fantasies of ethnic cleansing. But the mutual hostility and deadlock caused by the disappointment of the revolution and so many unfulfilled political and social demands had given rise to an undeniably volatile state of affairs. Furthermore, the national movements had formulated clear, exclusive territorial claims during the revolution, which extended far beyond the heartland of the respective nations and added to the tensions.

A case in point is the German national movement, which ended its alliance with the Polish national movement of the *Vormärz* period in 1848. When the German national assembly discussed the territory of the future German nation-state, it was agreed that it should include the Prussian partition of Poland, where the German-speaking population was in the minority. Liberal assembly member Wilhelm Jordan justified this as "healthy national egotism."[11] This imperial stance was one of the factors prompting the mobilization of the Polish national movement in

Poznań, which for the first time united nobility, urban bourgeoisie, and peasantry. In turn, an active national minority was formed in Prussia.

Prussia now had to address the question of how to deal with this minority. From the Congress of Vienna to the founding of the empire, Prussia wavered between pursuing an active policy of Germanization and making limited concessions to the Polish elites. For many years, it hoped that the situation would sort itself out eventually. This attitude was widely held among Europe's liberals. John Stuart Mill proposed that developed nations should simply absorb the minorities in their territory, since they were considered "backward parts of the human race."[12] Friedrich Engels, too, assumed that the "unhistoric" nations would eventually disappear.

When assimilation failed to happen as expected, the liberal ideologues of the nation in Germany and other countries grew more aggressive. In his 1855 novel *Soll und Haben,* Gustav Freytag portrayed the German-Polish conflict as a life and death struggle.[13] According to Freytag, the Germans' supposedly higher culture gave them the right to rule over the Polish partition and Germanize its population. He justified this with racist arguments that gave a foretaste of his later activities in the German colonial association. *Soll und Haben* was the biggest-selling German novel of the nineteenth century. It disseminated prejudices against Poland, and Slavs in general, among a huge readership. In reaction to Freytag, among other things, the later Nobel Prize winner for literature Henryk Sienkiewicz portrayed the Germans as ruthless colonizers and archenemies of the Polish. But Sienkiewicz's own views of the Poles' eastern neighbors reflected some of the colonial attitudes he criticized. According to him, the Ukrainians were merely raw material in need of stern guidance.

Belligerence and antagonistic nationalist attitudes took on epidemic proportions in Europe. The consequences were only kept in check by the stable international order and increasing economic prosperity. Why did so many European intellectuals support an aggressive, even racist nationalist stance? One explanation is that 1848, the year of revolutions, sparked a destructive competition between writers, journalists, artists, and even composers. There was considerable personal advantage to be gained by distinguishing oneself as a champion of "national interests," against foreign cultures. This is again illustrated by Gustav Freytag, a lesser realist in comparison to Émile Zola, who published as widely in his capacity as German colonial association activist and "Poland-eater" as he did as a novelist.

Nationalism became further radicalized in the light of Darwinism. Since the Age of Reason, nations had been perceived as organisms. Applying Darwin's theories, they were the product of a selection that only the fittest survived, analogous to evolution in the animal kingdom. As a consequence, nations grew more aggressive and imperialist toward the outside world and more discriminatory toward their own societies. Soon all the nations of Europe felt existentially threatened by the great powers' mounting imperialism, prompting them to condemn not only their international rivals but also the minorities in their own countries.

Modern racism was fueled by the experience of colonial rule. In the overseas territories, racism was part of everyday life and legitimized European domination. The principle of ethnic and racist purity determined life in the colonies, from bans on "mixed marriages" to mass resettlements of unwanted population groups. Colonial rule also went hand in hand with ruthless violence, leading to the first genocide—that of the Hereros—of the twentieth century.

While the impact of the colonial experience on Europe is disputed, it is widely agreed that World War I was attended by a massive increase in violence and radical nationalism, both on the battlefields and the home fronts. Even relations between formally neutral nations became strained. Widespread nationalist violence continued after the war and was commonly regarded as a legitimate means to assert "national interests," both by the nation-states deploying state-sanctioned violence and by various European societies. German *Freikorps* fought Polish paramilitary units in Upper Silesia; Polish and Lithuanian and Polish and Ukrainian units clashed further east; Southeastern Europe knew no peace for years. What all these conflicts had in common was the fact that they were not conventional wars between states. The aggressors were groups that had mobilized and organized themselves in the name of the nation. These groups rallied together under ethnically defined criteria of nationality. On a social level, too, unequivocal loyalty was demanded.

The Nation-State in Theory and Practice

The French Revolution marked not only the dawn of modern nationalism but also the arrival of a new concept of state. In feudal systems, the state was removed from its inhabitants, who were mostly serfs. Individuals rarely came into contact with the state and if they did, it was only indirectly. This changed in the modern nation-states and empires. Their citizens—de facto, for many years, wealthy, male elites—could at least in theory now determine who ran the country. As a consequence, the state became dependent on their loyalty and participation. Governments hence had a vested interest in molding their citizens and societies into a cohesive unit.

The project of the nation-state was originally one of peace. Liberals believed that a nation-state order in Europe would bring an end to the frequent wars between the anciens régimes.[14] Friedrich List, Guiseppe Mazzini, and the leading supporters of the various national movements in Europe hoped that nation-states would not battle each other if they were territorially saturated and democratically governed. This utopian liberal vision, which was revived after World War I, proved untenable for a number of reasons.

For one, nation building in Europe triggered an unexpected dynamic, causing the number of national movements to double over the course of the nineteenth century. Although some national movements were initially prepared to accept a future within an empire, they all demanded their own, unified territory. This was the logic of "territorialized" thinking, as Charles Maier put it, which had been a powerful force in the revolutions of 1848.[15] In many parts of Europe, there were not only one but several active national movements. Conflicts multiplied in regions that could not be easily allotted to any one potential or existent nation-state.

Second, the maxim that every nation should have its own state shook the foundations of the international order. The multinational empires were the first to falter. The Ottoman and Habsburg Empires successively lost power and territory during the nineteenth century. In 1859, 1871, and 1878, the Italian nation-state, Germany with its halfway position between empire and nation-state, and the Balkan states, respectively, were founded at the expense of the Ottoman or Habsburg Empires. In 1918–19 there was a further wave of nation-state founding, this time to the detriment of the Russian and German empires.

As the situation in many border regions illustrates, the new order did not bring peace but sparked further conflicts. The dispute between France and the German Empire over Alsace and Lorraine poisoned relations between the two neighbors and created a permanent trouble spot in Central Europe. The Southeastern European nation-states fought against the Ottoman Empire and among themselves over border regions such as Macedonia. The contemporary European public, however, did not perceive the Balkan wars in 1912–13 and the brutality with which they were fought as a consequence of the new order of nation-states but as a problem peculiar to "the Balkans."[16] The Paris Peace Treaties of 1919–20 replicated the order set up after the Balkan Wars in Central and Eastern Europe and equally failed to establish lasting peace.

Furthermore, the new nation-state order gave rise to new minorities. In each phase of nation building, some national groups were completely passed over, such as the Poles in the nineteenth century and the Ukrainians at the Paris Peace Conference. After World War I, the former members of imperial nations, such as the Germans in Poland and the Hungarians in Slovakia, saw their status shrink. Rogers Brubaker has described this problem in his book *Nationalism Reframed* as a triangular conflict between a nationalizing nation-state, an external homeland, and an irredentist minority.[17]

It is important to note that national minorities often first emerged when nation-states were created. The colonists who settled in eastern Galicia under Joseph II, the German-speaking urban bourgeoisie in Austrian Silesia and the Prussian Junkers in the Grand Duchy of Posen before 1918, for example, had hardly anything in common or any contact with each other. But over the course of the interwar period, they were forged together as the German minority in Poland. Similarly, the so-called Sudeten Germans were a product of Czechoslovakia.[18] These and other cases illustrate a dual process of nation building, defining the titular nation on the one hand and the respective minorities on the other.

Perhaps the nation-states' internal conflicts could have been resolved with the help of intergovernmental organizations and a longer, lasting peace. Developments in the Austrian half of the Habsburg Empire seemed initially promising in the early twentieth century, when a number of regional "compromises"[19] were reached. By the late 1920s, the Central European nation-states had achieved a level of domestic and international stability. Compromise was considerably more easily reached in states that were perceived as permanent and that had various instruments of conflict mediation, such as a democratically elected parliament and an independent judiciary. It would be wrong, then, to view events between the wars as an inevitable progression barring any chance of the various nation-states ever coexisting with their minorities.

Nation building was more liable to trigger conflicts the later it occurred. In the eighteenth and nineteenth centuries, little resistance was offered to the constitutional nation-states emerging from the old dynastic states. But the wave of nation-state founding in Southern, Central, and Eastern Europe between 1859 and 1878 was accompanied by several wars. The third phase of nation building after 1918 remained contested for years afterward. In much of Europe, World War I dragged on in a number of regional conflicts: at Germany's and Poland's eastern borders, in Southeastern Europe, and in some parts of Western Europe, such as Ireland. All these conflicts were fought over the borders of nation-states, not only by the armies of the respective warring parties but often by the members of rival national movements. Even in areas where agreements seemed to be reached fairly swiftly over contested borders, such as in Alsace and Bohemia, mastery was ultimately gained by violent means. One case illustrating this is the Kaaden massacre in 1919.[20] War was a constant but poor founding father of nation-states. World War I, especially, which continued de facto into the early 1920s across much of Europe, caused the collapse of administrative, legal, and communication systems as well as widespread impoverishment.

In spite of all the unifying utopias of nationalism, modern European nation-states had only limited powers of integration, at least compared with the empires preceding them. In the early modern era, the Polish Noble Republic, the Russian Empire, the Habsburg Empire, and the Ottoman Empire co-opted regional elites by raising them to the nobility or granting them local self-government. Hence, Tatars became loyal Russian and Polish citizens, the members of various regional elites became loyal citizens of the Habsburg Empire, and southern Slavs could become Muslim subjects of the High Porte. This diachronic comparison shows that while nation-states succeeded in vertical nation building—aligning all social classes nationally—they did not achieve the horizontal integration of culturally or linguistically distinct groups in the same way.

To counter their inherent instability, the nation-states founded after the mid-nineteenth century installed centralist administrations. Although the German Empire technically forms an exception here, it did not advertise its federal structure to the outside world. State elites determined how the nation was to be defined—what was to be considered German, Polish, or a hybrid national identity, such as Czechoslovakian or Yugoslavian. Such impositions met with considerable resistance from an early stage. There were several revolts in Sicily that, though mainly rooted in social grievances, also contained a regionalist element. The Italian state continues to suffer from internal differences to the point of separatism to this day. The regions of the German Empire grew together between 1871 and 1914, in spite of the many social and denominational divisions, not least on account of state efforts to promote nationalism. But there were breakaway movements in Germany after World War I, most notably in Upper Silesia, and intermittently in Bavaria and the Rhineland. The Spanish Civil War was not only a conflict between Leftists and Fascists but also between the centralist nation-state and the regions that had their own national movements.[21]

As Eugene Weber has shown in his classic book *Peasants into Frenchmen,* of all the large European nation-states, France was the most successful at engineering the vertical integration of the nation.[22] But in the interwar period, resistance grew even here toward the centralist order and the definition of the nation. France's nationalizing policy in Alsace, based on the maxim "purifier, centralizer, assimiler," was a failure.[23] Even the relatively well-established, older nation-states in Western Europe were, then, not assured a smooth ride. Ultimately, the older nation-states in Europe stabilized thanks to the long period of peace preceding 1914 and, above all, the economic upturn it facilitated. The nation-states in East Central and Southeastern Europe were in a less favorable position from the outset. They struggled not only with the consequences of war but also with huge internal differences on a political, economic, and cultural level. The regions making up Poland, Czechoslovakia, Romania, and the Kingdom of Serbs, Croats and Slovenes (renamed Yugoslavia in 1929) possessed very different traditions. Some of them had enjoyed regional self-government for decades before they were suddenly expected to submit to the rule of newly formed states. The elites and authorities from the respective capital cities were frequently perceived as aliens. The economic challenges were equally daunting, since there had been no common market prior to 1918 in Poland, Romania, Czechoslovakia, or Yugoslavia (or Ireland).[24] In the process of rebuilding Poland, even the rail tracks were found to not fit together. There was a consensus among the respective elites that this challenge could only be surmounted by a unitary state with a strong government. For this reason and following the French example, centralism became the main model for the domestic organization of newly founded nation-states. This pattern was consolidated by France's victory in World War I, which raised the republic's status even higher.

The European nation-states would have been better advised to make concessions toward their regions and minorities, and to regard national alignment as an option and not an obligation, but the fear was too great that any kind of cultural or local autonomy would undermine the state and the nation. Even municipal self-government was severely limited in all nation-states founded or expanded in 1919. This had unforeseen consequences, since it immediately shifted political conflicts to a national level and made the nation-state responsible for problems it had not necessarily caused.[25] The weaker the state and its government, the more it relied on a policy of nationalization and the more it repressed its minorities, if necessary by violent means.

These in turn resorted to violent and, in some cases, terrorist methods. Radical Ukrainian, Croatian, Macedonian, and Irish nationalists fought the nation-states they rejected at home and abroad in ways reminiscent of the Islamist terror attacks of recent years. There were, it is true, phases of détente in all nation-states founded after World War I, especially during the period of economic recovery in the 1920s. But violence remained a generally accepted means of asserting "national interests."[26]

Holm Sundhaussen has proposed that the structural causes of ethnic cleansing in Southeastern Europe lie in the fact that the two least flexible models of nation-building were employed here: the German model of ethnic nationalism and the French model of the centralist nation-state.[27] This theory can be applied with some modification to the countries of East Central Europe and parts of Western Europe (e.g., Ireland). Sundhaussen's observation of a process of negative learning is, however, certainly right. The model of the liberal nation-state was followed in parts of Europe where the demographic, social, and political circumstances and even the timing made it inappropriate. In spite of intensifying conflicts and successive crises, authorities mobilized all their powers to achieve the goal of a homogenous nation-state rather than adapting the model to the given situation. The established states set a bad example in this respect, especially Germany before World War I with its destructive policy toward Poland and its Polish minority and, later, France with its *épuration* of Alsace and Lorraine.

"Minority Problems"

On the whole, absolutist states regarded immigrants as a boon. This is illustrated by Prussia's absorption of Huguenots, who went on to contribute to the country's upswing, just as its rulers had hoped. Russia and Austria also enlisted the help of thousands of specialist and agrarian colonists to strengthen their economies. This policy of active settlement, or *Peuplierung*, introduced groups that could be anachronistically labeled minorities. But it did not cause any major political problems for the anciens régimes as long as societies attached more importance to status than to linguistic or cultural peculiarities.

This changed with the rise of modern nationalism. Integrating those imagined to belong to the national group in a modern nation implied excluding others. This mechanism worked outwardly—the antagonism between the "archenemies" Germany and France illustrates this—as well as inwardly, against fellow countrymen and women who spoke a different language, observed a different faith, or came from a different background. Attempts made by nation-states during the nineteenth century to enforce a standard culture and language proved counterproductive, especially in their borderlands.

The Polish partition in the east of the German Empire was a case in point. Prussia had legitimized its rule by arguing that German culture was superior and that the Poles were not in a position to build their own state. By this logic, the Germans were the vehicle of culture, or *Kul-*

turträger, to which the Poles would have to conform. Other European nations were similarly convinced of being the "bearers of culture" for "lesser" nations, such as Serbia in relation to the Slavic Muslims and the Albanians, and the Poles in relation to the Ukrainians, Byelorussians, and Lithuanians.

When it became clear that assimilation was not going to be achieved, more radical solutions were sought. Heinrich Wuttke, a Silesian-born, Leipzig-based history professor and member of the German national assembly in 1848, called for giving Poles the choice between assimilation and expulsion.[28] The influential scholar and writer Paul de Lagarde wrote in 1855: "It is doubtless unacceptable for any nation to exist in another nation; it is doubtless imperative to dispose of those who ... have caused this decomposition."[29] The fantasies of ethnic purity harbored by the revolutionaries of 1848 were crystallizing into concrete demands, since there was a state with the mechanisms in place to realize them.

Although Bismarck could not and would not go as far as Wuttke and Lagarde demanded, he incorporated Poznań into the North German Confederation in 1866 without making any concessions to the resident Polish. The suppression of Poles was also legitimized with religious arguments. Prussia, a predominantly Protestant state, attempted to reduce the influence of the Catholic Church. Soon after the foundation of the German Empire, Bismarck started the so-called *Kulturkampf.* He clamped down on the Catholic clergy and institutions, e.g. by imprisoning priests and closing Catholic schools. The Kulturkampf was also used to suppress the Polish population. In 1885–86, when the government struck a deal with the Catholic Church, it continued its anti-Polish policy by other means. In a cloak-and-dagger operation, 32,000 Poles and Polish Jews were deported to the Russian partition of Poland.[30] A "settlement law" was passed soon after, which provided for German farmers to migrate to the Prussian partition and was specifically aimed at demographically undermining the Polish minority and especially its aristocratic elite. Yet all this pressure from one of the most powerful states of Europe had little effect other than to consolidate the resistance of the Polish minority.

The state's "negative policy on Poland"[31] influenced and hardened attitudes within Germany. Gustav Freytag was joined by the writer Theodor Fontane in articulating vague fears of foreign infiltration. The sociologist Max Weber offered concrete suggestions on how to keep the Poles in line, and the anti-Polish sentiments of the pan-German nationalists entered into the political mainstream, with the imperial diet voting in favor of expropriating Polish landowners in 1908.[32] While this was in fact in breach of the constitution, as critics pointed out, dealing with an unwanted minority took priority over such technicalities.

Where Alsace and Lorraine were concerned, the German Empire was forced to show more consideration. Here, ironically, France contributed to the demographic manipulation. In the Franco-German Peace Treaty of 1871, Paris had secured a "right of option" for French citizens who found themselves on German territory after borders were redrawn.[33] These citizens could retain their French nationality by leaving their homes and immigrating to France. There was no option allowing citizens to be simultaneously French and German, or simply Alsatian. The nation-state required citizens to align themselves unequivocally.

This compulsion toward clear national identification also played a major role in establishing the nation-state order in Southeastern Europe. At the Congress of Berlin in 1878, Greece, Serbia, Romania, and Bulgaria signed agreements committing themselves to tolerate religious minorities. At first glance, these documents look like precursors to the minority protection devised after World War I. But the negotiations were mostly concerned with the Jewish minorities in the Balkan countries.[34] The Southeastern European Muslims had no lobby. Consequently, when the Muslims remaining in Serbia, Romania, and Bulgaria gained the right to opt for Ottoman citizenship, they launched a wave of emigration. Greece and Serbia tried the hardest to urge their Muslim minorities to emigrate. Romania set about nationalizing the Dobruja region, acquired in 1878, primarily by settlement and education measures.[35] Bulgaria tolerated Turks and Pomaks (Bulgarian-speaking Muslims) on the premise that they were ethnic Bulgarians of Muslim faith. Serbia took a similar approach after 1912 in Sandjak and Macedonia. It was assumed that these minorities would eventually assimilate or emigrate of their own accord.

As is shown in greater detail in the following chapter on the first phase of ethnic cleansing, the drive toward national homogenization gained a new dimension with the Balkan Wars of 1912–13. All the belligerent states tried as far as possible to reduce their minority populations, especially in their newly acquired territories, where they also settled members of the titular nation. Not only were Muslims targeted, as after 1878, but also ethnonationally defined minorities, such as the Bulgarian-speaking population in northern Greece and the Greeks in Bulgaria. Several hundreds of thousands of people were forced into exile during the Balkan Wars. Willful expulsions continued even after the armistice and the conclusion of peace treaties.

The latter deserve special consideration because they reflect the changed attitudes toward minorities across Europe. At the peace conference in Bucharest in 1913, the Southeastern European states opposed any protection of minorities on principle, although their newly expanded territories came with substantial populations not belonging to the titular nations. Though aware that new minorities were thus being formed, the great powers did not undertake to defend them. The United States was alone in intervening on their behalf in Bucharest, no doubt prompted by the disturbing report by the Carnegie Endowment for International Peace, one of the first NGOs set up to help minorities and protect their human rights.

Afforded little protection, minority members continued to flee throughout Southeastern Europe after the Balkan Wars. In 1914, Greece and Turkey conducted intense negotiations over an "exchange" of minorities, which would have affected considerable areas of both countries and about a million people. The outbreak of World War I prevented a final agreement from being reached. But in 1919, in the Paris suburb of Neuilly, two other former opponents, Bulgaria and Greece, arranged the "reciprocal emigration" of their minorities in Macedonia and Thrace, which ultimately dictated the fates of 153,000 people. The treaty is of crucial importance, marking the first time an ethnic border was drawn across an extensive geographical area under the aegis of the European great powers. Moreover, state authorities had never before driven such a large number of people into exile during peacetime. The population removal was combined with a settlement policy aimed at dominating disputed border regions by members of the titular nation. These two sides of ethnic cleansing were closely linked on an ideological and a practical level.

Minorities were viewed in an increasingly negative light across Europe during World War I. Especially in the Russian and Ottoman empires, they were suspected of being enemies of the state and potential traitors and deported en masse. A million Jews and Germans, who lived close to the front or on supply routes, were deported within the Russian Empire. The Ottoman Armenians suffered an even worse fate, and Serbs were deported from and within the Habsburg Empire. Often, military security was cited as the reason for the deportations, but negative stereotypes that had emerged prior to 1914 were a deeper-rooted cause. Russian officers' textbooks of 1907, for example, warned readers that Jews, Poles, and Muslims were disloyal and untrustworthy.[36] It seems highly improbable that the Germans living in Russia would actually have collaborated with the German Empire. Moreover, the Russian Jews possessed no external homeland with which they could have allied themselves. The danger of collaboration was perhaps more real in Asia Minor, where Armenian nationalists demanded their own nation-state at the expense of the Ottoman Empire and did in fact fight on the side of the Russians. In Anatolia, however, the actual military threat posed by the Armenians was already diminishing when the Young Turk government started the mass deportations. Since it was clear that few of the deportees would survive the march through the Anatolian highland and parts of the Syrian Desert, this deportation is commonly regarded as a case of genocide.

Even in places far away from all fronts, a radical view of minorities was gaining currency. In 1915, Swiss ethnologist Georges Montandon publicly supported the "massive transplantation" of minorities in Europe in a pamphlet entitled *Frontières nationales: Détermination objective de la condition primordiales nécessaire à l'obtention d'une paix durable.*[37] He called for minority exchanges between states as well as one-sided "transfers." As the title of his publication indicates, Montandon was already thinking about a postwar order in Europe. German-Jewish writer Siegfried Lichtenstädter was another advocate of population shifts for securing peace.[38] In England, the spectrum of politicians and experts supporting an "exchange of populations" ranged from the right wing of the Conservative Party through to the Labour Party.[39] The apparently rational solution they propagated was based less on knowledge of the regions in question than on colonial ideas. Montandon obviously did not believe that less-developed nations would be capable of resolving their conflicts in as civilized a manner as his native Switzerland. Lichtenstädter did not foresee the devastating implications of the actions he demanded for the minority to which he himself belonged.

Most writings on minorities in the run-up to World War I and between the wars applied a striking lack of differentiation. There were three basic types of minority: first, population groups related to coethnic states; second, stateless minorities such as the Ukrainians; and third, diaspora ethnic groups with no clearly defined territory, such as the European Jews and the German colonists in the Russian Empire. Although not all minorities held the same potential for political conflict, they were all put under increasing pressure to assimilate. Simply being termed a "problem" was stigmatizing—in contrast, nobody spoke or speaks of "nation-state problems."

Over the course of World War I, nationalist views became intensified, not only by the propaganda filtered in from above, but also from below and in everyday life. Heightened nationalisms could be observed among societies coexisting in the same country or region, such as the Poles and Ukrainians in Galicia. In these and other multiethnic areas marked by extreme poverty and hunger, such as Krajina and Kosovo, sufferers turned to the support of their ethnic kin.[40]

After World War I, popular opinion on minorities sank further across Europe, not only in view of the numerous armed conflicts that flared up over the new national order. US president Woodrow Wilson's "Fourteen Points" speech of January 1918 and Charles I of Austria's manifesto of October 1918 seemed to invite the use of force in drawing the borders of the collapsing empires' successor states. In the confusion that followed the war, haphazard demobilization allowed the remains of regular armies and paramilitary units to step into the power vacuum and continue the hostilities. In many parts of Europe, then, World War I did not end in 1918, but dragged on de facto until the early 1920s. Fighting continued in the east of Germany and Poland from the Baltic Coast to the Carpathian Mountains, the eastern Adriatic Coast, the southern part of the Balkan Peninsula, and western Asia Minor. Europe was pocked from north to south and west to east with fault zones where battles were fought over who would claim majority or minority status in future.

The latter was obviously not an inviting prospect. Many people felt there was no place for them in the new or expanded nation-states in East Central and Southeastern Europe, and a major wave of migration began after 1918. More than 1.2 million Germans and Hungarians emigrated from their countries' lost territories. Migratory routes varied in popularity according to how attractive the countries of origin and destination were. Far more members of the new minorities emigrated from Poland and Serbia, for example, than from Czechoslovakia. This illustrates the fact that ethnic migration, that is, the emigration of a group defined by nationality or ethnicity, is not necessarily equivalent to organized and violently enforced ethnic cleansing. Neither was migration among minorities after World War I confined to Eastern Europe. About 150,000 people classified as German were forced to leave Alsace. A debate was recently sparked in Ireland on whether the emigration of more than half of the republic's Protestants following independence constitutes ethnic cleansing.[41]

Rogers Brubaker has summarized the mass population movements after World War I as "post-imperial migration"[42] in reference to the collapse of the European empires. A more accurate term would be "nation-state-induced migration," since countless members of minorities left their homes not as the empires were collapsing, but after the postimperial nation-states had been founded and the borders had been redrawn. These migratory movements were very much in the interests of the nation-states and the League of Nations, since they considerably reduced the minority populations of many countries and took the nations closer toward their goal of ethnic homogeneity.

In the various regional conflicts following World War I, minorities were rarely on the side of the nation-states that ultimately prevailed. There was, then, a deep sense of mistrust within societies, especially toward the "losers" of the war: the Germans in Poland and Czechoslovakia, the Hungarians in Romania, Slovakia, and Serbia, and the Bulgarians outside their truncated territory. But even minorities that had taken no side during the phase of violent nation building, such as the Jews in eastern Galicia, were held to be suspect. Polish troops had barely put down the Ukrainian insurgents in November 1918 when a pogrom broke out in Lwów (L'viv in Ukrainian) against the Jewish population, which claimed the lives of at least seventy people.[43] In Alsace, where the arrival of French troops in 1918 was generally welcomed, the French state monitored and persecuted the population. Not only potentially irredentist minorities were viewed with suspicion, then, but all groups obstructing the ideal of a homogenous nation-state.

The violence toward minorities during World War I and attending the creation of nation-states was etched onto the memories of its victims. But it did not prevent some national minorities from participating in the governments of newly founded nation-states in the 1920s. One example is the German parties in Czechoslovakia, the most stable and liberal of the nation-states founded in 1918–19.[44] But the memory of the dead of any given group, whether among the majority or minority population, could be harnessed at any time to legitimize further violence.

The protection of minorities inscribed in the Paris Peace Treaties did nothing to change either the negative attitudes toward or the actual discrimination against these population groups. The treaties did not address the Western European nation-states or Germany. Not even Italy was required to commit to protecting its minorities, although it had absorbed sizable German-speaking and Slovenian minorities as a consequence of its territorial expansion in the north and east. There were, it appeared, two classes of international law: one for the "young" East Central and Southeastern European nation-states and one for the longer-standing nation-states, which were presumed by the international community to be already homogenous. Those states required to observe minority protection saw this as an infringement of their sovereignty and became even more determined to achieve homogenization.[45]

Moreover, the treaties provided for concrete measures to reduce minorities. The second treaty in the Paris series, the Treaty of Neuilly between Bulgaria and Greece, another two opponents during World War I, contained a passage on the "reciprocal and voluntary emigration" of ethnic minorities.[46] This planned migration, which took on an increasingly compulsory nature over the years, provided the blueprint for the 1923 Treaty of Lausanne, in which the great powers, Greece, and Turkey resolved the first extensive ethnic cleansing of two European states. It was neither of the two former enemies who proposed an "exchange of populations" but the British foreign secretary, Lord Curzon, who chaired the peace conference. Lord Curzon introduced this technocratic term to the debate and insisted that "exchange" on a voluntary basis would not be sufficient: it would have to be compulsory and without exception.

The bracketing together of very different groups as one minority in the Lausanne proceedings and other peace negotiations shows the extent to which the dominant great powers adhered to dialectical and mutually exclusive categories of majority and minority. Many Anatolian Christians affected by the Treaty of Lausanne did not speak Greek at all; there were many Albanians and Pomaks among the Muslims in Greece. The people targeted by resettlement schemes could not align themselves with a nation by making a declaration or even "converting" nationally; they were assigned nationality by the state authorities.

Initially, East Central Europe was not affected by population shifts on this scale, although here, too, reducing minorities took priority over protecting them. Evidence of this can be found, first, in the continuing stream of emigrants from the newly founded or expanded nation-states, especially from Poland and Romania, and, second, in the provisions of international agreements made at the time. The Geneva Convention on Upper Silesia of 1922, for example, granted the minorities in this multiethnic region, which had been divided up in 1921 following armed conflicts and a plebiscite, the right to emigrate to their external nation-states. About half of the new minorities took advantage of this "right of option." The Geneva Convention's main achievement was therefore to reduce the population not belonging to the titular nation. The remaining minorities could petition the League of Nations on issues of basic minority rights, such as maintaining cultural institutions and ensuring free access to education, but it took years to process these petitions, let alone yield any benefit for a minority.

A key international player must be mentioned at this point, who was not involved in either the Paris Peace Treaties or the League of Nations: the Soviet Union. In the mid-1920s, the Soviet Union pursued a very different policy on minorities than the Western great powers and the nation-states of East Central and Southeastern Europe. During this phase, the party leadership was engaged in consolidating the individual Soviet republics. By supporting their various national cultures, the regime hoped to implant Bolshevism in the minds of the Soviet peoples (a procedure known as *korenizatsiya*). At the same time, the minorities in the various republics enjoyed relatively high levels of autonomy. They were able to provide education in their national language and form their own political organs. *Korenizatsiya* did not necessarily have a peacemaking effect and often triggered violent struggles for domination of the nationally defined republics and autonomous regions. But in contrast to the post-World War I nation-states, the Soviet Union did not perceive its various minorities as a danger in the 1920s.

The public reception of the Treaty of Lausanne will not be considered in depth here since it overlaps thematically with how ethnic cleansing was executed, which is explored in the next chapter. It should be noted, however, that for a time, the plight of the refugees from Asia Minor deterred other states and the League of Nations from taking similar action. Even Lord Curzon outwardly distanced himself. But by the 1930s, the recurring violent clashes, endless quarreling before the League of Nations, and virulent nationalist terrorism placed ethnic boundaries and large-scale population shifts back on the international agenda. In 1937, a British government commission proposed an "exchange of populations" to end the rising Jewish-Arab tensions and violence in Palestine. This proposal was abandoned due to Arab resistance, but it was not the last time the seemingly rational solution found in Lausanne was advanced by international politicians.

The United Kingdom was foremost in accepting a new order of congruent state and ethnic borders. The Munich Agreement of 1938 was drawn up not only with a view to appeasing Hitler and avoiding another world war but also to solving the problem of minorities in Central Europe. It was made at the expense of Czechoslovakia—ironically, the European state that had pursued the most liberal policy toward its minorities in Central Europe—and created a new Czech minority. The signatories of the Munich Agreement silently expected the Czechs in the Sudetenland to adapt or emigrate.[47] The agreement, moreover, not only responded to the situation there but also actively provided for ethnic borders to be drawn in the Danube River Basin. Almost concurrently, Yugoslavia and Turkey arranged the transportation of 40,000 Muslims from the former Sandjak and Kosovo to Turkey; almost the same number again emigrated from Romania. When Hitler agreed to Mussolini's resettlement plans in South Tyrol, partly out of gratitude for the latter's support in Munich, it was received by the foreign press with suspicion but not outright condemnation.[48] This was another "minority problem" on the verge of being "solved." Six months after war broke out, a group of experts in the British Foreign Office recommended proceeding in a similar way with the German minority in Poland and Czechoslovakia after the Allies' projected victory.[49]

The British War Cabinet took over these recommendations, but did not yet envisage population shifts of the scale decided on in Yalta and Potsdam.[50] However, the principle was the same: if possible, there were to be no minorities in postwar Europe, or at least none that a neighboring country could mobilize to its own ends. As is shown in chapter 3, the victorious powers' plans were made not only with the Germans in mind but also the other minorities in East Central Europe. The Soviet Union had no part in the British resolutions of 1942. They were the result of negotiations with the governments in exile of Czechoslovakia and Poland, made by representatives of a democratic nation-state. When Stalin later became involved in organizing postwar Europe, he supported the principle of ethnic cleansing. The United States followed the British line, albeit hesitantly. Consequently, after World War II, the UN, successor organization to the League of Nations, had no minority protection function.

European Modernity

What caused national governments and international organizations to differentiate so crudely between majorities and minorities and to classify populations according to specific criteria? Why did individuals' personal sense of identity come to be disregarded in favor of criteria of language and extraction? Is there a connection between the categorization of populations and later processes of ethnic cleansing? These questions cannot be answered just by looking at the ideology of nationalism and mass movements. They also address the nature of the modern state.

In the late eighteenth century, Europe's absolutist monarchies began to carry out regular demographic inquiries into their populations. These were principally designed to gauge tax revenue and numbers of potential army recruits. By the mid-nineteenth century, more sophisticated data was being gleaned from the censuses and used to develop infrastructure such as school systems. Europe experienced a veritable craze for statistical methods and their potential for planning "progress." In 1853, a group of experts from a number of countries convened for the world's first International Statistical Congress. The Prussian delegation claimed that nationalities could be ascertained by applying the criterion of language. Austrian experts dismissed this as simplistic in view of their experience of a multinational state. But by the third International Statistical Congress in St. Petersburg in 1873, the Prussian—and now German—view prevailed. Over the next two decades, all continental empires, including the Ottoman Empire, set up central statistical offices. They all proceeded to carry out censuses inquiring into linguistically defined nationality.[51] In this way, theorists made a major contribution to narrowing conceptions of nation down to one specific, supposedly objective criterion.

From the outset, statistics on nationality were compiled with a political agenda in mind. As early as the 1830s, Prussian inquiries into regional language use in religious rites and education prompted the first wave of Germanization in the Grand Duchy of Posen. The increasing erosion of the rights of Poles in the German Empire was a reaction to demographic changes. Prussia responded to the information that the number of Germans in the eastern territories was steadily sinking by expelling Poles in 1885 and enacting the settlement law of 1886. In this way, Bismarck aimed to forcibly change the composition of the population in the east of the empire in order to support the German state's claim to power on demographic grounds. Gathering statistics on the population therefore led to modern population policy.

Statisticians and demographers were among the chief proponents of national homogeneity. Richard Böckh, a senior member of the Royal Statistical Office of Prussia in the latter nineteenth century, rejected assertions of bilingualism. In 1869, he wrote: "The individual can change his everyday language but not belong to two at the same time, since something completely equal, which does not even occur in nature, should not be adopted by statistics." He also ruled out dual or multiple identities, which were widespread in the eastern borderlands of Prussia, insisting, "There is no intermediary link, no halfway house."[52]

The geographer and demographer Dmitry Milyutin pioneered modern population policy in Russia. On a trip through Europe in the 1850s, he was particularly impressed by the Prussian army and its use of military statistics. He later introduced the concept to the Russian officers' training program and went on to plan the Russian army's Caucasus campaign of 1860–64, sending several hundreds of thousands of Muslims into exile. Russian Cossacks were subsequently able to take control of the northern Caucasus.

German population policy, like the Prussian method of compiling statistics it was based on, caught on in Europe. The Polish National Democrats included a purposeful settlement policy in their party program in the early twentieth century. The nation's leading political party at the time, it called for Poles to be settled in regions inhabited by ethnic Ukrainians in order to strengthen local "Polishness." When Poland was reestablished after World War I, the government put some of these plans into practice in the eastern Polish territories.[53] Similar population policies were pursued between the world wars by Italy in South Tyrol, by Yugoslavia in Kosovo, Macedonia, and Vojvodina, and by Romania in Transylvania and Dobruja.[54] The settlers became the personified symbols of the nationalizing state.

Such policies were indicative of their authors' static conception of nation. Germanization, Italianization, Polonization, or Serbianization by means of demographic manipulation could only work if the newly settled section of the population retained its national identity over the generations. The various governments' planning staff apparently ruled out the possibility of the settlers adapting to their surroundings. Here again, scientists and not only nationalist ideologues played a central role in defining immutable ethnic differences.

An increasingly objective definition of nation was meanwhile gaining acceptance even in nations that did not pursue an ethnic population policy and that viewed modern nationalism with skepticism. Austria's approach to its nationalities following the liberal 1867 constitution was diametrically opposed to Prussia's. The Austro-Hungarian Compromise and Galician autonomy were based on a policy of recognition. Each of the "peoples" within the monarchy had recognized rights; there was to be no discrimination on account of nationality. In this multinational state, the monarchy took the role of mediator; the emperor was to be the pater patriae. But since compromises had only been drafted with a few of the monarchy's nationalities, there was still widespread political dissatisfaction. The Czechs and the Ruthenians had been overlooked in the Austrian half of the empire, while in Hungary the government elites pressed ahead with the Magyarization of the entire population.

In the Austrian half of the empire, the government responded to the continuing conflicts by separating cultural, educational, and professional institutions along national lines, decentralizing power, conceding more responsibilities to local authorities, and democratization. These strategies, which were partially adapted for today's Bosnia and Herzegovina under the Dayton Accords, had the unintentional side effect of stimulating national movements to mobilize their populations. Political power was distributed and state and public institutions allotted in proportion to the numbers representing each nationality in the national censuses. As Bohemian statistician Heinrich Rauchberg pointed out, this caused the dispute over nations to shift to a local, even personal level: "It splintered into thousands of individual battles over households, families, lone souls."[55] Emotions ran especially high where the school system was concerned, since the education of the young was considered a crucial factor in securing the future of the nation. This wrangling over the distribution of power obscured the fact that the censuses were hopelessly narrow-sighted. Every citizen of Austria was required to declare *one* language, although multilingualism and mixed marriages were still common. Here, the demand for black-and-white statements was not the work of radical nationalists but of a modern bureaucracy trying to avoid political conflicts between the nationalities.

The manner in which these conflicts were resolved in the early twentieth century reflects the continuing nationalist dynamic in modern Europe. In 1905, the Austrian government tried to end the ongoing struggle for rights and political power between Germans and Czechs at least on a regional level. Representatives of German and Czech parties entered into negotiations that eventually produced the Moravian Compromise. This involved separating all public institutions, introducing a cantonal constitution, and registering Czech and German voters in separate electoral lists. As a result, Czechs could only vote for Czechs and Germans only for Germans. There was no option of changing lists or nationalities; nationality was now hereditary. Thus, the principle of extraction took precedence over free declarations of nationality.

Moravian civil liberties were cut on nationally motivated grounds in 1909. A number of Moravian families, who spoke partly or predominantly Czech at home, sent their children to German-speaking schools. Some were acting on practical considerations, some were following family traditions, and some simply had no exclusive sense of nationality. Czech politicians objected to this practice, fearing it would weaken their nation. The matter was taken to Austria's highest administrative court, which ruled against the free choice of schools. The children of parents who classified as Czech were required to attend Czech schools. This ruling signified a victory for administration—in this case, the school authorities—over personal liberty and parents' custody rights. Though Michel Foucault did not consider these particular cases, they corroborate his theories on the power dispositive.[56] In spite of the difficulties experienced in Moravia, similar rulings were made in two more parts of Austria—Bukovina and Galicia—in 1910 and 1913. Nations became objectively defined, then, not only as a result of state-led nationalism, such as in the German and Russian Empires, but also of modernizing processes in Europe.

The Moravian scenario repeated itself in other European regions in the interwar period. In the Polish part of Upper Silesia, there was controversy over the fact that parents in mixed families often sent their children to German schools. Here, again, their motives were pragmatic rather than ideological. While knowledge of two languages was an obvious advantage for future career prospects, German schools also provided more generous free school meals. Fearing growing support for the German minority, the Polish authorities denied parents the right to choose schools.[57] Fierce protests ensued and the dispute was referred to the League of Nations. The League of Nations' mediators cited objective criteria of nationality to rule that only families who spoke German at home could send their children to German elementary schools. This failed to take the reality of many multilingual families into account. The authorities now determined nationality in their own rational manner. Families were spied on to find out which languages they spoke in private. Public monitoring and repression also occurred in the German part of Upper Silesia. In this way, the League of Nations created a clear division between majorities and minorities. Changing nationality or taking an individual position between nationalisms was no longer possible. Such vital factors as schooling were governed by questions of origin and the apparently objective principles adhered to by modern administrations.

While the League of Nations applied dialectical criteria, France had already gone one step further. French national censuses had never allowed for identification with a national minority. But in Alsace, the *Commissions du Triage,* or selection committees, proceeded on the basis of an even more rigorous scheme. This divided the population into four categories: descendants of French citizens; progeny of mixed marriages in which at least one parent had French ancestors; citizens of third countries; and Alsatians classified as Germans.[58] This selection and the mass expulsions it gave rise to are considered more closely in the next chapter. In terms of European modernity, it is above all the refined categorization of the population that is of interest. The authorities worked toward determining as precisely as possible how closely each citizen identified with the French nation in order to proceed purposefully with reeducation, assimilation, or expulsion as required.

Identifying nationality became an increasingly depersonalized and bureaucratic process, not only in the nation-states but also in the Soviet Union. The policy of *korenizatsiya* was based on extensive data on nationality distribution. Soviet bureaucracy required, moreover, that holders' specific nationality (*narodnost'*) was entered alongside their class in their Soviet passports. When Stalin abandoned his minority-friendly policy in the early 1930s and began persecuting the national elites formed during *korenizatsiya,* the state had information at its disposal that its citizens could not evade. It goes without saying that the state and not any individual declaration determined one's national affiliation.

Nationality in Europe became depersonalized, then, in three stages. From about 1870, national censuses were conducted using rigid categories. Citizens were compelled to choose between them and select one nationality for statistical inquiries. From about 1900, state bureaucracies allotted nationality according to seemingly objective criteria. In the interwar period, the League of Nations supported the claims of state authorities to determine nationality in a number of conflicts. The categorization of the population inevitably led to minorities being isolated and discriminated against in many areas of life. Following the rationale of modern nation-states, forcibly resettling unwanted minorities was acting consistently.

Other achievements of modernity also contributed to preparing the ground for ethnic cleansing, such as the transportation system. Without dense shipping, rail, and road networks, the mass, organized removal of millions of people would not have been possible. At the same time, modern transportation helped to prevent even greater catastrophes. Modern shipping, for example, transported an unprecedented number of refugees across the Aegean Sea in 1912–13 and 1922–23. Without it, the refugees would perhaps have faced the same fate as the Armenians in eastern Anatolia in 1915. This illustrates modernity's deep ambivalence.

Improved infrastructure also played a pivotal role in the ethnic cleansing that took place between 1938 and 1948. Ever greater distances came into play, with ethnic Germans from Bukovina being resettled fifteen hundred kilometers away in the recently annexed Warthegau. The local Poles and Jews, meanwhile, were driven out to make way for the region's Germanization. The only moderating factor now was the war economy. Deportations to the Soviet Union could be effected much more swiftly, often taking only a few days or weeks. Cleansing at this stage was, moreover, not only faster but also more complete. Entire population groups could be rounded up, transported away, and barred from returning within a couple of weeks.

Technological advancements such as improved maps, aerial photography, and telephone communications were not merely inanimate tools facilitating ethnic cleansing, but actually had a critical influence on perceptions and attitudes. At the Conference of Lausanne in December 1922, chief negotiator Lord Curzon expressed his confidence that the transport and resettlement of the population groups in question could be completed within a few months. He felt optimistic that the forcibly resettled Turks and Greeks would be able to till the fields in their new home in the spring. An attitude of feasibility pervaded the negotiations and was articulated using medical terminology, conveying the impression that the forced resettlement of 1.5 million people would be a painful but swiftly executed "operation" to "cure" an ailment by a straightforward "transplant." Not one line in the protocol of the negotiations considers the plight of those affected or any potential victims. When an estimated twenty million Germans, Poles, and Ukrainians were to be "transferred" at the end of World War II, the Allies were again confident that such population shifts could be organized without difficulty. The fact that cattle cars were frequently used for these transports is indicative of attitudes toward the application of technology in human lives.

More sophisticated weaponry and modern warfare also advanced ethnic cleansing. Bayonets and rifles were the weapons used in the wars of the nineteenth century. If the situation arose, people could defend themselves with scythes and hunting weapons or hide from aggressors in the woods. Hence, they had some scope for reacting to war and violence. The invention of the machine gun and the development of artillery irrevocably changed the balance of power between military and civilian populations. The founding of the Red Cross after the Battle of Solferino and the Hague Convention of 1907 marked attempts to ease civilian suffering caused by war. But they could not avert the violence, which in the Balkan wars and World War I was aimed more than ever at the civilian population. By the time of World War II, even more sophisticated transportation and arms were capable of sending hundreds of thousands of people into exile within the space of a few months. The fate of the Croatian town Vukovar, razed to the ground by the Serbian paramilitary and the Yugoslav National Army in a matter of weeks in 1991, is a reminder of the efficiency of late twentieth century artillery. The refugees had no choice either with respect to their nationality or their course of action, faced with the superior strength of a hostile army.

Norman Naimark has pointed out that most instances of ethnic cleansing were only made possible by the context of war.[59] This was due to a number of factors: the more radical nature of nationalism in wartime, populations becoming generally brutalized, and the availability of technical resources making deportations feasible. Mechanisms ensuring the rule of law, which could have prevented ethnic cleansing, were deactivated by war. The reins of power were held by the military and technocrats, who dealt ruthlessly with supposed or actual enemies. Consequently, mass refugee movements increased as the population in war zones feared the worst from the enemy. This again demonstrates the growing asymmetry between military violence and the scope for action of the civilian population.

In the twentieth century, ethnic cleansing became an objective of war. Since the British experts concerned with the territorial reorganization of Southeastern Europe worked on the basis of "ethnological arguments," they encouraged the states of the region to collate population statistics. In the Balkan Wars, the hostile factions simply turned this logic around. They sent masses of people into exile in order to strengthen their claim to disputed territories at the projected peace negotiations. Creating an ethnopolitical fait accompli became a matter of course for the planning staff of various armies as well as international politics. Yet even though wars were not only a precondition but also an important factor in the practice of ethnic cleansing, it is important to note that by far the most forced resettlements in twentieth-century Europe took place during times of peace.

Christian Intolerance

Although ethnic cleansing was a modern phenomenon, comparable religious "cleansing" occurred in early modern Europe. These cases and their *longue durée* legacy throw light on the question of why ethnic cleansing was invented, developed, and practiced in Europe. Spain drove out its Sephardic Jews who were not prepared to convert to Christianity during the *Reconquista*. Despite pledges to the contrary, it did not treat its Muslims much better. Baptism was made compulsory in Granada in 1502 and in the rest of Spain in 1527. In 1567, the curtailment of the rights of converted Moriscos triggered an uprising. After it was quashed, in 1570, all Andalusian Moriscos were deported to other parts of the country. Finally, in 1609, Philipp III issued a decree for the expulsion of all converts.[60]

The Spanish king sought to consolidate royal power by pursuing a policy of "one state, one nation, one faith." In the eyes of the Inquisition, moreover, expelling Jews and Muslims and their converted descendants served to purify Christian Spain and cleanse it of sin. Conversion began to be deplored as a sign of religious weakness and betrayal. As in the twentieth century, ideology was informed by political interests. The crown and the Inquisition wanted to control all of Spanish society. They found allies in members of the petty nobility and urban lower classes who were envious of the Jewish and Muslim middle classes and their prosperity.

Another interesting parallel to the twentieth century can be observed in Spain's attempts to objectify religious affiliation. Servants of the Inquisition were required to submit family trees to prove that neither they nor their ancestors were converts. By the same token, the Inquisition investigated the origins of suspected heretics in order to ascertain their religion. Individual religion was, then, determined by extraction, similarly to the ethnic interpretation of nationality in the late nineteenth century. Equally, personal professions of affiliation carried no weight. The matter was decided entirely by the state administration, which by the day's standards was tightly organized.

In some ways, however, early modern cleansings differ distinctly from later cases in Europe. Expulsions of Spanish Muslims and Jews and their descendants went on for more than a hundred years. Not all areas under Spanish rule were affected equally. Many Moriscos and Marans were able to avoid persecution and many returned to their former homes after expulsion. Many were protected by their employers, enabling them to stay in Spain.

Another case suitable for diachronic comparison is that of the Huguenots in France, although this conflict involved two Christian denominations. French Protestants, known as Huguenots, emigrated or were expelled from Catholic-ruled France over the span of more than a hundred years. Ethnic cleansing, by contrast, mostly occurs in short periods of up to three years. The majority of Huguenots opted to convert, whereas changing one's nationality was rarely an option in the twentieth century. Recent research estimates that only one-fifth of the Huguenot community actually left France,[61] and when they did so, it was not only on account of "push factors"—which were dominant in the twentieth century—but also because of the "pull factor" of a welcome from other countries.

The last case of extensive cleansing of a religious nature in Central Europe—that of Salzburg's religious exiles—took a similar course. When Salzburg's Protestants were forced out by the Catholic archbishop, they found a warm welcome in Prussia. The religious exile of over 30,000 of the archbishop's subjects was not only economically disastrous but also severely damaging to his reputation. To the European public he seemed an intolerant zealot, while Prussia glowed in the friendly light of religious tolerance.[62] It was partly this moral turnaround that brought an end to interreligious expulsions in Europe from the early eighteenth century.

A line of continuity, on the other hand, runs right through to the modern age where European antipathy toward Muslims is concerned. In response to the failed siege of Vienna of 1683, the Habsburgs drove the Ottomans out of Hungary and parts of today's Croatia, causing the mass expulsion and emigration of Muslims. Since the victims were mostly converts from the region, their language and origins cannot have been the grounds for their expulsion. It was possible to evade expulsion by (re)converting to Christianity. But as Karl Kaser and Hannes Grandits have shown, neo-Christians were rarely able to settle permanently along the military frontier.[63] Most migrated to the Ottoman Empire a generation later, if not before, under pressure from the new regional ruler and the local population. Once on Ottoman territory, they usually converted again, to which the Ottoman authorities and regional societies apparently objected far less than the Christians on the other side of the border. The frequent persecution and emigration of neo-Christians in the Austrian-held territories indicate that here, as in early modern Spain, faith was not an attribute that could be abandoned at will. Later generations were held liable for the religion of their Muslim ancestors. In contrast to the ethnic cleansings informed by modern racism, however, this form of persecution was not based on any (pseudo)scientific findings.

Christian intolerance was also a major factor in the liberation of Greece and Serbia, the first Southeastern European nations to successfully revolt against the Ottoman Empire. In the early nineteenth century, Orthodox Christianity was the dominant component of the Greek and Serbian identities. Religious motives pervaded the devout Christians' struggle for independence from the Muslim Turks. A modern national identity based on language or origin, in contrast, had not yet developed.

The liberation wars in Greece, especially, were accompanied by willful violence against civilians. In 1821 there were massacres on the Peloponnese, claiming 8,000 lives in the town of Tripolis and between 15,000 and 25,000 throughout the peninsula.[64] Contemporary reports on Greece's liberation should be approached with caution, since newspapers and the newly fashionable travel reports had a tendency to dramatize and only rarely distinguished between the military and civilians. But there can be no doubt about the Greeks' objective to drive out all the "Turks."

There was less pronounced violence in Serbia, and several thousand Muslims remained in the country after its autonomy was recognized by the sultan in 1815. This was even true in the former Ottoman garrison and new capital of Belgrade. One reason for the divergence between Serbia and Greece is the varying influence of European ideas of civilization on each country. The philhellenes celebrated Greece's liberation from Ottoman rule as a victory of civilization over barbarism. While many Western observers were quietly horrified at the brutality with which the Turks were treated, there were no public protests. Indeed, in the figure of Lord Byron, English poet and occasional leader of the Greek military who died in 1824 near Missolonghi, the philhellenes saw a martyr in the struggle for civilization. Idealization of ancient and contemporary Greece went hand in hand with contempt for Ottoman culture, all traces of which were destroyed. Just a few years after Greece's liberation there was barely a minaret to be seen in the Peloponnese or Athens. In the principality of Serbia, too, Western influences played a major role in obliterating the last vestiges of Ottoman rule—albeit initially on a diplomatic level. In 1862 there were clashes between Christian Serbs and the Muslim population still remaining in Belgrade and the surrounding area. The European great powers responded to the escalating violence by resolving to resettle all Serbian Turks.[65]

This decision was made in the context of even more radical action being taken in the Russian Empire. As Peter Holquist has shown in his studies on the Caucasus campaign of 1860–64, at least 80 percent of the Muslim population of roughly half a million was forced to leave the western Caucasus.[66] Superficially, this mass migration resembles a preliminary stage of ethnic cleansing. But it was exacted as punishment for

alleged wartime pacts with the enemy, and so had more in common with
the Russians' treatment of the Crimean Tatars in the eighteenth century. The Russian army, moreover, barely distinguished between different ethnicities, such as Circassians (or Cherkess), Abkhaz, and Tatars,
but lumped together all Caucasian Muslims, who were indeed united by
their special loyalty to the sultan-caliph. This was, then, a case of religious cleansing, and not rigorously pursued. Since some Muslims managed to hide in the mountains and return to their villages when the front
line moved away, Russian statistics on refugees are unreliable. Meanwhile, Christian land takeover and settlement proceeded slowly.

The extent to which the creation of modern nation-states in the Balkans in the latter nineteenth century was accompanied by organized
ethnic cleansing is disputed. Kemal Karpat and his students emphasize
the forced nature of the migration of Southeastern European Muslims.[67]
The countries of Southeastern Europe and the older Western literature
tend to either play down the violence against Turks or legitimize it as
retribution for the massacre of Christians. As happens so often in history, it is important to differentiate between times and places. In the
heartlands of Greece and Serbia, there were very few Muslims remaining. Many had fled during the wars of liberation, fearing military brutality, the revenge of the local Christians for their earlier repression, or in
order to avoid being forced to convert.[68] But these refugee movements
were limited simply because the area "liberated" was relatively small.

The constellation changed with the Congress of Berlin in 1878. Serbia and Greece gained territories in regions where members of the nation and the national religion made up a distinctly smaller proportion of
the population than in the heartlands. By Southeastern European standards, these were imperial projects that needed to be shored up with ideology. Fear of the Turks was gradually turned into contempt, fuelled by
prejudices against the Orient. The Muslims remaining in the heartlands
were treated as uneducated and backward and eventually degenerated
into an underclass.

But the minorities that had been absorbed with the new territories
were so large that their swift and large-scale forced resettlement was
more than the Greek and Serbian governments could enforce. Consequently, they were driven out by other, longer-term measures. The new
nation-states expropriated wealthy Muslim landowners, destroying social fabrics that had evolved over many years. In turn, it became harder
for Muslim farm laborers to find regular work. Careers in state or local
administration were not open to Muslims. In view of this political and
economic discrimination, the prospect of starting a new life in the still
Ottoman regions of Southeastern Europe or Asia Minor had consider-

able appeal. Sultan Abdülhamid II (1876–1909) encouraged the "return" of devout Muslims from the lost territories by inviting all *Muhacır*, as they were known, to inhabit the sparsely populated Anatolian lands.

As a consequence of this combination of violence, discrimination, and better prospects across the border, at least a million Muslims emigrated from the Christian Balkan states in the first twenty years after the Congress of Berlin.[69] Justin McCarthy interprets this as a Turkish martyrdom, but the differences between this migration and the population removals of the twentieth century predominate. For one, emigration in this case took place over a long period, as in the early modern era, in contrast to the rapid and total ethnic cleansing of the twentieth century. Although there is little doubt about the forcible nature of the Muslims' migration, there were "pull" as well as "push" factors at play. And thirdly, population policy here was simply not pursued as systematically as in later years, either with regard to removing certain people or settling others.

It was not until the Balkan wars of 1912–13—in which the Ottoman Empire lost almost all of its European territories—that the stream of Turkish refugees became a flood. Muslims were now exposed to a second means of homogenization: the purposeful and mass resettlement of members of the respective titular nations. In the Balkan wars, moreover, the main impetus propelling conflicts in the region was no longer primarily religious but ethnonational. This was evident in the Christian antagonism not only toward Muslims but also toward other Christians. Serbia and Greece on the one side and Bulgaria on the other fought each other in 1913 with the same ferocity as they had previously fought the Turks. The Greek and Bulgarian clergy played a major role in spreading nationalist propaganda, participating in acts of violence and massacres and even organizing paramilitary units.[70] Hence, the violence against Muslims not only continued but also gained an ethnonational thrust. Ascribing this to a tradition of violence within Eastern Christianity, and the ethnic cleansing in Southeastern Europe to specific characteristics of the "Balkan peoples," would be simplistic. A number of factors contributed to engendering violence, including the Catholic Habsburg monarchy's obliteration of the Ottoman heritage, the fate of Muslims and converts in the conquered territories of Southeastern Europe, and Russia's policy in the Caucasus and the Crimea. The brutality and willfulness with which Christians persecuted European Muslims stemmed from the conviction that the latter's lives were worth less than their own.

Finally, consideration of the geography points to how Christian intolerance and ethnic cleansing were linked. Ethnic cleansing began where

Christian and Muslim areas of settlement overlapped. Even if religious differences and conflicts were a secondary cause of cleansing in the twentieth century, Europe should face up to this legacy.

Conclusion

To summarize, five basic preconditions of ethnic cleansing can be identified. The first of these is modern nationalism, which became increasingly restrictive over time. By the late nineteenth century, nations were regarded as static entities, defined by their members' origins and histories, which had to fight to survive. Modern nationalism was also linked to a new awareness of territorial claims. This inevitably led to deep-rooted conflicts, especially in the regions of Europe where several national movements operated and where national affiliation was ambiguous.

Modern nationalism's conception of nation and the idea of the nation-state were both based on an ideal of homogeneity. For many years, the liberal elites in Europe in particular believed that homogeneity would be achieved "naturally" by marginal population groups assimilating to the majority or titular nation. When this expectation failed to be fulfilled, the nation-states and nationalizing empires resorted to compulsory measures, ranging from enforcing a national language in schools to pursuing a nationalizing population policy. Attempts to repress existing or potential minorities were, however, by and large counterproductive. Exerting pressure on minorities to assimilate ultimately stimulated the resistance of these groups. The nation-states' demand for exclusive loyalty from their citizens placed their minorities in an increasingly precarious position. In addition to domestic conflicts, international conflicts arising from Europe's nation-state order caused further destabilization. A temporal dynamic can be observed here. The later a nation-state was founded, the more conflicts it entailed.

Minorities became the scapegoats of these structural problems. This is evident in the contemporary usage of the term "minority problems," apportioning blame to minorities rather than the nation-state order. From the mid-nineteenth century, minorities were perceived as a burden, an obstruction to the development of nations and nation-states, and as aliens in terms of a biological concept of society. Fantasies of purity and of eliminating these minorities gained currency early on. But they were not realized as long as the international order and the borders in Europe remained stable, which was by and large the case until 1912–13. In the decade of World War I, which de facto lasted until the early 1920s across much of Europe, the fantasies became real possibilities.

Ethnic cleansing was a consequence of the interplay of a radical form of nationalism with modern nation-state mechanisms. The (Western) European great powers played a leading role in this respect, first in the Balkans and then in other parts of the continent. The great powers established a nation-state order in Southeastern Europe at the Congress of Berlin, supported ethnic homogenization following the Balkan Wars, and, in the course of the Paris Peace Treaties, tended ever more toward the reduction rather than the protection of minorities. More importance was attached to minority protection in Central Europe after World War I, but even here, in cases of conflict, the League of Nations usually supported the nation-states.

Utopian ideas of homogenization also informed the black-and-white approach of national censuses. From about 1870, populations were counted and classified according to ethnic categories in most European states. While the continental empires at least recognized different nationalities, the nation-states refused to acknowledge the existence of minorities or other nationally divergent groups. In modern states, the population was forced to affiliate itself unambiguously. It was only possible to have one nationality; there was no place for multiple identities, at least not in population counts or other bureaucratic procedures. Recording populations in this way helped to put a seal on nations. The belief prevailed that individual nationality could be determined by objective criteria. Personal alignment was overridden by anonymous bureaucratic classifications.

As soon as statistical data on population nationality became available, it was misused. Censuses provided the basis for Prussian and German population policies in the eastern territories, where the ethnic composition of societies was manipulated by means of purposeful colonization. In the interwar period, several nation-states followed this example by settling members of the titular nation in disputed areas in attempts to homogenize and gain mastery of them. Precisely because this policy failed, states turned to other, more radical solutions: removal instead of active settlement.

Population policy was based on a static and one-dimensional picture of national affiliation. Turkish-speaking Christians in Asia Minor did not comply with it any better than Alsatians or Upper Silesians who identified primarily with their region. The "ethnological argument" propounded by Lord Curzon at the Conference of Lausanne became the decisive criterion for allotting disputed territories, positively inviting the manipulation of population structures by settling some population groups and expelling others.

Discourse on ethnic cleansing, both in the context of early fantasies and concrete proposals from the twentieth century, borrowed terminology from the field of natural science. Paul de Lagarde spoke of a "decomposition" that needed to be stopped, Georges Montandon of a "transplant." Later, transportation terms were added to this physiological vocabulary. People spoke of the "exchange of populations," "transfers," and "resettlement."[71] This utopian language of feasibility and its technical-sounding vocabulary were also rooted in the nineteenth century.

Modernity in Europe, then, has a Janus-headed nature. The once brotherly ideal behind the national movements gave rise to violent competition; the nation-state order brought war instead of peace; counting populations led to their selection; settling led to expelling. Ethnic cleansing is a European phenomenon not only because it first occurred on a large scale in Europe or in European-controlled territories. All the preconditions of ethnic cleansing—modern nationalism, the creation of nation-states, the attitudes toward minorities, and the technological utopias they gave rise to—were of European origin. This is also true of Christian intolerance. It is important to confront these traditions to discuss the deeper causes of ethnic cleansing. This inhuman practice was not the invention of an unscrupulous dictator or an accident of history; it emerged from the foundations of today's Europe and its nation-state order.

Notes

1. Among the defining characteristics of European modernity, Bauman names the tradition of rational thought, the development of modern administrative techniques, and the assertion of the individual in parallel to the formation of mass societies. See Zygmunt Bauman, *Modernity and the Holocaust* (Cambridge, 1991).
2. A more accurate distinction is made by Miroslav Hroch between stateless national movements and those operating in the context of nation-states. See Miroslav Hroch, *Das Europa der Nationen: Die moderne Nationsbildung im europäischen Vergleich* (Göttingen, 2005).
3. Source of the English translation: Ernst Moritz Arndt, "The German Fatherland," in *The Poets and Poetry of Europe*, ed. H. W. Longfellow (Philadelphia, 1845), 322–23. The original poem is titled "Was ist des Deutschen Vaterland?"
4. Quoted and translated from Siegfried Weichlein, *Nationalbewegungen und Nationalismus in Europa* (Darmstadt, 2006), 38–39. On Barère and the ethnolinguistic definition of the French nation, see also Hobsbawm, *Nations*, 21.
5. See Theodor Schneider, "Typologie und Erscheinungsformen des Nationalstaats in Europa," in Otto Dann and Hans-Ulrich Wehler, eds., *Nationalismus und Nationalstaat: Studien zum nationalen Problem in Europa* (Göttingen, 1991), 65–86.
6. See Ernest Renan, "Qu'est-ce qu'une nation?" in *Oeuvres Complètes*, vol. 1 (Paris, 1947), 887–907.
7. Translated from Erich Botzenhart, ed., *Freiherr vom Stein, Briefe und amtliche Schriften*, vol. 5 (Stuttgart, 1964), 1–3.
8. See Philipp Ther, "Deutsche Geschichte als imperiale Geschichte: Polen, slawophone Minderheiten und das Kaiserreich als kontinentales Empire," in *Das Kaiserreich*

transnational: Deutschland in der Welt 1871–1914, ed. Sebastian Conrad and Jürgen Osterhammel (Göttingen, 2004), 129–48.

9. See Jan Křen, *Die Konfliktgemeinschaft: Tschechen und Deutsche 1780–1918* (Munich, 1996), 108.

10. See Silviu Dragomir, "Nicolae Balcescu in Ardeal" [1930], reproduced in Silviu Dragomir, *Studii privind istoria revoluției române de la 1848,* ed. Pompiliu Teodor (Cluj-Napoca, 1989), 121.

11. For more on this debate, see Michael G. Müller, Bernd Schönemann, Maria Wawrykowa, eds., *Die "Polen-Debatte" in der Frankfurter Paulskirche* (Frankfurt, 1991).

12. See Hobsbawm, *Nations,* 34. The quote is taken from Chaim Gans, *The Limits of Nationalism* (Cambridge 2003), 16–32.

13. The last edition of the novel was published in 1996. See Gustav Freytag, *Soll und Haben. Roman in Sechs Büchern* (Karben, 1996).

14. See Roman Szporluk, *Communism and Nationalism: Karl Marx versus Friedrich List* (Oxford, 1988), 125–30.

15. Charles S. Maier, "Consigning the Twentieth Century to History: Alternative Narratives for the Modern Era," in *American Historical Review* 105 (2000): 807–31.

16. See the Carnegie Endowment for International Peace's report on the Balkan Wars: International Commission to Inquire into the Causes and Conduct of the Balkan Wars, ed., *The Other Balkan Wars: 1914 Carnegie Endowment Report of the International Commission to Inquire into the Causes and Conduct of the Balkan Wars* (Washington DC, 1993), 73. On the stereotyping of the Balkans, see Maria Todorova, *Imagining the Balkans* (New York, 1997).

17. See Rogers Brubaker, *Nationalism Reframed: Nationhood and the National Question in the New Europe* (Cambridge, 1996), 55–78.

18. On the German minority in Poland, see Winson Chu, *The German Minority in Interwar Poland* (Cambridge, 2012). On the Sudeten Germans, see Rudolf Jaworski, *Vorposten oder Minderheit? Der Sudetendeutsche Volkstumskampf in den Beziehungen zwischen der Weimarer Republik und der SR* (Stuttgart, 1977).

19. See Gerald Stourzh, *Die Gleichberechtigung der Nationalitäten in der Verfassung und Verwaltung Österreichs 1848–1918* (Vienna, 1986).

20. The unrest in Bohemia and northern Moravia cost the lives of fifty-eight people, including six policemen and members of the military. There are many German, Czech, and English books about the "Sudeten Germans," but one of the best on the subject so far is a Polish publication. See Piotr M. Majewski, *Niemcy Sudeccy 1848–1948: Historia pewnego nacjonalizmu 1848–1948* (Warsaw, 2007), 175–76.

21. Josep M. Fradera, "Regionalism and Nationalism: Catalonia within Modern Spain," in Ther and Sundhaussen, *Regionale Bewegungen,* 3–18.

22. See Eugene Weber, *Peasants into Frenchmen: The Modernization of Rural France, 1870-1914* (Stanford, 1976).

23. On French policy in Alsace during the interwar period, see Christiane Kohser-Spohn, "Staatliche Gewalt und der Zwang zur Eindeutigkeit: Die Politik Frankreichs im Elsass nach dem Ersten Weltkrieg," in Philipp Ther and Holm Sundhaussen, eds., *Nationalitätenkonflikte im 20. Jahrhundert: Ursachen von inter-ethnischer Gewalt im Vergleich* (Wiesbaden, 2001), 184–94.

24. On this structural problem facing not only East Central Europe, see Ivan Berendt, *Decades of Crisis: Central and Eastern Europe before World War II* (Berkeley, CA, 1998).

25. On centralization in the Kingdom of Serbs, Croats and Slovenes, or the later Yugoslavia, see Ivo Banac, *The National Question in Yugoslavia: Origins, History, Politics* (Ithaca, NY, 1988), 214–25. On Poland, see Brubaker, *Nationalism Reframed,* 84–103. On Czechoslovakia, see Jeremy King, *Budweisers into Czechs and Germans: A Local History of Bohemian Politics, 1848–1948* (Princeton, NJ, 2002).

26. In view of the vast amount of literature on minority conflicts, only a selection of books is given here. In addition to the works mentioned above, on Polish-Ukrainian relations between the wars, see Jerzy Tomaszewski, *Rzeczpospolita wielu narodów* (Warsaw, 1985), 67–104.

27. Holm Sundhaussen, "Bevölkerungsverschiebungen in Südosteuropa seit der Nationalstaatswerdung (19./20. Jahrhundert)," in: *Comparativ* 6 (1996), 25–40.

28. See Heinrich Wuttke, *Polen und Deutsche. Politische Betrachtungen* (Schkeuditz, 1846). Find more anti-Polish statements in Ther, "Deutsche Geschichte".

29. Quoted and translated from Friedrich Heckmann, *Ethnische Minderheiten, Volk und Nation: Soziologie inter-ethnischer Beziehungen* (Stuttgart, 1992), 45. On Lagarde, see Ulrich Sieg, *Deutschlands Prophet: Paul de Lagarde und die Ursprünge des modernen Antisemitismus* (Munich, 2007).

30. On the *Kulturkampf,* see Helmut W. Smith, *German Nationalism and Religious Conflict: Culture, Ideology, Politics, 1870–1914* (Princeton, NJ, 1995). More specifically on Poland, see Lech Trzeciakowski, *Kulturkampf w zaborze pruskim* (Poznań, 1970). On these deportations, see Helmut Neubach, *Die Ausweisung von Polen und Juden aus Preußen 1885–1886: Ein Beitrag zu Bismarcks Polenpolitik und zur Geschichte des deutsch-polnischen Verhältnisses* (Wiesbaden, 1967).

31. The term "negative Polenpolitik" was coined by Klaus Zernack in *Preussen—Deutschland—Polen: Aufsätze zur Geschichte der deutsch-polnischen Beziehungen* (Berlin, 1991).

32. On Weber, see Ther, "Deutsche Geschichte". On Freytag, Fontane, and other writers, see Kristin Kopp, *Germany's Wild East: Constructing Poland as Colonial Space* (Ann Arbor, MI, 2012), 29–123.

33. See article 2 of the treaty at http://www.documentarchiv.de/ (accessed 16 August 2010).

34. See Carole Fink, *Defending the Rights of Others: The Great Powers, the Jews and the International Minority Protection* (Cambridge, 2004), 29 and 37.

35. On the migration of Muslims from the Balkans since the late nineteenth century, see Alexandre Toumarkine, *Les migrations des populations musulmanes balkaniques en Anatolie 1876–1913* (Istanbul, 1995). On Romania's policy in the regions acquired from the Ottoman Empire in 1878, see Constantin Iordachi, *Citizenship, Nation and State-Building: The Integration of Northern Dobrogea into Romania, 1878–1913* (Pittsburgh, 2002).

36. See Peter Holquist, "To Count, to Extract and to Exterminate: Population Statistics and Population Politics in Late Imperial and Soviet Russia," in *A State of Nations: Empire and Nation Making in the Age of Lenin and Stalin,* ed. Ronald Grigor Suny and Terry Martin (Oxford, 2001), 115.

37. See Georges Montandon, *Frontières nationales: Détermination objective de la condition primordiales nécessaire à l'obtention d'une paix durable* (Lausanne, 1915). The text is reproduced in Ferdinand Seibt, Jörg Hoensch, Horst Förster, Franz Machilek and Michaela Marek, eds., *Mit unbestechlichem Blick ... Studien von Hans Lemberg zur Geschichte der böhmischen Länder und der Tschechoslowakei: Festgabe zu seinem 65. Geburtstag* (Munich, 1998), 377–96.

38. Lichtenstädter's first work (1898) focused on the Ottoman Empire. A publication of 1917 bore the universal title *Nationalitätsprinzip und Bevölkerungsaustausch* (The Principle of Nationality and Population Exchange). On Lichtenstädter, who often used the pseudonym M. E. Efendi, see Mihran Dabag, "National-koloniale Konstruktionen in politischen Entwürfen des Deutschen Reiches um 1900," in *Kolonialismus, Kolonialdiskurs und Genozid,* ed. Mihran Dabag, Horst Gründer and Uwe-K. Ketelsen (Paderborn, 2004), 19–66.

39. On this debate in England in the last months and aftermath of World War I, see Matthew Frank, *Expelling the Germans: British Opinion and Post-1945 Population*

Transfer in Context (Oxford, 2007), 19. This book was the first to trace the discourse on population shifts in a major Western European country.

40. This is illustrated by the case of eastern Galicia. See Philipp Ther, "Chancen und Untergang einer multinationalen Stadt: Die Beziehungen zwischen den Nationalitäten in Lemberg in der ersten Hälfte des 20. Jahrhunderts," in Ther and Sundhaussen, *Nationalitätenkonflikte*, 123–46.

41. One of the triggers of this debate was the publication of Peter Hart's *The IRA at War, 1916–1923* (Oxford, 2003).

42. See Brubaker, *Nationalism Reframed*, 167.

43. On the pogrom, which had major repercussions for the international protection of minorities, see Jerzy Tomaszewski, "Lwów—22. listopada 1918," *Przegląd Historyczny* 75 (1984): 279–83.

44. On "activism" in the German parties, see Majewski, *Niemcy Sudeccy*, 276–98.

45. On contemporary views on the minority treaties, see Josef Chlebowczyk, "W kwestii genezy międzynarodowej ochrony mniejszości po I wojnie światowej," in *Narody: Jak powstawały I jak wybijały się na niepodległość?*, ed. Marcin Kula (Warsaw, 1989), 427–34.

46. The text of the Treaty of Neuilly is reproduced in H. W. V. Temperley, *A History of the Peace Conference at Paris, vol. 5: Economic Reconstruction and Protection of Minorities* (London, 1969), 305–58; on this specific passage, found in paragraph 67, see 317.

47. Jan Gebhart, "Migrationsbewegungen der tschechischen Bevölkerung in den Jahren 1938–39, Forschungsstand und offene Fragen," in *Erzwungene Trennung: Vertreibungen und Aussiedlungen in und aus der Tschechoslowakei 1938–1947 im Vergleich mit Polen, Ungarn und Jugoslawien*, ed. Detlef Brandes, Edita Ivaničková, and Jiří Pešek, 11–22.

48. See, for example, the relevant article in *The Times* (London), 18 July 1939, 15.

49. Detlef Brandes, *Der Weg zur Vertreibung 1938–1945: Pläne und Entscheidungen zum "Transfer" der Deutschen aus der Tschechoslowakei und aus Polen* (Munich, 2001).

50. On the negotiations of 1940 and the resolutions of 1942, see Brandes, *Der Weg*, 424–27.

51. On the history of statistics and national censuses in the Ottoman Empire, see Kemal Karpat, "The Ottoman Adoption of Statistics from the West in the 19th Century," in Karpat, *Studies on Ottoman Social and Political History: Selected Articles and Essays* (Leiden, 2002), 132–45. Karpat points out that the statistics bureau was run until 1908 by members of Christian minorities who had studied in Western Europe and transferred the Western view of nationalities to the Ottoman Empire. It involved, then, a transfer of ideology and knowledge from Western Europe. The first Muslim head of the bureau, Ziya Gözalp, went on to become the ideologue of the national Right in Turkey, which called for ethnic purity in Asia Minor and supported pan-Turanism.

52. Quoted and translated from Morgane Labbé, "Institutionalizing the Statistics of Nationality in Prussia in the 19th Century (from local bureaucracy to state-level census of population)," *Centaurus* 49 (2007): 302. On the long-term legacy of this categorization, see Mark Levene, *Genocide in the Age of the Nation State*, vol. 2 (London, 2005)

53. On the parallels between German and Polish settlement policies, see Brubaker, *Nationalism Reframed*, 101. On the minority question in Poland, see Jerzy Tomaszewski, *Mniejszości narodowe w Polsce XX wieku* (Warsaw, 1991).

54. On settlement policy in the Kingdom of the Serbs, Croats and Slovenes, and the later Yugoslavia, see Milicia Zarkovic Bookman, *The Demographic Struggle for Power: The Political Economy of Demographic Engineering in the Modern World* (London, 1997), 121–46. The Serbian historian Zoran Janjetović has published a number of articles

on minorities and minority policy in interwar Yugoslavia, some of which have been translated into German. See also his monograph *Deca careva, pastorčad kraljeva: Nacionalne manjine u Jugoslaviji. 1918–1941* (Belgrade, 2005).

55. Quoted and translated from Emil Brix, *Die Umgangsprachen in Altösterreich zwischen Agitation und Assimilation: Die Sprachenstatistik in den zisleithanischen Volkszählungen, 1880 bis 1910* (Vienna, 1982), 13.

56. See Michel Foucault, *Power*, ed. James D. Faubion; trans. Robert Hurley et al. (New York, 2000).

57. See Tomasz Fałęcki, *Niemieckie Szkolnictwo mniejszościowe w województwie śląskim w latach 1937–1939* (Katowice, 1967), 67.

58. On French policy in Alsace, see Christiane Kohser-Spohn, "Die Vertreibung der 'Altdeutschen' aus dem Elsass 1918–1920," in *Die "Volksdeutschen" in Polen, Frankreich, Ungarn und der Tschechoslowakei: Mythos und Realität*, ed. Jerzy Kochanowski and Maike Sach (Osnabrück, Germany, 2006), 79–94; David Allen Harvey, "Lost Children or Enemy Aliens? Classifying the Population of Alsace after the First World War," *Journal of Contemporary History* 34 (1999): 537–54.

59. See Naimark, *Fires of Hatred*, 185–201.

60. On the various waves of compulsory conversion and expulsion in Spain, see Leonard P. Harvey, *Muslims in Spain 1500 to 1614* (Chicago, 2005). On the parallels between early modern and modern policies of homogenization, see Heather Rae, *State Identities and the Homogenisation of Peoples* (Cambridge, 2002).

61. See Barbara Dölemeyer, *Die Hugenotten* (Stuttgart, 2006), 26.

62. For an in-depth account that also elucidates the public perception of events, see Mack Walker, *The Salzburg Transaction: Expulsion and Redemption in Eighteenth Century Germany* (Ithaca, NY, 1992).

63. Hannes Grandits and Karl Kaser, "Familie und Gesellschaft in der habsburgischen Militärgrenze: Lika und Krbava zu Beginn des 18. Jahrhunderts," in *Microhistory of the Triplex Confinium*, ed. Drago Roksandić (Budapest, 1998), 27–68.

64. The latter figure is estimated by Justin McCarthy, *Death and Exile: The Ethnic Cleansing of Ottoman Muslims 1821–1922* (Princeton, NJ, 1995), 12. However, this number includes members of the military, so McCarthy's victimology should be approached with caution.

65. See Holm Sundhaussen, *Geschichte Serbiens, 19.–21: Jahrhundert* (Vienna, 2007), 130.

66. Holquist estimates that between 400,000 and 480,000 Muslims were forced to leave the western Caucasus. On these figures and Milyutin's career, see Holquist, "To Count," 113–19.

67. See Karpat, *Studies;* and among his former students especially McCarthy, *Death and Exile.*

68. On forced conversions during the Balkan Wars, see International Commission, *The Other Balkan Wars,* 77 and 155–56.

69. This figure is based on calculations in Toumarkine, *Les migrations.* This book, which is rarely cited by English-language scholars, draws on a convincing source of data and, in contrast to McCarthy's *Death and Exile,* has an impartial tone.

70. On the role of the clergy, which extended to involvement in pillaging and massacre, see the report by the Carnegie Endowment for International Peace, International Commission, *The Other Balkan Wars,* 72 and 93.

71. See endnotes 29 and 37.

CHAPTER 2

ETHNIC CLEANSING AS AN INSTRUMENT OF INTERNATIONAL POLITICS
1912–25

᷒᷒᷒

The history of ethnic cleansing in the twentieth century can be divided into four main periods. The first phase began in 1912 with the First Balkan War and ended in the 1920s with the implementation of the Treaties of Neuilly and Lausanne. During this period, ethnic cleansing became an internationally sanctioned and legitimized political means of solving conflicts between states and of consolidating the nation-state order. At least 2.8 million people were forced to permanently leave their homelands during this phase. The number is double that if the civilians deported during World War I and other borderline cases are included. While it is true that most ethnic cleansings were carried out in Southeastern Europe, contrary to the prevailing opinion, they were also implemented in other parts of Europe.

The second phase lasted from the signing of the Munich Agreement in 1938 until 1944—a time of German hegemony in Europe. The ethnic cleansings during this period took place in the Axis-allied states of East Central and Southeastern Europe and in territories annexed or occupied by the German Reich. Mass deportations of nationally defined groups were now also effected in the Soviet Union, which had hitherto used such measures primarily to remove unwanted social groups. At least six million people were forced into exile, expelled, deported, or resettled on account of their origins or nationality during this period.

The third phase was prompted by the new postwar order in Europe and lasted until the outbreak of the Cold War. During this period, ethnic cleansings were implemented across an even larger area, stretching from the Baltic Sea to the Aegean Sea and from the Vosges to the Caucasus. If we add comparative conflicts in the former British Empire to the list, at least thirty million people were affected.

In the fourth phase, in the 1990s, the former Yugoslavia and the Caucasus were the scenes of the worst ethnic cleansings; about five million people were put to flight or expelled. By this time, the international context had changed: the great powers no longer supported ethnic cleansing and finally tried to contain it. The next four chapters seek to give a comprehenisve empirical account of these phases and to present the main agents of ethnic cleansing. In the light of the previous chapter's findings, special attention will be paid to the consequences of nation-state building, the radicalization of nationalisms and hostility toward minorities, population policy under various regimes, and the complex of European modernity.[1]

An additional aspect considered here is the momentum ethnic cleansings gathered. This was propelled by three mechanisms: first, violence escalated to the point of becoming self-justifying; second, the absorption of refugees led to subsequent violent conflict and population movements, and the blurring of categories of victims and perpetrators; third, the international community removed further constraints by endorsing ethnic cleansings. In the first three phases especially, the policies of the Western great powers played a central role. They shaped the Paris Peace Treaties, which shifted the priority from protecting to reducing minorities, the Conference of Lausanne, the Munich Agreement, and the Allied conferences after World War II, from Tehran to Potsdam. This consensus only began to dissolve well after the war. But even in the 1990s, in the former Yugoslavia and the Caucasus, basic human rights counted for little in the power games played by nation-states and their representatives.

What were, then, the mechanisms of international diplomacy employed to "solve" interethnic and international conflicts? Who were the main agents of ethnic cleansing beyond the "usual suspects" Stalin and Hitler or lesser dictators such as Slobodan Milošević? Why did rationally conducted negotiations so often result in the drastic increase of mass forced migrations? How did an international policy become legitimized that, though rooted in the principle of the liberal constitutional state and facilitating humanitarian relief for refugees, raised public acceptance of forced population removals? Its adoption as a rational and legitimate instrument of politics throws light on the workings of European modernity. Ethnic cleansings were never prompted by irrational hatred but by concrete political objectives, incentives, and previous examples. But why were negative examples so consistently followed, causing millions of people misery and trauma? The following four empirical chapters will attempt to answer these questions by considering the agents of ethnic cleansing on various levels: international, national, and local.

The Balkan Wars and their Consequences

The entire region of Southeastern Europe was involved in the two Balkan wars of 1912 and 1913 in various constellations. In the First Balkan War of fall 1912, the Ottoman Empire was defeated by the united forces of Bulgaria, Greece, Serbia, and Montenegro, losing all its European territories with the exception of a small strip of land west of the capital, Istanbul. Subsequently, the allied Balkan states could not agree on how to divide up the Ottoman inheritance. And so the Second Balkan War broke out in summer 1913, in which the former allies defeated Bulgaria and the Ottoman Empire recaptured territory stretching to Edirne (Adrianople).

Despite only brief periods of actual fighting, lasting no more than a month in each case, the Balkan wars marked a critical point in modern warfare. The rearmed forces, mobilizing more than 750,000 soldiers, deliberately attacked civilian populations. The commission sent by the Carnegie Endowment for International Peace, which traveled to the affected areas shortly after the cease-fire, observed the same terrible scenes along a number of fronts: "Houses and whole villages reduced to ashes, unarmed and innocent populations massacred *en masse,* incredible acts of violence, pillage and brutality of every kind."[2]

When the hostilities began, Muslims were the main target of pillage, rape, massacre, and other crimes. According to the French historian and migration expert Alexandre Toumarkine, an estimated 200,000 Muslims lost their lives as a consequence of willful violence, starvation, and epidemics, or about 5 percent of the entire Muslim population of 4.3 million in the territories "liberated" from Serbia, Greece, and Bulgaria.[3] The Carnegie Endowment found evidence of systematic persecution: "The Muslim population endured during the early weeks of the war a period of lawless vengeance and unmeasured suffering. In many districts the Muslim villages were systematically burned by their Christian neighbors."[4] As in the Turkish wars of 1876–78, the "vengeance" mentioned here was triggered less by grievances suffered under Ottoman rule than by a deep-rooted contempt for Turks stemming from religious and Orientalist prejudice. The violence often escalated when the enemy was already defeated, defenseless and humiliated.

In the Second Balkan War, the Christian Balkan states fought each other as fiercely as they had previously fought against the Ottoman Empire. Immediately after each invasion, there was pillaging, rioting, and, in some places, massacre. This has often been explained by a specific Balkan propensity for violence, but the main reason was the viciousness of modern warfare.[5] Soldiers were imbued with a sense of duty and nationalist hatred. Moreover, there was a military logic behind attacking the civilian enemy population, which was a potential source of support for armed resistance and guerilla-style warfare and not easy to control.

Indeed, a logic of violence also prevailed when it came to creating a postwar order. At the negotiations in London after the First Balkan War in winter 1912–13, the British government repeatedly referred to "ethnological arguments" for determining which country the disputed territories should go to. These were based on the population statistics with which the conflicting parties had armed themselves prior to the war. In 1910, the Ottoman Empire had conducted a general census, following the European model, to count the population down to the humblest souls in the remotest villages.[6] The eight-figure population counts show that even newborn babies were identified by nationality. The Greek government responded to the Ottoman Empire's demographic campaign by ordering its own census of the Greek minority, to be carried out by the diplomatic missions and Orthodox dioceses in 1910–12. Though preceding the actual military conflict, this war of statistics was also an integral part of it: having put the populations of their respective enemies to flight, the conflicting parties could support their claims to disputed territories on "ethnological" grounds.

As occurred again at the other end of the twentieth century, there were now incidents of execution, mutilation, rape, and occasionally violation of corpses.[7] This symbolic violence was used to intimidate the remaining members of minorities and induce them to flee. The perpetrators could moreover garner kudos within their own circle by such excesses. When the hostilities ceased, the systematic discrimination of minorities continued via special taxes, expropriations, and the dismissal of employees and agricultural workers from their jobs. Many Muslims, in particular, lost their livelihoods in this way.

The extent of the refugee problem arising from the Balkan wars was as unprecedented as the number of civilian casualties. While the fighting raged, mostly Muslims took flight. Symptomatic of the growing asymmetry between the military and civilians, they often did so before the armies invaded. By fall 1913, over 150,000 Muslims had fled to Saloniki alone. In Thrace, along the Bulgarian-Turkish front, roughly 50,000 Bulgarians and the same number of Turks escaped abroad. During the Second Balkan War, roughly 80,000 Bulgarians and 100,000 Greeks took flight.

Yet the population shifts *after* the two Balkan wars were even more extensive than the refugee movements along the various front lines of the conflict. About 240,000 Muslims were shipped to Asia Minor; a further 40,000 journeyed overland via Kavalla. Greece supported this exile, even allowing Turkish ships to dock at Greek ports. By 1914, the Ottoman Empire had absorbed 413,000 Southeastern European Muslims. Another wave of migration moved toward Greece. By spring 1914, roughly 170,000 Greeks had fled Asia Minor and Bulgaria; Bulgaria registered 150,000 refugees in the same period. These figures point to a total of at least 890,000 individuals forced to permanently leave their homes as a consequence of the two Balkan wars.[8]

The link between the collapse of empires and ethnic conflict often propounded by historians hardly goes to explain the situation in Southeastern Europe. Here, large-scale population shifts took place in the context of wars between aggressive nation-states, while the drastically reduced Ottoman Empire was about to become one. The composition of populations in Southeastern Europe and Asia Minor had been fundamentally changed. In the Greek part of Macedonia, only about one-quarter of the prewar Muslim population remained; in parts of Thrace, ethnic borders were already in place.

Not only flight and expulsion but also settlement measures played a major role in homogenizing this large area. Serbia, Greece, Bulgaria, and Turkey took advantage of the refugee movements to populate their newly gained territories with their own nationals. The Greek government was the most active in this respect, even calling Greeks from the Russian Black Sea coast back to their supposed homeland. Unlike the nation-states born in 1878, all these countries adopted and enforced purposeful population policies on a broad scale.

The influx of refugees from the Balkan wars caused new expulsions in many regions. A well-documented example is that of eastern Thrace, where the Greek population had participated in pillaging the Turkish quarters of towns and neighboring villages along the Marmara coast in 1912–13.[9] When thousands of embittered refugees from the Balkans joined an already scarred local population, it sparked riots against the local Greeks, who escaped to the refuge of only a few isolated towns. This case of local disturbances illustrates the blurring of categories of victims and perpetrators of ethnic cleansing. The Muslim exiles of the Balkan wars initiated expulsions themselves, with government backing. The situation was similar in northern Greece, where a further 50,000 Muslims were driven into the Ottoman Empire over the course of 1914.

In western Asia Minor, too, a new dynamic emerged in 1914. Despite fierce protests from the Ottoman Empire, the European great powers decided to cede the Aegean islands close to the mainland to Greece. This intensified Turkish fears that Greece would soon expand toward Asia Minor following the *Megáli Idéa* (Great Idea), aiming for a Greater Greece on both sides of the Aegean Sea, including Constantinople.[10] In response to Greece's annexation of the Aegean islands near the coast, the Ottoman government began deliberately settling Turks in the provinces of Izmir and Aydin. They hoped to achieve two goals in this way: to put an end to the continuing refugee crisis and to defend the new border demographically. As previously in eastern Thrace, where refugees settled, further expulsions followed. According to Greek estimates, 100,000 people were forced to leave Asia Minor in 1914 alone.[11]

This was the inevitable consequence of a new order of nation-states in Southeastern Europe, which was finally resolved at the peace conferences of London and Bucharest. Despite the fact that all the states of Southeastern Europe had substantially larger minorities as a consequence of the Balkan wars, protecting them was a matter of only secondary or tertiary importance at the peace conferences.

The desire for lasting peace, however, eventually convinced Bulgaria and the Ottoman Empire to enter into negotiations. In September 1913, the two states signed the Treaty of Constantinople, which is often regarded as the precedent for contractual agreements on ethnic cleansing.[12] But this view does not stand up to closer consideration. In formal terms, it is true that Bulgaria and the Ottoman Empire agreed on an "exchange" of minorities. But it was confined to a fifteen-kilometer stretch of land along the new border, from which each country's minorities had fled over the course of the 1913 war. No other more extensive population movements were arranged.

On the contrary, Bulgaria and the Ottoman Empire agreed on comprehensive minority rights. Their property was declared inviolable; religious institutions were placed under special protection and became legal entities; the Muslims in the Bulgarian-won territories were even permitted to retain their Ottoman citizenship. In return, the Ottoman Empire committed to quickly "pacifying" the Muslims in western Thrace, who still made up the majority in the region around Dedeağaç (Greece, which gained the region after the treaty of Neuilly, renamed the city

Alexandroupoli), thereby confirming their status as a minority in Bulgaria. The Young Turk government, meanwhile, granted freedom of religion and education to the Bulgarian minority.[13] Protecting minorities was, then, discussed and resolved to a far greater extent here than at the previous international peace conferences, including the Congress of Berlin. This shows that on a regional level, compromise in favor of minorities was possible, contradicting the stereotypical view—as widely held then as now—of inherently aggressive Balkan states. Crucially, the parties to this agreement were the two losers of the Balkan wars. Both sides renounced their mutual regional imperialist demands and committed to refraining henceforth from encouraging their external minorities' irredentist tendencies.

Half a year after the Treaty of Constantinople was concluded, Greece and the Ottoman Empire entered into negotiations over a "population exchange."[14] Greece, concerned with improving the treatment of refugees, initially intended to confine the migration of the respective minorities to Thrace and Macedonia. The Turkish side, however, pushed for extending the scope of exchange to include western Asia Minor and Epirus. Greek prime minister Elefthirios Venizelos acquiesced, insisting only that emigration be voluntary. In June 1914, the two sides proposed forming a four-man commission to come up with concrete proposals on four specific points: the principle of voluntariness; a balanced "exchange"; compensation for abandoned property; and the possibility of return, which Greece demanded with an eye to future expansion. Since both sides basically agreed on the principle of voluntariness, Greece withdrew its demand for numerical balance. A generous solution was found for the question of abandoned property, with population exchange participants and even previous refugees conceded the right to compensation for property they were forced to leave behind. All contentious issues were to be resolved by a mixed commission in which Switzerland was also represented. In spite of the tense relationship between Greece and the Ottoman Empire, the negotiations went remarkably smoothly, since the two sides shared the goal of creating a homogeneous nation-state. The only disputed points were some details of the "population exchange" and the unspoken question of whether the future, ethnically consolidated border should run directly along the Aegean coast or further inland, as Greek nationalists envisaged. But the outbreak of World War I put an end to negotiations over the treaty.

In general terms, the negotiations of 1914 were held in a strikingly rational manner. Certainly, diplomats still today must maintain sangfroid, but these negotiations were so coolly conducted that, combined with the population utopias informing them, they launched a remarkable dynamic toward abandoning scruples. Some months after the Greek and Turkish negotiators initially met to discuss Thrace and medium-sized population groups, they were considering about half of Greece and the entire western portion of Asia Minor. The talks concerned the fate of far more than a million people. These were not refugees, but for the most part native citizens. It was not, then, a matter of confirming the status quo resulting from war, but of forward-looking measures.

This pattern was repeated at the negotiations in Lausanne, Yalta, and Potsdam several years and decades later. As soon as a population exchange or transfer was agreed on in principle, the project escalated during diplomatic negotiations. One might speak of a rationalist dynamic at work, which is characteristic of European modernity and has little in common with hate, revenge, or other emotions by which ethnic cleansing is often explained. But unlike later, in Lausanne, minorities at this earlier stage were not driven out of the affected areas wholesale. Just under half of all resident Muslims remained in Serbia, more than half in Bulgaria and Greece, and even more in Romania. This shows that the states in question, despite demonstrating an aversion to minorities, were not yet striving toward the total homogenization of their populations. Governments were satisfied for the time being if the titular nation had supremacy throughout the national territory. It was, then, a regional imperialism at work, which did not yet completely rule out ethnic diversity. The Ottoman Empire, by contrast, having written off the territories lost in 1912–13, became all the more determined to consolidate Asia Minor as a bulwark of Turkishness. In the case of Turkey, the utopia of ethnic purity was borne out of a defensive stance that engendered internal aggression.

Deportations in World War I

World War I brought about huge changes on all these levels and beyond Southeastern Europe. Since international diplomacy was put on ice, "population exchanges" could no longer be arranged and the flow of refugees in conflict zones such as western Asia Minor abated. The organized resettlement of refugees came to a standstill.

But minorities now faced persecution in other parts of Europe too. All resources were mobilized for war. Nationalist attitudes radicalized in the light of military dominance, and fears of subjugation and suspicions that certain sections of the population might support the enemy or prevent supplies from reaching the front line abounded. This paranoia was especially marked in the weakest continental empires, the Russian Empire and the Ottoman Empire. Population groups that asserted no territorial claims—and were in no position to do so—such as Russia's Jews and the Armenians in central Anatolia bore the brunt of it. The Russian military leadership ordered the expulsion of about a million Jews and Germans, who had barely had any contact with modern national movements, from the west of the empire. In some regions, such as western Lithuania, Courland, and Volhynia, deportations were enforced across the board.[15] It should be noted, however, that these were preventative rather than conclusive deportations.

While mostly Armenians and Greeks were threatened with deportation from the Ottoman Empire, large numbers of Greeks fled across the Aegean Sea in order to avoid conscription.[16] The situation in the eastern half of Anatolia was more volatile, first, because Armenians were fighting in the Russian army and, second, because Armenian nationalists were calling for an autonomous Armenian state, compounding Turkish fears of secession. In order to prevent another defeat as in the Balkan wars, the Young Turk government ordered the deportation of all Armenians close to the eastern Anatolian front. Armenians were removed from cities farther afield, too, but not to their potential external homeland of Russian Armenia. The authorities were well aware that the deportees had only a small chance of surviving the long march across the Anatolian highlands to the Syrian coast. Furthermore, rather than protecting the Armenians from pillaging by local Turkish and especially Kurdish populations, they actively encouraged it.

Ethnic cleansing did not take place on a mass scale within the German army's direct sphere of influence. But the army leadership, a circle around Reich chancellor Theobald von Bethmann-Hollweg, and several provincial administrations discussed concrete suggestions for the mass expulsion of Poles. A "border rampart" colonized by German settlers was to stretch right up to the Russian partition.[17] After the collapse of the tsarist empire in 1917, these plans gained increased relevance and were extended to the occupied territory in eastern Poland and the Baltic regions (the so-called *Oberost*). When the German Empire was forced to surrender just a year later, all these projects were abandoned. But their long-term effects should not be underestimated, since they formed the blueprint on which Nazi policy in Warthegau and West Prussia was based.

Unlike the Central Powers, the French army did not harbor any colonial fantasies in Europe, partly because they were fighting on almost exclusively home territory, together with the British. But the influential Alsatian government advisor Abbé Emile Wetterlé promoted the "selection" (*triage*) of the population in Alsace and Lorraine after these territories had been regained.[18] For him, as for most of French society, coexistence with the Germans was unthinkable. Thus, World War I gave rise to concrete plans for ethnic cleansing in several countries and, in two cases, their implementation.

Even far from all fronts, attitudes had become more radical. In 1915, Swiss ethnologist Georges Montandon defended the idea of a "great transplantation" of minorities in Europe.[19] Montandon's vision of a postwar order in Europe involved exchanges of minorities between states as well as one-sided "transfers." German-Jewish journalist Siegfried Lichtenstädter also argued for population shifts in order to secure peace.[20] These theses betray the influence of colonial attitudes, since they were concerned primarily with the Balkans, Asia Minor, and other "Eastern" regions. Population shifts were always proposed for areas that were perceived to be outside of the commentator's own "civilization."

Postwar Migrations

The full extent of the catastrophe of World War I became apparent as masses of uprooted or directly endangered people took flight in its aftermath. The civil war in Russia, continuing regional conflicts, and the new order of nation-states in Europe caused the legions of refugees in Europe to swell after 1918. While only a few of the refugee movements affecting millions were caused by purposeful and total ethnic cleansing, the borderline cases also warrant closer consideration here.

The hitherto most extensive case of flight in European history was caused by the collapse of the tsarist empire and the Russian Revolution. By 1922, the civil war had caused about two million Russian civilians to flee, most of them abroad, in addition to the roughly six million war refugees and evacuees. Meanwhile, nearly 250,000 Muslims fled the Armenian-Azerbaijani war in the Caucasus.[21] In the turmoil of the revolution, moreover, more than a million Polish nationals abandoned their homes in Russia.[22]

Among the refugees were also innumerable Eastern European Jews fleeing poverty, hardship, and pogroms. Hundreds of thousands were cared for by US Jewish aid organizations. Pogroms should not, however, be bracketed together with ethnic cleansing.[23] Although Jews in Russia were at greater risk of persecution after 1917 and pogroms spread to eastern Poland, this violence was mostly local and scarcely organized.[24] Most incidents were cases of "communal violence," though one-sided.[25] Concurrently, hundreds of thousands of Poles, Greeks, Germans, and members of other minorities fled the anarchic conditions left by the collapse of the state's power monopoly and the plundering and requisition-ing by Bolsheviks, Whites, and various paramilitary units.[26]

Pogroms proliferated as originally political conflicts took on ethnic di-mensions and intolerance of minorities rose to murderous levels. Flight was rarely to safety, since Russia's neighboring states to the West—often the refugees' first destination—did all they could to get rid of the new influx. The victorious powers consented to the municipal govern-ment of Vienna engineering exactly that; in Romania, only 4,000 of the 22,000 registered Jewish refugees were issued new residence permits in 1921; Poland had tens of thousands of Jewish refugees transported to the free city of Gdańsk.[27] It would be simplistic to attribute these enforced movements to a specifically Eastern European tendency to-ward anti-Semitism. The Soviet Union's immediate neighbors faced a far greater burden in terms of the sheer number of people fleeing the Russian Revolution than Germany or the countries of Western Europe. Yet the eagerness of various nation-states to absorb coethnic "repatri-ates" is evidence of their black-and-white views on citizenship. As long as refugees provided additional members of the majority nation they were welcome, regardless of the burden on the social system. In Poland, for example, a "repatriation commission" was especially set up to attend to their needs.

In contrast to these "repatriates," who were also responding to "pull" factors, the former imperial elites were simply under pressure to leave. By the early 1920s, over 600,000 Germans had left the former Prussian partition of Poland; at least 100,000 had left the eastern part of Upper Silesia for the German Empire. Around the time the Treaty of Trianon was signed, 425,000 Hungarians migrated from Slovakia, Romania, Ser-bia, and Croatia to Hungarian territory, now shrunk to one-third of its former size.[28] Roughly 150,000 refugees sought exile in Bulgaria.

In the past, German-language literature has often portrayed the Ger-mans' emigration from Poland as a form of expulsion. It is true that the proportion of Germans among the population of western Poland shrank dramatically, from more than 40 percent before the war to about 5 per-cent in 1921 in the regional capital Poznań (Posen). But the German minority in the Poznań district still numbered 327,000, and over a mil-lion in all of Poland.[29] With the exception of the Poznań uprising of 1919 and the Silesian uprisings, they were not affected by mass violence. It is therefore inappropriate to liken this migration to the expulsions after World War II or describe it as "ethnic cleansing."

Nevertheless, there were masses of people compelled by circumstances to migrate. Prussian officials, businessmen, and traders—in short, the social elite among the German minority—felt there was no future for them in the Polish nation-state and decided en masse to emigrate. Land-owning farmers and third-, fourth-, or fifth-generation town dwellers, on the other hand, tended to stay. The situation was similar for the Hungarians who left Slovakia, the Banat, and Transylvania. These were all elite migrations on ethnic grounds. One alternative was to become a "national convert." Several million people who had previously aligned themselves with imperial nations claimed different nationalities in national censuses in the early 1920s.

Triage in Alsace

Minority conflicts are frequently reduced to an Eastern or Southeastern European problem, and more often than not attributed to a peculiar brand of nationalism native to this part of Europe. But, in the immediate aftermath of World War I, it was France that devised the most efficient policy to deal with an unwanted minority. About 200,000 people had migrated to the Alsace-Lorraine region from the German Reich since 1871. By 1918, many of them had lived there for decades, raised families there, and become barely distinguishable from those whose families had been resident in the region for many generations.

The French policy of *épuration* aimed to cleanse the country of all legacies of German rule, including these former immigrants. Under the armistice agreement of November 1918, members of the German military were required to leave Alsace within two weeks. Many German administrative officials, teachers, and public figures subsequently followed suit. Similarly to the emigrants from the former Prussian partition of Poland, they were mostly reacting to "situative force," feeling they had no future in a French Alsace. When power was ceded to the French, migration was organized. Emigrants were required to report to the authorities, who ensured that they took no more than the maximum permitted 2,000 reichsmarks in cash and thirty kilograms of luggage with them, and confiscated any excess. This "voluntary" procedure, then, bore the marks of ethnic cleansing in the way it was enforced as well as in the professional and material consequences it entailed for the emigrants.

As the following letter of December 1918 from an "old Alsatian" to the French high commissioner shows, arbitrary deportations also took place:

> For about eight days now, male as well as female persons, officials and tradesmen, have been deported out of the country. Most of these people are granted a period of 24 hours to order their affairs. It goes without saying that this is not enough! How incredibly hard this measure hits families! Men, some

of whom have already reached an advanced age, are torn from the bosom of their families and driven out to the ruins of Germany, where they no longer have any home or place of refuge, where they are strangers without any income.[30]

On their departure and before crossing the bridge over the Rhine at Kehl, locals often hurled abuse at the refugees and sometimes spat or threw stones at them.[31]

The high commissioner's response to this appeal is not known, but the authorities continued to organize the swift *épuration* of Alsace. The process was based on two main tasks: ascertaining nationality and issuing identification papers. The objective of the "selection commissions" (*commissions du triage*) was to identify enemies and potential traitors, to secure a nationally loyal population, and to make Alsace French.

Selection among this very mixed population was a major logistical challenge. Toward the end of the war, Alsace had a population of about two million. While a plebiscite around this time would certainly have resulted in a clear majority for France, the new authorities did not want to rely on subjective opinions. So the government took the matter of Alsatian nationality into its own hands, issuing a decree on 14 December 1918 that distinguished between four main population groups. Residents with two French or Alsatian parents fell under category A, whereby only those with ancestors in the region before 1871 counted as Alsatians. Residents with one Alsatian parent fell under category B. Category C comprised foreigners not of German or Austrian descent, while category D applied to residents with German or Austrian backgrounds (*Altdeutsche*) and their children.

The members of each of the four groups were issued with symbolically decorated identity papers according to their category, which were required for traveling abroad and within France, to vote, and to maintain a position of employment. The 1,082,650 members of category A received identity papers with a *tricolore* red, white and blue stripe. The 183,500 members of category B had to make do with just the red stripe. The 55,050 category C papers were marked by two blue stripes, and the 513,800 category D documents had no stripes at all and put the holders at a considerable disadvantage.[32] They were sold French francs at an exchange rate of 1.25 reichsmarks instead of the 75-pfennig rate available to others. Furthermore, their freedom of movement was restricted and they often lost their jobs.

In addition to this discriminatory system of categorization based on parentage, the government installed the "selection commissions," made up of two representatives of the French army and local notables who were considered loyal Frenchmen. In January 1919, the French presi-

dent Georges Clemenceau gave the commissions the following instruc-
tion: "Whenever the presence of Germans seems to disturb the public
order, you should not hesitate to remove this danger."[33] In concrete
terms, he was endorsing deportations across the Rhine.

Over the course of 1919, about 150,000 people whom the French
state classified as German were forced to leave Alsace and Lorraine.
Many other people were interned and one-quarter of the population suffered the discrimination caused by their new, inferior identity papers.
Christiane Kohser-Spohn has summed up this French policy as one of
"purifier, centraliser, assimiler." Similar to later cases of ethnic cleansing, it was partly motivated by material and political interests within
the region. A neighbor or colleague denounced as German left property
behind that could then be appropriated. However, since denunciations
were difficult to verify and many people were wrongly identified as enemies to the nation, the French government dissolved the commissions
in October 1919. This marked France's return to the rule of law after a
period of arbitrary command. In the end, two-thirds of the members of
category D were able to stay in France.

Nevertheless, the selection that took place in Alsace set negative
standards in Europe. French nationality was not decided by personal
allegiance but by the authorities' classification. Nobody could elude the
state's system of registration and powers of definition. The extent to
which the state involved society in its selection was also unprecedented.
Although the government retrospectively viewed the work of the commissions as problematic and in some cases revoked their decisions, the
deportees had no chance of returning.[34]

The Protection and Reduction of Minorities
in the Paris Peace Treaties

On an international level, too, France took a tough stance on minorities
after 1918. Clemenceau's government tried to limit minority rights as
far as possible in the Paris Peace Treaties. But the news of pogroms in
Odessa, Lemberg (Lwów, L'viv), Pińsk, and countless other Eastern European cities swayed opinion in the opposite direction.[35] Pressure grew
to combine the goal of establishing a framework for peace in Europe with
an international agreement on protecting minorities. All newly founded
or expanded nation-states in East Central Europe and Southeastern
Europe were required to commit to protecting their minorities. According to Carole Fink, this "little Versailles" affected twenty-five million
people in twelve European nation-states, from the Gulf of Finland to

the Aegean Sea.[36] The countries concerned rejected the requirements on principle, perceiving them as discrimination by the Western European nation-states and as an intrusion into their sovereignty.

Eric Weitz has advanced the provocative thesis that from the outset, minorities were exposed to dual mechanisms of expulsion and protection and that neither can be viewed in isolation. In the Paris Peace Treaties, moreover, he discerns a dynamic toward "deportation," culminating in the Treaty of Lausanne.[37] A number of historical details clash with his argument, such as the fact that the Treaties of St. Germain and Trianon called for the protection of minorities while the Treaty of Neuilly—the second in the series of the Paris Peace Treaties—was designed to eliminate minority population groups. There was, then, no clear chronological progression toward "deportation." Furthermore, it is questionable whether the Treaty of Lausanne, which revised the Treaty of Sèvres, can be considered to be one of the Paris Peace Treaties. Nevertheless, in broad terms, Weitz's findings are compelling.

The minority rulings were officially supplementary agreements to the international treaties recognizing Poland and all other nation-states formed or expanded in 1918–19. Protecting minorities was not, then, of equal diplomatic importance as recognizing nation-states and their borders. Moreover, the victorious powers did not agree on any sanctions to penalize the violation of minority rights. Since members of minorities were explicitly not subjects under international law, they could not refer problems directly to the League of Nations—a body supposedly guaranteeing minority protection—but only through a member of the League of Nations.

Furthermore, as time progressed (though not in the sequence of the Paris Peace Treaties), a trend toward resettlement emerged. In the case of East Central Europe, this is demonstrated by the Geneva Convention on Upper Silesia of 1922. Although the German-Polish agreements extended minority rights in this region, they served mainly to advance national homogenization on both sides of the new border. The Geneva Convention included a "right of option" that legalized and facilitated the migration of around 100,000 individuals on each side who had voted against Germany or Poland, respectively, in the plebiscite of 1921.

The German minority remaining in Poland referred the matter of their discrimination to the League of Nations to little effect. The Hungarians, Albanians, and Lithuanians who protested in Geneva against the treatment of their minorities in Czechoslovakia, Romania, the future Yugoslavia, and Poland were similarly disappointed. Carole Fink's comprehensive study concludes that the League of Nations was inherently biased in favor of the new nation-states.[38] The League of Nations, as later the UN, was indeed an amalgamation of nation-states whose ultimate goal was the national homogenization of their respective populations. Correspondingly, its support for minorities was at best half-hearted.

This is shown as early as the Treaty of Neuilly, which Bulgaria concluded in November 1919 with the victorious powers and a total of sixteen signatory states. Superficially, it reads like any other treaty with the losers of World War I. Bulgaria was required to cede territories, including its Aegean coast in Thrace, drastically reduce its army, and pay reparations. In addition, like all the other states of East Central and Southeastern Europe, Bulgaria was called on to protect its minorities, as set out in a separate section comprising a noteworthy eight articles.

But this was also the first internationally sanctioned ruling on the deliberate reduction of minorities. In the second paragraph of Article 56 it succinctly states: "Bulgaria commits to recognizing the provisions considered expedient by the allied and associated main powers concerning the mutual and voluntary emigration of individuals belonging to racial minorities."[39] This referred to the Convention between Greece and Bulgaria Respecting Reciprocal Emigration, an agreement concerning the Greek and Bulgarian "ethnic, religious and linguistic" minorities in the two neighboring countries, which was signed on the same day as the Treaty of Neuilly.[40] As the title suggests, a principle of reciprocity was to apply, emigration was to be voluntary, and the property of the "emigrants" was to be protected. A mixed, international commission was to supervise the course of resettlement and compensation for abandoned property.

The circumstances in the two affected countries were very different. The parts of Greece settled by Bulgarian speakers stretched as far as the Aegean; some Greek towns, such as Saloniki, had a Bulgarian intelligentsia. While the Greek diaspora hardly threatened the dominions of the Bulgarian state, the Greek government had some reason to fear the formation of a Bulgarian irredenta. Consequently, Greece was far more interested in eliminating its minority than Bulgaria. Moreover, Prime Minister Venizelos had plans for the returning Greek minority from Bulgaria to Hellenize northern Greece. However, recent research has questioned whether these minorities had a distinct sense of national awareness at all or whether other forms of geographical and social identification predominated.[41] Simply describing oneself as Bulgarian or Greek is problematic in some areas and for many individuals. It was precisely this state of affairs that the two nation-states wanted to change by enforcing ethnic and cultural homogeneity and unambiguous loyalty in their territories.

Greece, Bulgaria, and the international commission originally planned to achieve "voluntary and reciprocal emigration" within two years.[42]

However, as the latest Greek and Bulgarian findings have shown, in this first phase, few members of the respective minorities opted for emigration. The Greek emissaries' propaganda did nothing to change this. By June 1923, a mere 197 Greek and 166 Bulgarian families had officially applied to migrate to the neighboring country.[43] "Voluntary" emigration turned out to be a fiction, then, since few actually wanted to leave their homeland. The contract's term and the mixed commission's brief were nevertheless extended several times, as the League of Nations and Greece held persistently to their vision.

The constellation changed with the arrival of the Greek refugees from Asia Minor. The Greek government channeled them to northern Macedonia and Thrace in order to demographically secure the country's northern border, destroying the local political and social balance in the process. The refugees, most of whom were utterly impoverished on arrival, needed housing, jobs, and farmland. The native population dismissed their demands or even chased them away. Moreover, they in turn began to eye the resident minority's houses and property with envy. There were local riots; private households were forced to accommodate refugees and land was divided up.

Ever more members of the Bulgarian minority were thus driven across the border. The same scenario was then repeated on the other side. The influx of refugees exerted pressure on the local Greek minority and disturbances erupted in many places. At the same time, attitudes toward the Turkish minority also hardened. It would be wrong, however, to attribute these conflicts primarily to local antagonisms, individual authors, or a regional tradition of violence. State population policy was the critical factor, as the comparison of different regions of northern Greece shows. Far fewer minority members emigrated from the border regions of western Macedonia neighboring Serbia than did so further east, because the Greek government's alliance with Serbia largely disposed of the need to settle refugees along this border.[44] Once again, state aggression was proven to have longer-term consequences than intercommunal ethnic violence, which usually abated after a period.

In response to the conflicts along the Greek-Bulgarian border, the League of Nations sent a commission to the area in 1925. It concluded that the "Macedonian question" could only be solved in strict adherence to the Treaty of Neuilly. In future, emigration was to take precedence over the protection of minorities.[45] Forced to acknowledge the failure of voluntary emigration, the League of Nations legalized forced migrations on an international level.

Under these circumstances, the principle of reciprocity could no longer be upheld. By the time emigration was phased out in 1931, the Treaty of Neuilly had caused the resettlement of nearly 102,000 Bulgarians and

53,000 Greeks. Most of them did not receive any compensation for abandoned property. While cattle breeders from the mountain regions were at least able to drive their cattle herds over the border under cover of darkness, most farmers and traders were not able to take any property with them. In Greece, the extreme strain placed on the national budget after the Treaty of Lausanne precluded the payment of compensation to the Neuilly migrants; Bulgaria also lacked the means after World War I to help refugees. Deprivation and embitterment prevailed on both sides of the border. On the Bulgarian side, it was compounded by a desire for revenge, which was eventually gained when Bulgaria occupied parts of northern Greece in 1941–44. Moreover, the Treaty of Neuilly limited the rights of the remaining minorities. The roughly 160,000 *Slavophonoi* (literally "Slavophones", a term invented by the Greek administration to avoid national designations) in Greece were now recognized only as a linguistic, not as a national, minority.[46]

Despite the vast problems caused by implementing the Treaty of Neuilly, contemporary observers viewed it positively. Lord Curzon, then British foreign minister, deemed "the scheme for the interchange of minorities" a success and of "great importance for the future peace in the Balkans."[47] While Dutch political scientist André Wurfbain, the first academic to publish a book on the enforcement of the Treaty of Neuilly, pointed out that it "did not do much credit to the history of the civilized world," he also saw in it an "innovation" of international policy.

In the mid-1920s, the League of Nations changed the previously liberal tenor of the Treaty of Neuilly, making forced migration out of what had originally been intended to be voluntary. Although the number of people forced to leave their homelands was relatively low in proportion to the population as a whole and the still-remaining minorities, the treaty nevertheless facilitated an instance of large-scale, organized, and compulsory ethnic cleansing.

The Treaty of Lausanne

The Treaty of Neuilly and its positive reception paved the way for the Treaty of Lausanne. No sooner had Greece achieved its military goals in Macedonia and Thrace than it opened up a new front in Asia Minor. In May 1919, with the tacit support of the British, Greek troops landed in Smyrna. Greece justified its actions by claiming there was a strong Greek minority in Asia Minor and a need to restore public order. In fact, Venizelos was acting on plans for not only a considerably larger but also a broadly homogenized Greater Greece. In 1919, he told *The Times* in

London of his wish for a "wholesale and mutual transfer of population"[48] with Turkey—following a border that was advantageous to Greece, of course. This probably marked the first use of the term "transfer" in an international context.

The Treaty of Sèvres of 1920, which reduced Turkey to a small part of Anatolia in accordance with Britain's wishes, included a passage on minority emigration similar to the corresponding article in the Treaty of Neuilly. Paragraph 143 of the Treaty of Sèvres provided for the "mutual and voluntary emigration" of the respective minorities along the new border. But Greece and Turkey were not able to agree on a convention analogous to the Treaty of Neuilly's supplementary agreements, providing more grounds for embarking on a new war.

As the Greek army marched into inner Anatolia in 1921, again with British approval, it left a trail of destruction.[49] This invasion—a colonial operation in terms of objectives and conduct—encountered determined resistance. Kemal Pasha, the later Atatürk, set about mobilizing Anatolia's Turkish population and especially the refugees from western Asia Minor. In August 1921, he defeated the invading Greek army seventy kilometers from Ankara. The Greek troops and also nearly all Christian civilians fled the counterattack. While they certainly feared suffering a similar fate to the Armenians in 1915 at the hands of the Turks, the scorched earth left by the retreating Greek army made fleeing practically their only option.[50]

Kemal Pasha and the new Turkish leadership had never made any secret of their contempt for the Treaty of Sèvres and the protection of minorities it stipulated. It not only opposed their plans in the conflict over western Asia Minor but also Kemal Pasha's basic convictions. As a pupil at the French grammar school in Saloniki, he had been brought up to admire a centralist and homogeneous republic. Lieutenant Aaron Stanton Merrill of the US Army, who had been sent to observe the situation, evaluated Turkish attitudes to minorities thus: "Their slogan is 'Turkey for the Turks'. They consider that all their troubles during the past 40 years can be attributed to the propaganda spread by the Christian minorities and that their only solution is to remove these minorities."[51]

By the time the Turkish troops moved into Smyrna/Izmir in September 1922, they had been preceded by hundreds of thousands of refugees. The invading army caused tumultuous disturbances; women were raped, people were killed in broad daylight, and the Greek Orthodox metropolitan Chrysostomos was lynched.[52] As in the Balkan wars previously, most of the atrocities were committed by paramilitary units. They were given free rein to inflict physical and symbolic violence in order to convey the message to the Greeks that there was no future for them in Smyrna.

The tragic climax of the Greco-Turkish War was the great fire of
Smyrna, which destroyed the Greek and Armenian quarters of the
town. Dreadful accounts of fleeing mothers carrying dead babies, people
plunging into the sea in desperation, and screams drowned out by the
loud music of military bands spread across the globe. The catastrophe
became a milestone in the collective memory of the twentieth century.
Ernest Hemingway, who was not in Smyrna himself at the time, probably based his short story "On the Quai at Smyrna" on an account by
lieutenant Merrill:

> The entire city was ablaze and the harbor was light as day. Thousands of
> homeless refugees were surging back and forth on the blistering quay—panic
> stricken to the point of insanity. The heartrending shrieks of women and
> children were painful to hear. In a frenzy they would throw themselves in
> the water—and some would reach the ship. The attempt to land a boat would
> have been disastrous. Several boats tried it and were immediately swamped
> by the mad rush of a howling mob.[53]

The destruction of Smyrna—an augury for the century of ethnic
cleansings—served to exacerbate the situation locally. It rendered the
town's Christian population homeless in addition to the refugees from
the interior. Like the Muslim refugees from Saloniki ten years previously,
hundreds of thousands waited to be taken across the sea. But unlike
then, the foreign media spread the news of the catastrophe throughout
the world. The public, not only in the United States and Britain, was
shocked.

The dramatic plight of the refugees moved the international community to intervene. The great powers sent ships to transport refugees to
Greece. In early October, the Allied high commissioner in Istanbul made
inquiries into whether the Turkish government would accept the offer
of a population exchange.[54] Eventually Turkey agreed to a peace conference led by the great powers in neutral Switzerland and an immediate
cease-fire.

The Conference of Lausanne was in some ways a continuation of the
bilateral Greco-Turkish negotiations of 1914, with one critical difference: it bore the distinct imprint of the great powers and the Treaties
of Neuilly and Sèvres.[55] In certain ways, in 1923, Greece got what it had
been demanding since 1919 and had almost achieved with the Treaty of
Sèvres: an ethnically consolidated eastern border. The only discrepancy
was that it followed a different course than Venizelos and his negligent
successors had envisaged.

Western historians have often taken the fire of Smyrna as grounds for
blaming Turkey or simply "the Turks" for "inventing" ethnic cleans-

ing.[56] But the Lausanne protocol clearly shows that it was the British foreign minister Lord Curzon who coined the term "exchange of populations" and suggested it to the two adversaries. Elsewhere in the protocol, Lord Curzon is recorded as proposing to "unmix the populations of the Near East." The leader of the Turkish delegation appeared surprised that this point was on the agenda at all.[57] The chief Greek negotiator—the experienced diplomat Venizelos had been reappointed after the disaster in Asia Minor—wanted the population exchange to at least take place on a voluntary basis, thus reiterating the position he had held at the Greco-Turkish negotiations of 1914.

However, at the decisive meeting of the "Territorial and Military Commission" on 1 December 1922, Curzon insisted that the transfer must be compulsory rather than voluntary.[58] The course of the debate is of interest for the history of ethnic cleansing not least because Curzon later accused the Turkish side of only deporting minorities and distanced himself from the idea of population exchange. "For his own part," the minutes of the next meeting two weeks later record, "he deeply regretted that the solution now being worked out should be the compulsory exchange of populations—a thoroughly bad and vicious solution, for which the world will pay a heavy penalty for a hundred years to come."[59] This comment by Curzon has been picked up by countless publications and used to apparently retrieve the honor of the British diplomats, the League of Nations, and their arbitration.[60] Nevertheless, it was Curzon who proposed a compulsory population exchange at the decisive moment in Lausanne.

Curzon's actions were informed by his experience of British colonial rule. As viceroy of India from 1899 to 1905, he had ordered the partition of Bengal into a region populated mostly by Muslims and a mainly Hindu region. Following fierce protests, the measure had been revoked some years after his return to London, but the idea of partition remained, to be realized with disastrous consequences in 1946–47.[61] A better-known example in Europe is the border of eastern Galicia, which Curzon introduced as British foreign minister to end the war between Poland and the Soviet Union in July 1920.[62] He proposed this almost dead-straight dividing line, which determined the course of the Polish-Soviet border in 1943–44, with little knowledge of conditions in the region. While Curzon cannot be blamed for later ethnic cleansings along the borders he drew either in Bengal or in eastern Galicia, he can be held responsible for proceeding without due knowledge of local settlement structures. Typically, the "ruler principle" was only used in regions that were considered backward. Partition aimed to divide political sovereignty along ethnically defined geographical boundaries. But rather than defusing power struggles between different ethnic groups or nations, it simply served to territorialize them.

The phrase "population exchange" feigned a reciprocity that only existed on paper, as in the Treaty of Neuilly, but suggested fairness and feasibility. The entire course of the negotiations in winter 1922–23 was characterized by a technocratic approach that masked the diplomats' ignorance of the region. The League of Nations' high commissioner for refugees, Fridtjof Nansen, declared his optimism that the Greeks and Turks who had been "exchanged" in the winter would already be tilling their fields in the spring. Consequently, he and Curzon pushed for an "immediate and efficient exchange."[63] It apparently did not occur to them that growing cotton in Macedonia and producing raisins near Izmir required different skills, knowledge, and local conditions.

The signatories of the Treaty of Lausanne justified it as guaranteeing "true pacification."[64] They defended the forced migrations it provided for by maintaining that this simply confirmed the reality of mass flight. In fact, the treaty extended the arena of ethnic cleansing. While the Greco-Turkish War had been confined to western Asia Minor, the Treaty of Lausanne also dealt with regions far removed from the hostilities, such as the Black Sea coast and the Anatolian highlands. Only western Thrace and Istanbul did not have to submit to a "population exchange," to the benefit above all of the Greeks and Armenians living there. (Despite the genocide of 1915, Istanbul still has a substantial Armenian minority today.) A total of 700,000 people were forced from their homes under the Treaty of Lausanne. On hearing news of the outcome of the conference, the minorities concerned in Greece and Turkey responded with protests and demonstrations.[65] As tense as the situation was, few were apparently willing to abandon their homes and property. But their resistance was to no avail; compulsory migration had been agreed on in the treaty, which ruled out exceptions.

Although the Treaty of Lausanne was designed to rescue the refugees, the situation in many areas did not improve for them. Beatings and pilfering were common. Contrary to the diplomats' confidence in technocracy, there were not enough ships waiting at the Black Sea coast to transport all the migrants in 1923. Greece was short of reception camps and accommodation. The "population exchange," which from a statistical perspective was not strictly reciprocal, was delayed. A lieutenant of the US Marines who was traveling through Trabzon in 1923 reported scenes of terrible deprivation:

> That sickness is general is shown clearly by the fact that litters of the dead are passing through the streets, many that are ill and unable to walk are being carried on the backs of their relatives, many are huddled in filth and

squalor by the roadside with evidence of extreme illness and expressions of pain in their faces and their audible groans add to the din and confusion. Many of the adults and most of the children are undernourished, skin condition, scabies and so forth are general.[66]

On arrival in Greece, they encountered equally dire conditions. As late as 1926, the Greek commission for refugees told the League of Nations: "On the humanitarian side, imagination cannot encompass the event. Only those can attempt to understand who have seen destitution, misery, disease, and death in all their possible forms, and the scale of disaster is so unprecedented as to demand a new vision even from such persons."[67] A correspondent for the magazine *Foreign Affairs* wrote in more sober terms: "[T]he refugees ... maintained a fox-like existence in tents, wooden barracks, shelters of twigs, or of turf, even in caves."[68]

There are no reliable statistics on casualties of the Greco-Turkish War and the ensuing ethnic cleansings. But official Greek statistics recorded the deaths of 75,000 refugees from malnourishment and disease following their arrival in their "home" country.[69] During the war, the death toll among the refugees must have been significantly higher. While under the Treaty of Neuilly almost two-thirds of the Bulgarian minority were able to stay in their homeland, with the exception of Istanbul and western Thrace, the "population exchange" sanctioned in Lausanne was wholesale. Henceforth, Turkey was deemed a homogeneous nation-state; the Greek population in Macedonia grew from 43 percent in 1913 to 90 percent in 1926. Moreover, the Treaty of Lausanne did not commit Greece or Turkey to recognizing national minorities, weakening the position of the Slavic population in Greece, which counted only as a linguistic minority, and the Kurds in Turkey, where only religious minorities were acknowledged.

The impact on the Greek national economy was equally catastrophic. Greece was hopelessly overtaxed by its additional 1.5 million citizens, who amounted to one-quarter of the population (officially there were 1,221,849 Greek emigrants from Turkey, according to the Treaty of Lausanne). It remained dependent on international aid, loans, and food donations until the outbreak of World War II. Not only that, the new influx of people gave rise to extreme tensions among the native population. Years later, former refugees were still physically assaulted and chased off farmland. One Greek politician even suggested marking them out with compulsory yellow armbands.[70] Conflict between the native population and former refugees, many of whom continued to speak Turkish, was one of the causes of the civil war in 1945–49. Right up until the late twentieth century, Greek politicians tried to divert attention from these inner conflicts by promoting an image of Turkey as a traditional enemy and cultivating the memory of the fire of Smyrna. Meanwhile, Turkey also suffered devastating damage to its national economy, but had less difficulty absorbing the refugees, since they made up a far smaller proportion of the total population. Nevertheless, the loss of Greek tradesmen and businessmen was sorely felt and agriculture around Izmir declined. The 355,635 Muslims who officially arrived in Turkey under the Treaty of Lausanne were in no position to replace the expelled Greeks.

How did the Treaty of Lausanne come to be regarded as a success in spite of all this? Part of the explanation can be found in the contemporary Western press. While Curzon regretted the mass expulsions in formulistic terms, he also underlined the peace that they had helped to achieve.[71] In a long speech to Parliament in fall 1923, he listed the advantages for Britain of free access to the Black Sea, the "liberation" of the Arab territories from the Ottoman Empire, and the increase in prestige for the British as chief negotiators. He did not mention the plight of the Greek refugees or any aspect of the humanitarian and economic disaster.

The Treaty of Lausanne became associated with an almost mythical peacemaking influence when Greece and Turkey signed a treaty of friendship in 1930, which indeed heralded a decade of unprecedented good relations between the two countries. For Turkey, which had gained full sovereignty under the 1923 treaty, Lausanne became a place of national remembrance, and was commemorated in the names of countless streets and squares. In Greece, in contrast, the events triggered by Lausanne and the expulsions from Asia Minor were remembered as national disasters. The only positive effect of the treaty was broadly felt to be the homogenization of northern Greece. To this day, nearly all Greek parties from the entire political spectrum support this development. Dimitri Pentzopoulos discussed this consensus in his influential book of 1962. Since, he claims, minorities pose a potential threat to the nation-state,[72] citing the example of the German inhabitants of the Czech borderlands (the Sudeten Germans), he writes: "National homogeneity, therefore, is considered a great advantage, intimately connected with the power of the state. Assuming the validity of this line of thought, it is evident that the exchange of populations immediately produces one desirable goal: it eliminates the heterogeneous element of a country."[73] Pentzopoulos also underlined the positive economic effects of the Treaty of Lausanne. Like other Greek, British, and American observers in the late 1920s, he stressed the importance of the refugees' contribution toward the economic development and urbanization of Greece.[74] Some commentators even drew analogies with the Huguenots and their contribution to Prussia's rise. The League of Nations meanwhile congratulated itself on the successful provision of care and accommodation to the masses of refugees, stating in 1928 that this proved that the scientific treatment of a migration problem can succeed with international support.[75]

Eliminating heterogeneity, scientific treatment, progress, economic growth—all these buzz terms that were in common currency for most of the twentieth century reflect the force of European modernity. If, like Pentzopoulos, one held ethnic homogeneity to be a precondition for the political stability of a nation-state, their effects seemed positive. Certainly, one might expect a sudden population growth to lead to a spurt of economic development.

But in the long term, did the Treaty of Lausanne really stabilize Greece and its relations with Turkey? State policy on assimilation and purposeful settlement was one of the factors driving members of the Slavic minority in Greece to support the Communists during the civil war in 1946–49. For many years, the urban slums inhabited by refugees from Asia Minor were among the flash points of disturbances in Greece.[76] There was also unrest in Turkey; many of the refugees transported to rural areas found it hard to settle and migrated to the cities.

Eventually, after 1945, events in Greece and Turkey showed that pursuing the utopia of ethnic purity can lead to increased minority persecution. Nearly all members of the Slavic minority who had not completely assimilated were driven out of Greece during the civil war. The 1955 pogrom (known as the *Septembrianá*) convinced most of the 125,000 Greeks remaining in Istanbul to leave. The political rapprochement between Turkey and Greece was not to last. In the postwar years, they reverted to their earlier antagonism despite their common membership in the North Atlantic Treaty Organization (NATO). The "consolidation of Hellenism" in Macedonia, moreover, which Pentzopoulos valued so highly, seems fragile to this day. When the former Yugoslav republic of Macedonia gained independence in 1992, there were Greek protests against the name of the state. Not only that, Greece obstructed trade with the young state and vetoed its membership of NATO. Evidently, the mere symbolic reminiscence of the old Macedonia was enough to rouse widespread fears of Slavic claims to Greek territory. Such reactions convey an impression of how deep the trauma of flight and forced integration is embedded. In regions that have been ethnically cleansed, it is passed on by the actual refugees to their descendants and society in general.

Conclusion

In the first phase of ethnic cleansing, the practice burgeoned on several levels. First, the size of the areas concerned grew dramatically. While in 1913 only small strips of borderland were affected, the enforced resettlements arranged in 1919 and 1923 dealt with far larger regions and eventually two entire nation-states. A total of 2.8 million people were moved in the following chronological order: 890,000 by ethnic cleansings as a consequence of the Balkan wars; 150,000 by *épuration* in Alsace; 156,000 under the Treaty of Neuilly; and 1,577,000 under the Treaty of Lausanne. These are all conservative estimates based exclusively on official statistics. They do not take into account either cases bordering on ethnic cleansing during World War I or migrations as a consequence of the new nation-state order after 1918, nor do they include the genocide of the Armenians. A broader definition of ethnic cleansing would point to a number twice as high.

The geographical ambit broadened as a result of diplomacy rather than the wars preceding ethnic cleansings. Instead of preventing ethnic cleansings, rationally conducted negotiations allowed them to escalate. Furthermore, ethnic cleansings became increasingly wholesale. While in Alsace and under the Treaty of Neuilly only about one-third of the minorities in question were forced to leave their homes, the Treaty of Lausanne provided for a total population exchange. It aimed to deal with each and every member of the respective minorities. It became increasingly difficult for individuals to evade the authorities performing selection by, for example, changing nationality. Again, this was not the result of irrational hatred but of deliberate planning.

The voluntary principle, which the Treaty of Neuilly originally included but which had unintentionally halted the migration of minorities, was increasingly disregarded and eventually abandoned in the Treaty of Lausanne. In parallel with this, the priority of international politics shifted from protecting to reducing minorities. Typically, the two processes were not regarded as incompatible. The resolutions on "voluntary emigration" formed part of the articles on minority protection in the Treaties of Neuilly and Sèvres. A dynamic from voluntariness to compulsion developed in the process of enforcing the individual treaties as well as from one convention to the next.

Eventually the great powers also abandoned the principle of reciprocity. In each of the cases considered here, minority migration was decidedly unbalanced. Under Neuilly, the ratio of Bulgarian to Greek "emigrants" was almost two to one (103,000 to 53,000); Lausanne affected three Greeks to every Turk (or Christians to Muslims, according to the treaty), or 1.2 million to 350,000.[77] But the great powers continued to speak of "reciprocal emigration" and "population exchange" and eventually also "de-mixing." Despite their euphemistic nature, these technocratic terms succeeded in raising public acceptance of the coercive measures they denoted.

The only civil rights respected by the treaties above were property rights. But in fact, conditions locally before leaving and on arrival in the refugees' "external homeland" did not allow compensation to be afforded in most cases. As a rule, ethnic cleansing left those affected destitute. Not only were they deliberately robbed by soldiers, the civil administration, and local residents, but many economic mechanisms proved vulnerable to the changes. Craft industries and local stores often went out of business after their original proprietors had been expelled and replaced by others. Agriculture, too, is dependent on local conditions and knowledge of them. Thus, the population shifts effected by the Paris Peace Treaties inevitably led to substantial material losses. But the detailed property regulations set out in the Treaties of Neuilly and Lausanne suggested that a liberal order and the rule of law could go hand in hand with ethnic cleansing, and that material belongings and human capital could be transferred easily.

On the one hand, the treaties saved the refugees from an even worse plight in their regions of origin and helped to organize their removal. For this reason, internationally arranged "population transfers" and their implementation should be distinguished from flight and unilateral expulsions. But on the other hand, the legitimization of ethnic cleansing raised judicial and public acceptance of such radical solutions on a national and an international level. Correspondingly, Lausanne was remembered not in the light of the refugees' misery and suffering but through the lens of belief in a rational and final solution, the utopia of feasibility, and the chimera of peacemaking. This was the truly fatal legacy of the treaty and indeed of the entire first phase of ethnic cleansing.

Notes

1. A similar periodization of ethnic cleansing in the twentieth century is provided by Donald *Bloxham*, "The Great Unweaving: Forced Population Movement in Europe, 1875–1949," in *Bessel* and *Haake, Removing Peoples*, 167–208.
2. International Commission, *The Other Balkan Wars*, 151. This quote is taken from a passage on the conduct of the Serbian army in Kosovo, but similar observations were made on the conduct of the Greek and Bulgarian armies. See International Commission, *The Other Balkan Wars*, 148–207 and the appendix, with eyewitness accounts.
3. See Toumarkine, *Les migrations*, 77.
4. See International Commission, *The Other Balkan Wars*, 72.
5. See Keith Brown, "'Wiping Out the Bulgar Race': Hatred, Duty, and National Self-Fashioning in the Second Balkan War," in *Bartov* and *Weitz, Shatterzones of Empires*, 298–316. This article also contains a convincing source critique of the Carnegie Endowment's report and its "Balkanist" way of explaining the violence.
6. Kemal Karpat, "The Ottoman Adoption."
7. See International Commission, *The Other Balkan Wars*, 148–49.

8. See Yannis G. Mourelos, "The 1914 Persecutions and the First Attempt at an Exchange of Minorities between Greece and Turkey," *Balkan Studies* 26, no. 2 (1985): 389 and 391.

9. See Eyal Ginio, "Paving the Way for Ethnic Cleansing: Eastern Thrace through the Balkan Wars (1912–1913) and Their Aftermath," in Bartov and Weitz, *Shatterzones of Empires,* 286 and 291.

10. See Mourelos, "The 1914 Persecutions," 396–98.

11. On this estimate, see Mourelos, "The 1914 Persecutions," 405.

12. See, e.g., Sundhaussen, "Bevölkerungsverschiebungen," 35.

13. A somewhat nationalist in tone but precise account is given by Georgi Markow, "Bulgarien auf der Friedenskonferenz in Konstantinopel (August–September 1913)," *Bulgarian Historical Review* (1990): 73–75.

14. On these negotiations, see Mourelos, "The 1914 Persecutions"; Harry Psomiades, "Fridtjof Nansen and the Greek Refugee Problem," *Deltio: Kentrou Mikrasiatikon Spoudon* 18 (2009): 308–11.

15. On expulsions during World War I, see Eric Lohr, *Nationalizing the Russian Empire: The Campaign against Enemy Aliens during World War I* (Cambridge, 2003). Almost one million Poles were also affected by evacuation and deportation.

16. Pentzopoulos estimates that 481,000 Greeks were deported, but this number is most probably exaggerated. See Dimitri Pentzopoulos, *The Balkan Exchange of Minorities and its Impact upon Greece* (London, 2002).

17. Broszat, *Zweihundert Jahre deutsche Polenpolitik* (Munich, 1963), 183; Hermann Graml, "Flucht und Vertreibung der Deutschen aus Ostdeutschland und Osteuropa: Ein Blick auf historische Zusammenhänge," in *Geglückte Integration? Spezifika und Vergleichbarkeiten der Vertriebenen-Eingliederung in der SBZ/DDR,* ed. Dierk Hoffmann and Michael Schwartz (Munich, 1999), 23.

18. See Harvey, "Lost Children," 539; Christiane Kohser-Spohn, "Die Vertreibung."

19. See Montandon, *Frontières nationales.*

20. On Lichtenstädter, see Mihran Dabag, "National-koloniale Konstruktionen," 62.

21. Peter Gatrell, "War, Population Displacement and State Formation in the Russian Borderlands, 1914–1924," in *Homelands: War, Population and Statehood in Eastern Europe and Russia 1918–1924,* ed. Nick Baron and Peter Gatrell (London, 2004), 13 and 26. Michael Marrus, *The Unwanted: European Refugees in the Twentieth Century* (Oxford, 1985), 60–61, gives a distinctly lower number. On Muslim refugees from the Caucasus, see Onur Yıldırım, *Diplomacy and Displacement: Reconsidering the Turco-Greek Exchange of Populations, 1922–1934* (New York, 2006), 89.

22. By 1925, the official number of repatriated persons in Poland was 1,265,000. See Konrad Zielinski, "Population Displacement and Citizenship in Poland, 1918–24," in Baron and Gatrell, *Homelands,* 105.

23. See Lieberman, *Terrible Fate,* 36–44.

24. On interethnic and other forms of violent conflict, see Ther and Sundhaussen, *Nationalitätenkonflikte.*

25. On the concept of communal violence and its antithesis, interethnic cooperation, see David Laitin, *Nations, States and Violence* (New York, 2007), 11.

26. Terry Martin describes some incidents as "popular ethnic cleansing." See Martin, "The Origins of Soviet Ethnic Cleansing," *The Journal of Modern History* 70 (1998): 813–61. Since ethnic cleansings are always predicated on their implementation by local actors, they are all "popular" to some degree.

27. Marrus, *The Unwanted,* 65. In 1926 several hundreds of thousands of Jews were given Polish nationality, indicating that minority policy was not always consistent.

28. On German emigrations, see Joachim Rogall, *Die Deutschen im Posener Land und Mittelpolen* (Berlin, 1998), 130; Antoni Czubiński, *Wielkopolska w latach 1918–1939*

(Poznań, 2000), 80; on Hungary, see István Mócsy, *The Effects of World War I: The Uprooted: Hungarian Refugees and Their Impact on Hungary´s Domestic Politics, 1918–1921* (New York, 1983), 12. For an overview, see Brubaker, *Nationalism Reframed*, 155–69.

29. See the statistics in Tomaszewski, *Rzeczpospolita wielu narodów*, 213.
30. I am grateful to Christiane Kohser-Spohn for making this document available from the Archives départementales du Bas-Rhin, FCGR, vol. 1/121/AL 899.
31. See Carolyn Grohmann, "From Lothringen to Lorraine: Expulsion and Voluntary Repatriation," *Diplomacy & Statecraft* 16 (2009): 578.
32. On these categories and statistics, see Harvey, *Lost Children*, 548–50.
33. Quoted from Harvey, *Lost Children*, 544.
34. See the enduringly relevant study by Swiss historian Karl-Heinz Rothenberger, *Die elsass-lothringische Heimat- und Autonomiebewegung zwischen den beiden Weltkriegen* (Frankfurt, 1976).
35. On Western reports on the pogroms, see Carole Fink, *Defending the Rights of Others: The Great Powers, the Jews and the International Minority Protection* (Cambridge, 2004), 133–264; see also Piotr Wróbel, "Polacy, Żydzi i odbudowa Polski na stronach The New York Timesa w 1918 i 1919 roku," in *Rozdział wspólnej historii: Studia z dziejów Żydów w Polsce, ofiarowane Jerzemu Tomaszewskiemu w siedemdziesiątą rocznicę urodzin* (Warsaw, 2001), 181–98. On Polish-Jewish relations in Congress Poland, see Konrad Zieliński, *Stosunki polsko-żydowskie na ziemiach Królestwa Polskiego w czasie pierwszej wojny światowej* (Lublin, 2005).
36. Fink, *Defending the Rights*, 236–64. The treaties on the protection of minorities with Poland, the Kingdom of Serbia, Croatia and Slovenia, Czechoslovakia, and Romania are reproduced in H. W. V. Temperley, *A History of the Peace Conference*, 432–70. On the previous negotiations, see 112–49.
37. ". . . deportation and protection ran together." Eric D. Weitz, "From the Vienna to the Paris System: International Politics and the Entangled Histories of Human Rights, Forced Deportations and Civilizing Missions," *American Historical Review* 113, no. 5 (2008): 1313.
38. Fink, *Defending the Rights*, 292.
39. Temperley, *A History*, 317. The term "racial minorities" implies an absolute and unalterable concept of nationality and national minorities.
40. A facsimile of the agreement is reproduced in André Wurfbain, *L´échange Gréco-Bulgare des Minorités Ethniques* (Lausanne, 1930). Greece tried to extend the "solution" by convincing Serbia to accede to the Treaty of Neuilly.
41. See Teodora Dragostinova, "Navigating Nationality in the Emigration of Minorities between Bulgaria and Greece, 1919–1941," *East European Politics and Society* 23 (2009): 185–212.
42. On the process of resettlement, see Stelios Nestor, "Greek Macedonia and the Convention of Neuilly," *Balkan Studies* 3 (1962): 175 and 180.
43. On these figures, see Dragostinova, "Navigating Nationality," 193. See also Iakō bos Michaēlidēs, *Metakinēsis Slavophōnōn Plēthysmōn (1912–1930): O polemos tōn Statistikōn* [Ιάκωβος Δ. Μιχαηλίδης, Μετακινήσεις Σλαβοφώνων Πληθυσμών (1912–1930): Ο Πόλεμος των Στατιστικών] (Athens, 2003). I am grateful to Jannis Panagiotidis for making this book available and translating excerpts. On the actual migrations, see esp. 135–64. See also Elisabeth Kontogiorgi, *Population Exchange in Greek Macedonia: The Rural Settlement of Refugees, 1922–1930* (New York: Oxford University Press, 2006).
44. On demographic border defense, see Kontogiorgi, *Population Exchange*, 208.
45. It was the Rumboldt Commission, named after its chairman. See Nestor, "Greek Macedonia," 181. On the preceding incidents, see also Kontogiorgi, *Population Exchange*, 85.

46. See chap. 8 (219–42) in Michaēlidēs, *Metakinēsis Slavophōnōn Plēthysmōn.*
47. Quoted by Matthew Frank, *Expelling the Germans: British Opinion and Post-1945 Population Transfer in Context* (Oxford, 2007), 19.
48. Quoted by Frank, *Expelling the Germans,* 19.
49. See the archival collection (also cited by Norman Naimark, *Fires of Hatred: Ethnic Cleansing in Twentieth Century Europe* [Cambridge, 2001]) "The Armenian Genocide in the U.S. Archives, 1915–1918" (hereafter AGUSA), microfiche 337, A6 (this particular file is a war diary).
50. Ibid., microfiche 337, A7, B9, and D12.
51. Ibid., microfiche 337, D6.
52. On rape and forced prostitution, see the report by another soldier of the US Marines in AGUSA, microfiche 47 (entry of 4 March 1923), 4.
53. AGUSA, microfiche 337, C12. For a more detached account of the tragedy, see AGUSA, microfiche 159, 27–29.
54. See Kontogiorgi, *Population Exchange,* 58.
55. See Lausanne Conference on Near Eastern Affairs 1922–23, *Records of Proceedings and Draft Terms of Peace* (London, 1923), 115.
56. As well as the Greek literature, see Naimark, *Fires of Hatred,* 72, according to which the Turks insisted on a compulsory exchange in Lausanne.
57. Lausanne Conference, *Records,* 118; Yıldırım, *Diplomacy,* 61 and 68. Yıldırım, however, also stresses the Greco-Turkish consensus on this issue (see 39).
58. See Lausanne Conference, *Records,* 120.
59. Ibid., 212.
60. See also the citation in Naimark, *Fires of Hatred,* 73.
61. On the Bengali partition, see the source documentation by Nityapriya Ghosh and Ashoke Kumar Mukhopadhyay, *Partition of Bengal: Significant Signposts, 1905–1911* (Kolkata, 2005).
62. On the Curzon Line in eastern Galicia, see Norman Davies, *God's Playground: A History of Poland, 1795 to the Present* (New York, 1982), 2:504.
63. Lausanne Conference, *Records,* 115.
64. Ibid., 114.
65. See Kontogiorgi, *Population Exchange,* 64; Yıldırım, *Diplomacy,* 79. On the number of persons uprooted under the treaty, see Yıldırım, *Diplomacy,* 3.
66. AGUSA, microfiche 47, file 131 (report by Lieutenant H. E. Gardner).
67. Greek Refugee Settlement Commission, *Greek Refugee Settlement* (Geneva, 1926), 15.
68. Quoted by Yıldırım, *Diplomacy,* 55.
69. Hirschon, *Heirs of the Greek Catastrophe,* 37.
70. Ibid., 187. On the other incidents of discrimination or persecution in Greece, see 174–75 and 182.
71. On Curzon's critique of the Treaty of Lausanne, see *The Times* (London), "Our Foreign Policy: Lord Curzon's Speech," 6 October 1923, 16.
72. Pentzopoulos, *The Balkan Exchange,* 125.
73. Ibid., 126. The myth of homogeneity has been countered by Anastasia Karakasidou, *Fields of Wheat, Hills of Blood: Passages to Nationhood in Greek Macedonia, 1870-1990* (Chicago, 1997).
74. Frank, *Expelling the Germans,* 23, cites this literature.
75. On the almost exclusively positive contemporary view of Lausanne, see Frank, *Expelling the Germans,* 25.
76. On Communist sympathizers among the refugees, see Pentzopoulos, *The Balkan Exchange,* 190–95.
77. Brandes, Sundhaussen, and Troebst, *Lexikon der Vertreibungen,* 273 and 387–88, gives higher numbers.

CHAPTER 3

TOTAL WAR AND TOTAL CLEANSING
1938–44

⌒⫯⫯⫯⫯⌒

From the Munich Agreement to World War II

The Munich Agreement of 1938 is remembered as symbolizing the ill-fated policy of appeasement toward Hitler and the Western democracies' moral bankruptcy. But it also marked a pivotal point in the history of national minorities and ethnic cleansing. This agreement between Great Britain, France, Italy, and Germany at Czechoslovakia's expense was based on the consensus that state and ethnic borders should henceforth correspond. In this sense, six months prior to its conclusion, high-ranking French and British politicians suggested a form of "population exchange" to Germany and Czechoslovakia in which the German-speaking diasporas in the interior of Bohemia would be dissolved and part of the border region ceded to Germany in return.[1] But by fall 1938, power relations between Germany and Czechoslovakia had become too imbalanced for the former to submit to bilateral population transfers.

Thus, the Munich Agreement made no further mention of the German islands in the Bohemian interior, stipulating only that Czechoslovakia cede all territories with a population that was more than 50 percent German. It was not deemed necessary to hold a general referendum on the issue since the results of national censuses were available, which were believed to hold all the relevant information. Local studies have shown, however, that populations in mixed settled areas could not be unambiguously divided into discrete categories of German or Czech.[2] But diplomacy made no allowance for subjective views of nationality. Thus, the dictate enforced by the European great powers on the most liberal of the nation-states founded in 1918–19 overturned the minority protection introduced by the Paris Peace Treaties. Anyone who found themselves on the wrong side of the new border had the choice of moving or assimilating. Not only the border regions known as the Sudetenland were affected, but also southern Slovakia: the four signatories called on Czechoslovakia and Hungary to agree on a new, ethnic border within three months. The crisis in the Sudeten border regions triggered by Nazi Germany was, then, merely the starting point of an extensive rearrangement of East Central Europe according to ethnic criteria.

This fateful development was the outcome of a fundamental change in mind-set that had evolved over a number of years. Since the world economic crisis, minority relations had deteriorated in most European countries.[3] Germans and Ukrainians rebelled in Poland; Croats, Albanians, and Bulgarians in Yugoslavia; Hungarians and Bulgarians in Romania; and Germans and Hungarians in Czechoslovakia. The countries defeated in World War I pushed for their postwar borders to be revised, especially Nazi Germany. Some radical groupings, such as the Organization of Ukrainian Nationalists (ONU) and the Inner Macedonian Revolutionary Organization (IMRO), used violence to fight the nation-states inhibiting their sovereignty. A wave of terror swept across Europe, which came to a spectacular climax with the assassination of King Aleksandar I of Yugoslavia and the French foreign minister Barthou in Marseille in 1934. The round of violence, petitions to the League of Nations, and disturbances in the newly founded nation-states threatened the fragile peace in postwar Europe. Minorities, rather than the upheavals caused by the new order of nation-states, were increasingly felt to be the root of the troubles.

The fact that the Munich Agreement actually created a new minority—Czechs living in the Bohemian borderlands—was largely overlooked by the diplomats negotiating it and the international public.[4] It was expected that "those Czechos," as a high-ranking member of the British delegation referred to the Czechs, would either conform or emigrate.[5] And it was Prime Minister Chamberlain who first uttered the word "resettlement" during negotiations over the future Czech minority in the Bohemian borderlands.[6] In order to channel this resettlement in an orderly fashion, the Czechs living in the borderlands were granted a six-month "right of option." Roughly 37,000 Czech officials and their families, who had moved to the borderlands since 1919, fled to the interior as soon as the Munich Agreement became public. Over the next weeks and months, 140,000 Czechs—some from families who had lived in the borderlands for generations—left their homes. Many did so under threat of violence[7] and arrived consequently embittered in the future protectorate. Although this case of ethnic cleansing was limited in scale compared to the measures under Lausanne, it was unprecedented in East Central Europe. A long-established regional population had never before been subjected to such swift and deep separation. Along with the Czechs, 18,000 Jews and 10,000 anti-Fascists fled into the remainder of Czechoslovakia.

The late 1930s also witnessed mass ethnic migrations in other parts of Europe. Between 1936 and 1939, about 100,000 Turks left Romania and Bulgaria on the basis of bilateral agreements. The same number again, if not more, emigrated on their own initiative, as well as about 20,000 Muslims from Yugoslavia, repelled by the continuing pressure to assimilate, everyday discrimination, and changes in the social structure.[8] Turkey adopted a plan in 1935 to increase population density by actively encouraging "home-comers." The Turkish authorities initially channeled most refugees to the borderlands in Thrace in order to demographically secure the region. This late resettlement in the 1930s was a continuation of the immigration of Southeastern European Muslims begun in 1878. It should, then, be viewed in sequence with earlier ethnic cleansings and not as the starting point of new population shifts. Nevertheless, the agreements between Turkey, Bulgaria, and Romania demonstrated once again that Lausanne was held as a model for resolving international conflicts by means of organized population removals.

This is also evidenced in an arena beyond Europe—the Middle East. In 1936, a British investigating committee was set up to analyze the violent conflicts between Arabs and Jews in the British mandate of Palestine. On the basis of its findings, the group, led by Lord Robert Peel, recommended dividing the region and enforcing a reciprocal population transfer across the new border.[9] This was to affect 200,000 Arabs but only 1,250 Jews. The Arab outcry was so huge that the British government dropped the plan. But the key words "partition" and "transfer" continued to be favored by international diplomats. On the eve of World War II, to resolve the conflict between Romania and Bulgaria, the British ambassador in Bucharest proposed a combined solution of border revision and population transfer in southern Dobruja.[10]

In June 1939, negotiations between the German Reich and Italy over South Tyrol followed a similar pattern, although the course of the border was not under discussion. Hitler styled himself the peacemaker by voting for the Brenner Pass as the ethnic demarcation line. Subsequently, a spokesman for the Italian government boasted that the Axis powers had solved the South Tyrolean problem with even greater statecraft and foresight than the authors of the exemplary Treaty of Lausanne.[11]

The British ambassador in Berlin met Hitler in August 1939 to discuss the possibility of a similar arrangement with Poland. According to Matthew Frank, the British government had two variants in mind: either a transfer of the respective German and Polish minorities across the existing border or a more extensive solution involving redrawing the border and shifting populations, which it referred to as a "progressive transfer." In a last-ditch attempt to prevent the outbreak of war, the French ambassador urged the Polish government to make a corresponding offer to Germany. Thus, Hitler was on the point of achieving a second Munich, both in terms of border changes to Germany's advantage and minority transfers. In contrast to Prague, however, Warsaw did not bow to international pressure. But the German Reich and the Soviet Union had already agreed on Poland's partition. At this point, even substantial concessions could not have prevented World War II. Germany's rapid victory in Poland enabled the German government to change the state and ethnic borders of *Mitteleuropa* as it saw fit. In the ensuing years, Adolf Hitler was to be the chief agent of ethnic cleansing in Europe.

Heim ins Reich

Hitler signaled the launch of his *Heim ins Reich* ("home to the Empire") policy initiative to bring diaspora Germans "back home" in his Reichstag address of 6 October 1939. He opened the speech with a lengthy invective against Poland and the Versailles peace settlement before addressing his core, forward-looking concern of rearranging the territories of Europe along ethnic (*völkisch*) lines. In order to establish a new framework for peace and a "feeling of European security," he claimed it was first necessary to "organize the entire *Lebensraum* according to nationalities, i.e. resolve the minority questions which not only affect this area but nearly all South and Southeastern European states." The primary means of achieving this should be to "resettle the nationalities … so that when this process is concluded there are better dividing lines than exist today."[12]

For the German Reich, Hitler envisaged a shift of its eastern border to correspond with the "historical, ethnographic and economic circumstances" but did not specify what he believed these to be. He addressed the "Jewish problem" only in an aside and largely refrained from making racist comments.[13] This was, then, one of the many speeches Hitler made in the second half of the 1930s that veiled his true goals.[14] Thus, he guaranteed the integrity of all the smaller neighboring states of the German Reich and called for reconciliation with France along the existing borders. Hitler evidently believed Europe's reorganization according to "ethnographic" criteria would find broad international acceptance and hoped Britain would eventually give way.[15] To underline his supposedly peaceful intentions, he announced the return to the Reich of "untenable splitter groups of German ethnicity," which were "a cause of continued international unrest." The ambiguity of this pledge became apparent when Hitler abused the ethnic German resettlers to colonize the annexed Polish territories rather than bringing them "back home" to Germany.

Germany and Italy signed a treaty on the resettlement of the German-speaking South Tyroleans only two weeks after Hitler made this speech. This agreement, the fundamentals of which had been settled in June 1939, was completely within the legal conventions established by the Treaties of Neuilly and Lausanne. Resettlement was to take place on a voluntary basis and property was to be registered and replaced wherever possible. South Tyroleans who opted for the nationality of the external state were, however, barred from returning to their homeland. The Italian newspaper *La Stampa* gladly predicted that the remaining German-speaking population south of the Brenner Pass would have to become 100 percent Italian, renounce their language and customs, and "dissolve themselves into the Italian race."[16] In practice, the "right of option" provided here, as in earlier cases, constituted a choice between a rock and a hard place, between the loss of one's homeland and compulsory assimilation. The population of South Tyrol responded with complaints, protests, and disturbances. But rumors of the imminent deportation of resisters to southern Italy or the Italian colonies eventually prompted a large majority to opt for German nationality.

At the same time as making these arrangements with Italy, Germany was also negotiating with Estonia and Latvia over its local minorities. Far more pressure was placed on the ethnic Germans in these Baltic states to emigrate than on those in South Tyrol in order to avoid conflict with the Soviet Union and bring movable assets back to Germany. Handbills, notices in the press, and public campaigns disseminated a doom-laden picture of a disenfranchised future for anyone intending to stay. "You don't want to?" asked one handout, which went on to warn:

Just so you know what you are opting for: 1) I, along with my children and children's children, disassociate myself from the German people. 2) I permanently relinquish my German status and hence all the protection that the German Reich has hitherto afforded me by its might. 3) I leave behind me all that is of my blood … 4) I prefer to remain isolated and alone.[17]

The last point, especially, touched a raw nerve. As soon as the first, typically younger, members of a family decided to emigrate, their relations, friends, and entire communities mostly followed.

At the same time, Nazi propaganda promised a bright future in the annexed Polish territories. Here, the resettlers were to fulfill a national mission and would be "afforded the utmost compensation" for the property they left behind. Nearly 62,000 people emigrated from Estonia and Latvia by late 1939. Following these countries' annexation by the Soviet Union, a further 17,000 initially hesitant resettlers followed.[18] Ultimately, only about 2,000 members of the German minority remained in these Baltic states, demonstrating the total nature of this resettlement action.

While the Germans from Estonia and Latvia were still embarking on the ships taking them "home," the German Reich concluded its next agreement on mass population removals. This time the deal was made, on 3 November, with the Soviet Union and concerned the descendants of German colonists in eastern Galicia and Volhynia. In formal terms, this was not to be a one-sided transfer, as from the Baltic states, but a reciprocal exchange of populations. It gave Byelorussians and Ukrainians living on General Government territory the "right" to register for resettlement in the Soviet Union. Soviet propaganda supported the registration by promising Byelorussians and Ukrainians national self-determination within the Soviet Union. Many of the former German colonists, for their part, were eager to escape collectivization, which was begun soon after the Red Army had invaded eastern Poland. The older generation, moreover, remembered the deportations enforced by Russia during World War I. Migrating to German-occupied Poland probably seemed the better alternative in the given circumstances. Nevertheless, here as previously in the Baltic region, the Nazi machinery left nothing to chance and applied extreme propagandist pressure. This set a group dynamic in motion that practically nobody in the tightly knit village communities could withstand.[19] A total of 137,000 people from eastern Galicia and Volhynia opted for resettlement in the German Reich. In September 1940, Germany and the Soviet Union concluded another treaty concerning resettlement from the Romanian regions that had been occupied by the Red Army. Subsequently, 93,000 ethnic Germans left Bessarabia and around 43,000 left the northern part of the Bukovina.

The German Reich's cooperation with the Soviet Union was not confined to diplomacy, extending to supervising resettlement locally. Authorized representatives and administrative staff from both states were deployed in the German- and Soviet-occupied territories and cooperated in mixed commissions. Joseph Schechtman reconstructed the process on the basis of contemporary reports and was evidently impressed by its efficiency when he wrote in 1945: "This was a well-balanced dual scheme, built from the apex downward and based on administrative German-Soviet parallelism; it reflected perfectly the cult of bureaucratic planning predominant in both the Reich and the Soviet Union."[20] Indeed, despite the freezing conditions in January and February 1940, the operation caused very few fatalities. The elderly, women, and children were transported by rail while most of the men formed wagon trains, taking their horses, cattle trucks, and farming equipment with them. Their reception was also efficiently organized, from medical care in the camps to the swift issuing of identification papers.[21]

In October 1940, the Nazis also concluded a treaty with Romania, under which 66,000 ethnic Germans emigrated from the southern part of Bukovina and Dobruja.[22] The resettlement from these regions posed the greatest logistical challenge so far, since in most cases it involved travel overland to the mouth of the Danube in Galati, then upriver by ship, and finally a last stretch overland to the places of destination. A Bessarabian German, who ended up in the town Ybbs on the Danube in Lower Austria, described his experience as one of an "emigrant, who feels like a fish that has been flung out of the water, fallen on dry land and tries to save himself, thinking he has reached the water that he now and again rushes along."[23]

The resettlers from Southeastern Europe, however, were not necessarily "German" enough for the Nazis, who proceeded to categorize them according to racial criteria. Only those who were classified as "pure-blooded" and "biologically valuable" were directed onward for resettlement. The resettlers who were put into the highest categories I and II did not have to wait long for apartments or farms in Warthegau and could set about starting a new life relatively quickly. The resettlers of category III, defined as "less balanced crossbreeds," however, did not receive any preferential treatment. Those of category IV—"completely imbalanced crossbreeds," those "of foreign blood," and the "genetically sick"—were mostly sent to the German heartlands to be Germanized. These lower-category resettlers were often housed in makeshift huts and made to perform forced labor. Several thousand people were even sent back to Romania. The racial selection of members of their own nationality marks the Nazis' population policy out from those of other European countries.[24] It also proved counterproductive to the Nazi objective of Germanizing western Poland, since it substantially reduced the number of people available to act as colonizers.

Those who did arrive in Warthegau or West Prussia faced a new start in a foreign land. The annexed territories were not flowing with milk and honey, as the propaganda had suggested, and conditions were often worse than in the resettlers' former homes. One ethnic German woman from Bessarabia complained to the Nazi authorities in 1942: "We have been here in Warthegau since November and I still feel as alien as I did on the first day. Warthegau has been a big disappointment to us all."[25] The German authorities' treatment of the Poles created less than ideal conditions for the new settlers. While the Polish residents of earmarked apartments and farms were usually evicted before the resettlers arrived, in rural areas, the latter sometimes witnessed these expulsions. In consequence, some resettlers came to doubt their legitimacy and even feel some sympathy toward the Poles who had to leave.[26] Compensation payments, moreover, proceeded very slowly. The ethnic Germans who had opted to resettle in South Tyrol, for example, only received about 10 percent of the compensation they were eligible for.[27] From summer 1940, less accommodation and fewer jobs were available to migrants. Thus, resettlement nearly always entailed a loss of income and social and professional status as well as personal networks. The situation in this respect was even worse in the *Altreich*. In Upper Bavaria the authorities noted the prevalence of prejudices toward the resettlers among the local population, a "stereotypical contemptuous disregard of their traditions and a tendency to lump them together with Poles and Czechs etc."[28] The refugees arriving in Germany after the war experienced similar prejudices some years later.

Most of the relevant literature, both old and recent, gives the total number of German resettlers as 770,000, on the basis of Nazi statistics. It is important to note, however, that the number of resettlers in the years 1939 and 1940 did not exceed half a million. The last third of the resettlers arrived in German territory on the tails of the retreating German army. They are, then, more accurately considered war refugees who were unable or unwilling to return to their homes after 1945.[29]

To what extent was the resettlement of the German minorities in Southern and Eastern Europe forced and therefore definable as ethnic cleansing? This question can only be answered on an individual level in the light of the resettlers' different regions of origin and social status. To the Nazis, the German resettlers were ultimately pawns to be used for realizing their short-term foreign policy goals as well as their longer-term ideological *Lebensraum* vision. Few were exposed to direct pressure to move—for example, by force of arms—but most were compelled by circumstances. They could not envisage a future as minority members, or under communism, in their homeland. The Nazi propaganda preyed on these misgivings while denouncing those intending to stay as traitors to the national community, the *Volksgemeinschaft*. At the same time, the German government lured prospective resettlers with fantastic promises. Eventually, even ethnic Germans who were skeptical of Nazi ideology or who were particularly attached to their homeland decided to emigrate.

One characteristic that these movements certainly had in common with ethnic cleansings was that they offered little chance of return. In 1941, the German authorities prohibited return movements despite the army's rapid advance on the Soviet Union. Later in the war, diaspora Germans desperately tried to escape westward from the Red Army. The roughly 50,000 Germans from Lithuania formed an exception in this respect, some of whom moved back to their old homeland in 1941. But their houses and farms had nearly all been occupied by Lithuanians who in turn drove out members of the Polish minority. These spontaneous expulsions illustrate the social dynamics and direct consequences triggered by ethnic cleansings on a local level. A return to the multiethnic status quo of early 1939 was almost impossible after a group had been absent for just one year.

Uniquely, the fate of the German resettlers was decided by the government of their coethnic state and nationalists within their own ethnicity. "Push" factors, in contrast, played a less important role. Negotiating this history in black-and-white terms of victims and perpetrators would be highly questionable—especially in view of the later histories of the German resettlers in occupied Poland, who were abused to complete the forcible Germanization of Warthegau and West Prussia. Another peculiar feature of the *Heim ins Reich* ("home to the Empire") policy, which was pursued in the context of war yet remained largely unaffected by it, was that most resettlers arrived on German territory outwardly unharmed. The efficiency of the Nazi bureaucracy corroborates Zygmunt Bauman's thoughts about European modernity. The Nazis' sophisticated administrative machinery indisputably saved tens of thousands of (German) lives, but also turned them upside down in a brutal and inhumane manner.

Under Nazi Occupation

The slogan "Heim ins Reich" was, like many Nazi slogans, a lie. The Nazis did not take the eastern and south European resettlers to the prewar territory of the German Reich, but to the annexed territories of occupied Poland. Polish historian Czesław Madajczyk and, more recently, Götz Aly have pointed to the connection between the resettlement of Germans, the expulsion of Poles and the genocide of the European Jews.[30]

However, the immense shadows cast by the Holocaust have obscured the fact that the German Reich initiated large scale ethnic cleansings in the areas it occupied and among the German allies (see the next chapter on ethnic cleansing in Germany's Sphere of Influence). All three of these main pillars of Nazi population policy in occupied Poland were based on the same racist foundation and ideological concept of a not only ethnically but also racially cleansed *Lebensraum*.

Despite these links, more differences than similarities can be observed in the Nazis' criminal treatment of non-Jewish Poles and Polish Jews. On the level of intent, the Nazis' approach to the two groups evidently differed: they quickly proceeded with killing Jews, whereas they initially expelled Poles en masse. According to the first versions of their "master plan for the East," the *Generalplan Ost,* the German government intended to resettle about ten million people from the Polish territories annexed by the Reich. By 1941 these plans had been extended to include the removal of seventeen million Poles to territories outside the Germans' *Lebensraum*. In contrast to the Jews, some Poles were considered suitable for assimilation or tolerable as labor slaves. Hence, the Poles were subjected to ethnic homogenization by a combination of expulsion, deportation, and forced assimilation, which was effected via the German People's List (*Deutsche Volksliste*). An additional difference lay in the fact that Poles were deported from Warthegau to the General Government, that is, to a clearly delineated reception area, which was occasionally referred to as *Restpolen* (remainder-Poland). The Jews of Poland and other European countries, in contrast, were rounded up in Nazi-established ghettos, or "Jewish reservations," as Himmler called them. These ghettos were created with the intent to destroy their inhabitants even before the Wannsee Conference was held. For this reason, the theory that ethnic cleansings escalated into genocide is even less convincing applied to the Polish Jews than to the German Jews.

There are nevertheless sound reasons for considering the ethnic cleansings in occupied Poland and parts of Yugoslavia as the first step toward a planned genocide. Immediately after the outbreak of war, the mass expulsions were accompanied by mass shootings. In the first three months after the German invasion, German soldiers and the SS shot 54,000 Polish civilians.[31] The primary goal of this organized mass murder was to destroy the local social elites, intelligentsia, and political representatives. The Jews were subjected to no such political and social selection, and instead were simply arbitrarily murdered. When the Poles formed resistance groups and made attempts on the occupiers' lives, however, the Nazis began terrorizing them as indiscriminately as they persecuted the Jews. The deportation of Poles from special regions, such as Zamość, also bore genocidal traits. These terrible experiences and reports from his homeland Poland motivated the Polish-Jewish lawyer Rafał (later Raphael) Lemkin to develop the concept of "ludobójstwo" (literally "genocide"). And yet the Nazis' treatment of Poles should still be classified as ethnic cleansing. The death toll is one reason. While only about 10 percent of Polish Jews survived the Holocaust, about 80 percent of the Polish population survived German occupation. But that is not to say that they survived unharmed. Many experienced sheer terror, especially the Poles expelled from Warthegau and West Prussia.

The expulsion of Poles from the German-annexed territories took place in three phases.[32] The first lasted from November to mid-December 1939 and affected about 90,000 people; the second ran from mid-February to March 1940 and uprooted about 40,000 people; the last phase dragged on over the second half of 1940 and affected 133,000 people. These extremely brutal expulsions were primarily intended to create space for the incoming German resettlers. On average, three Poles had to make way for every new arrival, with a higher ratio of Poles hit in rural areas. In this way, the Nazis aimed to install a modern, more economic population structure.[33] The German authorities parallelized removal and settlement more effectively than ever before in the history of ethnic cleansing. The police and SS often timed their expulsions of Polish farmers to the moment they had fed and milked their cows. Later the same day, German resettlers took over these farms and all their livestock, fixtures, and fittings. Some Poles tried to hide in the woods or in neighbors' houses,[34] but faced Draconian punishments if caught. Consequently, most Polish expellees packed only a few belongings and arrived penniless and homeless in the General Government.

As was often the case, the Nazi regime's brutality and contempt for human lives had unintentional effects. More Polish expellees were flooding into the General Government than the occupation administration could deal with. Fearing unrest and growing support for the resistance, General Governor Hans Frank opposed any further population removals. In March 1941, the deportations were stopped, mainly because Germany had to focus its efforts on the war economy in preparation for invading the Soviet Union. The victims of ethnic cleansings in Warthegau were now sent to the interior of the Reich. In total, 365,000 Poles were expelled to the General Government; 475,000 were deported within the German Reich and made to perform forced labor.

While the latter issue deserves special consideration, it is well researched and will only be outlined here.[35] Like the deportations to the General Government, forced labor under Nazi rule was based on ethnic selection and carried out in a systematic way, under violent and coercive

circumstances. Performing forced labor often proved to be just as traumatic as being forcibly uprooted. The victims, euphemistically called
"civilian workers" (*Zivilarbeiter*), were so mercilessly exploited that
about half a million died before the war ended.[36] An uncertain number
became chronically ill. In contrast to ethnic cleansing, however, forced
labor did not necessarily entail a change of location or have a permanent
character. The scale on which the two practices were enforced also differed. The Nazis made a total of about 8.4 million people perform forced
labor, 2.8 million of whom were Polish, that is, nearly 10 percent of the
Polish population.[37]

The number of those expelled and deported from the annexed territories, in contrast, amounted to "only" 840,000. In view of the Nazis' original aims and compared with later population movements, this
number seems relatively low. But it should be considered in the light
of the brutality with which the removals were enforced and the precedent they set. In western Poland, the Polish population's experiences
under German occupation—whether they were actually expelled or
not—made the thought of coexistence with the Germans unbearable.
Since members of the former German minority had actively taken part
in the ethnic cleansing, this feeling even permeated to a local level. Not
only had these Germans acted on their chauvinistic ideological convictions, they had also sought material advantage. The owners of the finest
apartments and largest farms were often at the top of the Nazis' lists of
Poles to be resettled.

While expulsions from the annexed territories were stopped in spring
1941, the same did not apply to the General Government or areas further east. Indeed, the Nazis' nationalist racism radicalized further after
the German invasion of the Soviet Union. Adolf Hitler, Heinrich Himmler, Reinhard Heydrich, and other leading ideologues forged plans for
the "reethnicization" (*Umvolkung*) of Eastern Europe by means of a
network of German colonies. A central element of these plans was the
establishment of an Aryan "bridge of settlement" reaching from East
Prussia to the Zips region in the Tatra Mountains. The Polish town
of Zamość lay along this route. In winter 1942–43, it was made a site
of demographic experimentation. SS leader Heinrich Himmler declared
Zamość to be a "German settlement area" and 110,000 residents were
deported to other places in the General Government—in most cases,
where Jews had lived until recently—or were sent to the German Reich
to perform forced labor. Resisters were shot on the spot. The occupying
power also imposed collective penalties on families and entire villages.[38]

The Poles were to be replaced by 60,000 German "defense farmers"
(*Wehrbauern*). In the event, only resettlers from Bessarabia and Vol-

hynia, who had been biding their time in reception camps, could be convinced to settle here. They found themselves facing a high risk of partisan attack, which even the SS's anti-Polish terror could not deflect. Attempts were made to create a buffer zone by expelling Poles from the surrounding areas and replacing them with Ukrainians. No more than about 13,000 German settlers were prepared to brave these inhospitable conditions. The operation was a failure, serving above all to strengthen Polish resistance. It was to be the last such experiment under German occupation, but it gives an indication of what Poland would have faced in the event of a German victory. According to the radicalized version of the *Generalplan Ost* of summer 1942, German *Lebensraum* was to stretch from Leningrad to the Crimea, thus forcing forty-five million Slavic *Untermenschen* out to the other side of the Urals. Population removals on this scale would certainly have resulted in genocide.[39]

Although the Nazis abandoned their most megalomaniac plans following Germany's defeat at Stalingrad, deportations and expulsions continued with dreadful regularity in occupied Poland. The fate of the civilian population of Warsaw in fall 1944 is a stark example. After the Warsaw Uprising, in which about 200,000 people were killed, roughly 350,000 survivors remained in the ruins of the devastated city. As punishment for the uprising, around 200,000 were deported to the General Government, 90,000 to perform forced labor in Germany, and 60,000 to concentration camps.[40] Subsequently, the German army razed the Polish capital to the ground using high-explosive bombs. The term "ethnic cleansing" does not quantify the extent of these measures, which marked the attempt to eliminate an entire metropolis.

The Nazis acted with comparable brutality in parts of occupied Yugoslavia. The situation here in many ways resembled that in Poland. The German Reich had annexed northern Slovenia and was trying to Germanize what it called Lower Styria by means of expulsions, deportations, and forced assimilation. In April 1941, Reinhard Heydrich proposed resettling 260,000 Slovenes. Ultimately, however, only about 30,000 Slovenes were sent to Croatia and Serbia and 11,000 to the German Reich for "reethnicization."[41] As in the annexed Polish territories, then, the main thrust of the Nazis' Germanization policy eventually shifted from expulsion to forced assimilation.

The annexed Slovenian territories were also targeted by extensive resettlement plans. About 60,000 Germans were to be introduced to the region. The largest single group—10,000 Germans—came from the Gottschee region in Italian-occupied southern Slovenia. They were brought "back home to the Reich" in winter 1941–42 under the Italo-German agreement. The case of the Gottscheers provides further evidence of the international repercussions of German policy, which is considered more closely in the next chapter.

Not even Western Europe was spared Nazi "reethnicization" measures. Two substantial deportation operations took place in Alsace and Lorraine, which now lay in different administrative districts of Germany. Immediately after the German invasion, the occupying forces expelled about 70,000 French citizens, Jews, and supposed criminals under the slogan "Hinaus mit dem welschen Plunder!" (Out with the shifty rabble!). Half a year later, a further 60,000 "evacuations" were enforced in another wave of Germanization.

In this case, however, the Nazi authorities actually planned to compensate the forced migrants for their abandoned property, revealing a fundamental contrast in their approaches to ethnic cleansing in Western and Eastern Europe. The expulsions in the West were executed along the lines of France's population removals of 1918–19, primarily on the basis of national categories. The SS and their racist motives did not begin to play a more influential role until the war progressed. In East Central Europe, in contrast, ethnic cleansing was carried out without any concessions to civil rights—murderous racism prevailed here from the start.

In winter 1942–43, several tens of thousands of people were again forced to leave Alsace and Lorraine before war production was prioritized, as in Poland. In total, about 100,000 people were driven out of Lorraine and 140,000 out of Alsace during German occupation.[42] Another means of ethnic homogenization, which had already been tested in the East, was the deportation of those considered "suitable for assimilation," including many children and adolescents, to the interior of the Reich.

The German People's List, which was introduced to the annexed Polish territories in March 1941, aimed to fulfill a similar function. It divided the population into four categories.[43] The first two identified members of the German minority who had proven their loyalty to the fatherland and those who were unambiguously German on account of their language and culture. The third category comprised persons of German descent who were considered "racially valuable" but who resisted Germanization. This referred mainly to the mixed population in Upper Silesia, Kashubia, and other regions with "unresolved ethnicity." The members of the fourth category were classified as renegades, who declared their support for Poland despite their German origins. This list was based on a mixture of apparently objective, racist definitions of nationality and subjective identification, which became less rigid after 1941. The list registered a total of 2.9 million people in the annexed territories of Poland, more than one-quarter of the resident population.[44]

The German People's List was introduced just as expulsions into the General Government were stopped and marked the regime's attempt to apply alternative, more inclusive methods of Germanization. Apparently the Nazi regime was prepared to resort to classic nationalizing methods from the standard repertoire of European politics should the circumstances and the growing need for conscripts demand it. The Jews of Europe, however, were exempted from such policies. From 1941, they faced industrial mass destruction.

The flexible combination of ethnic cleansing and forced assimilation was not new to Europe. Many nation-states operated in a similar way in the first phase of ethnic cleansing. It was its dependence on a racist selection, even classifying bodily features, which set the German People's List apart from other "ethnicizing" policies. Yet despite its detailed, ostensibly subjective definitions, it could not possibly account for the innumerable variations caused by social blending in the supposed "German East." The Zamość experiment and a similar abortive attempt to determine the population composition in Ukrainian Zhytomyr are further evidence of the Nazis' unique position in the history of ethnic cleansing. They not only deported and expelled the inhabitants of border regions neighboring coethnic lands, as other states did, but they also targeted remote diaspora settlements.

The policy of demographic Germanization failed even in the annexed territories. In spite of all the coercive measures, ranging from arbitrary expulsions to the abduction of children, in 1941 there were still more than three million Poles living in Warthegau, as opposed to just over one million Germans. While the proportion of Germans in the population tripled from 6.6 percent to 22.8 percent by 1944, this was due to the arrival of refugees fleeing the advancing Red Army as well as the active resettlement of ethnic Germans from Eastern Europe. In Upper Silesia and Gdańsk/West Prussia, the number of Germans grew faster on paper, since nearly 2.5 million people had themselves registered in the German People's List.[45] But the extent to which they actually and irrefutably considered themselves German must remain uncertain. After Germany's defeat at Stalingrad, there were increasing breakaway movements from the supposed "master nation" in Upper Silesia.[46] Expulsions on a far broader scale would have been necessary to change the ethnic composition of the annexed territories but were precluded by the need to focus on war production.

Although the Nazis' population removals ground to a halt before they had even achieved half they had aimed for, they were regarded as opening floodgates by international observers. This is true both in an admiring sense, by Germany's allies, who followed the Nazi's example, and in a damning sense, by its enemies. The *Heim ins Reich* resettlement campaign and the expulsion of the Poles had a deep impact on public opinion in Britain. The magazine *Fortnightly* published an article in early 1940 stating, "Hitler has burnt his boats ... He is daily setting precedents which cannot be forgotten when the reckoning comes." Some members of the House of Lords called for German minorities to be resettled according to Hitler's methods.[47]

Despite decrying the Nazi government's population removals, the British government commissioned a panel of distinguished experts, the Foreign Research and Press Service (FRPS) at Balliol College, Oxford, to ascertain how far population transfers could be "desirable, realizable and permanent." The FRPS found that the exchange or transfer of large-scale population groups could be a suitable means of reorganizing Europe. The historian Arnold Toynbee, the panel's chairperson, was especially convinced of this. Toynbee had observed the Greco-Turkish conflict at close range and published a book on it in 1923. He was a vocal supporter of the Lausanne model. Panel member Carlile Macartney, author of a book on nation-states and national minorities published in 1934, however, opposed this view. He objected to "the present fashionable panacea for all difficulties connected with national minorities." But he saw it as a "last resort" for a state that finds "its minority quite intolerably disloyal and constantly used as a catspaw by the neighbouring State," alluding to Poland and Czechoslovakia. During 1941, this academic "team of stars" fell into the background as the war progressed, but in January 1942 it received a second major government commission. Following British-Soviet discussions on the postwar order, the British government requested an investigation into "[l]essons to be learnt from past exchanges of populations, particularly the Greco-Turkish exchange and the forced removal of populations by the Germans and in territory now occupied by Germany."[48]

The wording of the commission betrays the exemplary role that the Nazis' policy played. The practical scope of this second study was far broader than the first in 1940 and included discussing the possibility of shifting the western border of Poland to the Oder River and thus "transferring" five and a half million Germans. Macartney and some of his colleagues did not think this was feasible and warned against reigniting German revanchism. But Toynbee, the oldest and most prominent of the scholars, insisted on keeping this point on the agenda.

The panel's debate illustrates how experts at desks and drawing boards toyed with the fates of millions of people. They were rarely troubled by moral qualms; if they had doubts or fears, they were that their plans might not be practicable or might provoke undesirable side effects. Over the years, moreover, the idea of population exchange was abandoned in favor of one-sided transfers affecting far more people than had originally come under discussion. Analogous to developments in international diplomacy after the Balkan wars and in Lausanne, then, a dynamic toward extending the geographic and quantitative range of plans can also be observed in academic circles. Götz Aly and Ingo Haar have shown how in Nazi Germany, academics and especially historians functioned as "mentors of destruction." Matthew Frank's book portrays some of their British counterparts as mentors of population removal. Contrastingly, other authors regard Eduard Beneš and the Polish government in exile in London as the main culprits responsible for the mass expulsion of Germans.[49] It is questionable, however, whether the representatives of two occupied countries really had such a profound influence on the political elites and public opinion in what was then a global empire.

Beneš's activities certainly had one decisive effect: they prompted the British government to declare the Munich Agreement null and void in July 1942. But while Whitehall wanted to revise the borders affected by Munich, it did not object to its lack of minority protection. To the horror of the anti-Fascist Sudeten Germans, the Czechoslovak government in exile was given free rein to expel most of the German minority. Ironically, by this stage Beneš was in favor of ceding the purely German-inhabited regions and keeping a million Germans in the country; however, a "transfer" had already been resolved.

Public opinion on population removals in the United States was less strong and more divided. A number of groups had lobbied vehemently for human rights and minority protection since 1918–19, breeding uncertainty among American observers. An article in the influential magazine *Foreign Affairs* supported only the return of population groups deported by Hitler to their homes.[50] But gradually the US government came into line with the British view. Former minister of trade and then president Herbert Hoover took a decisive step in this direction when in 1942–43, even before the Tehran Conference, he called for reorganizing Europe along ethnic borders, citing the great Lausanne model.[51]

Similar to the plans Hitler announced in his Reichstag address of October 1939, then, the West's vision of postwar Europe was based on a framework of homogenized nation-states. Was the contemporary public aware of these parallels? It was certainly possible to condemn Hitler's crimes in the German-occupied countries at the same time as viewing his type of resettlement policy as a feasible option.

More Cases in Germany's Sphere of Influence

Germany's racist policies and utopias of homogeneity had an impact far beyond the countries it had occupied. While the German army, the SS and the civil administration carried out ethnic cleansing on a far smaller scale than originally planned—hence ethnic cleansing was not a specific feature of National Socialism—the population shifts in the countries allied with Germany escalated in terms of numbers and brutality. The authoritarian and outright fascist regimes in Central and Southeastern Europe removed at least 1.65 million people,[52] triggering cycles of violence, which in some areas took on a genocidal character.

Again, these mass scale ethnic cleansings began at a negotiation table. As is mentioned above, the four signatory states of the Munich agreement not only redrew the German-Czech border but also demanded that Czechoslovakia and Hungary resolve their territorial disputes within three months. In effect, this amounted to partially sanctioning Hungary's revisionism, which called for a new border in southern Slovakia. Consequently, in November 1938, Germany and Italy compelled Czechoslovakia to cede its predominantly Hungarian-populated regions to Budapest.

Following the Munich model, the enforcement of the new ethnic border under the First Vienna Award was to be accompanied by extensive population shifts. All Czech and Slovak state officials were required to leave the ceded territory. Pressure was also put on other groups to leave, especially those who had received parcels of land during the Czechoslovak land reform of 1920. Often they had to hastily pack their bags to avoid violence; in some places there were riots. According to the secondary Slovakian literature, at least 100,000 Czechoslovak citizens fled the territories ceded to Hungary.[53] It was not until spring 1939 that tensions began to ease thanks to a change in government policy in Budapest. Hungary now returned to an imperial concept of nation building in southern Slovakia, tolerating a remainder minority population as long as it was kept on the political and economic margins.

Most members of the Slovak National Party (SLS), however, strove toward establishing an ethnically "pure" nation. At a demonstration in Bratislava in October 1938, SLS supporters chanted "Česi peši do Prahy!" (Czechs go back to Prague!). The autonomous Slovak government negotiated the resettlement of 10,000 Czech officials and their families with the former central government. Once again, the powerless authorities in Prague had no choice but to agree to a population transfer from which they drew only disadvantage. When Slovakia declared independence in 1939, moreover, the resident Czechs became aliens overnight.

Not only public servants but also employees and businesspeople now had to leave the country. Often Slovaks were eager to appropriate the Czechs' houses and apartments. Resettlement was enforced according to criteria of place of residence before 1918 and political conduct until 1938. Anyone considered to be a convinced supporter of Czechoslovakia had to go. This applied to 20,000 Czechs in the capital of Bratislava alone and at least 50,000 across Slovakia. Slovak historian Valerián Bystrický describes this process as "expulsion" (*vyst'ahovanie*).[54] It was soon to influence Slovakia's relations with its Jews, which is considered below.

Hungarian revisionist demands, meanwhile, were by no means exhausted with the acquisition of southern Slovakia and Carpatho-Ukraine. Hungary now turned its attentions to Transylvania, the most important of the regions lost in 1920. The conflict between Hungary and Romania over Transylvania illustrates the consequences of the Nazis' reorganization of Europe and the pursuit of ethnic borders. The fundamental problem in Transylvania was that the demographic lines of separation that Hitler demanded were not apparent on any map, no matter how detailed. Romanians and Hungarians lived door to door; few areas could be unambiguously identified as settled by one particular nationality. Although the Hungarian minority was especially large in the northwest half of the region, it still only made up a relative majority, as the Romanians did in southern Transylvania.[55] Transylvanian Saxons, Jews, Slovaks, and other small groups tipped the balance one way or another in this ethnic patchwork.

While Romania refused all Hungarian demands until 1939, its position was distinctly weakened by the Molotov-Ribbentrop Pact and the subsequent Soviet occupation of northern Bukovina and Bessarabia. Romania was only guaranteed independence by the Germans under the proviso that it made some territorial concessions toward Hungary and Bulgaria. With this *Pax Germanica,* the German Reich pursued its aims of stemming conflicts within its own sphere of influence, maintaining access to the Romanian oil fields, and gaining Hungary's and Romania's support in the war against the Soviet Union.

In August 1940, Hungary and Romania were finally bullied into negotiations by Germany and Italy. In line with Hitler's Reichstag address of October 1939, the pertinent issue was the redrawing of borders along ethnic lines of separation. There was considerable support in both the countries concerned for securing peace by means of a "population exchange." Leading Romanian and Hungarian politicians cited the Lausanne model, while Romania made the cession of northern Transylvania dependent upon the removal of the remaining Hungarian minority in southern Transylvania,[56] for fear that Hungary might one day claim the other territories lost in 1920.

Like the Munich Agreement and several earlier settlements, the borders enforced by the Second Vienna Award of August 1940 were linked to a "right of option." Hungarians were granted a period of six months to emigrate from Romania and vice versa. Romanians who wanted to stay in northern Transylvania were automatically given Hungarian citizenship. Those who opted to emigrate were entitled to take their movable property with them and claim compensation for immovable property from the reception state. Thus, the agreements complied with international standards of the interwar period established by treaties such as Neuilly and Sèvres as well as the Geneva Convention on Upper Silesia, once again demonstrating continuity with the Nazis' plans for reorganizing Europe.

But rather than bringing peace, the Second Vienna Award exacerbated the situation for minorities on both sides of the new border. Violence broke out in fall 1940, especially on the Hungarian side. It was sparked not only by protests against the changeover but also, more concretely, by the armed resistance of radical Romanian nationalists and the reprisals by the Hungarian army this provoked. Hundreds of people were killed in a number of massacres, the worst of which was in the town of Ip, where 155 lives were lost. The former office holders of the Romanian state, railroaders, post office employees, many teachers, and those who had merely received farmland during the land reform of 1921 were forced to leave the Hungarian-occupied territory. Orthodox priests and members of the educated classes, that is, the potential leaders of a national minority, made up a second group of refugees. While many refugees from rural areas were able to take some cattle, farming equipment, and furniture with them, refugees from urban areas were deported in sealed trains. It was, then, not a case of "redressing injustices" caused during Romanian rule, as Hungarian politicians claimed, but of permanent ethnic transformation.[57]

The reprisals suffered immediately after the Hungarians assumed power were followed by purposeful discrimination. Independent professionals lost their licenses; Romanians were de facto excluded from public service under an ambiguous clause concerning political conduct in the interwar period. Farmers who had benefited from the Romanian land reform lost their land. Moreover, the state seized all "abandoned" property. In 1942, a German-Italian investigating committee found that the Hungarian government was leading "a battle to reduce or even eliminate the influence of the Romanian minority in northern Transylvania on economic life."[58] Teaching in Romanian was axed and two-thirds of the region's Orthodox parishes were dissolved. As in Croatia and western Ukraine, then, the conflict was also fought on a religious front.

The discrimination of Hungarians in the Romanian region of southern Transylvania was less systematic but just as difficult to bear for those affected. Punitive taxes were imposed on independent professionals, ruining them or compelling them to emigrate. About one-third of the Hungarian schoolteachers were dismissed. Farmers were required to hand over their grain harvests. In the Council of Ministers, Romanian dictator Ion Antonescu purposefully added fuel to the conflicts with minorities: "I was raised to hate Turks, Jews and Hungarians. This feeling of hatred toward the enemies of the fatherland must be taken to its ultimate consequence." The refugees arriving on both sides of the border certainly had reason to hate. The Romanian Association of Expellees and Refugees from Northern Transylvania (Asociația Expulzaților și Refugiaților din Transilvania de Nord)[59] demanded that accommodation for the refugees take priority over housing the Hungarian minority. This was not the only aspect of coexistence to be affected by a negative bilateral dynamic. Any measure against the minority in one of the countries was soon followed by diplomatic protests, threats, and retaliation on the other side of the border. According to the statistics collated by the German-Italian investigating committee, by 1942, a total of 200,000 Romanians had fled the Hungarian part of Transylvania; there were also more than 100,000 Hungarian refugees from the southern part of the region. More recent publications indicate that the total number of refugees is probably higher, since not all were officially registered.[60]

Nazi Germany played a dual role in this conflict and the ethnic cleansing resulting from it. On the one hand, Berlin was party to the Second Vienna Award, which provided for the formally voluntary but de facto forced emigration along the new Romanian-Hungarian border in Transylvania. On the other hand, the German-Italian committee sent to investigate the situation tried to exercise a restraining influence in order to prevent war from breaking out between Hungary and Romania. Ultimately, up to 370,000 people, or one-sixth of the minority population, were forced to leave their homes. Although this was far less than intended, there was much embitterment on both sides, which resulted in Romanian retaliation actions after the Hungarian army's retreat in fall 1944.

As well as southern Slovakia and Transylvania, Hungary's revisionist plans were aimed at the lost territories in Vojvodina. Germany's attack on Yugoslavia in April 1941 provided an opportunity for Hungary to act. The Nazis left the thus captured regions of Bačka and Baranya to the Horthy regime, partly in order to relieve their own troops. The

Hungarian government then proceeded with its usual merciless persecution of the elites of the opposing nation-state in these regions. All Yugoslav public servants and the potential leaders of a Serb minority were expelled. Up to 50,000 Serbs were deported over the border into German occupation territory in just a few months. Massacres claimed at least 5,000 lives.[61] The Hungarian authorities acted even more ruthlessly toward the prospective minority than the Nazis in the annexed part of Slovenia. This can only be partially explained by the dynamic of the Serbian-Hungarian conflict. Hungarian policy toward minorities grew more radical in a number of stages, signposted by the annexations of southern Slovakia in 1938, Transylvania in 1940, and Bačka and Baranya in 1941. As in Romania, this increasing radicalization also affected attitudes toward Jews. In the heartland, most Jews survived, but almost all from the regained territories were deported.

The government in Budapest combined the removal of minorities with the purposeful settlement of coethnic citizens, some of whom were from the most distant regions. One example is the Szekler (Székely) of Bukovina, who were taken to Bačka and Baranya to promote Magyarization. People of Bosnian descent were also sent to create Hungarian pockets of settlement here. Germany was not alone, then, in pursuing a *Heim ins Reich*–style homogenizing settlement policy. The expulsions from the Hungarian-occupied territories would no doubt have continued had Germany, the dominant power in the region, not had other priorities. For example, Hungary had originally planned to deport 150,000 Serbs from Bačka and Baranya. But the German occupation government in what remained of Serbia was already struggling with the influx of refugees from Croatia and refused to cooperate. Moreover, at this point Germany was concentrating all the resources at its disposal to prepare its invasion of the Soviet Union.

Similar to the Hungarian-Romanian conflict, the deeper causes of the Bulgarian-Romanian conflict lay in the regional imperialism of the Southeastern European states. After the Second Balkan War, Romania had acquired southern Dobruja despite the fact that Romanians did not even make up 3 percent of the total population of 282,000 here in 1913.[62] The victors of World War I confirmed this border in the Treaty of Neuilly. Over the next twenty years Romania pursued a tough policy of nationalization in the conquered territory. First, Bulgarians were deliberately disadvantaged in education, during land reform, and in the job market. Second, over 40,000 Romanian colonists were settled in the region. The proportion of Bulgarians in the total population therefore sank from an absolute majority to under 40 percent, while that of the Romanians rose to 20 percent. These figures reflect the utopian nature of the goal of establishing a homogenous nation-state in southern Dobruja. Romania would have had to continue its settlement policy at the same pace as in the years 1920–40 for another thirty years or more to finally make up the majority population. Sofia, meanwhile, never accepted the loss of the region. Bulgarian gangs attacked Romanian colonists and institutions, provoking the state to deploy paramilitary units as a countermeasure.

In view of the continuing tensions, Britain proposed a population transfer along a revised border in 1939. But the Molotov-Ribbentrop Pact had put an end to Britain's status as a peacekeeping power in Southeastern Europe. Henceforth, the German Reich determined the course of the conflict together with Italy—and espoused the British idea. On 7 September 1940, Bulgaria and Romania signed the Treaty of Craiova, which in principle reestablished the borders of 1878. It also provided for the removal of the Bulgarian and Romanian minorities in Dobruja. It was entirely at the discretion of the two states' authorities to determine who belonged to these minorities. Those affected had no right to object or petition but were to submit to the "population exchange" without exception. By interwar standards, then, this was a harsh settlement, similar to that provided for by the Treaty of Lausanne. But it differed from the latter by restricting the forcible removals to the Dobruja region. Elsewhere in Romania and Bulgaria, the minority Bulgarians and Romanians, respectively, had a voluntary "right of option."

All in all, between 7 November and 14 December 1940, 61,000 people left northern Dobruja for Bulgaria, while Romania absorbed about 100,000 new nationals. Romania therefore had more new arrivals to accommodate than Bulgarians who had left, but space had been created and farms left behind by the Dobruja Germans returning via *Heim ins Reich*. In contrast to the population removals in Transylvania, the forced resettlement of the Bulgarian and Romanian minorities occurred without bloodshed. Those affected were able to take much of their household goods and livestock with them: 215,000 sheep, 18,500 horses, 12,500 cows, and various small animals thus accompanied their human owners over the border in a mass migration of man and beast that defies the imagination.[63] This transfer illustrates the difference between a consensual and organized "population exchange" and expulsions in civil war–like conditions. But the comparison leads to a somewhat alarming conclusion: the total cleansing of Dobruja's Bulgarian and Romanian minorities proved to be the more stable "solution" than the partial, continuous, and to some extent revised ethnic cleansing in Transylvania. At least, this was the view held by the Allies, who tacitly confirmed the Treaty of Craiova in 1944. A chain of ethnic migrations had completely changed the face of Dobruja. The first minority to go was the Turks in

1936–39. They were followed in November 1940 by the Dobruja Germans and, a short time later, by the Bulgarian and Romanian minorities. Two years later, most of the region's Jews left under far worse circumstances. The centuries-old ethnic and denominational diversity of the region was to a large extent homogenized in the space of just five years.

Ultimately, however, Dobruja was less important to the Bulgarian revisionists than having access to the Aegean Sea and controlling Vardar-Macedonia for securing the country's status as a major power within Southeastern Europe. When the German Reich invaded Greece in 1941, Bulgaria occupied the northeast of the country. According to Schechtman, about 100,000 Greeks were consequently forced to migrate. Most of them fled to Thessaloniki, inadvertently placing the area's Jews under intense pressure. Soon afterward, the entire Jewish minority in Saloniki was deported to Auschwitz.[64] The policy of removal was combined with the purposeful settling of Bulgarian nationals. In late 1941, the Bulgarian Ministry of the Interior called on ethnic Bulgarians to settle in the regained regions. The plea was primarily addressed to former refugees under the Treaty of Neuilly, but other citizens could also apply for land and living space there. According to the government, by 1943, 122,000 Bulgarians had migrated to the Bulgarian-occupied parts of Thrace and Macedonia.

The situation in Vardar-Macedonia was initially less volatile than in the Bulgarian zone of occupation in Greece, since the government in Sofia accepted Macedonians as ethnic Bulgarians. For this reason, expulsions immediately after the region's annexation were confined to about 26,000 post-1918 Serb immigrants. But the enactment of a new, more restrictive citizenship law in July 1942 triggered further removal actions, affecting at least another 110,000 people who were defined as Serbs or other unwanted minorities.[65] Kosovo, bordering Macedonia, was another conflict zone. In 1941, Albanian nationalists expelled Montenegrins and Serbs who had received land and farms since 1913, especially in the area around Peć. These actions were arranged with the German army, who initially occupied the area, and who merely warned the Albanians not to act too hastily. By the time the Italian army took over occupation, about 20,000 Serbs had been expelled and many colonists' houses burned down.[66] After Italy changed sides in World War II and the German army resumed occupation, a second wave of ethnic cleansing began that went far beyond merely settling scores with the local elites of the former nation-state. With German consent, the Albanian nationalists formed military units and persecuted the Serbian minority. Now trains were organized to carry out deportations from Kosovo. The

German army calculated that at least another 20,000 Serbs were forced to leave Kosovo.[67] Although this was not, then, a total ethnic cleansing, most of the Serbian refugees did not return after 1945, preferring to stay in more shielded areas in the Serbian heartland.

Most of the half a million Serbian refugees from Croatia, Bosnia, Vojvodina, and Macedonia arrived penniless in occupied Serbia, where they faced a day-to-day struggle to survive. In view of this huge influx of refugees and the daily terror of German occupation, it is perhaps not surprising that nationalist victimization myths were still rife in Serbia in the 1980s. Slobodan Milošević harnessed the memories they invoked to bolster his aggressive brand of nationalism, which ostensibly pledged to "defend" the nation.

In all the regions examined here, refugees suffered considerable trauma. Even when the population removals occurred in peacetime and on the basis of bilateral treaties, they nearly always involved humiliation and physical abuse, periods in transit camps, journeys in overcrowded cattle trains, deprivation, and hunger. Furthermore, the refugees forfeited most of their property.

A pattern can be discerned in Hungary's and Bulgaria's policies in their regained territories. These two revisionist states took especially radical action against national minorities in historically contested regions. The main targets of their persecution were the elites who had been settled there in the interwar period by the Romanian, Yugoslav, and Czechoslovak governments. But even poor smallholders were ousted if they had received farmland during the various national land reforms. It was therefore a case of retrospective revisionism on the one hand and forward-looking homogenization on the other, forming a "dual revenge."

Romanian policy in northern Bukovina and Bessarabia, which was recaptured from the Soviet Union in 1941, followed the same pattern. Immediately after invading these regions, the Romanian foreign minister, Mihai Antonescu, outlined his position at a cabinet meeting thus:

> I am for the forced emigration of the entire Jewish element from Bessarabia and Bukovina, which must be thrown over the border. I also favor the emigration of the Ukrainian element. I do not know when, after how many centuries, the Romanian nation will again enjoy this total freedom of action with the possibility of ethnic purification and national revision. This is the hour when we are masters on our territory. Let it be used![68]

As in the formerly Soviet-occupied part of Poland, Jews were accused of being Stalin's fifth column and collectively branded "Judeo-Communists." The Ukrainians were lumped together with the Russians and the

Soviet Union because of their Slavic roots. However, as in Hungary and Bulgaria, minorities were relatively secure in the heartland of the Romanian state.[69] The policies of the newly founded states of Slovakia and Croatia did not follow this pattern. The members of various minorities were persecuted throughout these countries.

The response of society in these states to violent ethnic homogenization was divided. While radical nationalists certainly operated locally to achieve the governments' targets, the expropriations and use of violence on a huge scale offended against traditional values, especially of the rural populations. The Hungarian consulate in Braşov reported from the Romanian part of Transylvania that the indigenous Romanian population took a passive role and did not participate in spontaneous disturbances. Reports from northern Transylvania contrast the conduct of the radical nationalizers sent from Budapest with the local populations, who were accustomed to living side by side with other nationalities. Yet there was very rarely any open resistance to the abuse of minorities, expulsions, or public shootings, especially where Jews were the victims. Throughout the war, in all the states of East Central and Southeastern Europe allied with Germany, violent nationalists prevailed.

This state of affairs shaped the experiences of the refugees, expellees, and resettlers considered in this chapter, who totaled at least two million.[70] This is a high number in relation to the total populations of these countries and compared with statistics on the Soviet Union. But far more extensive population removals had originally been planned. In the event, the Nazis' reorganization of Europe dissolved in a permanent state of war. The "feeling of European security" that Hitler invoked in his Reichstag address of October 1939 did not manifest itself in any of the German-allied countries. On the contrary, the attempt to draw ethnic borders only sparked new hatred, violence, and desires for revenge.

Soviet Ethnic Cleansing

The Soviet Union first arranged a "population exchange" on an international level in the secret protocol supplementing the Molotov-Ribbentrop Pact. However, as Terry Martin and other historians have shown, ethnic cleansings took place in the Soviet Union as early as the mid-1930s.[71] Despite being the subject of much research, the issue of Soviet ethnic cleansing in a European context still leaves many questions unanswered. Why did a state that had fostered the autonomy and cultures of its different subject nationalities in the 1920s begin deporting them en masse to Central Asia and Siberia in later years? When and in which cases did the goal of national or ethnic homogenization supersede that of social homogenization? Did this development follow a linear progression or did it occur in spurts by a process of reaction and counterreaction? These questions seem all the more compelling since ethnic cleansing was not an intrinsic aspect of Soviet ideology put into practice, in contrast to Nazism. The Bolsheviks were primarily concerned with changing the social order and are therefore more typically associated with "social cleansing."

Identifying the many kinds of population cleansing that took place in the Soviet Union in the 1930s is complicated by the fact that, as in all multinational empires, social and ethnic boundaries intersected. Despite the Bolsheviks' expropriation of major landowners, industrialists, property owners, and other wealthy members of society, in some rural areas, the tsarist-era social structure remained to some extent intact. If a wave of deportation predominantly affected one nationality, it did not necessarily signify the deliberate persecution of this ethnicity, but the fact that its members frequently represented unwanted social characteristics.

The case of the Polish minority—the first nationally defined group to be affected by purposeful mass deportations—provides a key to understanding ethnic cleansing in the Soviet Union.[72] Despite the mass flight movements triggered by the revolution, the civil war, and the Polish-Soviet War, there were still hundreds of entirely or predominantly Polish-inhabited villages in the Byelorussian Soviet Socialist Republic (SSR) and central Ukraine. The local landowning farmers here, as all over the Soviet Union, resisted collectivization in 1929–30. In order to detract attention from this social conflict, the Politburo of the Soviet Communist Party singled out the Polish minority as troublemakers and branded them as traitors to communism. In March 1930, the Politburo accused "Kulak-Polish elements" of counterrevolutionary activities and espionage and ordered the deportation of about 15,000 families to avert the danger of a Polish attack.[73] The Ukrainians were also blamed for the Soviet Union's inherent political and social problems. Once collectivization had been accomplished, however, the regime stopped these deportations. In 1932, Stalin even had a Polish district established near the western border of the Soviet Union. These concessions revived some elements of the *korenizatsiya* tradition of the 1920s, promoting the culture and autonomy of the various Soviet nationalities. The minorities inhabiting the border regions were even advantaged in many ways so that they might promote the Soviet cause to their countrymen on the other side of the border.

But Soviet hopes of exporting the revolution were soon displaced by fears of importing the counterrevolution. The first ones to bear the

brunt of this 180-degree turnaround were the Soviet Poles. Stalin interpreted the nonaggression pact made by Poland and Germany in 1934
as a prelude to their attack on the Soviet Union. For this reason, he
instructed the NKVD, the People's Commissariat for Internal Affairs, to
preventively "cleanse" (*ochistit'*) the areas close to the western border
of Poles and German colonists.[74] This first major wave of deportations of
"unreliable elements" to Central Asia and Siberia lasted from 20 February until 10 March 1935 and affected 36,000 Poles and 9,000 Germans.
It heralded a new dimension in ethnic cleansing, especially in terms
of pace. By 1938, about half of the Polish minority in Byelorussia and
Ukraine had been deported for being linked to "Polish sabotage and
espionage groups."

In spring 1935, 23,000 Finns from the Leningrad area suffered a similar fate. In 1936, 171,000 Koreans were deported,[75] followed by tens
of thousands of Estonians, Latvians, Greeks, Bulgarians, Romanians,
Persians, and various Turkish peoples by 1941. These ethnic cleansings
were symptomatic of Stalin's phobic fear of military isolation, prompting the Soviet authorities to target all nations with cross-border ties.
The dynamic of the "great purge" was another significant factor. Having
achieved collectivization and hence social homogenization, the NKVD
channeled its energies into removing all kinds of national "deviants."

According to Terry Martin, about 20 percent of the cleansings during the great wave of terror from July 1937 to November 1938 were
motivated by national or ethnic criteria.[76] He places the total number
of people arrested, deported, or executed on account of their nationality
in the late 1930s at around 800,000. This would seem to undermine the
premise of Soviet ethnic cleansing, since it falls way below the number
of those affected by social and political cleansing.

Furthermore, this was not the first time in Russian history that
entire population groups had been removed from border regions. As
mentioned above, the tsarist empire carried out comparable preventive
deportations during World War I. The Soviet Union was, then, another
empire seeking to reinforce its shaky foundations by removing certain
"unreliable" groupings within its own civilian population. Yet this had
never before been done on such a scale or at such a pace, or combined
with measures aimed at social homogenization. In the course of collectivization, Ukrainians and above all Poles were singled out for branding
as exploiters and class enemies. This added a national element to the social cleansings, which became increasingly significant in the late 1930s.

Different utopias of homogeneity also interacted on a local level. By
1932, Soviet society had been divided into farmers, workers, and intelligentsia following collectivization and the deportation of 2.3 million

people. Henceforth, the regime tackled ethnic differences. Members of minorities were easy targets, even if they behaved unobtrusively. Not only had many played an active role in the *korenizatsiya* phase, from 1932 their ethnicity (*narodnost'*) was legally required to be entered in their personal identification papers. The regime's nationalization of society made the citizens of the Soviet Union tangible as individuals and as a group. This process, too, can be regarded as a result of European modernity, or more precisely of Stalin's modernization of Russia.

The mass deportations continued after the Red Army's invasion of eastern Poland in September 1939. Similarly to previous developments in the prewar territory of the Soviet Union, a dynamic could be observed away from social toward ethnic cleansing, but at an accelerated pace. The Soviet leadership portrayed the invasion as a Ukrainian and Byelorussian national revolution and referendums were held the next month on the annexation of the "liberated territories." The rigged results served to legitimize the territories' absorption into the Byelorussian and Ukrainian SSRs, which, according to the propaganda, unified all the members of the titular nations. The Soviet press called for the Byelorussians and Ukrainians to "strike the Polish lords."[77] There was indeed rioting, plundering, and manslaughter, mostly targeting landowners, military settlers, and former policemen. But the promised changeover of elites did not take place as the local populations had imagined. The new men installed at the reins of power were primarily Russian and eastern Ukrainian party cadre.

Instead of nationalization, a process of "Sovietization" was now enforced by means of extensive expropriations. In the same month as the vote on annexation, the NKVD compiled lists of persons to be arrested or deported. These included mostly Polish settlers (*osadnicy*) who had immigrated to the eastern territories after 1918, police officers and regional and local government officials, landowners, company owners, and businesspeople—in short, society's former elite. The Soviet occupiers sentenced 37,000 people to terms of imprisonment and 1,208 to death; 7,300 were shot without sentencing. On 9 February 1940, mass deportations from the former territory of eastern Poland began. Special units set out before dawn to drag victims from their beds, order them to pack a few belongings, and take them to stations serving as assembly points in freezing conditions of as low as forty degrees below zero centigrade. In just two days, 140,000 Polish nationals were rounded up and sent far north to Central Asia or Siberia.[78] The bureaucratic efficiency came to an abrupt end, however, when they arrived there. Often the deportees were simply turned out of the train in the middle of the steppe or the Siberian tundra and left to fend for themselves. The second major wave of deportations on 13 April affected about 61,000, mostly relatives of those deported in February and other state employees, shopkeepers, and white-collar workers, including many Polish Jews. The third wave of deportations on the night of 28–29 June 1940 affected 78,000, mostly refugees from the General Government. By the second half of that year, resistance toward Sovietization had been broken, and the occupying administration largely stopped the deportations. But in June 1941 a last thrust of about 50,000 people were deported. Furthermore, members of the NKVD murdered about 9,500 prison inmates before beating a hasty retreat from the Germans. After the German invasion, the SS blamed the Jews for this atrocity, fanning the flames of anti-Semitic sentiment.

In total, about 325,000 people, including 200,000 Poles and 70,000 Jews but relatively few Ukrainians and Byelorussians, were deported from the former territories of eastern Poland to the interior of the Soviet Union. Thus, 63 percent of the victims were Polish and 21 percent Jewish.[79] Since Poles made up 40 percent of the population in the region, they were clearly overrepresented among the deportees. But the disproportion of Polish Jews is even more striking, since they made up only 10.7 percent of the population according to a national census of 1931. From about fall 1940, Ukrainian and, to a lesser extent, Byelorussian nationalists were increasingly at risk of arrest and deportation.

The common social characteristics of the deportees point to the primarily sociopolitical objective of the occupying Soviets. Their goal was to remove the old elites in order to subsequently break any remaining resistance toward collectivization and other forms of expropriation. De-Polonizing the annexed territories was of secondary importance and mostly pursued by other means, such as forcibly conferring Soviet nationality, abolishing the use of Polish in education and administration, and ousting Poles from government and the economy. But since Stalin was no fonder of Ukrainian nationalists than he was of Poles, the expanded Ukrainian SSR was only half-heartedly nationalized and not by means of *korenizatsiya* policies. For this reason, in the Polish (and Romanian and Baltic) territories annexed in 1940, the Soviet Union remained a multiethnic state.

Karelia, which Finland lost to the Soviet Union after the war in winter 1940, forms a notable exception here. Most of the Karelian population was evacuated to more westerly areas of Finland by the Finnish military or fled the advancing Red Army. All Finns still remaining behind the front line were interned and deported to Finland under the Treaty of Moscow of 1940.[80] This was, then, a contractually agreed forced resettlement, and a sign of how the Soviet victors intended to deal with conquered territories. In 1941, the NKVD ordered the deportation of 89,000 Finns from the Leningrad area to Kazakhstan and Siberia.[81] Later, many Karelians were able to temporarily return following the German invasion of the Soviet Union. About 280,000 Finns, or 70 percent of the refugees, took advantage of the Finnish army's invasion of the territories ceded in 1940 to return to their homeland.[82] But in 1944, following their recapture by the Red Army, a second and final flight from Karelia began, which was eventually acknowledged by the international community at the Paris Peace Conference and subsequent treaties of 1946–47.

Repeated flight was a merciful fate compared to deportation within the Soviet Union. The NKVD's victims were given minimal forewarning to pack a few belongings and provisions and thus set out poorly prepared on journeys that often lasted several days or even weeks. Many deportees fell ill or died due to the cold and insanitary conditions on the trains. According to the NKVD's internal reports, 10,557 of the 140,000 people deported from eastern Poland in February 1940—or over 7 percent—died en route or immediately on arrival.[83] Few of the expulsions discussed in this book and none of the forced resettlements claimed such a high toll.

The removal of 900,000 Germans in August and September 1941 marked a new extreme in the scale of deportations in the Soviet Union.[84] This case is especially interesting for the history of Soviet ethnic cleansing for three reasons: first, it affected the hitherto largest group by far; second, it targeted an exclusively ethnically defined and not sociologically defined group; third, it combined the preventive goal of removal with deliberate, collective punishment. All the Soviet deportations carried out later in World War II, of Crimean Tatars, Chechen-Ingush, various Turkish peoples, Kurds, and Greeks—in total, almost a million people—bore the stamp of this intent to punish.

The deportations of summer 1941 were enforced against the usual Stalinist background of paranoid suspicion of traitors, spies, and collaborators. In the case of the Germans, these fears were not entirely unfounded, since the German army filled its shrinking ranks with any men of German extraction it could find as it advanced. But the ethnic cleansing of regions such as the southern Urals, which lay far from the front line, had no founding in military logic. The grounds for these deportations, the deportees' status as *specpereselenci* (special settlers),[85] and the mode of their accommodation in Siberia and Central Asia are all suggestive of punishment. Many Germans were deported to sites that had previously been used as penal colonies for Kulaks. But here they at least had a roof over their heads, unlike the Chechens and Crimean Tatars deported in 1944.

Despite the German army's surprisingly rapid advance, the Soviet deportation machinery continued to run smoothly. The removal of the Germans from the Volga region, decreed by the NKVD on 27 August 1941, was completed in only seventeen days. Deportations from regions further from the front line in fall of that year were carried out even faster.[86] In terms of ethnic selection, too, the process was wholesale, with families of mixed marriages being deported almost without exception. Finally, the permanence of the deportations proves their totalitarian character. After the war, the NKVD deported a further 200,000 members of the German minority who had returned to Germany during Nazi resettlement campaigns or as refugees. The British and American occupation authorities unwittingly played their part by handing over these Soviet Germans, who were registered as displaced persons in their occupation zones, to the Soviet Union.[87] The Soviet Germans were not even released after Stalin's death, but remained in exile until the collapse of the Soviet Union, or until they received authorization to emigrate to Germany.

The next group to be collectively penalized was the Chechen-Ingush, whose dogged resistance to collectivization had made them a thorn in the side of the Soviets. The NKVD further honed selection and removal processes so that it took just six days to deport 496,460 Chechen-Ingush. As soon as the trains moved away, however, the efficiency came to an end. Tens of thousands did not survive the cold on the long journey in the middle of winter, and many more died later in the work camps.[88] As a result of their removal, 23.7 percent of the deportees died by 1948.

This death toll, by far the highest among all the nationalities deported within the Soviet Union, gives cause to consider the case of the Chechens genocide. But it did not involve mass slaughter, as in 1994 in Rwanda, or industrially executed mass murder, as in the German concentration camps. The Soviet victims of deportation died of exposure, starvation, and exhaustion. This was ethnic cleansing compounded by three longer-term factors: the Soviets' contempt for the Muslim people of the Caucasus, influenced by a Russian strain of colonialism and Orientalism; a desire to punish earlier resistance toward collectivization; and the internal dynamics of the NKVD, which after years of terror and war had lost all sense of moderation and human suffering.

The next substantial number to be deported was 189,000 Crimean Tatars over two days in May 1944. They were followed by about 15,000 Greeks, 13,400 Bulgarians, and nearly 10,000 Armenians, also from the Crimea. While the emptied regions of the northern Caucasus were only slowly recolonized, the Crimea was more easily resettled. Many Russians were willing to migrate to this peninsula, with its mild climate, making up the demographic losses of 1944. In this way, the Crimea gained a distinctly Russian character.

From a long-term perspective, Stalin thus completed what the Ottoman wars had begun in the nineteenth century. By late 1944, there were no Muslims living along the northern and eastern Black Sea coasts apart from a few isolated groups, such as the Abkhaz and the Georgian-speaking Adjari. Religious differences were not officially grounds for deportation; the groups affected were defined by nationality. But anti-Muslim attitudes, which had developed in the tsarist empire, still endured[89] and had been internalized by the Georgians Stalin and Beria. Mass deportations to Central Asia and Siberia also continued a tsarist tradition. However, these measures did not affect the ethnic homogenization of the Soviet Union as a whole. On the contrary, collective banishment preserved and strengthened the sense of community within the affected groups.

The Soviet Union was the only state to change the objective of its ethnic cleansings from forward- to backward-looking. It enforced deportations in the latter 1930s in preparation for an anticipated attack from the West. In 1941, it expelled the Germans partly for reasons of military strategy. But even this and certainly all later deportations were primarily prompted by retrospective motives. They targeted groups that had been stigmatized during collectivization and World War II and exacted retribution for past offenses. Unlike the European nation-states, Stalin was not primarily concerned with ethnic homogeneity. The Soviet Union remained a multiethnic state; its deportations did nothing to change that. The total of 2.5 million people removed on account of their ethnicity in the period between 1935 and 1948 may seem staggering, yet the number of people deported in the 1930s for sociopolitical reasons was far higher.[90]

Outside of its borders, the Soviet Union pursued a more instrumental approach to ethnic cleansing. At the first Soviet-British negotiations in Moscow in late 1941, the Soviet leadership expressed its support for reorganizing Europe along ethnoterritorial lines.[91] Its motives were similar to those of the British: preventing further German aggression, making peace between enemy neighboring states, and establishing an enduring postwar order. Another incentive was the spoils of war from the Nazi-Soviet pact. The negotiations between the "Big Three" concerning these are considered in chapter 4.

Wars within the War: The Ukrainian-Polish and Serbo-Croatian Conflicts

One of the bitter discoveries of the two world wars was that modern warfare and occupying regimes could cause tensions to rise and violence to break out between nations that were not, formally speaking, enemies.

Galicia is a case in point, where World War I prevented the implementation of a 1914 compromise between Poles and Ukrainians in the region.
When Russia occupied eastern Galicia in 1915, it favored the junior nation of the Ukrainians. On Galicia's recapture, the Habsburgs tended to
rely on the Poles as allies. Informers on both sides took advantage of the
general state of lawlessness, in which arbitrary punishments and mutual distrust between the different national groups were rife. In 1919,
civil war broke out in the power vacuum left by the war to determine the
hegemon in the multiethnic region.

The occupying powers in World War II repeated the strategy of "divide
and conquer," with even worse consequences. In the Soviet-occupied territories, most posts in local administration and the newly nationalized
industry and collectivized agriculture were assigned to Ukrainians and
Byelorussians, but not all Poles were dismissed. If the installed Ukrainians and Byelorussians appeared unsuitable for political or personal
reasons, they could easily be replaced by Poles. An embittered sense of
rivalry came to pervade all areas of daily life and was often accompanied
by informing, intrigues, and mutual accusations of collaboration. Even
schoolchildren became selective about their playmates and avoided direct contact with their peers of other ethnicities.[92] But the threat of
Soviet terror loomed over all and mostly prevented interethnic mistrust
from erupting into violence.

Jews were made scapegoats by all sides. As previously in the Polish-
Soviet War of 1920, the propagandist term *Żydokomuna*—an Eastern
European equivalent of the Nazis' "Judeo-communism"—gained currency. The hostility toward Jews, who were given many positions in
the lower- and mid-level Soviet administration, came to a head in June
1941, after the German invasion. Local residents in several towns in the
formerly Soviet-occupied part of Poland took part in pogroms, claiming
far more lives than in 1918–19. These attacks were steered by the German army and the SS, who also initiated the violence if the indigenous
populations proved hesitant. About a week after the German invasion,
the persecution of the Jews reached a new, genocidal level. The German
army and the SS began carrying out mass shootings that horrified even
confirmed anti-Semites. The atrocities committed in full view of the
public, thus bearing a symbolic character, caused attitudes within the
local population to change. Human life was treated as worthless before
the eyes of Poles and Ukrainians on a daily basis. A scenario almost as
terrible could be observed in the Romanian territories occupied by the
Soviet Union in summer 1940 and recaptured by Romania in June 1941,
with the Romanian army and police acting as initiators instead of the
Germans.

For the Organization of Ukrainian Nationalists (Orhanizacia Ukrains'kych Natsionalistiv, OUN), Poland's suppression and the Red Army's defeat by the Germans provided an opportunity to finally establish a Ukrainian nation-state after the previous failed attempt in 1919–20. Ukraine declared its independence in L'viv on 30 June 1941. The Nazi authorities had not been consulted. The Germans responded by interning OUN leader Stepan Bandera in Sachsenhausen concentration camp, but cooperated with radical Ukrainian nationalists nonetheless. It was assumed that the latter would support German rule on the lower rungs of the hierarchy and provide additional troops for the campaign against the Soviet Union. The OUN had not included any clear demands for ethnic purity in its prewar programs. But following the German invasion, and in view of Ukraine's meager chances of permanently subjugating the Poles or gaining any substantial concessions from Poland, it radicalized its stance in step with the negative model provided by the Nazis. In a handbill circulated in October 1941, Ukrainian nationalists cried: "Long live the great, independent Ukraine without Jews, Poles and Germans. Poles go back behind the San, Germans go to Berlin, Jews go hang."[93]

German economic policy exacerbated the rising tensions between Poles and Ukrainians. While the Soviet Union had for a time prioritized the territories occupied in 1939–41 when supplying food and consumer goods in order to promote integration, the Nazis' strategy was to exploit the occupied territories as thoroughly as possible. As a result, the supply situation rapidly deteriorated and poverty and hunger spread, engendering conflicts over distribution. Poles and Ukrainians once again accused each other of seeking advantages at the other's cost. The occupying forces fostered the mutual mistrust by sometimes cooperating with the Ukrainians, sometimes with the Poles.

While life in the cities remained largely unaffected at first, mass violence broke out in the parts of eastern Poland where military colonizers had been settled by the Polish government from 1919. In late 1942, Ukrainian nationalists murdered the Polish population of a binational village in Volhynia for the first time. The violence soon spread to Galicia. In fall 1943, the archbishop of L'viv (Lwów), Twardowski, wrote to his colleague in the Eastern Catholic Church, Andrei Sheptyts'kyi: "The incidents occurring on the territory of my diocese, the murders of my chaplains and the population of the Latin faith have now transcended the boundaries of individual revenge or even of personal, private and political score-settling." Twardowski went on to list the priests murdered and the many places from which Poles had been expelled.[94] In spite of the two churchmen's appeals for peace, the fighting spread to epidemic proportions, consuming the whole of the southeast of the Second Polish Republic. East of the Bug River, Poles were only safe in the villages and small towns known as "self-defense centers." Meanwhile, west of the Bug, the Polish Armia Krajowa forces (AK) maintained military control and carried out retaliatory strikes against the Ukrainian population.

The distance in space and time between the massacres east and west of the Bug River indicate that these were not cases of spontaneous revenge or local "excesses" but the outcome of processes steered from above. The retaliatory strikes were carried out on orders from the command of the Ukrainian rebel army, the Ukraiins'ka Povstans'ka Armia (UPA), and the AK, who were informed of the course of the conflict on both sides of the Bug and the San. Many of these massacres can therefore be regarded as acts of retribution, which also characterized the conflict between the Ustasha and Chetniks in the Independent State of Croatia and other comparable constellations.

In January 1944, the Red Army crossed the Polish-Soviet border of 1939 for a second time. In an attempt to silence the nascent political competition of the Moscow-loyal Polish Committee of National Liberation (Polski Komitet Wyzwolenia Narodowego) in Lublin, the Red Army and the NKVD dissolved the self-defense centers and arrested members of the AK. But Soviet security was not able to protect the Polish population from UPA attacks, which were stepped up again in spring 1945. Countless village churches were burned down, sometimes with the village residents gathered inside. Crosses were carved into the corpses of ritually murdered pregnant women and infants.[95] The brutality displayed in this civil war was a sign of the Ukrainian nationalists' weakness rather than their might. In their desperate struggle against the NKVD and allegedly collaborating Poles, the UPA resorted to any means available to them. And yet they were not alone in using such intense violence: the NKVD and especially the SS had acted even more brutally during occupation. This war within the war was following a dreadful pattern that had been set by warfare internationally and the negative example of the Holocaust. About 30,000 to 50,000 Polish civilians lost their lives as a result of the fighting in Volhynia and eastern Galicia.[96] At least 300,000 fled across the Bug to areas controlled by the AK. About the same number sought refuge in Polish self-defense centers. It is therefore barely possible to retrospectively distinguish flight from unofficial expulsions, although it is certain that most migrations were in direct reaction to violence.

The situation was similar west of the Bug, but with the roles reversed. In today's southeastern Poland, Ukrainians were expelled or fled attacks by the AK. Massacres occurred here too, such as in April

1945 in the town of Piskorowice (Pyskorovychi in Ukrainian), where hundreds of people were murdered. According to Ukrainian calculations, more than 300 predominantly Ukrainian-inhabited villages were burned down, claiming 4,670 lives. The number of refugees cannot be calculated with any certainty, since there was no official system of registration, but it is known that the large majority of Ukrainians was forced to leave the postwar territory of Poland after conclusion of the Polish-Ukrainian evacuation treaty in September 1944.[97] This agreement was made in the context of establishing a postwar order in Europe and is therefore considered in greater detail in chapter 4.

As in other cases of wartime flight and expulsion, the ethnic cleansing of and by Ukrainians and Poles took a heavy toll. Victims often fled in several stages and phases, first from their home village to the next town and from there to an urban center or across the Bug. This scenario recalled the flight of the Balkan Muslims in 1912–13 and of the Greeks of Asia Minor in 1923. All these cases of ethnic cleansing in the context of war had a particularly high mortality rate, reaching 10 percent and more in some areas of Volhynia. Another typical feature was symbolic violence, which did not usually occur during contractually arranged forced resettlements. The "enemy" was publically abused, stigmatized, and executed in order to induce his fellow civilian countrymen and women to leave. Furthermore, ethnic cleansing during wartime went hand in hand with the near total loss of victims' personal property. Most refugees from Volhynia and comparable regions were only able to take a small bundle and the clothes they stood in with them.

The Polish-Ukrainian conflict served the Allies as further justification for completely reorganizing East Central Europe by territorial and ethnic criteria. As early as 1944, they began discussing where to direct the future refugees and expellees. Parts of the former territories of eastern Poland had been reduced to scorched earth. The regions west of the Bug were already overcrowded and still contested and therefore also unsuitable. So the Allies and the Polish government focused on the eastern German territories.

The Serbo-Croatian conflict of 1941 to 1945 claimed the most lives of the wars within the war. As well as being directly influenced by the Nazis, regional actors in the conflict gained considerable scope for action. On 10 April 1941, five days after the German army's invasion of Yugoslavia, the radical Croatian nationalists of the Ustasha (*Ustaša,* "insurgents") proclaimed the Independent State of Croatia (Nezavisna Država Hrvatska, NDH), which encompassed most of today's Croatia and Bosnia and Herzegovina and some counties in the north of Serbia. Unlike Ukraine's aspirations toward independence, the German government supported this new nation-state, seeing the Ustasha as a shortcut to securing mastery over Yugoslavia, while taking much of the burden off the occupying power as well as forming a counterbalance to allied Italy.

Ustasha ideology was more profoundly Fascist than that of the OUN. Even before 1941, striving for an ethnically pure nation-state had been one of the programmatic aims of the radical Croatian nationalists, who had operated in exile in Italy since 1929. Not content with minorities being subjugated, they demanded that they assimilate or be eradicated. The Serbs were the largest minority group targeted by the Ustasha, followed by Jews, Sinti, and Roma. Bosnian Muslims, in contrast, were regarded as Croatian converts and even permitted to build a large mosque in the capital, Zagreb. According to Ustasha ideology, violence was not just a means to an end but a political principle, and glorified in aesthetic terms.

The problem for the Ustasha was that the Croatian state was inhabited by nearly 1.9 million Serbs (constituting about 30 percent of the population), as well as about 40,000 Jews and 30,000 Sinti and Roma. Radical Croatian attitudes toward these minorities were summed up in a handbill circulated after the German invasion of Croatia bearing the motto: "No Serbs, gypsies, Jews or dogs."[98] By bracketing together minorities with animals, the Ustasha publicized their inhumane, racist convictions. Milovan Žanić, the chairman of the executive council in the first Ustasha cabinet, declared in a speech on 2 May 1941:

> This must be the land of the Croats and no one else's. There is no method that we, as Ustashas, will not use to make this land truly Croatian and to cleanse it of Serbs who have endangered us through the centuries and would endanger us again at the first opportunity. This is not a secret, this is the policy of our state.[99]

Just a few weeks after seizing power, Ustasha units began mass murdering Serbs in multiethnic areas such as Slavonia and northern and southern Bosnia. The worst of this phase of massacres took place in Glina, a small town in western Slavonia, 55 kilometers south of Zagreb. Here, the Ustasha drove 260 Serbs into an Orthodox church, stabbed and shot at the crowd, and set the church alight.[100] In 1991, Glina caught the public eye again when the first armed conflicts between Serbs and Croats took place here in July of that year. In spring 1941, state functionaries and Serbians who had arrived in the interwar period—that is, the elite of the Yugoslav settlers—were the first victims of the violence. But what began as a political settling of scores mutated into a chaotic wave of interethnic violence.

The expulsions of Serbs gained a new dimension through the agreements made with Germany on 4 June 1941. Zagreb and Berlin arranged for Croatia to take in 170,000 Slovenes who were obstructing the Germanization of annexed territories, like the Poles in Warthegau. Ustasha leader Ante Pavelić agreed to these population shifts on the condition that Croatia would be able to deport at least as many Serbs from Croatia. About 9,000 Slovenes—alleged supporters of the Yugoslav state—were to be deported directly to Serbia.[101] Hence, the German Reich triggered a chain of ethnic cleansings ending in occupied Serbia, which, similar to the General Government, was to serve as a kind of dumping ground for deported Slavic *Untermenschen*. Hitler met Pavelić in Berlin two days after the treaty was signed and made him swear again to the agreed population shifts. Hitler reiterated the point he had made in his Reichstag address of October 1939 that only clear borders between nations could achieve lasting peace and insisted that the pain of resettlement was better than endless misery. Later, the Ustasha cited the same arguments and the Treaty of Lausanne to justify its own actions. And inspired by the case of Greece, it even requested international loans to help finance the transportation and resettlements.[102]

The rationality at the core of the Croatian policy on Serbs was reflected in the names of the offices dealing with it. The State Administration for Economic Renewal, set up in June 1941, was responsible for organizing the deportation of Serbs; the task of the Colonization Institute was to help repatriated or landless Croats to resettle. The name of the former agency was not just camouflage; its second main task was to oversee the transfer of deported Serbs' and expropriated Jews' property. This was redirected to the Croatian middle class and peasantry, who were even more glorified in Ustasha ideology than German farmers were by the Nazi state.

The State Administration for Economic Renewal launched a second wave of ethnic cleansing in August 1941. Tens of thousands of Serbs were forced to leave their homes practically overnight. The fifty kilograms of luggage they were permitted to take was often confiscated as they made their way to the assembly camps and on to Serbia. As well as these organized deportations, "wild" expulsions also took place. By 20 September, 118,000 refugees had left Croatia, according to the German occupation government in Belgrade. Every day 2,500 mostly impoverished people arrived in Serbia, in need of food and accommodation.

The situation on the banks of the Drina, marking the border between Bosnia and Serbia, was especially precarious. In summer 1941, local Ustasha functionaries drove 20,000 people out toward the river and shot at them from the slopes of the riverbank.[103] Many people drowned as they tried to cross the river. The Drina Valley was also the site of the worst massacres of the war in Bosnia in 1992 and 1995. During World War II, units of the German army deepened the tragedy by refusing to receive refugees. Eventually Croatia and the German Reich agreed to set up a bilateral commission to organize the "resettlement" of the Serbs more efficiently, but to little effect. Since the ethnic cleansing was causing intractable problems for the occupation government in Serbia as well as strengthening the partisans' cause, in October 1941 Himmler intervened. Concurrently, the SS stopped resettling the Slovenes from so-called Lower Styria. As in Warthegau, the Nazis' attempt at changing the ethnic composition of the population had proven unfeasible and counterproductive.

Once officially arranged population shifts were abandoned, a new, even more fatal dynamic began. The Croatian transitory camps that had been used in summer 1941 to detain Serbs now became concentration camps where the Ustasha interned Serbs, Jews, Sinti, and Roma. Fighting the partisans, whom the Ustasha provoked with their ruthless violence, became a pretext for persecuting Serbs en masse. In July 1942, the Croatian government issued a vague "decree to suppress punishable actions against the state,"[104] which was open to broad interpretation but effectively gave the state the right to arrest the relatives of those who had gone underground. The Ustasha occasionally sent entire villages to the camps in order to deter resistance within the population and induce flight to Serbia. Moreover, in summer 1942, responsibility for the roughly twenty larger camps was passed from the Ministry of the Interior to the Ustasha supervisory service. A Catholic priest in Jasenovać noted the effect this had on conditions in the camps: "The concentration camp at Jasenovać is a real slaughterhouse. You have never read anywhere—not even under the GPU or Gestapo—of such horrible things as the 'Ustashi' commit there."[105]

Later, in Communist Yugoslavia, the toll taken by the Ustasha camps became a political issue of the highest order. In order to justify their claim on reparations and to emphasize the genocidal nature of the Ustasha regime, the Communists placed the total number of victims at 700,000 in the Jasenovać camp alone. Croatian nationalists such as the future president Franjo Tudjman, in contrast, maintained that no more than 60,000 died in all the camps. On the basis of reliable research, Joso Tomasevich has estimated the number of Serbs who died during the war in Croatia and Bosnia and Herzegovina to be 334,000.[106] Since there had been 1.9 million Serbs in the Independent State of Croatia at the time of its founding, this would signify a loss of over one-sixth of the population.

In addition to the mass killing in the camps, there were countless local massacres, even of Serbs who were desperately trying to conform outwardly.[107] If one deducts the victims of the bloody partisan fighting from the total number of Serbian casualties in the period 1941–44, the number is still about equal to that of refugees who arrived in Serbia by 1944 (241,000). For this reason, the ethnic cleansings in Croatia should be regarded as attempted or partial genocide.

This murderous violence can be explained by a combination of internal and external factors. While still in exile in Italy, the Ustasha fostered a cult of violence that they put into practice on a national and local level after seizing power. The Independent State of Croatia developed genocidal traits precisely because of its weak organization. Pavelić did not have the local Ustasha functionaries fully under control. They consequently acted with even greater ferocity than the government in Zagreb or the Germans on the ground wanted. Thus, a few thousand violent radicals were enough to terrorize the entire country. A typical element of Ustasha terror was to collectively punish extended families (*Zadruga*), especially to combat partisans. But this was the only distinctive aspect of violence that can be attributed to "the Balkans" and used for constructing a specifically regional explanation. The instigation and indirect influence of the Nazis appears to have been a far more significant factor. Without this, the Ustasha might have been content to settle old scores with the Yugoslav elites, Serbian colonists, and prominent supporters of a Serbian national identity, such as the Orthodox clergy. As in western Ukraine, the Nazis' persecution of Jews and their general ruthlessness set a negative example.

Furthermore, the immense scale of the homogenization project in Croatia launched a trajectory toward genocide. The Ustasha aimed to expel or assimilate one-third of the population of the NDH. Ethnic cleansing on this scale—the only other case where the ratio between the majority nation and the minority to be removed was two to one was that of the Sudeten Germans—would have required a smooth-running state apparatus, a modern transport system, and the complete disarming of the minority. The Ustasha were far from being able to organize such a complex procedure, even with German support. The Serbs in Croatia, moreover, offered resistance, unleashing a spiral of violence that ultimately claimed the lives of one-sixth of the Serbian minority.

Finally, Serbian royalist and nationalist counterviolence must be taken into consideration. At certain points in the war, in parts of Serbia and eastern and southern Bosnia, the Chetniks gained the military advantage. Their guerilla attacks on the occupying Germans and offensive action along a wide front against the Ustasha led to massacres above all of the Muslim population in the upper reaches of the Drina.[108] The mass murder in and around Foča took place in the context of the region's brutal partisan fighting but was rooted in the ideology of Chetnik nationalism. Chetnik leader Draža Mihailović and his closest advisers strove toward an ethnically pure Greater Serbia and called for the "cleansing of the [Serbian] state territory of national minorities and non-national elements."[109] Like the Ustasha, they destroyed religious monuments such as mosques and Catholic churches to this end. But unlike the Ustasha, the Chetniks did not have a state apparatus to organize ethnic cleansing. Any analogy drawn between the two organizations, then, must conclude that the differences outweigh the similarities, especially where the effect of ideology is concerned.

With no place to deport unwanted minorities to, massacres and "wild" expulsions were the only methods by which the Chetniks could attempt to ethnically homogenize Serbia. Here again, the escalating violence repeated the negative pattern set by the Germans. For every German soldier shot by partisans, the occupying forces in Serbia retaliated by killing between fifty and one hundred Serbs. In the six months from September 1941 to February 1942, the German army killed over 20,000 people in this way.[110] The executions took place in public in order to intimidate the Serbs and deter further resistance. The extreme brutality of all later partisans, including the Communists, was certainly more deeply influenced by these experiences than the often-cited tradition of violence in the Balkans.

When the Communist partisans gained the advantage in spring 1943, they vowed to end all interethnic violence and to unite all the nationalities of Yugoslavia. The popularity of Tito's partisans indicates that the vision of a peaceful multiethnic state found broader support than the murderous ideology and methods of the Croatian and Serbian nationalists. From 1945, the mythology of common partisan struggle against the Fascists formed the bedrock of official remembrance. But in the privacy of homes and local communities, memories of massacre and expulsions survived. However, the Germans' share of the responsibility for the traumatic war within the war was largely disregarded. This was partly due to the fact that on a day-to-day basis, the occupying forces remained in the background. Their persecution of Jews and retaliation measures against partisan attacks formed isolated incidents in the local public's perception. Hitler's extensive plans for reorganizing Europe and the chain of population shifts he had arranged with Paveli may have been the cause of untold suffering, but they were not part of the population's everyday experience of war. For this reason, here as in western Ukraine, public memory focused on local and regional perpetrators and directly experienced violence. The Ustasha, Chetniks, OUN, UPA, and AK were far more likely to be remembered as enemies and perpetrators than the *Hitlerowcy* (Hitlerists), as the anti-Fascist propaganda referred to the Germans.

The Ukrainian-Polish and Serbo-Croatian wars within the war had different outcomes. Ethnic borders were erected in eastern Poland at the end of World War II. Henceforth, western Ukrainians and Poles could only fight each other retrospectively, which often occurred in both popular and academic literature. The Serbo-Croatian conflict, in contrast, ended inconclusively. The radical nationalists on both sides, the Ustasha and the Chetniks, were defeated, but neither the germ of nationalism nor the memories of conflict were eliminated.

Nevertheless, the similarities between the Ukrainian-Polish and Serbo-Croatian conflicts outweigh the differences. The violence in both of these wars within the war was sparked by attempts to establish a homogenous nation-state during World War II. There was no place for minorities in the nationalists' ideology. The Ustasha enforced more extensive ethnic cleansings because it was able to use the mechanisms of its own Independent State of Croatia, whereas the OUN and the UPA had to operate from the underground. In both conflicts, flight often took place in stages or across several fronts, entailing heavy losses and particularly severe trauma.

Ethnic Cleansing of Jews

Historical comparisons can be elucidating, but also lead to false conclusions. It would be wrong to treat the ideology, planning, and enforcement of Nazi policy on Jews as "ethnic cleansing." The Nazis' pseudoscientific racism and fantasies of destruction lent the persecution of Jews in the German Reich and the occupied territories unique dimensions from the outset. For this reason, the escalation theory—that the prewar goal of ethnically cleansing Germany of Jews mutated from 1939 or 1941 into plans to destroy German Jewry—does not hold. It would, moreover, suggest that the reasons for the Holocaust were more functionalist than intentionalist.

Yet to ignore the fate of the European Jews in this context seems equally inappropriate. Below, I will consider the extent to which the German-allied states' policies on their Jewish minorities can be considered ethnic cleansing. The term "cleansing" frequently appears in contemporary sources and Nazi documents in reference to the Jews. Nevertheless, one might still question what Romanian foreign minister Mihai Antonescu and his "conducator" Ion Antonescu meant when they spoke of "cleansing" in reference to Jews in 1941, or the Slovakian president Josef Tiso a year later.[111] To understand the semantics of the terminology and the various countries' policies on their Jewish minorities, one must consider the broader context and the specific characteristics of East Central European anti-Semitism.

Romania, Hungary, and Poland displayed tendencies toward a modern form of state-sanctioned anti-Semitism even before 1939.[112] Although the same is not true of Czechoslovakia or Yugoslavia, almost all radical Slovak and Croatian nationalists held anti-Semitic views. This East Central European anti-Semitism contrasted with that of the Nazis by stemming from traditional stereotypes fostered by the various national movements rather than pseudoscientific racist theories. In rural areas, especially, Jews were commonly held to be henchmen of the big landowners who exploited the native farmers. Anti-Semitism was manifested in most of these countries in quota systems, professional and economic discrimination, and expropriations, which were resolved in the late 1930s and accelerated after the outbreak of war. The anti-Semitism of the two newly founded states of Croatia and Slovakia could even be called constitutive.

Anticommunism underpinned the region's anti-Semitism. Societies in the territories occupied by the Soviet Union in 1939 and 1940 accused Jews wholesale of collaborating with the Communists. Tadeusz Tomaszewski, a doctor and psychologist in Lwów (L'viv), noted in his compelling journal: "The conquered nations trust the subjugators more than those with whom they were subjugated. This at least applies to mixed territories, where there are lots of old conflicts, like here."[113] After the German invasion, in the eastern half of Poland, this animosity was vented in dozens of major and many more minor pogroms, which would not, however, have occurred without German approval and support. Solidarity was shown in many individual cases, but not for Jews as a group. Besides the traditional and modern anti-Semitism that was fostered by the myth of *Żydokomuna*, Nazi terror played a major role. The Nazis punished anyone caught actively assisting Jews by death but rewarded denunciations.

German instigation played a lesser role in the territories recaptured by Romania from the Soviet Union in June 1941. In Bessarabia and northern Bukovina, members of the Romanian army and paramilitary groups organized the hounding, lynching, and massacre of Jews. The pogrom in Iasi alone claimed 3,000 lives. Subsequently, in July and August, the Romanian government began expelling Jews from Bukovina and Bessarabia across the old Romanian-Soviet border to Transnistria. Since the German army blocked the border crossings over the Dniester, Bucharest had transit camps and two ghettos set up to hold 100,000 people at the border.

Once Transnistria had been handed over to the Romanian military, there were no limits to the mass expulsions. The province or "republic" of Transnistria (Guvernământul Transnistriei) became a vast labor camp for Jews and Roma, where less than one-third of the 125,000 deportees survived the winters of 1941–42 and 1942–43.[114] The cold, malnourishment, and disease claimed most of these lives in conditions that mirrored the Soviet gulags. This death toll and the use of an entire region as a death camp indicate that the Jewish minority in northern Romania was subjected to genocide rather than ethnic cleansing. But, significantly, this was also one of the few cases of aborted mass murder. In summer 1943, Romanian dictator Ion Antonescu allowed the survivors of Transnistria to return to Romania and refused to hand over Romanian Jews to the Nazis. This case again refutes the theory that there was a direct trajectory from ethnic cleansing to genocide. Fascist Romania committed partial genocide of the Jews in parallel with the ethnic cleansing of other minorities. Furthermore, the Romanian government only took such murderous action against the Jewish minority in Bessarabia and Bukovina. In the Romanian heartland, in contrast, measures did not go beyond extortion, expropriation, and professional discrimination. This regional difference shows that anti-Semitism and anticommunism went hand in hand and reinforced each other.

Anti-Semitism in Bulgaria was traditionally less pronounced and only increased slightly from 1941. But here, too, the government acted ambiguously toward the Jewish minority. While the Jews in the Bulgarian heartland were protected from exposure to the Nazis, as in Romania and Hungary, their property was confiscated and they were professionally disadvantaged. Meanwhile, 14,000 Jews in the Bulgarian-occupied territories were classified aliens and handed over to the Nazis. These Jews were persecuted along with other groups, such as Serbs and Greeks. But they suffered a different fate because there was no external destination for them. The only imaginable place of reception was the Middle East, in fact not such a huge leap from the Black Sea states.

International literature deals with the persecution of the Jews in the German-allied states in the same context as the Holocaust. Certainly, the Nazis' machinery of destruction can be seen to have effected both deportations and mass murder, but this presupposes a view of events from the end, from the perspective of Auschwitz. Romania, Bulgaria, Hungary, Croatia, and Slovakia rigorously pursued certain sociopolitical aims, especially the building of a broad national middle class. But it does not necessarily follow that they therefore organized the complete genocide of their Jewish minorities, not even the Independent State of Croatia. For a time, the Ustasha leadership proved reluctant to hand over Jews and left industrial mass murder to the Germans. Without wishing to split hairs or exculpate the guilty, this distinction should not be ignored.

Three factors support classifying the treatment of Jews in the German-allied states as ethnic cleansing: the successive and alternate intensification of the persecution of different minorities, the motivation or intent behind it, and its spatial dimensions. Below, observations on these and how they differed from the Nazi treatment of Jews are followed by an examination of the repercussions of the Nazi persecution of Jews in the immediate postwar period. This era will not be defined in strict terms as starting on 8 or 9 May 1945 but will include the period following the invasion of the Red Army, which occurred at different points during the course of 1944–45 in different regions.

Developments in Slovakia illustrate the manner in which utopias of ethnic purity were applied to combat successive minorities. Against the background of anti-Semitic propaganda, the Hlinka Party first turned against the Czechs residing in Slovakia, drove them out of their homes and jobs, and eventually organized their removal. Subsequently, it was the turn of the Jews. However, their discrimination and persecution was far more drastic, caused rapid impoverishment, and held no prospect of a coethnic nation-state or place of reception. The ideological and social mechanisms of radical, purgative nationalism led to this sequence of persecution. Once the Czechs had disappeared from Bratislava or declared themselves Slovak, the Jews were the next visible and targetable minority. In the space of just two years, they were stripped of all their rights, socially degraded, and most of them deported. The sequence of minority persecution was different in the German Reich before 1941. Here, the Jews were targeted first, followed by the Poles and other, supposedly racially inferior, groups.

The motives behind the deportation of Jewish minorities also differed between Nazi Germany and the German-allied states. While the Nazis demonstrated a clear intent toward mass destruction right after the beginning of the war, in Slovakia, the Jews were persecuted for a number of reasons.[115] Expropriated and dismissed from their jobs, the Jews—once resented as the exploitative rich—became a burden on society. Deporting them seemed a solution to this problem. The sociopolitical objectives common to all the German-allied states were another motivating factor. Following their radically nationalist rationale, Jews obstructed the development of national economies and modern, productive societies. The technical-sounding names of the state authorities organizing the expropriation and expulsion of the Jews reflected this: the Ministry for Economic Development in Slovakia; the State Administration for Economic Renewal in Croatia. With the exception of Croatia, the German-allied states ran deportation and labor camps, but no extermination camps. While all are deplorable, they are not the same. These states were concerned with removing Jews but not with completely destroying them. Nevertheless, from 1942, higher-ranking Slovakian, Hungarian, and Romanian government members were aware of the final destination of the deported Jews. For this reason, these can be assumed to be cases of genocide by ethnic cleansing but not of independently planned and deliberately wholesale genocide, apart from the exceptions in Croatia and northern Romania mentioned above.

Public reactions in the German-allied states were also distinct from developments under Nazi rule. When news spread of the existence and function of the death camps in occupied Poland, even avowed anti-Semites came to disapprove of deporting Jews. In August 1942, Slovakian president Josef Tiso spoke out against any further deportations, although by this point his government had already deported two-thirds of the Jews on Slovakian territory. Hungary refused to cooperate with the Nazis in this respect for the entire duration of the war, not least because the complete elimination of "Jewish capital" from the Hungarian economy would have exposed it to Germany's clutches. It was only when Germany occupied Hungary in March 1944 that the Nazi mass murderers were able to do as they pleased there. Romania refused to hand over its Jewish citizens from 1943. But the representatives of these states merely tacitly disassociated themselves from the German extermination machinery. Anti-Semitism remained a component of their official policy and propaganda.

Yet the public's reactions to returning survivors of the Holocaust from late 1944 showed that these societies had presumed the Jews would be gone for good. When they reemerged from hiding places or concentration camps, they often encountered disbelief and dismay that they still existed. Attempts by Jews to gain occupancy of their former homes often sparked outbreaks of anti-Semitic violence. The myth of *Żydokomuna* endured to motivate pogroms in 1945–46 in towns such as Krakow, Bratislava, and Kielce.

The public's refusal to reintegrate Jews demonstrates the devastating effect of the Nazi terror. Especially in Poland, many previously Jewish-owned properties were inhabited by people who had lost their own homes and property. The idea of a homogeneous nation-state, which had seemed completely utopian in 1939, had to a large extent become reality during the war. Societies now clung to it like an anchor in stormy seas. Public support for the negative utopia of homogeneity was consequently far greater after the war than before 1939, and Jews were more than ever regarded as an alien element of society.

Conclusion

In the years 1938–44 an unprecedented number of people were affected by ethnic cleansing in Europe. Even leaving aside the Jewish minorities persecuted, expelled, and deported by or on the instigation of the Nazis and the millions made to perform forced labor, at least 6.4 million people were uprooted as a result of ethnic cleansing. This figure comprises the following chronologically ordered cases: 500,000 Germans resettled (1939–42); 1.3 million expelled or deported from the territories annexed by Nazi Germany in the West, East, and Southeast (1940–41); 110,000 deported during Operation Zamość (1942); 2.5 million deported from the Soviet Union (1935–44); 2 million expelled and resettled under German supremacy in Central and Southeastern Europe (1940–42). This list conveys an impression of the destructive dynamic of the Nazis' plans to reorganize Europe.

But this reorganization had already begun before the war, with the Munich Agreement. Hitler was referring to the consensus on ethnic borders achieved here when he spoke of a new "feeling of European security" in his Reichstag address of October 1939. The four signatory states of the Munich Agreement had determined that the future borders in Europe were to follow ethnic lines of separation. Protecting minorities was henceforth not on the agenda; they had the choice of emigration or assimilation. This applied not only to the Sudeten regions but also to the Danube area. The First and Second Vienna Awards of 1938 and 1940 therefore followed a pattern set by the Munich Agreement and that resulted in the mass removal of minorities.

At the same time, the Vienna Awards also connect with longer lines of continuity. The minorities in southern Slovakia and Transylvania officially had a "right of option," under the legal façade of voluntariness, and their rights of ownership were respected. These two settlements made under Nazi hegemony, then, resembled the Treaties of Neuilly and Sèvres, whereas the Treaty of Craiova, between Romania and Bulgaria, contained more parallels with the Treaty of Lausanne. The elements of the Vienna Awards based on the rule of law can hardly be attributed to the Nazis; they were legacies of the liberal nation-state order of the interwar period. It is striking that these treaties caused more extensive ethnic cleansings than the Nazis' unilateral expulsion campaigns. While only about 10 percent of the intended ethnic cleansings were actually carried out in the German-annexed territories, the Romanian-Hungarian agreement (the Second Vienna Award) affected about 20 percent of each state's minorities. In Dobruja, homogenization was almost total.

Although only a small proportion of the planned population shifts actually took place, in the period 1938–44, processes of ethnic cleansing were intensified in terms of totality, pace, and spatial dimensions. As the Soviet example shows, by this point it was perfectly feasible to round up half a million people within two weeks and transport them thousands of kilometers away. The number and size of the regions affected also grew, and with it the extent of the suffering and trauma. Population removals in occupied Poland and Yugoslavia were now coordinated: Slovenes had to make way for Germans, some of whom came from the Italian-occupied territories; the arrival of uprooted Slovenes in Croatia gave the Ustasha an opportunity to expel as many Serbs as possible. Nazi-occupied and dominated Europe became an enormous marshaling yard, where minorities were shunted around with far-reaching consequences. Even when population removals took place under contractual agreements and undisturbed by hostilities, the utopia of ethnic purity and the revision of state borders it demanded engendered further violence and hatred. Hitler's framework for peace in Europe was actually a blueprint for more bloodshed and war.

It emerges that there were two contrasting motivations for ethnic cleansing. The first was a backward-looking revisionism, fueled to a large extent by the memory of past conflicts; the second was a forward-looking utopia of homogeneity. While the Nazis and their allies focused increasingly on their visions for the future, the Soviet Union did the opposite. Here, minorities were collectively penalized for alleged offenses in the past. The utopia of national homogeneity did not play a significant role in and was not achieved by the deportations under Stalin. The allies of the German Reich, meanwhile, treated minorities in their border regions differently from those in their heartlands. Finally, a comparison of ethnic cleansings once again reveals the Nazi regime's unique position in history. Only the German Reich put its racist and nationalist utopias of purity into practice on such a comprehensive scale. By doing so, Hitler provided terrible inspiration for his allies and set countless precedents for the postwar period.

Notes

1. See Frank, *Expelling the Germans*, 30n73.
2. See King, *Budweisers into Czechs*.
3. For an intelligent and largely neutral account, see Majewski, *Niemcy Sudeccy 1848–1948*, 300–98.
4. See *The Times* (London), "An Impregnable Case," 4 October 1938, 15. Chamberlain and Hitler discussed the Sudeten Germans' "unification" with the Reich and the cession of the Sudeten regions. Logically enough, this combination of a territorial with a group principle did not take the Czech minority into consideration. Chamberlain made a few feeble attempts at addressing their prospects and simply accepted Hitler's evasive replies. On this aspect of the negotiations, see *Akten zur Deutschen Auswärtigen Politik 1918–1945: Aus dem Archiv des Deutschen Auswärtigen Amtes. Serie D (1937–1945), Band II: Deutschland und die Tschechoslowakei (1937–1938)* (Baden-Baden, 1950), 634–35, 732–34, 755–56 (hereafter *ADAP*).
5. On the matter of gaining the consent of the government in Prague, Neville Chamberlain's personal adviser, Sir Horace Wilson, is quoted in German sources as saying "I will still try to make those Czechos sensible." See *ADAP 1918–1945, D/II*, 633.
6. See *ADAP 1918–1945, D/II*, 633.
7. See Gebhart, *Migrationsbewegungen*. On the pressure exerted on the established Czech population, see the local study by Paul Mähner, "Gnadlersdorf (Hnanice): Ein südmährisches Dorf an der Grenze," in *Bevölkerungstransfer und Systemwandel, Ostmitteleuropäische Grenzen nach dem Zweiten Weltkrieg,* ed. Helga Schulz (Berlin, 1998), 163–210.
8. On Turkey's agreement with Romania and Bulgaria, see Joseph Schechtman, *European Population Transfers 1939–1945* (New York, 1946), 488–96. In 1939, Turkey was on the verge of signing a similar agreement with Yugoslavia, but this was precluded by the outbreak of World War II.
9. The Peel Commission is considered in more detail in chapter 4.
10. See Frank, *Expelling the Germans*, 37. Britain aimed to forge ties with Romania and Bulgaria by this involvement. The Treaty of Craiova, which is discussed below, largely adhered to the British proposal of late 1939.
11. On these negotiations, see Karl Stuhlpfarrer, *Umsiedlung Südtirol 1939–1940* (Vienna, 1985), 49–86. The quote is from Schechtman, *European Population Transfers*, 53.
12. For the original quotes, see http://www.reichstagsprotokolle.de/Blatt2_n4_bsb00000 613_00067.html and http://www.reichstagsprotokolle.de/Blatt2_n4_bsb00000613_00 052.html.
13. However, in a discussion with the head of the Supreme Commander of the German army, Wilhelm Keitel, on 17 October 1939, Hitler demanded that "the Reich territory be cleansed of Jews and Polacks." See Götz Aly, *"Endlösung": Völkerverschiebung und der Mord an den europäischen Juden* (Frankfurt, 1995), 63 and 177.
14. Secondary literature mostly emphasizes the racist element of these speeches. See the analysis by Michael Wildt, "'Eine neue Ordnung der ethnographischen Verhältnisse': Hitlers Reichstagsrede vom 6. Oktober 1939," *Zeithistorische Forschungen* 3 (2006): 1, quoted by http://www.zeithistorische-forschungen.de/16126041-Wildt-1-2006 (accessed 25 June 2009).
15. The message was positively received in Belgrade. In response to this speech, the Yugoslav government proposed a population transfer of the border-region Slovenian and German minorities. See Milan Ristović, "Zwangsmigrationen in den Territorien Jugoslawiens im Zweiten Weltkrieg," in *Zwangsmigrationen im mittleren und östli-*

chen Europa: Völkerrecht—Konzeptionen—Praxis (1938-1950), ed. Ralph Melville, Jiří Pešek, and Claus Scharf (Mainz, 2008), 309.

16. Quoted by Schechtman, *Population Transfers*, 54.

17. For the original wording of this handbill aimed at the Germans in Latvia, see Dietrich Loeber, ed., *Diktierte Option: Die Umsiedlung der Deutsch-Balten aus Estland und Lettland 1939-1941* (Neumünster, 1972), 170.

18. On the number of resettlers, see Valdis Lumans, *Himmler's Auxiliaries: The Volksdeutsche Mittelstelle and the German National Minorities of Europe 1939-1945* (Chapel Hill, NC, 1993); Markus Leniger, *Nationalsozialistische "Volkstumsarbeit" und Umsiedlungspolitik: Von der Minderheitenbetreuung zur Siedlerauslese* (Berlin, 2006), 89.

19. See Dirk Jachomowski, *Die Umsiedlung der Bessarabien, Bukowina und Dobrudschadeutschen: Von der Volksgruppe in Rumänien zur "Siedlungsbrücke" an der Reichsgrenze* (Munich, 1984), 104.

20. Schechtman, *Population Transfers*, 155.

21. See Lumans, *Himmler's Auxiliaries*, 169.

22. On migration from southern Bukovina and Dobruja, see Lumans, *Himmler's Auxiliaries*, 174. Facsimiles of the treaties are reproduced in the appendix of Jachomowski, *Die Umsiedlung*, 209–25, also 68–69 and 93–95. A total of 52,400 people migrated from southern Bukovina; 13,968 migrated from Dobruja.

23. Quoted and translated from a report made in a reception camp in 1941. See Leniger, *Nationalsozialistische Volkstumsarbeit*, 120n378.

24. On the selection and categorization of the resettlers, see Isabel Heinemann, *"Rasse, Siedlung, deutsches Blut": Das Rasse- und Siedlungshauptamt der SS und die rassenpolitische Neuordnung Europas* (Göttingen, 2003), 232–50.

25. Quoted and translated from Jachomowski, *Die Umsiedlung*, 176–77.

26. The Nazis noted "incomprehensible feelings of sympathy with the Polish." See Jachomowski, *Die Umsiedlung*, 165.

27. See Pertti Ahonen, Gustavo Corni, Jerzy Kochanowski, Rainer Schulze, Tamás Stark, and Barbara Stelzl-Marx, *People on the Move: Forced Population Movements in Europe in the Second World War and its Aftermath* (Oxford, 2008), 20.

28. Quoted and translated from Leninger, *Nationalsozialistische Volkstumsarbeit*, 129.

29. On the official statistics, see Ahonen, *People on the Move*, 19.

30. See Czesław Madajczyk, *Die Okkupationspolitik Nazideutschlands in Polen 1939–1945* (Cologne, 1988); Aly, *"Endlösung,"* 14 and 21.

31. See Włodzimierz Borodziej, *Geschichte Polens im 20. Jahrhundert* (Munich, 2010), 193. For an in-depth account of German warfare in Poland, see Jochen Böhler, *Auftakt zum Vernichtungskrieg: Die Wehrmacht in Polen 1939* (Frankfurt, 2006).

32. Maria Rutowska, *Wysiedlenie ludności polskiej z Kraju Warty do Generalnego Gubernatorstwa 1939-1941* (Poznań, 2003), 61–93.

33. See A. Ebbinghaus and K. H. Roth, "Vorläufer des Generalplans Osts: Eine Dokumentation über Theodor Schieders Polendenkschrift vom 7. Oktober 1939," *1999* 7 (1992): 62–91.

34. See Aly, *"Endlösung,"* 109–14, 213, and 215. On Polish attempts to escape expulsion, see 98. For a detailed account of the misery endured by Polish expellees, see Zygmunt Klukowski, *Zamojszczyzna*, vol. 1, *1918–1943* (Warsaw, 2008), esp. 126–27, 177–79, and 197. This diary from the Zamość region is one of the best ego-documents about the German occupation (and the subsequent Stalinization of Poland).

35. As well as the older publications by Ulrich Herbert on forced labor, see the survey by Mark Spoerer, *Zwangsarbeit unter dem Hakenkreuz: Ausländische Zivilarbeiter, Kriegsgefangene und Häftlinge im Deutschen Reich und im besetzten Europa* (Stuttgart, 2001). For a victims' perspective, see Alexander von Plato, Almut Leh,

6

and Christoph Thonfeld, eds., *Hitlers Sklaven: Lebensgeschichtliche Analysen zur Zwangsarbeit im internationalen Vergleich* (Vienna, 2008).

36. The mortality rate among prisoners of war and concentration camp inmates was far higher if they were made to perform forced labor. For an estimate of the number of victims, see Spoerer, *Zwangsarbeit*, 223–29.

37. Borodziej, *Geschichte Polens*, 200.

38. See the vivid journal account in Klukowski, *Zamojszczyzna*.

39. On these plans, see Czesław Madajczyk, *Vom Generalplan Ost zum Generalsiedlungsplan* (Munich, 1994); Aly, *"Endlösung,"* 33–34.

40. See Włodzimierz Borodziej, *Der Warschauer Aufstand 1944* (Frankfurt, 2004), 205–6.

41. See Ristović, "Zwangsmigrationen," 319; see also Stevan K. Pavlowitch, *Hitler's New Disorder: The Second World War in Yugoslavia* (New York, 2008), 33. Aly gives more precise statistics on deportees to the Reich in *"Endlösung,"* 286. On deportations, see "Die Okkupationspolitik des deutschen Faschismus in Jugoslawien, Griechenland, Albanien, Italien und Ungarn (1941–1945)," in *Europa unterm Hakenkreuz: Die Okkupationspolitik des deutschen Faschismus (1938–1945)*, vol. 6, ed. Bundesarchiv (Berlin, 1992), 170–71.

42. See Heinemann, *Rasse, Siedlung*, 306–31; Lumans, *Hitler's Auxiliaries*, 180.

43. To what extent this categorization was inspired by French practice in Alsace in 1919 has not yet been researched. The form of categorization was similar, but the German People's List was based on uniquely racist principles, and did not include a category for foreigners (such as category C in Alsace; see chapter 2).

44. See Borodziej, *Geschichte Polens*, 194.

45. See Madajczyk, *Okkupationspolitik*, 240–42.

46. See Philipp Ther, "Die einheimische Bevölkerung des Oppelner Schlesiens nach dem Zweiten Weltkrieg: Die Entstehung einer deutschen Minderheit," *Geschichte und Gesellschaft* 26 (2000): 407–38.

47. Quoted by Frank, *Expelling the Germans*, 42, from the magazine *Fortnightly*. On the House of Lords, see Detlef Brandes, *Der Weg zur Vertreibung: Pläne und Entscheidungen zum "Transfer" der Deutschen aus der Tschechoslowakei und aus Polen* (Munich, 2005), 52.

48. On the FPRS's debates and recommendations, see Frank, *Expelling the Germans*, 45–56, esp. 50 and 52. High-ranking officials in the British Foreign Office expressed similar opinions; Frank, *Expelling the Germans*, 78.

49. See Brandes, *Der Weg zur Vertreibung*, 5–104.

50. Hedwig Wachenheim, "Hitler's Transfers of Population in Eastern Europe," *Foreign Affairs* 20, no. 4 (July 1942): 705–18.

51. See Herbert Hoover and Hugh Gibson, "The Problem of Lasting Peace," in *Prefaces to Peace* (New York, 1943), 289–91.

52. This number does not include deported Jews from the region and German refugees. For a precise calculation, see the end of this sub-chapter.

53. See Martin Vietor, *Dejiny okupácie južního Slovenska 1938–1945* (Bratislava, 1968), 42. This figure is confirmed by a more recent publication by the Slovakian Academy of Science. See Elena Mannová, ed., *A Concise History of Slovakia* (Bratislava, 2000).

54. See Valerián Bystrický, "Vyst'ahovanie českých štatných zaměstnancov zo Slovenska v rokoch 1938–1939," *Historický Časopis* 45 (1997): 596–611. On the statistics, see 606. This case of ethnic cleansing has hitherto been entirely overlooked by German and English research literature.

55. The population statistics continue to vary according to their national provenance. See Ottmar Trașcă and Rudolf Gräf, "Rumänien, Ungarn und die Minderheitenfrage zwischen Juli 1940 und August 1944," in Ralph Melville et al., *Zwangsmigrationen*, 271.

56. Ibid., 267.

57. Ibid., 267.
58. Quoted and translated from ibid., 293.
59. On the previous quote and this association's activities, see ibid., 301.
60. The Romanian government registered 218,000 refugees by 1944. See Dumitru Şandru, *Mişcări de populaţie în România (1940–1948)* (Bucharest, 2003), 9; Corneliu Pădurean, "Contribuţii la problematica refugiaţilor din Nord-Vestul Transilvaniei în judeţul Arad (1940–1942)," in *Mişcări de populaţie şi aspecte demografice în România în prima jumătate a secolului XX: Lucrările conferinţei internaţionale "Mişcări de populaţie în Transilvania în timpul celor două războaie mondiale. Cluj-Napoca, 24-27 mai 2006*, ed. Sorina Paula Bolovan, Ioan Bolovan, Rudolf Gräf, and Corneliu Pădurean (Cluj, 2007).
61. See the figures in Michael Portmann, *Die kommunistische Revolution in der Vojvodina 1944–1952: Politik, Gesellschaft, Wirtschaft, Kultur* (Vienna, 2008), 92.
62. On Bulgarian population statistics, see Andrea Schmidt-Rösler, *Rumänien nach dem Ersten Weltkrieg: Die Grenzziehung in der Dobrudscha und im Banat und die Folgeprobleme* (Frankfurt, 1994), 25.
63. On these figures, taken from contemporary media, see Schechtman, *Population Transfers*, 407.
64. Schechtman, *Population Transfers*, 418.
65. On these figures, see Björn Opfer, *Im Schatten des Krieges: Besatzung oder Anschluss—Befreiung oder Unterdrückung? Eine komparative Untersuchung über die bulgarische Herrschaft in Vardar-Makedonien 1915–1918 und 1941–1944* (Münster, 2005), 264–65.
66. See Noel Malcolm, *Kosovo: A Short History* (New York, 1999), 293–94.
67. See Malcolm, *Kosovo*, 305.
68. Quoted and translated by Dinu C. Giurescu, "Romania During the Second World War," in *Romania: A Historic Perspective*, ed. Dinu C. Giurescu and Stephen Fischer-Galaţi (Boulder, CO, 1998), 366. According to the plans of the head of the central statistics office in Romania, 3.5 million people were to leave Romania; Hungarians, Serbs, Bulgarians, and Ukrainians in the context of population exchanges, Jews and Roma on the basis of one-sided population transfers. See Mariana Hausleitner, Brigitte Mihok, and Juliane Wetzel, eds., *Rumänien und der Holocaust: Zu den Massenverbrechen in Transnistrien 1941–1944* (Berlin, 2000), 18. See also Vladimir Solonari, *Purifying the nation. Population exchange and ethnic cleansing in Nazi-allied Romania* (Baltimore, 2010).
69. The one exception here was the Roma, who were pursued throughout the country from 1942. Ultimately nearly 25,000 mostly nomadic Roma were deported to Transnistria, where over 75 percent of them perished. See Brigitte Mihok, "Die Verfolgung der Roma: Ein verdrängtes Kapitel der rumänischen Geschichte," in Hausleitner, *Rumänien*, 25–32.
70. This figure comprises 500,000 Serbs, 540,000 Romanians (although 220,000 refugees were able to return to the territories annexed by the Soviet Union in 1941), 280,000 Czechs and Slovaks, 200,000 German resettlers from the prewar territory of Romania, 150,000 Hungarians, 120,000 Greeks, and 60,000 Bulgarians. The Jews deported from states allied with Germany are special cases that are discussed in the chapter on the ethnic cleansing of Jews. The figure of approx. two million people encompasses only the groups who fled or were transported across international borders, not internal refugees.
71. See Martin, "The Origins"; see also the monograph by J. Otto Pohl, *Ethnic Cleansing in the USSR 1937–1949* (Westport, CT, 1999), 30.
72. See the publication by Russian historian Nikolaj Iwanow, *Pierwszy Naród ukarany: Polacy w Związku Radzieckim 1921–1939* (Warsaw, 1991).

73. Martin, "The Origins," 839.
74. On Stalin's exact wording, see Martin, "The Origins," 854. On the model character of this wave of deportations, see Nikita V. Petrov and Arsenii B. Roginskii, "Pol'skaia Operatsiia' NKVD 1937–1938 gg.," in *Repressii protiv poliakov i pol'skikh grazhdan,* ed. Memorial (Moscow, 1997), 31.
75. In the 1930s the Koreans were the largest single group to be deported. On their history, see Alexander Kim, "The Repression of the Soviet Koreans during the 1930s," *The Historian* 74, no. 2 (2012): 267–85. German Kim is the most prolific Russian-language author on the Soviet Koreans. See German Kim, *Istoriia immigratsii koreitsev,* 2 vols. (Almaty, 1999–2000).
76. Martin, "The Origins," 855.
77. See Jan Gross, *Revolution from Abroad: The Soviet Conquest of Poland's Western Ukraine and Western Belorussia* (Princeton, NJ, 1988), 26 and 35.
78. On the different phases of this deportation campaign, see Stanisław Ciesielski, Grzegorz Hryciuk, and Aleksander Srebrakowski, eds., Masowe *deportacje radzieckie w okresie II wojny światowej* (Wrocław, 1994), 40; Ahonen et al., *People on the Move,* 126–28.
79. See Stanisław Ciesielski, ed., *Umsiedlung der Polen aus den ehemaligen polnischen Ostgebieten nach Polen in den Jahren 1944–1947* (Marburg, 2006), 19; Piotr Eberhardt, *Polska Granica Wschodnia 1939–1945* (Warsaw, 1993), 73.
80. The amount of international literature on the flight and forced resettlement of the Finns is negligible. Consequently, the subject is overlooked in all recent monographs and anthologies on ethnic cleansing. The information here is based on Schechtman, *Population Transfers,* 389, and Brandes, Sundhaussen, and Troebst, *Lexikon der Vertreibungen,* 334–36.
81. On the deportation of Soviet Finns, see Pohl, *Ethnic Cleansing,* 21–25.
82. On these statistics and local resistance to refugees, see Schechtman, *Population Transfers,* 392–93.
83. See Ciesielski et al., *Masowe Deportacje,* 61; Ahonen et al., *People on the Move,* 126.
84. See Pavel Polian, *Ne po svoei vole: Istoria i geografia prinuditel'nykh migratsii v SSSR* (Moscow, 2001), 114. Polian estimates the number of deported Germans to be 905,000, rising to 1.2 million toward the end of the war due to the removal of ethnic Germans from Romania, Yugoslavia, Poland, and other countries as well as the "repatriation" of former Nazi resettlers.
85. On this term and the status it implied, see Polian, *Ne po svoei vole,* 115.
86. On these deportations, see Pohl, *Ethnic Cleansing,* 27–60.
87. According to Pohl, the Allies handed over 203,000 Germans between September and December 1945. See Pohl, *Ethnic Cleansing,* 46.
88. See the numbers in Naimark, *Fires of Hatred,* 125; Pohl, *Ethnic Cleansing,* 49.
89. See Holquist, "To Count," 115.
90. This number includes the nearly two million "national deportees" of 1937–44, plus the "repatriated" German Soviet citizens who were immediately deported to Central Asia in 1945–46, as well as the Poles and Baltic people deported in 1940–41 and from 1944 onward.
91. See Frank, *Expelling the Germans,* 52.
92. See Philipp Ther, "Chancen und Untergang einer multinationalen Stadt: Die Beziehungen zwischen den Nationalitäten in Lemberg in der ersten Hälfte des 20. Jahrhunderts," in Ther and Sundhaussen, *Nationalitätenkonflikte,* 123–46. On interethnic relations in Galicia, see the compelling eyewitness report by doctor and psychologist Tadeusz Tomaszewski, *Lwów 1940–1944: Pejzaż psychologiczny* (Warsaw, 1996).

93. Quoted by Dieter Pohl, *Nationalsozialistische Judenverfolgung in Ostgalizien 1941–1944: Organisation und Durchführung eines staatlichen Massenverbrechens* (Munich, 1996), 177.

94. See Józef Wołczański, "Korespondencja Arcybiskupa Bolesława Twardowskiego z Arcybiskupiem Andrzejem Szeptyckim w latach 1943–1944," *Przegląd Wschodni* 2, no. 2 (1992–93), 475 (letter of 15 October 1943). On the Polish-Ukrainian conflict and the ethnic cleansing of Poles, see Timothy Snyder, *The Reconstruction of Nations: Poland, Ukraine, Lithuania, Belarus, 1569–1999* (New Haven, CT, 2003), 158–78.

95. See the eyewitness reports recorded in Archiwum Instytutu Śląskiego w Opolu (hereafter AIS), "Pamiętniki trzech pokoleń mieszkańców Ziem Odzyskanych," *Pamiętnik*, nos. 82 and 95; Jeffrey Burds, "Agentura: Soviet Informant's Network and the Ukrainian Underground in Galicia 1944–48," *East European Politics and Societies* 11, no. 1 (1997): 106 and 118.

96. In Ciesielski, *Umsiedlung*, 23, the number given is 70,000, but this is most probably exaggerated.

97. On the flight and expulsion of Poles and Ukrainians, see Ivan Bilas, *Represyvno-karal'na systema v Ukraini 1917–1953: Suspil'no-politychnyi ta istoryko-pravovyi analiz*, vol. 1 (Kiev, 1994), 213–37. The best Polish book on the subject is by Grzegorz Motyka, *Tak było w Bieszczadach: Walki polsko-ukrainskie 1943–1948* (Warsaw, 1999).

98. Quoted from Pavlowitch, *Hitler's New Disorder*, 32. On Ustasha ideology, see the seminal work by Alexander Korb, *Im Schatten des Weltkriegs: Massengewalt der Ustasha gegen Serben, Juden und Roma in Kroatien* (Hamburg, 2013).

99. Quoted by Jozo Tomasevich, *War and Revolution in Yugoslavia, 1941–1945: Occupation and Collaboration* (Palo Alto, CA, 2001), 392.

100. See Tomasevich, *War and Revolution*, 398.

101. On this agreement, see ibid., 393.

102. I am grateful to Alexander Korb, University of Leicester, for pointing this out.

103. On the situation in the Drina Valley, see Tomasevich, *War and Revolution*, 394.

104. See ibid., 399.

105. Quoted by ibid., 400.

106. Ibid., 738. The same figure is given by Aleksa Djilas, *The Contested Country: Yugoslav Unity and Communist Revolution 1919–1953* (Cambridge, 1991), 126.

107. The Nazi authorities recorded eighty-seven cases of the willful massacre of Croats claiming one hundred victims in the year May 1941 to May 1942. See Tomasevich, *War and Revolution*, 413. In the latter half of 1941, about half of the Orthodox clergy was also murdered.

108. Recent estimates point to between 86,000 and 103,000 war victims among Bosnian Muslims, that is, many more than in the 1990s. See Sundhaussen, *Geschichte Serbiens*, 339.

109. Quoted and translated from Sundhaussen, *Geschichte Serbiens*, 321n622. The original wording is: "Čišćenje državne teritorje od svih narodnih manjina i ne-nacionalnih elemenata."

110. See Sundhaussen, *Geschichte Serbiens*, 327.

111. On the two Antonescus, see Giurescu, *Romanians*, 366; Radu Ioanid, "The Deportation of the Jews to Transnistria," in Hausleitner, *Rumänien*, 70; Radu Ioanid, *The Holocaust in Romania: The Destruction of Jews and Gypsies under the Antonescu Regime, 1940–44* (Chicago, 2000), 92. On Tiso, see Tatjana Tönsmeyer, *Das Dritte Reich und die Slowakei 1939–45: Politischer Alltag zwischen Kooperation und Eigensinn* (Paderborn, 2003), 96. The head of the central statistics office in Romania referred to the expulsion of the Jews as a "one-sided population transfer." See Ma-

riana Hausleitner, "Großverbrechen im rumänischen Transnistrien 1941–44," in Hausleitner, *Rumänien,* 18.

112. On Hungary, see Christian Gerlach and Götz Aly, *Das letzte Kapitel: Der Mord an den ungarischen Juden* (Stuttgart, 2002).
113. Translated from Tomaszewski, *Lwów 1940–1944,* 84.
114. See Ioanid, "The Deportation of the Jews," 97.
115. See Tönsmeyer, *Das Dritte Reich,* 137–61.

CHAPTER 4

THE BIG SWEEP

POSTWAR EUROPE AND BEYOND

1944–48

⊙ℰℱℱ⤳

Another Escalation: The Allied Plans 1943–45

The Allies' postwar framework for peace was just as closely related to the Munich Agreement as the Nazis' reorganization of Europe—but in reverse. Germany's annexation of the Sudetenland in 1938 had launched a series of population shifts in East Central and Southeastern Europe. Britain's revocation of the Munich Agreement in July 1942 prompted other population transfers. The dialectical thread linking the conclusion and revocation of the Munich Agreement was an intolerance of national minorities.

Over the course of the war, the focus of Allied plans for Central Europe shifted from forcibly assimilating to removing (the German) minorities. The terminological trend changed accordingly. From 1942, despite frequent references to Lausanne, "population exchange" was rarely mentioned in talks in London, which now centered on the idea of "population transfer." Plans were initially made for no more than the German resettlers, who were to leave Poland again, and a few areas of strategic and economic importance such as Upper Silesia and East Prussia. In the opinion of President Beneš, some of the German minority could stay in Czechoslovakia. The way things stood in 1943, no more than five to six million Germans were to be affected by the projected removals.

But Germany's defeat at Stalingrad changed the course of the war and the scope of Allied designs. From 1943, not only Germans fell into their ambit but also several other nations in the eastern half of Europe, mainly due to Soviet claims to the spoils from the Nazi-Soviet Pact and especially the eastern half of Poland. For a time, it was not clear how far west the Soviet Union would expand and whether it would annex major Polish towns such as Lwów. At the Tehran Conference in November 1943, the "Big Three" agreed on the Oder River as Poland's western border. The Soviet Union was awarded a large part of the Polish eastern territories and the ice-free port of Königsberg. Churchill demonstrated the border changes to Stalin by pushing matches around the conference table.[1] Poland, the country most affected by the deals, was not represented, echoing the situation five years previously at the conference in Munich. The Allies, meanwhile, agreed to combine the redrawing of state borders with the "disentanglement," as Churchill put it, of ethnic borders.

As the British prime minister admitted in his memoirs, he and President Roosevelt were fully aware in Tehran "that the three or four million Poles who lived on the wrong side of the line would have to be moved to the West."[2] A year later, Churchill acted as bearer of the bad tidings. In a speech to Parliament on "the future of Poland" in December 1944, he declared: "There will be no mixture of populations to cause endless trouble ... A clean sweep will be made."[3] Yet he was optimistic that these population shifts would not present too many difficulties thanks to modern transportation methods and technologies. Nevertheless, he warned the Polish government in menacing tones to comply with this Allied diktat.

By the time of Churchill's speech, Stalin had already created precedents. In early 1944 he installed a Moscow-loyal government, the Polish National Liberation Committee (PKWN), in Lublin. The PKWN accepted the new Polish-Soviet border, although it entailed the loss of Vilna, Lwów, and nearly half of the former national territory. Not content with these gains, Stalin also ethnically realigned the border. In September 1944, he made the PKWN sign treaties with the three most westerly Soviet republics of Ukraine, Byelorussia, and Lithuania on the "evacuation" of their resident Polish minorities. In formal terms, these were bilateral evacuations that also applied to the Ukrainian, Byelorussian, and Lithuanian minorities in Poland.

Although the Allies excluded Poland from the Big Three's negotiations, they could not completely dupe this first victim of Nazi aggression, which had offered tough resistance and contributed tens of thousands of volunteers to the Western armies. It was agreed that Poland should receive adequate compensation in the west for its losses in the east. At the Yalta Conference, the Allies placed the western border of Poland at the Oder and Neisse Rivers, and thus in regions that not even the Polish government in exile had claimed in 1944. This gave Stalin the advantage that Poland was henceforth dependent on the protection of the Soviet Union.

German expellee literature and, inspired by this, Norman Naimark tend to underline the role of Poland and Czechoslovakia in expelling the Germans. But the role of the Allies, who were the authors of the postwar order, should not be underestimated.[4] Britain and, from 1944, the Soviet Union determined the course of events in East Central Europe. The British government was the most vocal champion of "population transfers," employing rhetoric of radical change in an apparent bid to compensate for its loss of influence in the region. Stalin proceeded more discreetly, mostly guaranteeing the Polish and Czechoslovak governments his support in dealing with the German minorities behind closed doors. In Yalta, Stalin maintained to the Western powers that most Germans had already left Poland fleeing the Red Army. Although this was a blatant lie—in early 1945, more than half of the German population was still resident in the eastern territories of the Reich—the Western powers were only too willing to believe him. At the same time, Stalin encouraged his allies in Poland and Czechoslovakia to exert extreme pressure on the remaining Germans. The general secretary of the Polish Communists, Władysław Gomułka, ordered conditions to be created that no Germans would want to remain in.[5]

Aside from removing the Germans, the Soviet leadership proved ambivalent toward ethnic cleansing. It did not even take consistent measures against Polish populations; only the Polish minority in western Ukraine and the urban elites in Lithuania and Byelorussia were quickly and brutally "evacuated." In rural areas, the Soviet authorities began registering Poles to be resettled but seemed in no hurry to complete the task. As is examined below, the Soviet Union even halted or helped to reverse ethnic cleansings that had begun in regions such as Transylvania.

In contrast to their rhetoric of cleansing in 1944, the Western powers acted more cautiously after the war, mainly on account of practical difficulties. In June and July 1945, more than 100,000 expellees fled to the ruins of postwar Germany every week, joining about five million war refugees. Neither the German authorities nor the occupation administrations could cope with the overwhelming flood of refugees. Consequently, it was resolved that the Potsdam Agreement should include a moratorium on mass expulsions and that the organization of the population removals was to be improved. In Article XIII, the Western powers stipulated a "humane and orderly transfer."[6]

The older literature and Western eyewitnesses often claim that Stalin took the Western powers by surprise by proposing the forced expulsion of the Germans in Potsdam. They portray the Western powers as taking a passive role or accepting the "transfer" in exchange for other benefits.[7] But Matthew Frank shows that mass population shifts were an integral part of British foreign policy. At most, the Western powers had pragmatic misgivings, but none on principle. Thus, the talks in Potsdam centered on the issue of how far west Poland should be moved and the mass migration this would entail, but did not debate the value of population shifts as a means of international politics. It was, moreover, Churchill who introduced the concept of "transfer," primarily to maintain Britain's influence on the Czech and Polish governments, according to Frank.[8] Hungary's inclusion in the Potsdam agenda still seems surprising today, since Hungary had been Germany's most faithful ally during the war. The German minority here had never challenged the state's territorial status quo and there was no tradition of interethnic conflict, as in Poland or today's Czech Republic. By including Hungary in the Potsdam scheme, Stalin was pursuing sociopolitical goals, such as extending the scope of the land reform planned by the Communists.

As in previous years, the mechanisms of international diplomacy allowed the scale of ethnic cleansing to increase at a dramatic pace. This is evidenced in the progress of the conferences from Tehran to Potsdam. In 1943, the Soviet Union confined its territorial demands on Poland to Vilna and mostly rural areas. Following the Red Army's invasion of East Prussia in 1944, Stalin claimed Lwów (L'viv) and eastern Galicia, including the oil fields around Borysław. Finally, in 1945, the Allies carved off almost half of the prewar territory of Poland, prompting extensive ethnic cleansings as a result.

No holds were barred in the case of the Germans, either. In 1943, the Allies debated the ceding of Upper Silesia and East Prussia. Including the German minority in central Poland and the resettlers, this would have forced some 3.5 to 4 million people to migrate. But under the Potsdam Agreement, twice as many Germans were removed from the postwar territory of Poland. In 1942, Edvard Beneš announced the Czech government's intention to expel about a million Germans; in the end it was three million. Finally, Churchill announced the "total expulsion" of the Germans from postwar Poland in a speech to Parliament in December 1944. At the Yalta Conference, Stalin and Churchill cynically calculated that seven million German war casualties should leave enough space for the expellees in Germany's postwar territory. Internally, senior officials and government advisers in Washington and London expressed misgivings about organizing a mass migration of this scale, but to the public it was presented as absolutely feasible.

The scope of ethnic cleansings also widened due to an inherent domino effect: border and population movements formed a chain, linking regions several hundred kilometers apart. Poles were to leave the eastern Polish territories at the cost of the Germans in the eastern German territories; they in turn were to spread across the different zones of occupation. Only the German-Croatian agreements of June 1941 had had comparable dimensions, moving Slovenes to Croatia and Serbs out of Croatia. Poland was also linked with the neighboring Soviet Union by the "population exchange" mentioned above.

By and large, the Allies left the enforcement of these unprecedented plans to Germany's East Central European neighbors, which is why they feature prominently in German remembrance of "expulsion." There can be no doubt that the resettlement, expulsion, transfer, or whatever one called it, of the Germans found broad popular support in Poland and Czechoslovakia. Poles and Czechs did not want to live in the same country as Germans. But the Allies' extensive border revisions had already made population movements inevitable. Without the Potsdam "transfer," Poland would have become a binational state, with the twenty-five million Poles who had survived the war living door-to-door with eight million Germans. In Czechoslovakia, Munich had resulted in traumatizing not only the elites. For the governments of both countries, then, the international context and public opinion at the end of the war offered a unique opportunity to finally deal with the German question. They attempted this at first by creating a fait accompli, as Stalin suggested, and later by means of the Potsdam Agreement.

The expulsion and forced resettlement of the Germans in Poland was closely linked to the arrival of the "evacuees" from the lost eastern territories of Poland.[9] It is therefore useful to analyze them in comparison. It is also important to compare different groupings among the German "expellees." Too often, flight, expulsion, and forced resettlement out of such different regions as East Prussia, the Sudetenland, and the Banat are treated indiscriminately. But there was much to distinguish them; one need only consider the differing courses of the "transfers" in Poland and Czechoslovakia, both of which were resolved in Potsdam. The former took place in an utterly devastated country, where governance was shared by the mutually distrustful national government and the Red Army.[10] Czechoslovakia, in contrast, had survived war and occupation relatively unscathed, largely retaining its sovereignty, and was thus in a far better position to ensure an "orderly" transfer. This was to have considerable consequences for the fate of the Germans who were removed from both countries.

The Westward Shift of Poles

It is important to make temporal as well as geographical distinctions when analyzing these cases of ethnic cleansing in a comparative vein. The point in time at which flight, expulsion, or eviction took place was critical for determining the course of events and the refugees' experiences. Flight occurs in anticipation of acts of violence. It is based on fear and a preassessment of the attitudes and conduct of the enemy army, paramilitary units or civil administration. Mere moments could separate flight from the start of actual violent expulsion, such as during the advance of the *Wehrmacht* or the Red Army. In the eastern Polish territories, various phases of mass flight, expulsion, and forced resettlement intersected in the course of the Red Army's invasion and the Polish-Ukrainian civil war. The "evacuation treaties" signed in September 1944 marked a turning point in this bloody conflict by providing for the protection of the lives and property of those concerned, at least on paper. The Soviet authorities committed to organizing migration and the Polish government gained the formal right to intervene against violations.[11]

The use of the term "evacuation" in the treaties of 1944 deserves special consideration. It equated the migrants' situation with a natural disaster or an imminent military threat, which made the removal of a certain population group to another place imperative for its own safety. Although the situation in many isolated Polish settlements under attack from the UPA was indeed disastrous, the Polish population feared a revival of the Soviet Union's deportations to Siberia and Central Asia at least as much. The authorities exerted extreme pressure on the Polish population, most notably in present-day Ukraine and Vilnius—regions that had been contested for years—by withholding food ration cards, confiscating housing, and making arbitrary arrests. For this reason, by fall 1944, at least 117,000 Poles had registered to be "evacuated."

The Soviet authorities launched the first refugee trains in late 1944, at the onset of a severe winter, when there were few places able to accommodate the refugees in western Poland. The forced resettlements continued under these conditions until spring 1945. Evacuees were mostly transported in cattle cars, some open, some enclosed, offering little protection against the elements. Most of them were pillaged on their way to the departure station and received only meager provisions during their long wait and transport. The trains often took several days or weeks to reach Gleiwitz, Allenstein, Gdansk, Breslau, or Stettin, having to navigate bombed and sabotaged railroads. When they finally reached their destinations, evacuees were often commandeered out and left to fend for themselves. But the former eastern German territories were practically in ruins. Food supplies were exhausted and many spring crops had not been sown. Poverty and hunger were inevitable. The region was known as the "wild west" in central Poland on account of its rampant criminality and general desolation.

The situation stabilized from summer 1945, when the Polish civil administration assumed responsibility for the former eastern German territories from the Red Army. But the following report from Bydgoszcz (Bromberg) records the hardship that eastern Poles were still experiencing that summer: "The long journey in open railcars, sometimes lasting seven to eleven weeks, with inadequate provisions—not enough fat and sugar—caused a state of exhaustion in the passengers, especially the children."[12] About one-quarter of the officially registered "repatriates" needed immediate medical attention upon arrival.[13] In view of the postwar context and the hitherto unprecedented scale of the undertaking, it is hardly surprising that these "evacuations" were poorly organized. As well as the 1.5 million "repatriates," about 300,000 refugees from the Polish-Ukrainian civil war and people who had not registered to avoid persecution by the NKVD were on the move. In addition, hundreds of thousands who had been made to perform forced labor by the Nazis were now homeless. All in all, the number of eastern Polish refugees, expellees, and resettlers totaled at least two million. It was the largest-scale population movement in European history up to this point.

But at least there were houses, jobs, and land available for these newcomers, in contrast to the situation awaiting the German refugees. The forced resettlements from the former eastern Polish territories reached a climax in spring and summer 1946. During this period, the *Sibiriacy* also arrived, survivors of Stalinist deportations to Central Asia in 1939–41. Unlike those forcibly resettled, these former deportees perceived their immigration to Poland as liberation. They were true "repatriates," to use the official post-1945 terminology, returning to their home country, if not their actual homeland in eastern Poland. A similar attitude was held by a number of Poles who had initially tried to remain in the former eastern Polish territories but applied to emigrate in 1946 to escape the NKVD's constant reprisals. Their applications were mostly successful because the local Soviet functionaries, especially in the cities, were keen to be rid of the unruly Poles.

In rural areas, however, Polish populations were under pressure to stay. The authorities especially in Byelorussia and Lithuania prevented several hundreds of thousands of Poles from emigrating in order to avoid losses in agricultural production. According to the Soviet Ministry of the Interior's concluding report on "resettlement" (*pereselenie*) from and to Poland in October 1946, 347,000 Poles who had originally registered for "repatriation" in the Byelorussian and Ukrainian Soviet Socialist Republics had "refrained from emigrating." Virtually the entire Polish minority in rural Lithuania stayed.[14] A quarter of a million Poles were not able to migrate to Poland from the Soviet Union until the late 1950s.

Even after their migration, there was still a huge statistical discrepancy between the number of returnees to postwar Poland and those who had declared Polish nationality in the last prewar national census. But where were those Poles who never arrived in postwar Poland? Had they all died as a result of German occupation and postwar ethnic cleansing? Taking the model of postwar statistics designed by the German Expellee Association (Bund der Vertriebenen) and adopted by various postwar governments, this statistical discrepancy would be interpreted as evidence that at least a million Poles were "victims of expulsion".[15] But the main cause almost certainly lies elsewhere: a large proportion of eastern Poles disappeared from the statistics because they changed nationality in order to evade forced resettlement. The Germans, in contrast, were expelled and "transferred" across the board, with the exception only of special cases such as the Upper Silesians. Little is known of the postwar history of the Poles remaining in the former eastern territories, since they neither fall into the category of victims of "Soviet ethnic cleansing" nor that of consistently patriotic Poles.

The "evacuations" from the eastern Polish territories were, then, not a case of total ethnic cleansing, but neither were they as voluntary as the treaties stipulated. Many official documents, journals, and memoirs provide evidence of the direct or indirect force and trauma that evacuees experienced.[16] The official allowance of two tons of possessions each family of "repatriates" was permitted to take was in practice rarely granted. Most of those arriving in the former eastern territories of Germany were therefore destitute as well as physically exhausted. On arrival, they had to vie with the many resettlers from central Poland, whose migration had been of a more voluntary nature. The question of why the latter had better prospects for making a new start touches on the topos of integration and goes beyond the ambit of this book.

De-Germanizing Poland and Czechoslovakia

The ethnic cleansing of Germans from East Central Europe took a similar course to that of the Poles, with the distinction that the individual phases were of differing duration. While the Germans' firsthand experience of war had been relatively short but intense, their contractually arranged forced resettlement took almost twice as long as that of the eastern Poles. This was due not least to the unprecedented number of those affected. The Yalta and Potsdam resolutions affected about eight million people, four times the number affected by the hitherto most extensive ethnic cleansing—that of the Poles. Today it is possible to reconstruct the history of the German refugees, expellees, and those forcibly resettled in precise detail thanks above all to the findings of Polish and Czech research.[17]

The case of the Germans took on unique dimensions for a number of reasons. The Allies and their East Central European partners held the Germans as a nation responsible for the world war and the crimes committed under German occupation. Collective punishment was a logical product of the construct of collective guilt. About four million Germans in the eastern territories guessed what would befall them if they stayed and fled of their own initiative in winter 1944–45. Often inadvertently caught in the front line, or subjected to willful attacks, by far the largest number of Germans died during this phase of the process that is summed up as their "expulsion." At this stage, the Nazis contributed significantly to the loss of lives among their own nationality. The *Gauleiter* of East Prussia, Erich Koch, forbade the civilian population from fleeing even when the situation was clearly hopeless. The severe winter also claimed a heavy toll, causing death due to hypothermia for a considerable number of infants, sick, and elderly people. Rape was inflicted on a large scale to purposefully humiliate the enemy, as Norman Naimark has insightfully examined.[18] The civilian German population was helplessly exposed to the revenge of Soviet soldiers; there were massacres in many places. But it is almost impossible to retrospectively distinguish between war victims in a narrow sense and victims of "expulsion," who were to play such a prominent role in the discourse generated during the Cold War in postwar West Germany.

Soviet forerunners such as the writer Ilja Ehrenburg provided the template for the Polish and Czech armies' treatment of the Germans. In early June, the "ten commandments" for Czech soldiers in the border regions ran: "The German remains our irreconcilable enemy. Do not stop hating the Germans ... Behave as victor toward the Germans ... Be hard to the Germans ... German women and Hitler Youth share in the blame for the German crimes. Be unyielding toward them."[19] The command of the Polish Second Army, which was stationed along the Oder and Neisse Rivers, gave its soldiers the following orders: "You must perform your tasks in such a stern and decisive way that the German vermin do not hide in the houses but flee of their own accord and back in their own country thank God for saving their skin."[20] In spring 1945, the political elites of these two countries and even church leaders stirred up public animosity toward the Germans, although this was hardly necessary in view of everything the population had been through since 1938. The above orders are remarkable not only for their inflammatory wording but also for the point at which they were given. In the minds of the public, the war, occupation, and Nazi terror did not end with the German Reich's capitulation. This is evidenced in the conduct of the individuals, groups, and institutions responsible for the worst violations of human rights. As Czech historian Tomáš Staněk has shown, it was the Czechoslovak army units who had fought for the Soviet Union at the eastern front and experienced the Germans' war crimes firsthand that now dealt with the Germans most harshly.[21]

However, too much importance should not be attached to the motive of revenge, which is often highlighted by the media and academic literature.[22] The Czechoslovak army was given the orders in question after the expulsion of the Germans had already been arranged. They were intended to accelerate an ideologically founded process that was steered from above and in which Czechoslovakia took the lead. Mass expulsions began in the interior in May 1945 and continued in northern Bohemia soon afterward, uprooting at least half a million Germans by late July.[23] The goal was to create a fait accompli to present at the projected peace conference.

Poland could not match this pace. East of the Oder and Neisse Rivers, the power struggle between the Red Army and the Polish army and civilian administration, among other things, delayed the launch of mass ethnic cleansings by a month. While the Polish government was eager to start expelling Germans as long as the course of Poland's postwar border with Germany was undecided, the regional and local commands of the Red Army flexed their muscles by insisting on keeping workers and farmers in the country. Hundreds of thousands of refugees who had fled from Silesia to Czechoslovakia or the Soviet zone of occupation even returned home. The Polish army was not able to create precedents along the Oder and Neisse until after 20 June. The military then began "de-Germanizing" a zone stretching from the border about fifty kilometers inland, which was to be colonized by demobilized soldiers and members of the military. By late July, about 300,000 Germans had been driven across the border after being robbed, beaten, and abused.[24]

The brutality of the Czechs' and Poles' treatment of the Germans prompted the occupying powers to intervene. The influx of beaten and starving refugees was an enormous strain on their capacities. The roughly one million expellees arriving in late July 1945 swelled the masses of homeless and war refugees in Germany, all desperate for somewhere to live. Typhoid and dysentery epidemics raged in the improvised reception camps, claiming many lives.

The acute refugee crisis was the second major topic of discussion at the Potsdam Conference, after the postwar order in occupied Germany. The United States and Britain voiced reservations about the scale of the planned population shifts,[25] but did not challenge the consensus on ethnic cleansings that had existed since Tehran. Eventually the victorious powers agreed on a compromise. In compliance with Stalin's wishes, the territories east of the Oder and the Neisse were placed under Polish administration and the "transfer" of all remaining Germans from Poland, Czechoslovakia, and Hungary resolved. The population shifts were to be halted for a time, however, in order to ease and improve the refugees' reception in the Big Three's zones of occupation.

Similarly to earlier, comparable settlements, the Potsdam Agreement's legitimization of ethnic cleansings had double-edged consequences. On the one hand, it dramatically extended the scope of removals, mainly because it included the German minority in Hungary and ruled out any exceptions. Even confirmed opponents of the Nazi regime, such as Sudeten-German anti-Fascists, had to submit to the "transfer." On the other hand, it provided a legal framework for intervening against grave human rights violations. Although these did not stop with the Potsdam Agreement, anti-German violence gradually abated from fall 1945. Massacres and pogroms, such as in early June in Postoloprty (Postelberg), Bohemia, or in late July on the bridge across the Elbe in Ústí nad Labem (Aussig), no longer occurred after the Potsdam Agreement. This was due not least to the fact that Poland and Czechoslovakia could now remove all the Germans from their national territory contractually. Symbolic violence, to induce the unwanted population to flee, was made superfluous by the Potsdam Agreement.

In postwar Czechoslovak and Polish society, desires for revenge gradually turned into contempt for the nation that had offended all standards of human coexistence by its invasions, occupation terror, and the Holocaust. The Germans found themselves at the very bottom of the social hierarchy, with fatal consequences, especially in the regions that struggled most with the devastating effects of the war. Once the often-starving Polish newcomers had been provided for, there was next to nothing left for the Germans. In parts of Pomerania, Lower Silesia, and the Kaliningrad area, conditions barely improved for some years.

Improvements were most noticeable in the migrants' reception situation. By organizing the "transfer," the Allies were able to distribute refugees between them and within their zones of occupation. The new arrivals in the reception camps received medical care and often their first hot meal in many days or weeks. Subsequently, the social welfare offices sought accommodation for them.

The difference in the consequences of expulsion from contractually arranged forced resettlement is strikingly illustrated by the fate of the German minority in Yugoslavia. By late 1944, most Germans had fled or been evacuated by the *Wehrmacht*. The Potsdam Agreement did not apply to the refounded Yugoslavia, and there were no organized mass transports of returnees from here after the war. The roughly 130,000 Germans still remaining in Yugoslavia were nearly all interned in camps to perform forced labor.[26] But even these austere camps were not worth running, since most of the internees were women, children, or elderly. The Germans became a burden. The authorities settled upon the pragmatic solution of loosening camp security so that more inmates might escape. But once outside, they were effectively fair game; they were without rights and faced a walk of several hundred kilometers to Germany, which they often tackled under cover of darkness for fear of persecution. The mortality rate was correspondingly high, and the highest among all the German minorities: about one-third of the German population remaining in Yugoslavia in 1945 perished.[27] The reception of those who survived the long trek to the Federal Republic of Germany (FRG) was complicated by the fact that they did not come under any international agreements. Some Banat-Swabians struggled until the 1950s to gain German citizenship and the benefits of "exile" status.

The Allied Control Council's agreements with Poland and Czechoslovakia in November 1945 marked a turning point in the course of the postwar forced resettlements. The Four Powers (the United States, Britain, the Soviet Union, and France) agreed to fixed arrival quotas in the zones of occupation in return for the countries of origin committing to the "humane" and "orderly" treatment of the Germans before and during transport. Detailed bilateral agreements followed in January and February between the American and British occupation authorities with Czechoslovakia and Poland, even determining the number and route of rail transports per week. About three million Germans were resettled in 1946 on the basis of these agreements. The organization and conditions of the "transfers" improved perceptibly, especially in Czechoslovakia. Physical violence and the pillaging of migrants' possessions became the exception rather than the rule. Moreover, the western Allies tried to mitigate the humanitarian disaster by providing international aid. The UN Relief and Rehabilitation Administration (UNRRA) sent large amounts of food to Europe, the Cooperative for American Remittances to Europe (CARE) distributed millions of packages.

But power struggles within the Polish government and with the Red Army continued to hinder improvements to the organization of forced resettlements. Several ministries, the inundated state repatriation office, and various civil authorities argued over the distribution of responsibilities. In these circumstances, the greatest danger to the health and lives of the remaining Germans was no longer deliberate physical abuse but the lack of provisions and care in assembly camps and during transport. In winter 1946–47, after many migrants had suffered or even died of exposure in trains that had been haphazardly diverted for days, or stood motionless at stations, Britain halted the cynically named Operation Swallow, tasked with resettling Germans from Poland. Not only Germans were affected by the abysmal organization of and conditions on the trains. In one of the fatal trains that prompted the operation's halting, three Polish returnees on their way to Silesia froze to death.[28]

Violent assaults on Germans decreased throughout 1946 and 1947, but their physical abuse continued via another channel. Before they emigrated, the Germans were exploited as workers in return for discriminatory payment and food rations. Thus they, too, arrived in their designated home, occupied Germany, exhausted and often physically ill. In some regions, Germans were compelled to stay rather than to go. Tens of thousands of qualified Silesian miners, Bohemian glass manufacturers, and employees in other branches of industry were prevented from emigrating until the mid-1950s. This situation parallels that in parts of the former Polish eastern territories, where agricultural workers were prevented from migrating.

The so-called autochtons in Upper Silesia and Masuria were a unique case. Combining historical with ethnic and biologically determinist arguments, the government in Warsaw concluded that the population in these two regions were of Polish descent and would sooner or later become patriotic Poles. The influential governor of Upper Silesia, Aleksander Zawadzki, defied the "transfer" and demographic strengthening of the German enemy, saying: "We will not give up a single Polish soul and we don't want a single German one."[29] From September 1946, former citizens of the German Reich were "verified" and persons registered in the German People's List "rehabilitated" as Poles. In this way, 1.1 million ex-German citizens were able to remain in Poland, including nearly all those classified under categories III and IV and some of category II of the German People's List, and even former members of the SS and the Nazi Party. The expulsions and forced resettlements from Poland were therefore not total, but allowed one-seventh of the population that came under the Potsdam Agreement to stay in the country.

In Czechoslovakia, no regional exceptions were made. Even many Czech spouses of mixed marriages and their children were expelled in 1945. The expulsions (*Odsun*) in Czechoslovakia were unique in other respects, too. Today's Czech Republic was populated by about two-thirds Czechs and one-third Germans (the next largest group had been Jews, but most of them were killed by Germans in the Holocaust). The violent removal of such a large minority by the titular nation has not been equaled by any other case of ethnic cleansing. Such radical action could only be taken in the context of utterly asymmetrical power relations. The German minority was completely impotent vis-à-vis the state and its agencies. Not only is the total of more than two million persons removed remarkable, but also the fact that hardly any of them attempted to defend themselves or evade transport by fleeing or going into hiding.

The totality of power or powerlessness shaped the conduct of both sides. Czechs took advantage of the civilian German population's defenselessness to inflict all manner of abuse, from humiliation to physical assault, rape, and manslaughter. But the Germans' lack of resistance also aided the rational organization of the "transfer," which ensured that the number of fatalities remained relatively low. According to the calculations of the joint German-Czech historical commission, the number of deaths as a consequence of expulsion and forced resettlement did not exceed 30,000. This figure even includes the suicides of convinced Nazis and deaths immediately after crossing the border, such as on the death march of Brünn.[30] In relation to the total number affected, the death toll was less than 1 percent—far lower than in other cases of ethnic cleansing.

Nevertheless, there is no cause to make light of these events. The total of 19,000 documented casualties is still equivalent to the population of a small town. As Tomáš Staněk has shown by highlighting many individual cases, there were countless incidents of torture resulting in death and unfounded shootings, as well as the infamous massacres of Prague, Postoloprty, Horní Moštěnice (Ober-Moschtienitz, where 74 children and 120 women were among the victims), and Ustí. Some victims were shot in the neck; some were buried alive. The death toll in the eastern German territories, which had been ravaged by embittered fighting in the last days of the war, was many times higher. Military historian Rüdiger Overmans estimates that about 400,000 people died in present-day

Poland in the course of flight, expulsion, and forced resettlement.[31] The chaos of flight and the last phase of the war was compounded by the severe winter of 1944–45 and the general crisis in spring 1945. This period certainly claimed by far the most refugees' lives. The organization of the "transfer" resolved in Potsdam in summer 1945 continued to be hampered by difficulties. In the ensuing years, most deaths occurred in the—now well-researched—labor camps of Potulice (Potulitz) and Łambinowice (Lamsdorf), many surviving internees of which were later "verified" as Poles. This illustrates the radical nature of Polish "de-Germanization" (*odniemczanie*), which, as in Czechoslovakia, even affected those who were German only in the broadest sense. As in the interwar period, individuals were forced to align themselves. Now, however, not only their identity but their very existence depended on it. Most fatalities in the camps were not the result of murder or manslaughter but of malnutrition, disease, and general neglect. The vanquished were, moreover, exploited to perform forced labor. This transition from revenge to exploitation can be regarded as another example of violence being rationalized, as also occurred in the process leading to the Holocaust. But while in the latter case, efficient planning facilitated mass murder in an industrial fashion, in the case of the "transfers" it increased the refugees' chances of survival.

This discrepancy can be explained by different intents. The goal of ethnic cleansing was the removal of a group from a certain area, not their destruction by mass killings. This also applies to the Germans remaining in the east, who might have suffered a far worse fate if the German Reich had existed longer and rallied its people to fight a guerilla war or exercise other forms of violence. Forced resettlements would then have taken place in the context of armed conflicts, comparable to events in parts of eastern Poland or eastern Bosnia in 1943–44. The collapse of the German Reich and the civilian German population's complete loss of sovereignty and rights was, ironically, a precondition for the legitimization and rationalization of this most extensive case of ethnic cleansing in modern European history.

The biblical scale of the Germans' exodus from the east, their physical and mental state on arrival, and their continuing plight in postwar Germany eventually caused people to view ethnic cleansing in a different light. Even though the Germans were no more popular with their Western enemies than with their foes in the East, over the course of the year, opinions in the West began to change. The Allies, who no longer shifted borders and nations around on drawing boards, were directly confronted with the consequences of their resolutions in their zones of occupation. The English media, which had paid little attention to the fate of refugees and expellees until summer 1945, began to cover it extensively after the Potsdam Agreement. Writers such as Victor Gollancz, grandson of a Polish rabbi, and various reporters for the British and US armies even compared the treatment of the Germans in Poland and Czechoslovakia with Nazi crimes.[32]

Furthermore, the arguments for ethnic cleansing, which had been held to be valid since Lausanne, began to be called into question. The Allies had agreed on the removal of all Germans from the eastern territories of the Reich and the Czechoslovak border regions partly in order to prevent Germany from declaring war on its eastern neighbors again and as a form of collective punishment. But as the flood of refugees continued ever more chaotically, the British and US governments increasingly feared sowing "the seed of hate" and reigniting German revanchism.[33] To deflect criticism in Germany and especially in their own countries, British and US politicians attacked Poland and Czechoslovakia and Stalin, who defended his allies. The nascent Eastern Bloc condemned Germans en masse for the terror inflicted during the occupation and had no sympathy for the discourse on human rights that the German refugees' plight had sparked in the West. Moreover, Britain and France had lost much of their moral credibility by their actions in Munich in 1938 and their failure to provide military support to Poland in 1939. When US foreign minister Byrne called Poland's western border at the Oder and Neisse into question in 1946 because of the spiraling number of refugees, the Cold War constellation had already crystallized. The Western powers, eager to shrug off responsibility for Yalta and Potsdam and the ethnic cleansings resolved there, opposed a hostile Stalin and his East Central European allies, who intended to continue the process of radical "de-Germanization."

The stereotypical image of Stalin as a "nation killer" stems more from Cold War attitudes than from Stalin's actual deeds. The Germans were the only nation he targeted by total ethnic cleansing. Like the Karelian Finns, he saw them as wartime enemies deserving of collective and rigorous punishment. Furthermore, by supporting the expulsion and contractually arranged forced resettlement of the Germans, Stalin pursued another strategic goal: in the event of the Germans' feared revanchism being roused, Poland and Czechoslovakia would be reliant on the Red Army for protection.

Homogenizing Postwar Poland

However, the history of post–World War II ethnic cleansing in East Central Europe should not be confined to that of the Germans. The goal of creating a homogenous or binational nation-state worked against all the minorities in Poland and Czechoslovakia. The second largest group to be affected after the Germans in Poland was the Ukrainians. Although the Ukrainian minority shrank to about one-sixth of its prewar size through the westward shift of Poland, there were still about 700,000 Ukrainians living in the southeast of present-day Poland in late 1944. Of these, 482,000 were removed to the Ukrainian SSR in 1945 and 1946 under the evacuation treaties.[34] On paper, this exodus was voluntary, as in the case of the eastern Poles. But it was attended by assaults prior to boarding and "acts of sabotage against rail transports," as the NKVD's concluding report of October 1946 laconically noted.[35] The sober language of bureaucracy did as little justice to the reality of the situation here as in the case of the forced resettlement of the Poles from western Ukraine. The Polish assaults prior to emigration ranged from beatings to entire villages being burned down. About 150,000 Ukrainians nevertheless resisted forced resettlement. They were deported within Poland in spring 1947 during *Akcja Wisła* (Operation Vistula). The totality and pace of this operation recalled the Soviet deportations of the Crimean Tatars and Chechens three years earlier. Like them, the Ukrainians were collectively accused of collaborating with the Nazis and the *Banderowcy,* supporters of OUN leader Stefan Bandera, who were habitually linked with the *Hitlerowcy.*

However, the NKVD's main motive for overseeing the Ukrainians' forced resettlement and deportation was to combat the anti-Communist UPA. The Ukrainian nationalists used southeast Poland, and especially the Bieszczady Mountains, as a base to hide and plan their bloody guerilla war against the Red Army and the NKVD. The complete ethnic cleansing of the voivodeships of Krakow, Lublin, and Przemysl was therefore in the Soviet Union's strategic interest, as well as being a step toward establishing a "monolithic" Poland. Operation Vistula served to tangibly weaken Ukrainian resistance. The Soviet state security organs killed about twenty times more UPA fighters (over 100,000) in the Soviet Ukraine than their Polish counterparts did. In this case, then, partisan war claimed far more lives than ethnic cleansing. But Russia did not collectively blame all Ukrainians, considering them a brother nation. The Ukrainians in Poland were the only ones to pay for the OUN's and UPA's resistance with eviction from their homeland. In this respect, they paralleled those ethnic Germans who paid the highest price for the war and occupation terror inflicted by the Nazis. In addition, several hundred thousand people, mostly relatives or alleged supporters of partisans, were incarcerated or sent to labor camps in the Ukrainian Soviet Socialist Republic.

The former eastern territories of Germany served as a Polish equivalent to the Soviets' Siberia and Central Asia, especially remote areas of Masuria, where deportees were dispersed among several places to be assimilated. There were strict limits on the number of *Akcja Wisła* Ukrainians to be absorbed by each district and village. This purposeful precision was barely matched by the NKVD in Central Asia and Siberia. The Soviet deportees, moreover, were allowed to return to their former homes after Stalin's death (with the exception of Volga Germans and Crimean Tatars). Polish Ukrainians did not enjoy the same privilege. This demonstrates once again that the Communist regime in Poland, though politically relatively moderate, was particularly severe with its national minorities. Former Ukrainian settlements in the Bieszczady, like their German equivalents in many parts of the Bohemian Forest and the Sudeten mountains, were left to go to ruin. Countless villages were deserted and eventually overgrown.

The extent to which the Polish government supported the revival of the country's third-largest national minority, the Jews, is still disputed today. Immediately after the war, it approved a number of independent Jewish organizations, including a subsidiary organization of the Polish Workers' Party. But in 1947, it began to crack down on these structures and all nonconformists. The pogrom of Kielce of July 1946 launched a huge wave of emigration, spelling the departure of about 90,000 Jews, or more than one-third of the postwar minority. Yet Jewish emigration after World War II was not only caused by "push" factors. Zionism and the prospect of starting a new life in Palestine, far from the sites of horror and destruction, was another significant motive. The next wave of Jewish emigration in the late 1950s was prompted by dissatisfaction with the Communist system. The emigration of almost all remaining Polish Jews in 1968, in contrast, can be more clearly defined as ethnic cleansing. Although there were no pogroms that year, an "anti-Zionist campaign" was launched that involved the wholesale dismissal of Polish Jews from their jobs and anti-Semitic attacks in the media. This persecution selectively targeted one distinct ethnic group. Even completely assimilated Jews were cleansed from the Communist Party, state apparatus, and economy on account of their origins. Two decades after the Holocaust, the distress of having their prospects in Socialist Poland reduced to nil prompted most Polish Jews to leave the country.

Another borderline case of ethnic cleansing is that of the Byelorussian minority in the Białystok area. Like the Ukrainians in southern Poland, this population group theoretically came under the bilateral evacuation treaties of 1944, but in the event only about 36,000 of the roughly 150,000 Byelorussians left the postwar territory of Poland. Most of them gained the permission of the local authorities to stay in Poland. The Byelorussians were treated with greater lenience than the Ukrainians in Poland because they were not linked with any history of violent conflict. Where peaceful coexistence had prevailed during World War II, the Communist security organs had difficulties dividing communities along ethnic lines. Nevertheless, minorities remained in Poland on the condition that they conformed outwardly, and even then they were at risk of attack, as the example of the Jews shows.

As a result of its radical policy on minorities, Poland became a 95 percent homogenous nation-state, according to the official statistics. The only recognized minority was the Czechs in the Cieszyn (Těšín) region, who were authorized to run their own schools and cultural institutions from 1947, mirroring the position of the Polish minority on the Czech side of the border. Not only national minorities but also regional groupings such as the Upper Silesians and Kashubs were affected by the utopia of a "monolithic" Poland. Although they were officially recognized as "autochtons," they were regarded as Germans, or a kind of German variant, by the new Polish residents, who marginalized them in the political sphere and discriminated against them in the professional sphere. As a consequence, these regional groupings soon turned their backs on Communist Poland, including many who had voted for Poland in the plebiscite of 1921 and who had welcomed the end of Nazi rule as their liberation. The vice governor of Upper Silesia, Arkadiusz Bożek, summed up their disappointment in the People's Republic of Poland with the words: "Only the masters have changed. The Berliners have gone and the Warsaw-Krakowers have come."[36]

Back to Interwar Models: Hungarians outside Hungary

Czechoslovakia took a similarly hard line with its minorities. In 1945, the government in exile in London and the government in Prague demanded the expulsion of all Hungarians from southern Slovakia. This followed the logic of reversing the Munich Agreement. Hungary had participated in suppressing the First Czechoslovak Republic and some 100,000 Slovaks and Czechs had been forced to leave the territory ceded to Hungary as a result of the First Vienna Award, which followed the Munich Agreement.

But the Allies were skeptical of the expulsion and forced resettlement of the Hungarians, in contrast to that of the Germans. Anxious not to alienate public opinion in Hungary, the Western powers blocked all official resolutions to this effect in Potsdam. In bilateral negotiations with the Czechoslovak government, the Soviet Union suggested making an arrangement similar to the Polish-Ukrainian evacuation treaties. But Stalin would not approve the mass expulsion of Hungarians to avoid causing further chaos and crisis in postwar Hungary, which was already overburdened with several hundreds of thousands of homeless Hungarians in early 1945.

Hungary itself played a significant role in avoiding another refugee disaster. In contrast to Germany, the country retained its own government even after its defeat in World War II. Hungarian Communists took advantage of their close links with Moscow to call on Russia's help in deflecting the Czechoslovak demands. Czechoslovakia was consequently forced to accept a bilateral population exchange in February 1946. Since the Hungarian government wisely refrained from urging its Slovak minority to emigrate, the minority "exchange" was limited to 140,000 people, or one-sixth of the Hungarian minority in southern Slovakia. They came mostly from Bratislava and Košice and were members of the urban middle class. Most Hungarian peasants stayed, but were forced to submit to "re-Slovakization" and outward assimilation.

Not satisfied with this, the Czech government went on to deport 53,000 Hungarians to the Bohemian border regions by 1947.[37] The inhabitants of the Croatian villages in South Moravia were also deported. The deportation of the Hungarians provoked such an outcry from the government in Budapest that the Soviet Union distanced itself from Czechoslovakia. Consequently, the Czech Communist Party was cleansed of "nationalist deviants" such as later Party leader Gustav Husák, who had been particularly active in stirring up hatred toward Magyars and "Magyarons" (alleged Slovaks who had assumed Hungarian identity), and Czechoslovakia returned to a more internationalist course following the coup d'état in February 1948.

In contrast to the Ukrainians in Poland, a large number of the Hungarian deportees in Czechoslovakia were able to return to their homeland a few years later, where they were conceded a measure of cultural self-determination, such as the right to elementary education in their own language. But the history of deportations to the inhospitable border regions of the Czechoslovak Socialist Republic did not end there. During Stalinization, ever more politically undesirable Czechs were interned in corrective labor camps or sent to mine uranium in Jachymov.[38] In this way, ethnic cleansing blended with political and social cleansing.

The comparison of Poland and Czechoslovakia shows that population removals took place in staggered phases in the two countries and that their Stalinist regimes acted ambivalently toward national minorities. While Prague followed an especially exclusionist course under the pre-Communist governments in power in the first two years after the war, it eased the pressure on minorities in 1948. Stalinist Poland, meanwhile, launched a purgative policy toward all its minorities as early as 1947. This is illustrated by the events following the revision of the Polish-Soviet border along the Curzon Line in 1951. All Ukrainians in the affected area were immediately sent to the Ukrainian Soviet Socialist Republic or deported within Poland.

Despite the fact that Hungary had been Nazi Germany's most loyal ally, the Soviet Union prevented Czechoslovakia from expelling its entire Hungarian minority from summer 1945. Hungary had neither instigated the Munich Agreement nor started World War II, nor set up concentration camps for the Jews. The Soviet authorities therefore evidently felt it could not be tarred with the same brush of collective guilt as the Germans, nor subjected to a total "transfer" by way of retribution. Nevertheless, the Hungarian minority in Slovakia lost its elite and minority rights from the interwar period and was socially degraded.

Resettling the Polish and Czech Borderlands

Typically, literature on the German expellees and most of the relevant English-language literature breaks off the narrative at the point when ethnic cleansing has been completed. Most of it, moreover, focuses on just one national group of victims, although the utopia of national homogeneity usually worked against all the minorities within a state. Shortening the perspective and temporal scope in this way obscures a second method of creating ethnic homogeneity: the settlement of members of the titular nation. As in earlier cases of ethnic cleansing, the expulsion and forced resettlement of minorities in Czechoslovakia and Poland was combined with the radical nationalization of the "cleansed" area by purposeful settlement. In the immediate aftermath of the war, large numbers of Czechs and Poles were channeled to the former eastern territories of Germany. The first arrivals were to serve as administrative staff to implement expulsions locally. The later influx was to serve in the Czechization or Polonization of the regions concerned.

Czechoslovakia not only removed its minorities faster, it also colonized the "cleansed" regions much more rapidly than Poland. In this respect, it had the advantage of a largely intact infrastructure and relatively short distances to cover. Following on the tails of the army were the revolutionary guard and the first administrative teams, consisting of many adventurers and criminal elements, most of whom were seeking easy material gain and who were responsible for the worst acts of violence against the civilian German population. By summer 1946, they were joined by the refugees of 1938 and about 1.5 million Czechs attracted by the promise of farmland, housing, and social advancement.[39] These settlers were to form a "Slavic buffer" in the former Sudetenland. To make up the demographic losses caused by forced resettlement, Czechoslovakia launched an elaborate "repatriation" program aimed at the diaspora Czechs and Slovaks in the Soviet Union, Poland, Austria, Hungary, Romania, Bulgaria, France, Belgium, Germany, and even overseas. Eventually only about 200,000 diaspora Czechs returned—far less than had been hoped.[40] But it was a huge radius of action for such a small country and shows how high a priority ethnic homogenization was. The settlers' expectations were only partially fulfilled; living standards in the border regions remained lower than in the interior of Bohemia and Moravia due to losses in production caused by the forced resettlement of the Germans. The population in the border regions never regained its prewar size. Two years after the war, it numbered 2.4 million, almost one-third less than before 1938. Many rural villages were deserted.

While the settlement campaigns of 1945 and 1946 had mostly proceeded peacefully—in stark contrast to the "transfers"—this changed after 1947. Only a small proportion of the settlers now came of their own accord. Many were politically persecuted Czechs or Hungarians and Roma sent from Slovakia to be assimilated. Parts of the former Sudetenland were reduced to a kind of Czechoslovak Siberia, damaging the profile of the entire region. The actual chances of social advancement were minimal due to collectivization and nationalization, which amounted to the renewed appropriation of recently redistributed German property. For this reason, a return migratory movement began from the border regions to the interior as early as 1947. While the population remained more or less constant due to the high postwar birth rate, many mountainous areas were entirely depopulated. The ethnic cleansing in Czechoslovakia, then, had a destructive effect, not only on those who were forced to migrate.

The settlement of the "regained territories" in Poland in 1945 and 1946 was far more chaotic. These regions lay mostly in ruins. The Polish administration, moreover, was beset with internal conflicts that impeded efficient organization, and the newcomers were a highly heterogeneous mix. The largest group was of "resettlers" from central Poland who had been enticed by promises of a land where milk and honey flowed.[41] In fact, they often found burned-down farms and towns reduced to rubble. But as in Bohemia, many of them did not intend to stay longer than it took to obtain some usable objects to sell on the black market. Local studies have shown that aside from these "looters" (*Szabrownicy*), only about half of the Poles who arrived in Wrocław between 1945 and 1949 settled permanently in the city.[42] The "wild west" was a place outside the law, not only with respect to the remaining Germans but also for the Poles. It remained intrinsically unstable until the Potsdam Agreement. Frequent raids by soldiers of the Red Army compounded the mood of insecurity.

The second largest group to arrive was that of eastern Poles. Unlike the resettlers from central Poland, they had no prospect of returning to their former homeland. The third largest resident group was the autochthons, who were commonly regarded as German and consequently discriminated against. The government also tried to convince miners of Polish descent from France, Belgium, and the Ruhr to return. Thus, the resettlement of the former German eastern territories was no less of a complex organizational feat than the "transfer" of the Germans. Yet the immigrant Poles did not make up the majority population until summer 1946. Their official mission of Polonizing the "recovered territories" and their tolerated inhabitants, the autochthons, proved difficult to accomplish because of the deep rifts within postwar Polish society. Immigrants from central Poland opposed those from eastern Poland in bitter and often violent disputes over farms, housing, jobs, and responsibilities.

In a bid to distract attention from the internal conflicts, official propaganda promoted the "re-Polonization" of the former eastern German territories with increased vigor, claiming that the regions east of the Oder and Neisse were ancient Polish lands. But the presence of so many Germans and their language emblazoned on street signs, storefronts, and gravestones seemed to make a mockery of the claim that this was "Piast" Poland, historically ruled by the Polish dynasty of that name until the late fourteenth century. There were too many advertisements to paint over, monuments to tear down, books to confiscate, and even beer coasters to destroy to ensure that the newcomers did not feel they were in a foreign land. Many immigrants were highly wary of national claims, having lived through changes to Poland's territory in 1939 and 1945 and, in some cases, even the Polish-Soviet War and the period of statelessness prior to 1918. In the aftermath of World War II, rumors of a third world war between the Western powers and the Soviet Union began to circulate. Some "repatriates" even welcomed the thought, hoping it would provide an opportunity to return to their homeland. Few believed that the former eastern German territories would ever become a permanent part of Poland. They kept their bags packed, ready to leave again at any time. Sociologists and social psychologists spoke of a "symptom of temporariness,"[43] which only began to dissipate in the era of détente and with the coming of age of a new generation in the 1970s.

The rootless and fragmented postwar society in the ethnically cleansed regions provided ideal conditions for Soviet experimentation with collectivization and the nationalization of small businesses and trade. The settlers had no titles to the land, businesses, or housing they had been allocated. Moreover, the "de-Germanization" of society increased its susceptibility to political dictatorship. The Communists had far more success in the 1946 elections in Czechoslovakia and the 1947 plebiscite in Poland in the ethnically cleansed regions than the other parts of the countries. Comparison of the frequency of strikes shows that settler societies tended to offer less resistance to the authorities.[44]

In the strongholds of the autochthons, Upper Silesia and Masuria, a nationalist dictatorship became established in the same year that the war ended. Polish settlers pried into their neighbors' affairs to find out if German was still being spoken or German books being read in private. Thus, the struggle for ethnic homogeneity prepared the ground for establishing the communist system of surveillance. But ultimately the utopias of a monolithic Poland and a purely Slavic Czechoslovakia proved to be unstable foundations for postwar societies. No sooner had Poland removed the hated enemy than new minority problems arose in the mixed populations of Silesia, Masuria, and other regions. In view of today's pluralist societies, it hardly seems surprising that it was not possible to eliminate cultural diversity. The "demixing" of the population in Czechoslovakia affected not only Germans and Hungarians but also the state's titular nationalities. Few of the Czechs expelled and forcibly resettled from Slovakia in 1939 ever returned to the east of the country. Furthermore, a new social rift emerged. Contrary to the Communists' promises of equality, the remaining minorities profited far less from the economic upswing of the 1950s and 1960s than the titular nations and effectively became second-class citizens.

The social divide and lack of prospects were among the main reasons why so many members of the German and other minorities registered to emigrate over the course of the postwar period. In the FRG, this was taken as evidence of the continuing pressure on them to leave the Communist countries. But when the West pointed an accusing finger at Stalin and the Communists, it ignored the Soviet Union's ambivalence on the issue of ethnic cleansing. This ambivalence becomes apparent, however, on consideration of the southern half of East Central Europe.

Soviet Restraint and Retribution

As is shown in chapter 3, the Nazis realized their plans to rearrange Europe along ethnoterritorial lines above all in Central and Southeastern

Europe. So when the Red Army crossed the mouth of the Danube and the Carpathian Mountains in summer 1944, the Soviet Union promised peace instead of nationalist violence. The first multiethnic area to act on this promise was northern Transylvania, which had fallen to Hungary after the Second Vienna Award. Despite the forced resettlement of 219,000 Romanians until 1944, according to official statistics, and the deportation of Jews organized by Adolf Eichmann, this was still an ethnically mixed region. But the resident Hungarians lived in fear of both the Red Army and the revenge of Romania, which had changed sides at the "right" moment in the war and was now among the victors. The Iuliu Maniu Guards, named after the leader of the National Peasant Party, and other paramilitary units marched into the contested region on the tails of the Romanian army. The conditions were ideal for enforcing a radical ethnic cleansing: a territorial conflict had been smoldering for decades, population shifts had already begun, the border was still disputed, and relations among the local population were strained by a history of violence. About 400,000 Hungarians—by no means only functionaries of the Horthy regime—evaded the anticipated reprisals by retreating with the Hungarian army to the interior.[45] About 200,000 Transylvanian Germans also fled for fear of retribution.

In the event, the invasion was less bloody than had been expected, since the Red Army disarmed the Romanian paramilitary units or forced them to retreat.[46] Ostensibly this was on account of assaults on the civilian Hungarian population. In fact, Soviet policy was not premised on respecting individual human rights, but on a dual political calculus. First, a Hungarian-Romanian civil war would have threatened reinforcements to the front and supplies to the occupying troops further west; second, Transylvania served as collateral for inducing the Romanian government to fall into line with Moscow. Stalin did not, then, put the region immediately under Bucharest's control, which would have been akin to revising the Second Vienna Award. Furthermore, the Red Army sealed off the prewar border with Hungary, halting the refugees' progress. Over the course of 1945, about three-quarters of the Transylvanian Hungarians as well as the population group that had been "exchanged" under the Second Vienna Award returned to their old homeland. Only functionaries of the Horthy regime and former soldiers of the Hungarian army were excluded from returning.

Transylvania therefore provides one of the few examples of an ethnic cleansing in European history that was halted and even reversed to an extent. Soviet policy in this case was based on Stalin's view that Romania was a "multi-national state."[47] Since he considered the Romanian Communists too weak to rule alone, Hungarians and Jews were permitted to supplement the Party leadership.

The extent to which the Transylvanian Saxons were included in the Soviet vision of a multinational Romania is not clear. In early 1945, about 70,000 Saxons, or one-sixth of the German minority in Romania, were sent to eastern Ukraine to perform forced labor. This served not only to provide much-needed manpower for reconstructing major industries, but also as a collective punishment. The NKVD deported men and women of working age almost indiscriminately for the purpose of reconstructing industry. At least 30,000 Upper Silesian miners and around the same number of Danube Swabians were also deported to perform manual work.[48] Hungarians and members of other nations who fell into the clutches of the NKVD by chance were also among those deported.[49]

The deportations to eastern Ukraine are a borderline case of ethnic cleansing insofar as they were not intended to be permanent and creating ethnic homogeneity in the victims' places of origin was at most a secondary goal. Some deportees were soon repatriated by the governments in East Central Europe. In 1946, the government in Warsaw, for example, convinced the Soviet Union to allow the deported Upper Silesian miners to be repatriated on the grounds that they were ethnic Poles. The Transylvanian Saxons, however, had no lobby, and many continued performing forced labor until the late 1940s. When their discharge finally came, it was too late for many camp inmates. About one-sixth of the forced laborers died in the first year after deportation,[50] most of malnutrition, repeated abuse, or disease. This death rate was far higher than among the deportees and forced resettlers from Poland and Czechoslovakia. The murderous conditions in the Soviet gulags have been much publicized; since the Germans were treated with special contempt, their prospects were particularly bleak. Corrective camps based on ethnic selection were among the most brutal phenomena that the gulag system produced. Nobel Prize winner Herta Müller testified to this in her harrowing novel *The Hunger Angel.*

In the late 1940s, the deported Transylvanian Saxons were allowed to return home. The turbulent history of the German minority in Romania shows that the ethnic cleansing of Germans in East Central Europe was no by means ineluctable, not even in regions under Soviet control. The decision whether to remove or tolerate minorities depended primarily on the resolutions of the Great Powers and the subsequent actions of the individual nation-states. The comparatively good relations between the Romanian majority and the German minority helped the latter to persevere, but local relations among nationalities did not decide the fate of minorities. If this were so, the Transylvanian Hungarians would have been expelled from their homeland on account of their long history of local conflict.

Was it a privilege to stay as part of a minority rather than to be expelled? There are many records of Transylvanian Saxons trying to defect to West Germany in the postwar period. They simply wanted to escape the low standard of living and lack of prospects in Communist Romania. Contrary to Stalin's claim, Romania was not and did not become a multinational state, but was firmly in the grip of a national-Communist regime by the 1950s. Long-standing Party leader Gheorghiu-Dej ended the country's internationalist episode by depriving the Hungarian and Jewish members of the Party leadership of power. From 1968, minority cultural and educational institutions were subject to increasing restrictions.

In some respects, developments in Yugoslavia immediately after the war took a similar course to those in Romania. Some of the Hungarian minority, mostly functionaries of the Horthy regime who had participated in the persecution of Serbs, fled the advancing Red Army and Tito's People's Liberation Army. As feared, there were riots, executions, and massacres in Vojvodina, which claimed the lives of about 2,000 Hungarians.[51] Some of the army command and Party leadership demanded the "cleansing" of the entire Hungarian minority (387,000 people according to a survey of December 1944) in retaliation for the terror of occupation.

But in late 1944 only those members of the minority who had actively participated in the crimes of the "occupying German-Hungarians" were due to be prosecuted. Yugoslavia no longer aimed to be a purely Slavic state, welcoming "untainted" Hungarians, Albanians, and Italians. Germans, however, remained personae non gratae.[52] Although it took some time for this internationalist policy to filter down to local administration practice, in contrast to the situation in Czechoslovakia and Poland, the pressure on minorities began to ease from spring 1945. The ethnic cleansing of Hungarians in Vojvodina was limited to the social elites and the occupation-era resettlers.

In 1946, however, the issue of population transfer was raised once again when Yugoslavia proposed the transfer of some 110,000 German camp internees, following the Potsdam model. The Allied Control Council refused on account of the existing burden of refugees from Poland, Czechoslovakia, and Hungary. Moreover, the Soviet Union objected to a transfer in the Soviet zone of occupation. But rather than sparing the Germans, this only served to prolong their suffering in the Yugoslav camps.

The Soviet Union also refused a one-sided transfer of the Hungarian minority from the Vojvodina region to avoid a further influx of refugees.[53] Eventually Tito proposed a compromise during the Paris Peace Conference in July 1946: a voluntary, reciprocal population exchange of up to 40,000 on each side. This reflected the international consensus on peacemaking by means of population transfers as well as the victorious powers' pragmatic reluctance to provoke another large-scale refugee crisis. In September 1946, Yugoslavia and Hungary arranged a bilateral agreement that essentially confirmed the flight of fall 1944 and the expulsion of the settlers. By 1950, the Hungarian authorities had registered a total of 65,000 arrivals from Yugoslavia.

Behind these statistics lies a confusion of entangled histories, as the example of the roughly 13,000 Székely among the refugees from Vojvodina shows. This group originated from Bukovina, which was divided up between the Soviet Union and Romania in 1940. In spring 1941, Hungarians and Romanians concluded an agreement on the resettlement of the Székely minority. Hungary felt the Székely were a lost cause in Bukovina, and could be put to better use promoting Magyarization in the annexed territories. But rather than settling them in northern Transylvania, they were moved to land held by Serbian colonists in Vojvodina, who had come to the multiethnic region as part of a post-1918 nationalizing campaign. The Székely's odyssey ended in 1945 in flight or deportation to the postwar territory of Hungary, where they were sent to districts predominantly inhabited by Danube Swabians, who were in turn forced out of their homes. This example demonstrates the ambiguity of categories of victims and perpetrators in cases of ethnic cleansing. The Székely of Bukovina were the object of a population policy that they had little influence on. The individual stages they went through of temporary and final settlement prompted the expulsion of Serbs and Germans, respectively.

The postwar history of Romania and Yugoslavia is another illustration of the unique fate of the Germans in comparison to other nations who participated in war and occupation crimes to a lesser degree. Germans were practically outlawed after the war. The significance of state-run politics for the course of ethnic cleansing is demonstrated by events in the regions along the Danube. Countries that defined themselves as multinational rarely carried out large-scale ethnic cleansings, although they did exact retribution. This opposes Benjamin Lieberman's claim that ethnic cleansings took place on popular demand.[54] The perpetrators were acting primarily on instructions from above rather than hatred from below. That is not to say that human rights counted for more in Romania or Yugoslavia in 1945 than in other states or regions, but violence here—once again, with the exception of that against the German minority—had a more political than nationalist thrust.

Finally, the example of Romania and Yugoslavia points to a congruity with Czechoslovakia. The pre-Communist government in Prague was far more discriminatory against its Hungarian minority than the Stalinists who came to power in 1948. Similarly, the Communists in Yugoslavia and Romania were more tolerant of minorities than the bourgeois or peasant parties preceding them. The Romanian Communist Party even integrated Hungarians and Jews into the leadership. The Soviet Union actually played a central role in stopping the exodus from all three countries, or even reversing it, despite its initial sympathies for a purely Slavic Czechoslovakia. Thus, Stalin prevented any further refugee crises comparable to that of the Germans. This pattern calls into question Timothy Snyder's focus on the Nazis and Soviets as the major perpetrators of ethnic cleansing.[55] Moreover, the Stalinist regimes acted very differently from the people's democracies. Poland is a notable exception. Here, the Communists promoted the national homogenization of the country by means of ethnic cleansing.

Despite limiting ethnic cleansings in the areas along the Danube after 1944, the states here retained the long-term goal of homogenizing their national societies. This is also true of Romania, which adopted the same nationalist-Communist course as Poland, Czechoslovakia, and Hungary in the early 1950s. If minority rights such as elementary education in the native language were conceded under Stalinism, it was done in the expectation that these minorities would eventually conform and their nationalism would flag. Furthermore, the Communists stigmatized minorities in a new way, not only as foreign bodies in the national fabric but also as exploitative landowners and capitalists. This had no founding in reality—in 1948 there were no major Magyar landowners or Jewish industrialists in Central Europe any more—but revisited old and remarkably persistent stereotypes.

Internationalism and the myth of the brotherhood of Socialist peoples were not conducive to overcoming old conflicts. Official remembrance in the Communist countries conflated the mythology of heroic resistance with that of popular antifascism and was rarely reconcilable with individuals' private recollections. But the interethnic conflicts during and immediately after the war, which were effectively denied, had caused lasting trauma. Even most internal refugees, such as the Czechs from Slovakia and the Serbs from Kosovo, did not want to return to their former homes as a consequence. Societies therefore tended to remain divided along the existing lines of conflict, especially in regions that had only been partially ethnically cleansed. On the whole, the remaining minorities responded by outwardly conforming but not participating in the majority societies. Since minorities withdrew, they profited relatively little from the economic upswing of the 1950s and 1960s. But there were no repeat cycles of repression, revisionism, war, and ethnic cleansing due to the fact that the borders in East Central Europe became cemented over two generations of Soviet hegemony.

In view of the events in the period 1944–48, the Soviet Union should not be seen to have played a one-dimensional role as an agent of ethnic cleansing. "Soviet ethnic cleansing" climaxed in the interior and internationally by summer 1945. Subsequently, a policy of pragmatism prevailed. If strategic interests such as Hungary's integration into the Communist bloc or pragmatic considerations such as containing the refugee crisis in the Soviet zone or securing agricultural production took precedence, the Soviet Union halted population removals or even reversed them. Conversely, the NKVD carried out further ethnic cleansings if it advanced its own interests as, for example, during Operation Vistula. But it did not share the Nazis' view of ethnic purity as a primary goal or a political principle of creating order.

Large-scale forced migrations of specific social, political, or ethnic groups were nevertheless a component of Communist rule. The procedure governing deportations such as Operation Vistula, from the comprehensive registration of victims to their removal to the remotest and most inhospitable parts of the country, followed the Soviet model. This practice continued in later years in Czechoslovakia, Romania, and other Communist countries. Preventing the return of internal deportees was as important to these countries as their previous removal. The Stalinist regimes built up totalitarian systems of surveillance to ensure that deportees did not remigrate to their old homes. Hence, deportation was applied as a variant of ethnic cleansing in the Soviet Union and its sphere of influence but not in the postwar liberal nation-states.

The emphasis on retribution, whether inflicted on former wartime enemies or on alleged collaborators, was another unique element of Soviet ethnic cleansing. In contrast, the liberal nation-states and the Nazis were less concerned with collective punishments for past offences than with creating a new European order without national minorities. Ethnic cleansings were most radically enforced in places where the originally liberal idea of a homogenous nation-state was pursued by Communists in government, such as in Poland and Czechoslovakia.

At the Fault Lines of the Cold War

Ethnic cleansing occurs most often in contested border regions. In the latter 1940s, a second line of conflict emerged in parts of Europe that was congruent with areas of interethnic and international dispute but of wider significance: the increasing antagonism between East and West.

Interestingly, both sides in the Cold War eventually participated in ethnic cleansing. In this section, the agenda of those nations and population groups that were compelled to align themselves locally in the East-West conflict will be examined.

One of the fault lines of the Cold War, running through an area to which no state or system had an undisputed claim, was northeast of the Adriatic Sea. This part of Italy, with the formerly Austrian port of Trieste as its economic and cultural center, was not liberated by British or American troops but by the Yugoslav People's Liberation Army. The hinterland was mostly populated by Slovenian and Croatian peasants, the towns along the coast by Italians. The delicate social and ethnic balance in the region had, however, been devastated by Italian occupation from 1941. In line with the Fascist ideology of *Mare Nostrum,* Mussolini annexed coastal towns such as Split and the hinterland of Rijeka and Zadar, which had been contested since World War I. Subsequently, the Fascists tried to cement their claim by Italianizing the population. To this end, they applied the usual national repertoire of assimilative language and education policies while also deporting the Yugoslav state functionaries and elites of the Slovenian and Croatian minorities. According to Gustavo Corni, some 50,000 to 100,000 Yugoslav citizens were forced to leave the areas annexed by Italy.[56] The Italian occupation policy in the interior of Yugoslavia provoked further armed resistance.

Italy's change of sides in World War II in September 1943 defused the conflict to a degree. Germany was now the occupying power and hence the main enemy here too. Perhaps this explains why Yugoslavia acted with relative leniency toward the Adriatic Italians in comparison to the German and Hungarian civilian populations in Vojvodina. Nevertheless, in the years 1943–45, about 3,000 to 4,000 people lost their lives as a result of Yugoslav retribution. In Italy this persecution is known as *foibe,* after the caves where a number of massacres took place and where the bodies of the dead were left.[57] These murders and the advance of the People's Liberation Army triggered a first wave of flight. In late 1945, the Yugoslav People's Liberation Army captured all of Istria, including Trieste. At this point, coexistence still seemed possible on a local level, since the region's Italian Communists were prepared to accept Yugoslav supremacy. But the Western powers were not, and arranged with Moscow the partition of the area around Trieste into two zones of occupation: a British-occupied zone A with Trieste and its immediate hinterland, and a Yugoslav zone B encompassing all of Istria apart from the exclave of Pula.

A second and more intense wave of repression began after partition in zone B. Any Fascist functionaries and collaborators who could be found were tried by war crimes committees, as in other parts of Yugoslavia. Dozens of death sentences and long terms of imprisonment in labor camps were imposed. A total of 5,000 Italians, as well as some Croats and Slovenes, died as a result of state retribution or spontaneous acts of revenge.[58] On a day-to-day level, schooling in Italian was drastically reduced. The relative wealth of the Italians made them much more vulnerable to Communist expropriations than their less well-off Croatian and Slovenian neighbors. Tito's regime, which transformed Yugoslavia into a Stalinist dictatorship ahead of Hungary and Czechoslovakia, responded to protests and resistance with iron resolve. In 1946, Italians were collectively condemned as reactionaries, national enemies, and Fascists; some were publicly executed. But evidently they did not all feel the situation was hopeless, as the actions of several hundred Communist workers from the industrial town of Monfalcone illustrate. In spring 1946, they migrated from an undisputedly Italian town at the northernmost tip of the Adriatic Sea to Yugoslavia to take over the homes of Italian refugees in Rijeka with the intention of helping to build communism. Some years later, following Tito's break with Stalin, most of them were interned in the notorious Goli Otok camp, accused of being Stalinist deviants. There was, then, no government-sanctioned plan to comprehensively deport or expel all Italians from Istria and Dalmatia.

It was the resolutions of the Paris Peace Conference in summer 1946 and the Italian-Yugoslav peace treaty of March 1947 that launched an irreversible mass exodus. Having suffered political repression, social degradation, and direct or indirect violence after the war, over 90 percent of the Italian population opted for citizenship of their external nation-state in 1947. As under earlier agreements, those who opted to emigrate automatically lost their right to return. About 200,000 people emigrated within two years. In 1950, when relations between Yugoslavia and the West had improved, the Italian government had the option clause renewed. Another 50,000 Italians left Istria and the villages and towns along the Adriatic coast, not due to acts or threats of violence but because of a perceived lack of prospects.[59] The Slovenes and Croats living in Italy also had a "right of option," but rarely asserted it for practical reasons—it involved registering with a Yugoslav consulate—and because of the political situation in Yugoslavia. A last mass wave of migration occurred in 1953, when Britain and the United States handed over administration of zone A around Trieste to the Italians while simultaneously vacating the exclave of Pula.

The case of the Italian-Yugoslav border region is interesting not only because of the high number (over 250,000) of people affected but also because of the dynamics of international diplomacy involved. As early as 1942, the British Foreign Office had proposed redrawing the Italian-Yugoslav border after the war on the basis of ethnic criteria. The population living "on the wrong side of the border"[60] was to be exchanged in an arranged transfer. This, once again, demonstrates a line of continuity from the Treaty of Lausanne and the various treaties under Nazi hegemony concerning bilateral population exchanges. The first Italian postwar prime minister, Alcide de Gasperi, responded positively to the suggestion by the British occupation authorities in Trieste to arrange an "exchange of populations" in 1948. The migration of the Italian minority was, then, politically overdetermined. The only uncertain factors were the actual course of the border and the number of people who would be affected. Here, again, the priority was not to preserve national minorities but to share out the territory of an ethnically mixed region. Retrospectively, it is hard to determine whether the antagonism between the two neighboring states or the East-West conflict between the two political systems played the more significant role. Since the Yugoslav state was not opposed to absorbing non-Slavic nationalities (apart from Germans), the latter seems more probable. This is supported by comparison with Vojvodina, where ethnic cleansings were stopped in 1945 (again with the exception of the Germans). Moreover, in counterfactual terms, there probably would have been no mass exodus from summer 1946 if the Communists had seized power in Italy—although this would not have prevented the spontaneous flight of 1945. Nevertheless, the ethnic Italians who stayed faced life as a politically and socially marginalized minority, similarly to the Hungarians in Vojvodina or the Kosovar Albanians. To most, then, migration to their external home country seemed preferable. Furthermore, they were ensured a welcome by the Italian state. Prime Minister de Gasperi, a Christian Democrat, anticipated the rhetoric of the Cold War when he likened their situation to that in the Buchenwald concentration camp. Any claims to the Italian territories in the East were laid to rest in contemporary discourse. Both the government and the affected populations spoke of an "exodus." The term *foibe,* remembering the massacres in the karst landscape of Istria and Dalmatia, gained currency in the 1990s.

A number of factors contributed to the "exodus." The first was the clash of systems at a fault line of the Cold War. Ironically, from 1947, the rapprochement between Yugoslavia and Italy cemented 1945's ahistorical boundary between the two states and systems as a clear ethnic border. This followed the logic of nation-states in the postwar period, which, despite having largely abandoned expansionist policies, still pursued utopias of homogeneity. An internal group dynamic was another important factor here, as in comparable cases. Once a substantial proportion of the minority had opted for Italy and emigrated, the evolved society and culture of their Istrian and Dalmatian places of origin ceased to exist. From this point, the "exodus" of almost the entire Italian minority became inevitable and was made possible by the rapprochement between Italy and Yugoslavia.

The Cold War, in contrast, had a mixed effect on ethnic cleansing in Central Europe. Initially, the East-West conflict, which began to loom in 1945, accelerated population removals. But from 1948, the political and ethnic status quo became cemented along with the bloc boundary; East-West migration came to an almost total standstill. This situation did not change until 1956, when de-Stalinization sparked a revival of earlier migratory movements. The "resettlement" of most of the Germans remaining in Poland and Czechoslovakia and the Poles and Polish Jews from the Soviet Union were follow-ups to the ethnic cleansings between 1944 and 1948, but occurred under different circumstances. As in the case of the Italians from Istria, these migrants' old homeland no longer existed; communism seemed alien to most of them (though many Silesians migrated to the German Democratic Republic [GDR] from Poland), so they eventually opted to make a new start in their—often equally alien—external nation-state.

Another fault line of the Cold War, and the site of a mass exodus of minorities, ran through northern Greece. Here, too, international and local conflicts overlapped. Theoretically, the Allies had agreed on Greece's place in the Western sphere of influence. But Communist partisans in northern Greece opposed the settlements between Churchill and Stalin and continued to resist the reestablishment of a liberal nation-state. They were supported by two groups: those refugees from Asia Minor who continued to suffer deprivation and discrimination, and the *Slavophonoi*. The disenfranchisement of this predominantly peasant population had begun under the dictatorship of General Ioannis Metaxas (1936–41), when they were placed under surveillance, public use of their language was prohibited, and their pasture rights were arbitrarily infringed. German occupation compounded their situation. Like occupied Poland and Ukraine, Greece was fully exploited by Nazi Germany and local populations were left to go hungry. Society fragmented into different ethnic groups as people turned to the support of their own kin in the daily struggle to survive. In the shadow of occupation rule, a legal black hole emerged in which various paramilitary units, including collaborators, Greek nationalists, and Communists, vied for power.

After Germany's withdrawal, the conflicts between these groupings intensified. Local paramilitary groups were dependent on the cooperation of villagers, whom they intimidated into providing support if it was not volunteered. Civilians were therefore also targeted by the continuing guerilla fighting, during which the inhabitants of several hundred Macedonian villages were expelled.[61] Populations in northern Greece had, then, already been uprooted by geographically small-scale cases of flight and expulsion when, in 1946, civil war broke out. In the formerly Bulgarian-occupied parts of Macedonia and Thrace, the conflicts between government-loyal units and Communists had an ethnic dimension from the start. Former refugees from the Bulgarian zone of occupation immediately drove out the Bulgarian settlers and their alleged or actual supporters among the local population. The Greek army continued the expulsions with the aim of starving out the partisans. The *Slavophonoi* were eventually faced with the choice of fleeing to the towns and trying to blend into the background or taking to the mountains and joining the partisans. Government propaganda placed the Greek Communist Party on a level with the sworn enemy, Communist-ruled Bulgaria. Greek newspapers recalled German occupation and warned the population that the *Slavophonoi* were a local equivalent of the Sudeten Germans.[62]

Toward the end of the civil war, 35,000 *Slavophonoi* fled or were expelled to Bulgaria and Yugoslavia, along with 25,000 Greek Communists.[63] Since a part of the minority still remained in Greece, this cannot be defined as an exclusively ethnic cleansing. A more clear-cut case is that of the 154,000 Turks who migrated from Bulgaria in 1950–51. Alarmed by the far higher birth rate among the Turkish minority, the government in Sofia began to fear its increasing size and the formation of an irredenta. Finally, the Korean War provided a pretext for repressing the Turks, with the aim of inducing as many of them as possible to flee—a policy that the national-Communist regime repeated from 1984.[64] Turkish residents of Bulgaria were required to change their names, religious rites such as circumcision were banned, and mosques were destroyed. By 1989, the pressure had grown so intense that around 320,000 people, or one-third of the Turkish minority, left Bulgaria across the temporarily opened border. Since the principle of nonintervention between the blocs still prevailed, little protest at this purgative side to national communism was voiced by the West. Slobodan Milošević surely noticed this, two years before he took even more radical measures in Croatia.

The connection between ethnic cleansings in the southern Balkan and northeastern Adriatic regions and the East-West conflict is verified by comparison with another interethnic constellation. Unlike the *Slavophonoi,* who virtually disappeared from northern Greece either by migration or assimilation, the Turkish minority in western Thrace was largely left unharmed. This was due not least to the fact that the

Western powers hoped to make allies of Greece and Turkey and were therefore concerned to avoid complications caused by local disturbances and large-scale ethnic cleansing.

The German-Danish conflict was settled in a similar context in the postwar period. In 1945, the situation in South Jutland (or North Sleswick; Nordschleswig in German) was comparable to that in areas contested by Germany and Poland, such as Upper Silesia. Like these regions, it had a history of territorial changeovers, irredentism, counterproductive attempts to enforce assimilation, and tense local relations between the majority and the minority.[65] The main difference in South Jutland was that the conflict here affected only a comparatively small region of minor strategic and economic importance. Moreover, while occupation by Germany had certainly been perceived as a breach of civilization, German rule had been less oppressive in Denmark than elsewhere. Relations between the two states were less strained as a consequence.

Similarly to East Central Europe, South Jutland had a German minority that was particularly supportive of Nazism and the local occupation regime. After the war, popular demands for the German minority to be collectively expelled were overruled by the Danish government, which decided to pursue individual prosecution. This juridical approach resulted in one-quarter of the male minority population eventually standing trial. The scale of this prosecution campaign conveys an impression of the problems the same juridical approach would have posed after the war and German occupation in Czechoslovakia, even if the country had been able to preserve its democratic and liberal traditions.[66] Would it have been at all possible to take several hundred thousand active Nazis to court, try them in proper legal proceedings, and sentence them justly? Denmark opted for individual prosecution at the cost of further alienating its German minority, who showed little remorse and felt they were being treated unfairly. A breakthrough in minority policy was finally reached in the region prior to the NATO founding, when the FRG and Denmark agreed to uphold the rights of the Danish minority in the German state Schleswig-Holstein and of the German minority in South Jutland.

A nonviolent solution comparable to that in South Jutland was also found in Alsace. Despite the extensive expulsions and deportations that had attended the Nazi occupation of the region, the French government did not inflict collective retribution, for three main reasons: first, many collaborators had already fled; second, neither the Germans nor the equally compromised autonomy movement posed a threat to the region's national integrity any longer; third, to avoid repeating the mistakes made after World War I. Thus, there was no categorization of the population equivalent to de-Nazification in the American zone and there were no mass expulsions tearing Alsatian families apart. Scores were settled only by means of legal proceedings against some 10,000 Nazi functionaries and collaborators. Most of these were concluded by 1946; in 1953 General de Gaulle proclaimed a general amnesty. From that point until the late 1960s, little was said about the Nazi period or France's failed minority policy between the wars. The collective silence rested on a social and political consensus that prevailed on a national and regional level. Interestingly, in contrast to the expellee associations of the Germans from East Central Europe, the "relief association of expellees from Alsace-Lorraine" (Hilfsbund der vertriebenen Elsass-Lothringer) did not have a high public profile in the postwar period.

With the passing generations, these conflicts became buried under silence. They were brought to light again during the student protests of 1968. At the same time, the regional movement in Alsace was revived in a left-wing political spirit. But processes of Franco-German reconciliation and European unification looked further back to the memory of World War I. This was symbolized in 1984 by Helmut Kohl and François Mitterand historically shaking hands at Verdun. Focusing on the more distant past in this way allowed such difficult issues as the expulsions after 1918 and under Nazi rule to be relegated to the background. Hence, consensual forgetting has proven to be just as conducive to peacemaking as active remembrance, which has become something of a mantra for dealing with the past. The forgetting effected during Alsatian and Franco-German reconciliation stands in stark contrast to the remembrance of the "expulsions" from the East that West Germany deliberately fostered in the context of the East-West conflict.

This ideational fault line of the Cold War, separating German victims from Eastern European and Communist perpetrators, emerged soon after the war ended. The Western powers increasingly distanced themselves from the policy of deportation and the Potsdam treaty, citing humanitarian concerns. In a speech given in Stuttgart in September 1946, US foreign minister James Byrne made the key statement that Poland's shift so far west had intensified the refugee crisis. In West Germany, and especially among former exiles, this was interpreted as questioning the legitimacy of the Oder-Neisse border and thus as a "speech of hope." In East Central Europe, in contrast, it was perceived as a further sign of betrayal by the West after the Munich Agreement and its failure to help in September 1939.

The rhetorical confrontation intensified after the founding of the Federal Republic of Germany. The West condemned the expulsions in parallel with asserting a fundamentally revisionist demand for the "right to homeland," or return, of the exiles; the East clung to the Potsdam Agreement and the fact that the "transfer" fulfilled its resolutions. Beyond these conflicting interests, however, there was an unspoken consensus on proceeding with the homogenization of postwar societies. The FRG, and to a lesser extent the GDR, perceived its territory as the homeland of all ethnic Germans and supported the resettlement of the remaining German minorities from the east. In the 1950s, moreover, their arrival was welcome, since there was a growing need for workers in both German states. Warsaw, meanwhile, saw the Germans' emigration from Masuria and Upper Silesia as the solution to an acute domestic problem and an opportunity to advance the building of a "monolithic" Poland. Czechoslovakia released the specialists it had previously held back for its own industries. Thus, the homogenization of the states of East Central Europe progressed further in the postwar period. The same is true of the FRG and Austria up until the arrival of immigrant workers from Southern Europe and Turkey.

Refugees suffered most under the utopia of national homogeneity. Despite official recognition of their status as exiles, the German expellees were commonly labeled "rucksack Germans," "Polacks," or other pejorative terms. Public skepticism toward the newcomers harked back to Nazi attitudes and contributed significantly to their sense of embitterment. But rather than challenging the majority society, the refugees and their political interest groups, the expellee associations, projected these negative experiences—the dual trauma caused by losing their homeland and being treated as outcasts—onto the states that had expelled them on the other side of the Iron Curtain.

On the British Track: India and Palestine

This book focuses on Europe because, compared with the rest of the world, it was the site of the most and most comprehensive ethnic cleansings in the twentieth century. Nevertheless, the continent cannot be viewed in isolation. Non-European nation-states such as the United States participated in arranging the postwar order of Europe; Great Britain with its global empire cannot be reduced to a merely European state in this period. It would therefore be wrong to draw an artificial dividing line between Europe and the rest of the world. Unfortunately, the reception of the Potsdam Agreement and the subsequent Paris Peace Treaties in countries outside Europe or at its margins has not yet been systematically researched. But there are a number of source examples showing that population shifts were received attentively and positively.

Greek newspapers lauded the "transfer" as an exemplary solution to minority problems. Not only Potsdam was discussed in British-ruled India but also the case of Trieste. While the Peel Commission's proposals of 1937 for Palestine were rejected, variations on this "solution" to the Jewish-Arab conflict continued to fuel political fantasies.

However one interprets the Soviet Union's role in the Potsdam Agreement, the treaty was signed by all three great powers. Even the United States, which had a tradition of supporting minority protection, ratified the agreement, thus legitimizing population transfers as an instrument of international politics. Similarly, the "solutions" found at the Paris Peace Conference by the great powers and other states involved were three large-scale forcible migrations: the Hungarian-Slovak, the Hungarian-Yugoslav, and the Yugoslav-Italian population exchanges. These settlements of 1946–47 sent out strong signals, especially since they were made in the context of peace treaties in one of the major capitals of the Western world.

The global order for which the United States was primarily responsible was predicated on the supremacy of the nation-state. The name "United Nations" is evidence of this, although "United Nation-States" might have been more apt. In contrast to the League of Nations, the UN charter did not recognize collective minority rights. Minority protection was henceforth to be based on universal and individual human rights. Theoretically, this outlawed large-scale forced population removals. But the Potsdam Agreement—which was concluded five weeks *after* the UN charter was signed—and the Paris Peace Treaties of 1947 were enforced regardless. Mass population shifts were therefore an integral component of the "European model" for creating an international order. The term "model" implies not merely the concept of a European nation-state order but also its implementation, transposition, and local adoption. The method for this kind of analysis is taken from the "transfer history" developed by Michael Werner and Michel Espagne in Paris.[67]

In concrete terms, this section investigates the connections between the postwar reorganization of Europe and the ethnic cleansing outside Europe in roughly the same period. Two cases will be highlighted: the flight and expulsion of at least twelve million people in consequence to India's partition in 1947 and that of over 800,000 people in Palestine in 1948–49. In both cases, the prehistory of the conflict will be considered first, which the existing literature tends to portray in a predominantly internalist manner, that is, focusing on the conflict region itself and hardly taking Europe or global relations into account. Second, the question will be addressed of why the processes of decolonization and the establishment of independent nation-states were accompanied by such mass violence. Third, although the ethnic cleansings here occurred just as the British Empire had begun withdrawing its troops and handing over power, the influence of London and the colonial administration must be examined and thus the extent to which the European model was directly transferred.

On the strength of the traditional literature on the British Empire, this question would not even arise. William Roger Louis, a doyen of research on the empire, describes Britain's handover of power in the former colonies as its "finest hour" in an essay on the partitions of India and Palestine.[68] Contrastingly, authors such as Stanley Wolpert and Shahid Hamid hold the British entirely responsible for the humanitarian disaster caused by decolonization in their evocatively titled books *Shameful Flight* and *Disastrous Twilight*.[69] To find a nuanced position between these two poles, some undisputed facts must be established. The ethnic cleansings in India and Palestine were not based on contractual agreements. This marks an important contrast to Europe. Nevertheless, the colonial elites adopted the idea of the European nation-state as the basis for a postcolonial order. They also knew about the contemporary population exchanges and transfers in Europe, which the British had in fact proposed for solving conflicts in India and Palestine.

In order to understand these primarily political conflicts and why they became ethnicized in such a fatal way, it is useful to analyze them in reference to two markers of European modernity: the idea and practice of the nation-state and the dynamic of violence as a political instrument. In this way, the long-term, mid-term, and short-term factors can be isolated and identified. Modernity seems an appropriate frame of reference for analyzing the events in India, since it was one of the most politically advanced British colonies. That is why it was decolonized earlier than the British colonies in Africa and France's colonies. India's independence movement was successful because the country had its own anti-imperialist brand of nationalism, a secular political elite, and a politically mobilized population.

European ideas were a formative influence on the leaders of the two largest Indian parties, the Indian National Congress, founded in 1885, and the Muslim League, established in 1906. Jawaharlal Nehru, who became leader of the Congress Party in 1930, and Muhammad Ali Jinnah, the long-standing president of the Muslim League, had both been educated at British schools and universities. Not only had they studied the basic principles of modern democracy and nation-states, they had experienced British nationalism firsthand and become advocates of the modern nation-state. Nehru and Jinnah were both liberal democrats, but disagreed on how an independent state of India should be organized even before World War II. Jinnah demanded more rights for the over ninety million Indian Muslims and autonomy for the predominantly Muslim provinces. The Congress Party, in contrast, insisted on preserving India's unity and a centralist order rejecting federalism and denying political minority problems. By the outbreak of World War II, essential components of modernity were in place in India, including a rail network, a growing middle class, a press and other media of mass communication, and a pluralist system of political parties, as well as an anti-imperialist nationalist movement. But the process of modernization did not affect all parts of society equally and simultaneously here, as elsewhere in the world. Religious and social divisions intersected; in many Indian principalities, Hindu rulers faced Muslim majority populations, or vice versa, as well as smaller minorities such as the Sikhs. The British colonial rulers drew advantage from the social and cultural differences and rivalry between groups by co-opting their support as required.

The dichotomous process of classifying, registering, and counting the members of these groups was another element of modernity and an aspect of colonialism. Despite the fact that Hindus of the highest and lowest castes had less in common with each other than Hindu traders had with Muslim traders, or landowners of both religions, the colonial rulers divided the population in censuses and other statistics by religious criteria. This division had a deep impact on everyday life. In major train stations, for example, there were separate water fountains and sanitary facilities for Muslims and Hindus. In this way, British colonial rule contributed to politicizing religion.

For many years, the Muslim League was not a compact political party but claimed to act in the name of all Indian Muslims. In 1936, Jinnah defined these as a minority forming a "separate unity within the state" and requiring its special protection.[70] In this way, he was challenging the Congress Party, which had won a comfortable majority in the 1936 elections and refused to let the Muslim League participate in government, in the British parliamentary tradition. While Nehru defined his party as secular and transreligious, it was indisputably dominated by Hindus. The distribution of political power thus followed the colonial pattern of a population divided according to religious criteria.

The extension of adult suffrage to about 30 percent of the male population marked a decisive step toward mobilizing the masses. It also helped mobilize the opposition Muslim League, which responded to its political marginalization by proclaiming the Muslim Nation in 1939. The Pakistan Declaration of Lahore, which was to become one of the flash points of interethnic violence, followed a year later. This directly challenged the Congress Party and its premise of a transreligious and unified Indian nation by announcing the birth of the independent nation of Pakistan (literally, land of the pure), encompassing all predominantly Muslim regions within yet-to-be defined geographical outlines.

Most of the secondary literature on the violent partition of India focuses on the period during World War II. The British viceroy halted democratization in September 1939 in order to avoid sparking any disturbances on the home front. When the Congress Party advanced its Quit India Resolution in August 1942, the party leaders were interned or placed under house arrest pending the end of the war. Any correspondence with the Muslim League was intercepted by the British, interrupting negotiations between the two major parties. In these repressive circumstances, which echoed those in the Habsburg Empire during World War I, political networks and platforms for dialogue could not exist. Moreover, the proposed constitution, which the colonial rulers had originally supported, could not be ratified.[71] But at this stage, the viceroy considered a weak legislature preferable to a united front pushing for independence. Meanwhile, the requisitioning of grain for the British market was causing social tensions to mount, especially in Punjab, the granary of India. A year later, the situation was even worse in Bengal, where a famine claimed the lives of two to three million people, many times more than the ethnic cleansing of 1946–47.

At the same time, other groups were clamoring for their political demands to be heard. Inspired by the Pakistan Declaration, the Sikhs, who had served loyally in the colonial army for many years, demanded the protection of their minority. Radical Sikh nationalists called for the founding of their own state, Sikhistan, though even in their most compact area of settlement, Punjab, they only made up about 10 percent of the population. Even smaller groups such as the Muslim Meos in Rajasthan demanded an autonomous province from which they could work toward independence or joining Pakistan.[72] These examples demonstrate how group-oriented nationalisms in India intensified by focusing on territorial possessions and the goal of separate nation-states. Also, in 1942, Jinnah claimed the "right to self-determination" for India's Muslims. Since the leadership of the Congress Party had been put out of action and their policies for a united India stifled, such discourses were able to make a deep impact.

By the time World War II ended, it was too late to ease the tensions, and they continued to mount instead. In 1946, the first elections in ten years were held, encouraging the political mobilization of the population. Despite the London Cabinet Mission's attempts to arbitrate at the subsequent negotiations, no compromise on the Muslim League's participation in government could be found. Whichever side was to blame for the failure of the constitution, the situation of political deadlock gave rise to two crucial developments: the British government abandoned the idea of a united India and the Muslim League called a general strike. On Direct Action Day on 16 August, severe disturbances broke out in Kolkata that claimed about 4,000 lives and rendered 100,000 homeless. Some weeks later, another pogrom took place in the Bengal province of Noakhali. On this occasion, the perpetrators blocked off potential escape routes. While mostly Hindus were targeted by the violence in Bengal, the roles were reversed in the neighboring region, Bihar. Here, radical Hindus attacked the Muslim minority; the death toll is estimated to have been between 5,000 and 10,000.[73]

Since the violence broke out immediately after government negotiations had broken down at flash points many hundreds of miles apart, it cannot have been spontaneous, or the involuntary eruption of long-festering interethnic tensions, but was certainly engineered. Yasmin Khan speaks of "propaganda networks"[74] that purposefully sowed hatred throughout the land. As in Transylvania and eastern Poland during World War II, the massacres thus committed were acts of retaliation by violent radicals who had been galvanized into action by victim narratives. Mahatma Gandhi's attempts to mediate were tragically doomed to fail. Traveling to the conflict zones where he publicly fasted, he risked his life to urge both sides to renounce the use of violence. Although he was able to pacify Bengal in this way, the pogroms spread to Punjab. The interethnic violence and paramilitary attacks had an especially deep impact on a local level. The populations in multiethnic quarters and villages separated and formed local self-defense organizations. About 100,000 people, mostly members of the upper classes, fled the affected areas in the first half of 1947.[75] The British army rarely intervened, against the will of many Indian politicians, instead concentrating on its retreat.

The new viceroy, Lord Louis Mountbatten, sent to India by the Labour government in March 1947, resolved to put an end to the troubles. The remedy he prescribed was the swift partition of India. Gandhi objected to this plan and was especially concerned about its effect on multiethnic Punjab, where Muslims made up about half, Hindus one-third, and Sikhs one-tenth of the population. In his view, there was no way to divide this region, with its twenty-eight million inhabitants—about equivalent to the contemporary population of Poland—and maintain peace. But Viceroy Mountbatten, like his predecessor, merely humored Gandhi as an eccentric fakir and failed to take his mediation seriously or consider his proposal of forming a united government with Jinnah as prime minister.[76] Unrest broke out in Punjab even before partition was announced on 3 June 1947. As on Direct Action Day, the violence was mostly instigated by Muslims and returned by Hindus, according to the principle of reciprocal retaliation. There was pillaging and rioting in multifaith cities such as Lahore, Amritsar, and Rawalpindi, which were partially laid to waste.

Mountbatten's negotiations with the leaders of the Congress Party and the Muslim League over India's partition stood in strange contrast to the violence that was raging all around them. In the viceroy's technical terminology, he was "the principal doctor in producing the treatment for the body as a whole." Nehru also spoke of a "cure"; Jinnah of a "surgical operation."[77] In spring 1947, the political leaders added demographic concepts to their medical metaphors. In the event of an independent Pakistan being founded, the Sikh leaders demanded comprehensive population transfers from and to central Punjab and repeated their demand for an independent state, Sikhistan. Viceroy Mountbatten cautiously addressed the issue of population transfers at a press conference on India's partition, saying:

> There are many physical and practical difficulties involved. Some measure of transfer will come about in a natural way … perhaps governments will transfer populations. Once more, this is a matter not so much for the main parties as for the local authorities living in the border areas to decide.[78]

This statement is reminiscent of Churchill's speech on the future of Poland in December 1944, with the distinction that Mountbatten avoided declaring the enforcement of transfers but indicated that they were likely. It also betrays his reliance on local authorities to deal with them, like natural disasters, although they were in fact a problem affecting the entire country. The governor of Bengal warned Mountbatten against a hasty partition of India, pointing out that it took a lot longer for Europe to find a solution for Gdańsk or Trieste.[79]

The fatal flaw of British partition plans was that they did not provide for either an orderly handover of power or a clearly defined border. The British troops' withdrawal left a power vacuum that was filled by paramilitary units. The Indian army was preoccupied with dividing its resources between India and the future Pakistan. Similarly, the state apparatus also had to be divided and Muslims were filtered out. Two-thirds of India's regiments and more than 25,000 civil servants, who had the right to choose which state they served after partition, were transferred in summer 1947.[80] Meanwhile, the exchange of state functionaries and movable property such as filing cabinets, typewriters, and other office equipment between present-day India and Pakistan went remarkably smoothly, creating the illusion that minorities could be moved just as easily.

The exact course of the border remained confidential until mid-August 1947. Mountbatten did not even familiarize himself with the geography until June. The task of drawing the dividing line was delegated to Cyril Radcliffe, a lawyer and former director-general of the Information Ministry in London, who was familiar with all the plans concerning the postwar reorganization of Europe but had never set foot in India. Radcliffe was given a mere six weeks to map out 5,000 kilometers of border.[81] He was obliged to maintain strict secrecy to avoid disruptions to the British colonial army's retreat. Radcliffe's method was straightforward and based on the black-and-white categorizations of national censuses: districts with a Muslim majority were to go to the future Pakistan, regions with a non-Muslim majority to India. This adherence to ethnographic data, as well as the ambiguous exceptions made for places with important transport connections and waterways, invited manipulation by paramilitary units such as the Muslim National Guard and the nationalist Hindu Rashtriya Swayam Sevak Sangh (RSSS), which carried out expulsions to determine the course of the border between India and Pakistan.

When the long-awaited border was announced two days after both states declared independence, on 17 August 1947, ethnic cleansing began immediately in Punjab, which differed from previous pogroms only in scale. Civilians and especially women were targeted by extreme violence, mass rape, and abductions. In the absence of boundary stones, the new municipal and state borders were marked with the bodies of the enemy dead. As in Croatia and western Ukraine during World War II, religious symbols were carved into the skin of enemy corpses and women were publicly abused to show contempt for their religion. At the same time, radical nationalists attempted to forcibly convert people, indicating that some fanatics still believed the enemy could be compelled to assimilate. While the deplorable forms of violence used were symptoms of the religious dimension of the conflict, this was a secondary aspect of the primarily political dispute over India's partition.

Nehru and Jinnah made dramatic appeals to stop the violence, promising equality for the minorities in India and Pakistan, in August 1947, but it was already too late. Several hundred thousand people left their homes on both sides during the monsoon, in conditions of extreme heat. Several refugee trains were hit by arson attacks. In view of the worsening humanitarian disaster, the best the two neighboring states could do was to start regulating the migrations. On 20 October 1947, the Indian and Pakistani armies arranged a Joint Evacuation Plan to supervise the resettlement of 10 million people. By November, 2.3 million Hindus and Sikhs had arrived by train in India; 850,000 left Pakistan in treks stretching up to 100 kilometers and over. By May 1948, 4.7 million Muslim Punjabis had fled in the opposite direction. The number of deaths en route is estimated at anywhere between 200,000 and 2 million, although the latter figure was certainly circulated for its dramatic effect rather than its accuracy.[82] Remarkably for a regulated population exchange, the targeted number of evacuations from Punjab—10 million—was not fulfilled.

This was mainly due to the strain the mass flight placed on the economies of Pakistan and India. There was staff lacking in administration, trade, and small businesses. Both sides therefore sought to contain the fighting and reestablish state control after the British troops' hasty retreat. But this was impeded by the arrival of the refugees, causing new conflicts over the distribution of accommodations and jobs. The main victims of the conflicts were the minorities who had stayed. A case in point is the Muslim minority in the capital Delhi, which shrank from about 40 percent of the population in 1941 to under 7 percent ten years later.[83] The Indian government was nevertheless able to prevent the fighting from spreading to the mixed population of the Ganges Valley. Even Bengal remained peaceful in comparison to Punjab. Bengal's relative stability was also due to the fact that the British troops retreated at a more gradual pace while the Indian and Pakistani army, police force, and civil administration were built up relatively rapidly. Ian Talbot's comparison of Punjab and Bengal refutes the claim that "ancient hatreds" or the escalation of the conflict were the main causes of the violence. If this were true, Bengal would have been first to go up in flames rather than Punjab, which had been comparatively peaceful and governed by a multifaith party until 1946.

But even Bengal was far removed from reaching a settlement between its majorities and minorities. Massacres continued to occur on both sides of the border, prompting about four million people to flee. In 1950, the governments of both countries finally took steps against the rampant violence. The prime ministers of India and Pakistan concluded the eponymous Nehru-Liaquat Agreement, providing for the return of refugees and compensation for lost property. Over a million people remigrated from refugee camps to their former homes under this agreement. It is interesting to note that it was made in the absence of British troops and colonial officials, who were no longer represented in the region. However, there were still up to 2,000 migrants crossing the border each day, even after India introduced passports and tighter border controls in 1952. About 200,000 people migrated annually until the mid-1950s.[84] As in much of East Central Europe after 1938 and 1944, the homeland had ceased to be home for many.

The continuing migration indicates how difficult it was for multiethnic regions to become stabilized once mass violence had destroyed the local social balance. In 1973, refugees made up one-quarter of the population in the slum metropolis of Kolkata. Conversely, the number of Hindus among the population of Dhaka, the capital of Bangladesh, which had broken away from Pakistan, sank from 58 percent before partition to under 5 percent.[85] In view of the differences between and within Punjab and Bengal, it cannot be claimed that all refugees suffered a collective fate. Similar to the case of the Germans from East Central Europe, the situation varied according to their place of origin and local conflict constellations. This has been demonstrated in Ian Copland's study of Rajasthan, where the ethnic cleansings were almost total in some areas but only affected the elite of the Muslim minority in others.[86]

Notwithstanding these regional and local differences, which gave rise to widely varying experiences of flight and trauma, the refugees' victimization became engraved in national memory, especially in Pakistan. The Indian government did not promote victim narratives to the same extent, fearing that the dissemination of antagonistic views of history might spark new conflicts with the still substantial Muslim minority. As in Germany, then, the priority in India was placed on distributing and settling the refugees and remigrants throughout the country and promoting their swift integration. Again, similar to Germany, in recent years second-generation authors have claimed that the plight of the refugees was made a taboo subject.[87] This is only true with respect to cases of mass rape, but not to India's partition or the ethnic cleansings in general. Happily, the trend toward remembering begun in the late 1990s has not generated any new conflicts. Authors from India, Pakistan, and Bangladesh have established that people on both sides went through very similar experiences. This realization should not, however, obscure the significance of huge social differences among the populations. Nearly 50,000 refugees could afford to flee by plane in late 1947. These passengers of the British Overseas Airways Corporation started a new life under very different circumstances than the millions of agricultural workers and day laborers whose poverty worsened and some of whom still reside in the slums of Kolkata and Karachi. Ethnic cleansing in India should therefore be considered in differentiated terms of local, regional, and social factors. But the same is true of Germany and other European countries.

At first glance, the ethnic cleansing in Palestine seems hardly comparable with that in India. Mandatory Palestine had two million inhabitants in 1947 when its partition was resolved, whereas India had four hundred million. The area affected by ethnic cleansing was far smaller than Punjab or Bengal alone. But the comparatively low number of 800,000 refugees in Palestine gains an added dimension when seen in relation to the total population. Moreover, the refugees were almost exclusively from one party in the conflict, the Arab Palestinians. And yet the two cases have a number of aspects in common, including the influence of European modernity, the context of nation-state founding as the colonial power withdrew, and the purposeful escalation of violence on a local level. These three interwoven issues will serve as a basis for elucidating the causes and development of ethnic cleansings in Palestine from a comparative perspective.

Ottoman rule shielded the Middle East from European modernity for a relatively long time. But the impact it eventually had on Mandatory Palestine was direct and asymmetrical. While anticolonial Arab nationalism was largely confined to the urban elites, most of Jewish society had a pronounced sense of national awareness. Zionism was indeed the main factor, alongside the experience of anti-Semitism, motivating Jews to migrate to the symbolically charged "Holy Land." The Arab and Jewish populations in Palestine also differed in terms of economic productivity. Although Jews made up only one-third of the population in 1946, they earned a far higher domestic product than the predominantly peasant Arab population. The Jewish underground army, which had been trained and armed by Britain in 1941–42 to defend the region in the event of the *Wehrmacht*'s advance, had a larger stock of more sophisticated arms and an efficient command.

The Jewish-Arab conflict stemmed from the Balfour Declaration of 1917, in which the British government promised the Jews their own "national home" in Palestine in response to the pogroms in Eastern Europe. Zionist-motivated immigration increased considerably as a result. The number of Jews in Palestine rose to 175,000 in 1931 and jumped to 475,000 by 1939, after the Nazis came to power. The Arab population rebelled against this immigration and the increasing economic competition from the Jews in several uprisings. While the disturbances in 1920–21 and 1929 were confined to a few towns and quarters, in the years 1936–39, Arabs across Palestine revolted, resulting in pogroms in some places that irreparably damaged the status quo in the binational state. In view of the apparently insoluble conflict, the Peel Commission proposed the partition of Palestine in 1937, suggesting a population *transfer* (rather than a population exchange) to solve a political conflict for the first time.[88] This commission also cited Lausanne as a model, once more revealing the connection between European history and the European colonies. The plan's bias, requiring 200,000 Arabs but only 1,250 Jews to emigrate, provoked massive resistance, which caused the British government to reconsider. For the next ten years, Britain supported a "binational state," partly because it hoped to retain more influence on an independent Palestine with a weak central power.

A binational state may seem preferable to an ethnically exclusive nation-state to anti-Zionists such as the historian Ilan Pappé,[89] but it was problematic for the same reason as in India: it demanded the binary division of a multiethnic society. Arab and Jewish societies in Palestine were far from homogeneous in 1937 and in 1947. Christian urban Palestinians, Muslim peasants, the Druze in the north, and nomadic Bedouin in the Negev Desert had just as distinct cultures as the Mizrahi and the Sephardic Jews, the Zionists, and, from 1945, the survivors of the Holocaust. This complex social fabric influenced interethnic relations and was by no means volatile or antagonistic in all places. The colonial authorities could have distinguished between the different groupings and allowed them to participate in a democratizing political system, as in India. The Habsburgs had effectively done this on the eve of World War I in Bukovina, where the Polish, Ruthenian or Ukrainian, Romanian, and German (and thus, indirectly, Jewish) populations were conceded political autonomy on their designated territories.[90] But colonial rule in Palestine, as in India, was based on a black-and-white approach that did not register these intraethnic nuances and thus split society according to a binary principle.

The extent to which the Zionists advanced the idea of population transfers during World War II is much disputed in the secondary literature. Palestinian authors such as Nur Masalha and advocates of "new history" in Israel have supported the argument that the Zionists had a master plan for the ethnic cleansing of Palestine from the start.[91] There is little evidence to support this claim. Pappé cites only the fact that leading Zionists insisted on a "transfer."[92] Crucially, the future prime minister David Ben Gurion favored a smaller state with a distinctly Jewish majority population over a larger binational state. He, then, laid the foundation stone for the homogeneous nation-state. The emir of Jordan, King Abdullah, shared Ben Gurion's preference for dividing Palestine into two nation-states, seeing in it the opportunity to expand his territory west of the River Jordan.[93]

British discourse on Palestine was considerably influenced by developments in India. The Labour government did not see any justification for maintaining colonial rule and the massive military presence of 100,000 troops (compared to 150,000 in the entire Indian subcontinent), which the empire could no longer afford on account of its huge international debts after World War II. Bloody terrorist attacks by the Jewish underground, moreover, were wearing the British forces down. In

February 1947, the government in London decided to give up Palestine and leave settlement of the conflict to the UN, almost concurrently with its resolution to grant India independence.[94] The United Nations voted by a small majority to divide Palestine into three parts, as the British government had proposed ten years earlier but now opposed. The first part consisted of Jerusalem, placed under international control; the second of an almost purely Arab state comprising today's West Bank, some bordering districts, Gaza, and parts of Galilee; and the third was a de facto binational Jewish state with a slightly larger Jewish than Arab population. It was a highly unbalanced proposal in many ways, including geographically, since the three compact Jewish and Arab parts of the country were only linked internally at a few small points. Whoever had military control of the connections between them effectively had power over all parts of Palestine.

As in India, the announcement of partition launched a wave of violence by the weaker party, the Arabs. This first phase of the civil war of December 1947 to March 1948 did not yet affect the entire country but was confined to the larger cities and major connecting roads, especially the road from Tel Aviv to Jerusalem. The British troops stationed in Palestine were far greater in numbers and military potential than the Jewish and the Palestinian units. But they were under orders to keep out of the hostilities and proceed with their withdrawal, as in India. This evasion of responsibility, which William Roger Louis euphemistically calls the "Indian solution,"[95] created a power vacuum into which paramilitary groups stepped. Up to 100,000 people—mostly members of the Arab elite—fled Palestine in this phase. The first villages along the connecting roads were razed to the ground and their inhabitants expelled.

Another issue of contention in the secondary literature is the extent to which this ethnic cleansing was a development of the war, designed to cut off the supply of reinforcements to the Arab Liberation Army (ALA), or an end in itself. Benny Morris supports the former theory and focuses on the various assaults, minor battles, and front lines; Ilan Pappé claims ethnic cleansings were planned well in advance, independently of military operations.[96] The minutes of internal government meetings seem to point to Pappé's version of events, such as the statement by future prime minister David Ben Gurion of November 1947—even before the UN announced partition—that only a state with a clear Jewish majority could survive. Ben Gurion viewed the Palestinians as a fifth column to be dealt with thus: "They can either be mass arrested or expelled; it is better to expel them."[97]

It is widely agreed that a new phase of ethnic cleansings began in March 1948. Arms supplies arriving from Czechoslovakia helped the

Haganah, the Zionists' military arm, to gain a clear military advantage. Whether the policy of *Odsun*[98] was imported from Prague along with the arms has not been researched, but the leading Zionist politicians were certainly well informed about the Potsdam Conference and the subsequent reorganization of Europe. They developed a so-called Plan D (or Plan Dalet) involving the complete occupation of the cities and the major routes connecting them. They gave the military clear orders: "In case of resistance, the armed forces must be wiped out and the population expelled outside the borders of the state."[99]

Even towns where interethnic relations had been relatively peaceful, such as Haifa, one of the principal British military bases along with Jerusalem, were devastated by ethnic cleansing. In early 1948, at least 15,000 members of the Palestinian middle and upper classes fled this predominantly non-Jewish town. In the last third of April, the Haganah forced the remaining 50,000 to flee under artillery fire during Operation Passover Purification (*mitzvah bi'ur hametz*).[100] The ethnic cleansing of Haifa is of particular interest because the town's mayor, Shabtai Levy, made a last-minute attempt to convince the Palestinians to stay. Meanwhile, the British troops and many Western journalists looked on as the atrocities unfolded before them. In fact, the British troops helped the desired exodus along by providing ships to transport the refugees to Akra or Lebanon. In Tiberias, the largest town on the shores of the Sea of Galilee, events took a similar course. Radical military units bombarded and destroyed the Arab part of the town, against the will of the dominant Sephardic Jewish community, who had been accustomed to living in a Muslim environment since Ottoman times.[101] Subsequently, the British army supplied the trucks with which the local Palestinians were "evacuated" to Nazareth or Jordan. Since the date of the British troops' withdrawal had been brought forward from August to May 1948, their primary goal was not to get entangled in the hostilities, as in India.

Similarly, the Western journalists in Haifa also exercised restraint. Although Palestinians from Haifa were driven into the sea like the Greeks in Smyrna twenty-five years earlier, it did not inspire any outraged reportage to form a *lieu de mémoire* like Ernest Hemingway's "On the Quai at Smyrna." Ultimately, this was due to the West's Orientalism, viewing Muslims either as brutal barbarians or as comic figures, but not as tragic victims. Western empathy was confined to European Christians, such as the victims in Smyrna. The fate of the Arabs, like that of the Turks, was of secondary importance. The events in Palestine were, moreover, overshadowed by the concurrent overtures to the Cold War and the Berlin blockade.

Following the attack on Israel on 15 May by its neighbor Arab states, the ethnic cleansings gained a new dynamic. The Israeli army, built up from the Haganah, tried to realign the various fronts in the country by means of population removals. The Palmach, an elite fighting force set up to perform guerilla operations during World War II, was under orders to expel Arab civilians at will in order to block supplies to the enemy by the flood of refugees.[102] Palestinian villages were set alight, bombed, and razed, often before the eyes of the evicted residents so that none could plan on returning. This tactic achieved the desired result and kept the Jordanian army in the West Bank occupied with supplying the refugees with water and food.

The evacuation and destruction of Palestinian villages prepared the ground for large-scale Israeli settlement. In June 1948, Ben Gurion gave the Israeli cabinet the order to acquire land, under strict confidentiality.[103] The fact that these settlement plans were not publicized using nationalist propaganda, as in postwar Poland and Czechoslovakia, marks a crucial change that had occurred since 1945, when the Western powers, the Soviet Union, and the East Central European states openly advocated mass population transfers in Europe. The humanitarian disasters in Europe and India had put an end to the international consensus in favor of ethnic cleansing. The expulsion of the Palestinians was therefore organized as a fait accompli and was not sanctioned by the international community.

Nevertheless, the influence of European models and concepts was clearly apparent in the Israeli government's Transfer Committee, which was made up of high-ranking members of the military, colonization experts, diplomats, and secret service agents. This committee named the primary objectives of the war: to destroy Arab villages; to ensure that Jewish settlers acquire land and reap the harvest; to prevent the return of refugees; to conduct negotiations with neighboring states on their permanent absorption of the Palestinians.[104] In the event, the last goal was not achieved, since the Arab states refused to recognize Israel's existence or integrate the refugees. They were held in transit camps to keep the conflict with Israel simmering, the trauma of their expulsion exacerbated by their rejection by the receiving Arab states and societies. Since no contractual settlement had been made, the ethnic cleansing of Israel remained a case of flight and expulsion without transfer.

The scope of the Transfer Committee's plans increased in the second half of 1948. Despite the military intervention of Israel's neighboring Arab states, the Israeli army was able to extend the areas it controlled from the coastal strip toward the West Bank and capture all of Galilee up to the source of the Jordan. Several massacres occurred in the process, which were not premised on any strategic considerations. The Palmach brigades left trails of destruction in their path, spurred on by Prime Minister David Ben Gurion, who declared before the Galilee offensive: "The Arabs only have one function left—to run away."[105] The extreme violence cannot be attributed to the effect of propaganda and orders from above alone. Like the special forces of other nations carrying out such orders, the Palmach developed a dynamic that eventually prevented it from distinguishing between civilians and the military.

It would nevertheless be wrong to equate the situation in Israel with that in Czechoslovakia or other East Central European states. The Jewish state did not attribute collective guilt to the Palestinians. It differentiated its expulsion procedure in towns such as Nazareth according to political criteria, especially the inhabitants' conduct during the uprising of 1936–39 and the civil war from 1947. Christian Palestinians, Druze, and the inhabitants of a number of villages in the mountainous region around Jerusalem, who had taken the side of the Haganah, were spared ethnic cleansing.

Any attempt to explain the brutality of the Israeli army and the Palmach brigades must factor in their own past history and experience of trauma as a motivating force. This aspect comes to the foreground if one considers other cases of ethnic cleansing, which frequently prompted a second wave of violence when the refugees reached their destination. Many of the Jewish inhabitants of Palestine had suffered the repeated trauma of anti-Semitism and pogroms in Europe firsthand, as well as the Arab Palestinians' revolt of 1936–39. The ALA's brutal attacks on civilians and the neighboring Arab states' invasion had compounded the sense of insecurity within the Jewish community, which numbered only 650,000 at the time. Self-defense, the relevance of which grew in relation to the Holocaust, has always been a very strong motivator to use violence. Ilan Pappé paints a simplified picture with his dialectic of Israeli superiority and Arab defenselessness, inverting the Israeli foundational myth of David (Israel) against Goliath (the Arab world).

The fact that the planned Israeli state took on ever-larger dimensions from summer 1948 is a different story. But wars are often characterized by a cruel banality. The winning side can dictate the conditions of peace to the losers. After the war, the new border separating Jewish from Arab Palestine, provided for by UN Resolution 181, ran much further north and east than originally projected. Instead of 200,000 Arabs to be resettled, as the Peel Commission had proposed, there were now over 800,000 Palestinian refugees. The purely Arab state that had been planned from the start—by expanding the Kingdom of Jordan to the west—now faced a largely homogenized Jewish state.

The cases of India and Palestine are further examples of conflicts engendered by nation-state building. But comparison of these two states also brings some important differences to light. While the Indian and Pakistani authorities tried to stem the flow of migrations from 1948, Israel purposefully extended its ethnic cleansing campaigns. The differing ratio of refugees to the total population testifies to this: while it was under one-third in even the most contested regions of India, such as Punjab, about two-thirds of the Palestinian Arabs were expelled. If the leaders of the Indian Congress Party had espoused as narrow a definition of the nation as the Zionists, the result would have been a catastrophe of apocalyptic proportions. The ethnic cleansing in India was stopped at a point when the colonial forces had already completely withdrawn and could no longer intervene. It would be wrong, then, to put the blame on the colonial power. In contrast to its involvement in Lausanne and Potsdam, the British government did not resolve any large-scale forced migrations for India or Palestine. Moreover, it held an ambivalent position on both partitions so as not to jeopardize its regional influence.

Yet there is evidence implicating Britain on several levels. British democracy, with its principle of exclusive majority rule—to take up Michael Mann's theories[106]—was unsuited to multiethnic spaces. The dichotomous political system compounded the minorities' fears of being bulldozed by the majorities. This explains why it was precisely the minorities asserting their right to self-determination and fighting for independence, also by violent means. The British forces would have been able to contain this violence, but concentrated on their withdrawal instead.

Finally, the peculiarities of nation building under British rule must be considered. Colonial societies were divided into two nations (or "races" in the terminology of the day), reducing their multiethnic plurality to a binary constellation of two opposing poles. The universality of the principle is demonstrated by the fact that it was applied in a number of cases. Society in India was organized according to ethnoreligious criteria, whereas the Palestinian Arabs were defined by their language. This constellation does not necessarily lead to ethnic violence or cleansings, as the example of Canada shows. But any conflicts it generates can only be resolved in the context of an established constitutional framework. Britain only approved such frameworks in the predominantly "white" settler colonies, not in India or the Middle East.

The colonial rulers had considered the principle of "partition" as a possible solution for apparently insoluble and violent conflicts in these regions long before World War II. But partition shifted the problem of political participation to a territorial level. In the age of modern nationalism, this had fatal consequences: colonized nations not only fought for power but also over their future territories. Equally fatally, it conveyed the illusion of an ultimate solution to a complex political problem, similar to population transfers. The two concepts seemed complementary, then, and were applied in parallel in India and Palestine, as previously under British influence in Trieste.

The global discourse on population transfers and the Israeli government commission set up specifically to implement them are symptoms of the widespread adoption of the postwar European order of homogenized nation-states. Partition and transfer were European concepts that were willingly adapted by local elites. While in India the transfer was eventually stopped, it escalated in Palestine. Here, the military of a society numbering only 650,000 forced more than 800,000 to flee. Yet this was not a total ethnic cleansing. In contrast to the postwar situation in several European countries, members of minorities still made up nearly 20 percent of the population of Israel. Nevertheless, the refugees and the remaining Arabs were not the only ones to suffer from the measures. The Mizrahi and Sephardi in Israel, who were accustomed to living in a multiethnic society, were marginalized for decades.

The ethnic cleansing of 1948 formed a prelude to longer-term processes of homogenization. The Mizrahi driven out of the Arab states and the millions of remigrants in Bengal since the 1950s show that the repercussions of the postwar reorganization of nation-states continue to be felt across ever wider geographical areas. In most cases, the refugees were cared for on reception, even in impoverished Pakistan. The flight and expulsion of the Palestinians, which took place nearly three generations ago, continues to be a source of embitterment because they received no such support in their Middle Eastern reception countries and were deprived of sovereignty. The cycle of violence in the Middle East has not yet been broken.

Conclusion

The ethnic cleansing between 1944 and 1948 was unprecedented in scale if not in terms of innovation. To convey an impression of the extent of the phenomenon, the numbers of those affected in each case are listed below in chronological order: 420,000 Finns (1940–44); 2.1 million Poles from the Soviet Union (1940–41 and 1944–46); 650,000 Ukrainians from Poland and within Poland (1944–46); 12 million Germans from East Central Europe (1945–48); 80,000 Hungarians from Yugoslavia and Serbs and Croats from Hungary (1944–46); 145,000 Hungarians from Slovakia and within Czechoslovakia (1945–47); 70,000 Slovaks from Hungary (1946–47); 250,000 Italians from the northeast Adriatic region (1945–48); 12 million Indians (1947–50); and 800,000 Arab Palestinians (1948–49). In total, then, almost 29 million people were forced to leave their homelands. Factoring in those who did not survive ethnic cleansing, the number rises to more than 30 million. This is, moreover, a very cautious estimate, which does not include smaller population groups, the temporarily displaced, or forced laborers. The figures above evidence a renewed, dramatic increase in ethnic cleansing after the second phase of the period 1938–44. Certainly, ethnic cleansing is linked to wars, but 90 percent of these population shifts took place *after* one side had secured victory.

Since most ethnic cleansings took place in the context of postwar borders being rearranged, it is imperative to maintain a nuanced view of interethnic violence. It has become fashionable in the last decade to focus research on the destructive impact of individuals or groups and their misdeeds rather than state institutions. The result is frequently a view of history reminiscent of Hobbes's *Leviathan* and—following Hayden White[107]—adhering to tragic conventions. An individualistic approach is certainly essential for prosecuting the perpetrators of ethnic cleansings via, for example, the International Court of Justice in The Hague. But the case studies analyzed in this chapter show that it was largely in the hands of the great powers and the individual states to either contain outbreaks of violence or allow them to escalate into ethnic cleansing. It is in any case remarkable how swiftly mass violence could be halted once state authorities or the military gave the order.

The tremendous increase in the number of refugees between 1944 and 1948—totaling four times as many as in the period 1938–44—can only be explained by orders from above. The victorious powers were instrumental in causing this escalation. At the conferences of Potsdam, Yalta, and Tehran, they spontaneously redrew borders and shifted states and societies across hundreds of kilometers. The resolutions by the "Big Three" between 1943 and 1945 affected about twenty million people. They were not only concerned with punishing the Germans and preventing another war of aggression, but also with territorially and demographically reorganizing an entire continent.

A line of continuity from the Nazis' reorganization of Central and Southeastern Europe in 1938–44 to the Allies' postwar order is evidenced by a number of factors. The primary objective of the latter was to homogenize nation-states and align state and ethnic boundaries. As previously in the interwar period, the great powers sought to maintain a façade of legitimacy for the Munich Agreement and the First and Second Vienna Awards. The bilateral settlements between Poland and

the western Soviet Socialist Republics, which were crucial for effect-
ing Poland's shift so far westward, and Hungary's agreements with its
neighboring states to the north and south, were based on the fiction of
the consensual and constitutional nature of population exchange. The
Treaty of Craiova of 1940, concerning the division between Bulgaria
and Romania and the ethnic cleansing of the Dobruja region, actually
retained its validity after the war.

Initially, the Germans were subject to the arbitrary prerogative of
the victor, which was not codified until the Potsdam Conference. The
ethnic cleansing of the Germans from East Central Europe was unique
in terms of scale, totality, and one-sidedness. It responded to the in-
comparable aggression and terror inflicted by the occupying Germans,
which transgressed all norms, even independently of the Holocaust. But
more than desires for retribution, it was motivated by forward-looking
concerns or, as Churchill succinctly put it in December 1944, the avoid-
ance of endless trouble with national minorities. The Allies began to
reconsider, however, when they were confronted with the consequences
of their resolutions. The acute refugee crisis in Germany in summer and
fall 1945 and the portrayals of misery in the Western media prompted
them to take a more critical view of ethnic cleansing. Article XIII of the
Potsdam Agreement demanded the improved organization of population shifts. But the Western powers did not abandon the principle of
"transfer."

In other cases, such as that of the Hungarian minorities in Romania,
Serbia, and Slovakia, ethnic cleansings were halted or even reversed.
This was not done to protect human rights but for pragmatic reasons.
Stalin was concerned with maintaining his political influence in Hungary and avoiding the chaos of another refugee crisis of German proportions in the regions along the Danube. In this way, he defined Romania
and Yugoslavia as multiethnic states rather than unitary nation-states.
Yet the Romanian-Hungarian conflict in Transylvania and the Serbian-
Hungarian conflict in Vojvodina were not perceived to have been ideally
settled either by Stalin or by the states affected. A more profound confrontation of the past would have been necessary to successfully resolve
conflicts in Communist multiethnic states, but this was impossible under Stalin. Thus, population transfers were arranged again in 1946–47
in the Danube region that conceptually linked up with Lausanne and
earlier settlements under German hegemony. To the rest of the world,
these partial ethnic cleansings conveyed the message that they were still
a relevant means of solving internal and international conflicts.

Europe's idea of the nation-state, its violent ethnopolitical conflicts,
and concrete examples of ethnic cleansing all contributed to such mea-

sures being taken on an extensive scale in India and Palestine. While attempts were made to limit the ethnic cleansings in India in 1948 on account of their negative repercussions for the economy and the risk of them sparking widespread civil war, the Zionists used ethnic cleansings in an expansionist manner as a means of acquiring land. Faits accomplis had previously been created in this way in East Central Europe, where many Jewish emigrants and the crucial arms supplies came from. Although Britain did not directly motivate ethnic cleansings in India or Palestine, as it had in Europe, it continued to uphold a strategy of divide and rule. The withdrawing colonial power indirectly fostered interethnic violence by a number of its measures and supported homogenization in concrete terms by transporting refugees. Societies in the Middle East responded to the mass population removals differently from those in Europe and India, with lasting consequences. While governments in Europe and India introduced measures to integrate refugees, the Palestinian refugees were left stateless, without rights and at the mercy of regional powers and their revisionist plans. In this case, no contractual settlements were made to provide for the status of the refugees as victims of forced resettlement or their integration into reception countries.

Despite the use of drastic measures and purposeful violence, the utopia of homogeneity was not realized. Poland was soon struggling with new minority problems. Yugoslavia, Czechoslovakia, Romania, and India remained multiethnic states. Conflicts continued in Pakistan between the ethnic subdivisions of the Muslim Nation. The exception is Germany, where society had indeed been homogenized in line with the Nazis' vision of a "national community" (*Volksgemeinschaft*), albeit on truncated territory. But although minorities had been removed or weakened, the pressure to conform remained. The German expellees from East Central Europe were among those to feel it most.

To return to the agents of ethnic cleansings: historians often blame Stalin for the ethnic cleansings in East Central Europe. But he was less of a breaker of nations, as Robert Conquest dubbed him four decades ago and Timothy Snyder recently paraphrased,[108] than a ruthless tactician. Events in southern Slovakia and Romania and the fact that the rural Polish population was kept back in Lithuania and Byelorussia show that the Soviet Union did not pursue a consistent policy of ethnic homogenization either in its external sphere of influence or in its own territory.

The Allies consensually resolved the ceding of the Polish and German eastern territories and hence Poland's shift westward, as well as the removal of all minorities in the northern part of East Central Europe. As Detlef Brandes has shown, Poland and especially Czechoslovakia were

actively committed to the "transfers," at a point when they were not
yet clearly aligned with the Soviet camp or ruled by dictatorships.[109]
A broad social consensus in favor of removing minorities prevailed in
these "people's democracies."

Within the Soviet Union, in contrast, Stalin avoided such harsh measures after World War II, although as victor he was in a position to enforce them and he faced armed resistance to Sovietization in the Baltic
states and Ukraine. The Stalinist regime that seized power in Czechoslovakia via a military coup in 1948 even allowed the deported Hungarians to return. This was not a sign of the Communist authorities'
humanitarianism but a side effect of prioritizing central Communist
projects such as social homogenization and the elimination of groups
that did not conform to the Marxist-Leninist system, such as industrialists, businesspeople, home owners, and independent farmers. While
Stalinist regimes kept a constant eye on "national deviants," their policies were primarily focused on creating a classless society and a "new
man." Similarly, ethnic cleansings were of secondary importance to the
Nazis. From spring 1941, their planned population removals had to
be deferred as they concentrated all resources on invading the Soviet
Union, total war, and annihilating the European Jews. However, more
extensive ethnic cleansings were carried out in the German-allied states
in Central and Southeastern Europe.

Ethnic cleansings were not, then, a characteristic feature of totalitarian dictatorships, which displayed ambivalence toward them. Democratic or authoritarian nation-states used ethnic cleansings to reduce
unwanted social plurality and consolidate power. Every political system has a catalog of reprisals that are intensified at moments of crisis.
The radical nationalism of the Nazis resulted in genocide; in the Soviet Union, the "class war" fought during collectivization led to state-
engineered "sociocide." The dark side of the nation-state and the international order of nation-states was ethnic cleansing.

This thesis is supported by the example of the regions affected outside Europe. In India and the Middle East, ethnic cleansing attended the
building of democratic states to replace British colonial rule. Michael
Mann's attempt to blame democracy for ethnic cleansing nevertheless
fails to convince.[110] Nation-states tended to resort to ethnic cleansing
when the rule of law was threatened by war or other destabilizing factors, making ethnocracies out of democracies. Ethnic cleansings were
most radical in places where democratic structures were combined with
authoritarian rule. Established democracies, in contrast, were able to
process interethnic conflicts and the consequences of war and occupation in other ways. Denmark and France after World War II are cases in

point. In addition, several examples of ethnic cleansing show that they weaken democratic structures. In Poland and above all in Czechoslovakia, they prepared the ground for the Communists' seizure of power.

Ethnic cleansings therefore cause profound loss, for individuals as well as for the states and societies that enforce them, especially with respect to the way of life in the affected regions. Only a few European cities that were ethnically cleansed still have as rich a social and cultural life as they did before 1938; life in rural areas was often permanently obliterated. In the Sudeten Mountains, the Bohemian Forest, and the Bieszczady, the vacant sites of former villages are still discernible. Loss is perhaps the common denominator linking all the individuals, societies, and states affected two generations later.

The mid- and long-term losses and the dire immediate consequences were indeed the main reasons why the international community gradually came to disapprove of the practice of ethnic cleansing in the postwar period. The effect of the UN Genocide Convention, which was rarely applied in the first forty years after its conclusion, is often overestimated today. The anti-Greek pogrom in Istanbul in September 1955, the actions of the conflicting parties in Cyprus in 1974–75, and even more extensive population removals in the Third World were not negotiated or criticized in the context of the Genocide Convention.[111]

A more important factor turning public opinion against ethnic cleansing seems to be the discourse on human rights that developed in Britain and the United States in response to the emerging Cold War and that became universalized and anchored in society after the student protest movement of 1968. In the Soviet sphere of influence, de-Stalinization allowed a paradigm shift to take place and the deportations of the 1940s to be revised. The Volga Germans, Crimean Tatars, and Polish Ukrainians were the only groups that remained deported until 1988–89. Finally, developments on the Indian subcontinent must be taken into account. The agreements between the Indian and Pakistani armies of late 1947 on the reciprocal evacuation of refugees were made with humanitarian objectives in mind and not the explicit goal of ethnic homogenization. With the Nehru-Liaquat Agreement of 1950, the two countries even attempted a return to multiethnic coexistence. The Paris Peace Conference of 1946–47 marks the finale of ethnic cleansing as a practice under international law, confirming the theory that it was a European phenomenon.

Large-scale population shifts such as the Potsdam Agreement provided for can only be enforced with the support of an international or at least a regional consensus. Thanks in part to the profound change in attitudes to such practices and the long period of peace after World War

II, no more major ethnic cleansings took place in Europe between 1948 and 1989.

Notes

1. See Brandes, *Der Weg zur Vertreibung*, 241.
2. W. R. Churchill, *Triumph and Tragedy (The Second World War)*, vol. 6 (Boston, 1953), 648.
3. See Churchill, *His Complete Speeches*, 7069.
4. See Naimark, *Fires of Hatred*, 108–38.
5. Quoted by Naimark, *Fires of Hatred*, 125.
6. A facsimile of the Potsdam Agreement is reproduced in *Ausgewählte Dokumente zur Deutschlandfrage 1943 bis 1949* (Berlin, 1971), 55–73.
7. See the preface by a high-ranking US diplomat in Alfred M. de Zayas, *Die Nemesis von Potsdam: Die Angloamerikaner und die Vertreibung der Deutschen* (Munich, 2005), 11 and 126–27. There are several English editions of the book; the latest was published as *Nemesis at Potsdam: The Expulsion of the Germans from the East* (Rockland, 2003). See also Klaus-Dietmar Henke, "Der Weg nach Potsdam—Die Alliierten und die Vertreibung," in Benz, *Die Vertreibung*, 80. It is portrayed as a marginal aspect of the negotiations.
8. Frank, *Expelling the Germans*, 116.
9. The intertwined character of the removal of Germans and the arrival of Poles has been stressed recently in an excellent local study. See Hugo Service, "Reinterpreting the Expulsion of Germans from Poland, 1945–9," *Journal of Contemporary History* 47 (2012): 528–50. See also Ther, *Gesellschaft und Vertriebenenpolitik*.
10. "Poland" is defined here as the national territory determined by the Potsdam Agreement and the subsequent Polish-Soviet border treaty. The eastern German territories were no longer under Allied rule after the Potsdam Agreement but part of Poland (or the Soviet Union, in the case of Königsberg).
11. "Evacuation" was originally planned to be completed within just four months. This again highlights the day's prevalent belief in a utopia of feasibility, in this case on the Soviet side. The implementation of the treaty is dealt with in greater detail in my dissertation published in 1998 and in Ther and Siljak, *Redrawing Nations*.
12. Archiwum Akt Nowych (archive for new files, AAN), MAP, 2488, 13.
13. See AAN, MZO, 70, 112.
14. On the statistics concerning the nonrepatriated Poles, see Rossiiskii gosudarstvennyi arkhiv sotsial'no-politicheskoi istorii (RGASPI), Font 17, op. 121, Tekhsekratariat Org. Buro, SK VKP (b), Delo 545, 47 and 50–51. According to Jerzy Kochanowski, 50 percent of the Poles registered to emigrate in the Lithuanian Soviet Socialist Republic and 45 percent in the Byelorussian SSR were held back. See Ahonen et al., *People on the Move*, 102. Cieselski, *Umsiedlung*, 40, maintains that only 158,500 of the 382,000 Poles registered in Lithuania were actually forcibly resettled in Poland.
15. This figure is deduced from the sum of 1.517 million official repatriates, 300,000 refugees, up to 50,000 victims of the Polish-Ukrainian civil war, 300,000 victims of forced labor, and 550,000 prospective emigrants who had to stay in the Soviet Union; in total about 2.7 million, as opposed to a prewar Polish population of over 4 million in the former eastern territories.
16. Many ego-documents from eastern Poland were collected by the KARTA Center and some of them published in the magazine of the same name. Further material is held in the archives of the Instytut Zachodni in Poznań and the Instytut Śląski in Opole.

17. See the publications by Czech historian Tomáš Staněk and the four-volume documentation by Borodziej and Lemberg.

18. See Naimark, *Fires of Hatred,* 195–198 (and more material in the individual chapters).

19. Quoted and translated from Tomáš Staněk, *Verfolgung 1945: Die Stellung der Deutschen in Böhmen, Mähren und Schlesien (außerhalb der Lager und Gefängnisse)* (Cologne, 2002), 161.

20. Quoted and translated from Borodziej and Lemberg, *Die Deutschen,* 1:161 (document 35).

21. See Staněk, *Verfolgung 1945,* 34.

22. For a typical example of a publication overstressing this motive, see Alfred-Maurice de Zayas, *A Terrible Revenge: The Ethnic Cleansing of the European Germans* (New York, 1994).

23. The exact amount of officially registered expellees was 448,000. See Tomáš Staněk, *Odsun Němců z Československa 1945–1947* (Prague, 1991), 76.

24. On these estimates, see Borodziej and Lemberg, *Niemcy w Polsce,* 69.

25. See Frank, *Expelling the Germans,* 92.

26. On the exact numbers, see Portmann, *Die kommunistische Revolution,* 255.

27. See Portmann, *Die kommunistische Revolution,* 257.

28. See Andreas R. Hofmann, *Die Nachkriegszeit in Schlesien: Gesellschaft- und Bevölkerungspolitik in den polnischen Siedlungsgebieten 1945–1948* (Cologne, 2000), 236.

29. "Nie chcemy ani jednego Niemca, ale nie oddamy ani jednej duszy polskiej." Quoted from AAN, MZO, 84, 37.

30. See Gemeinsame deutsch-tschechische Historikerkommission, ed., *Konfliktgemeinschaft, Katastrophe, Entspannung: Skizze einer Darstellung der deutsch-tschechischen Geschichte seit dem 19. Jahrhundert* (Munich, 1996), 69.

31. See Rüdiger Overmans, "Personelle Verluste der deutschen Bevölkerung durch Flucht und Vertreibung," *Dzieje Najnowsze* 26, no. 2 (1994): 60.

32. See Frank, *Expelling the Germans,* 122–63.

33. On the concept of revanchism, see Frank, *Expelling the Germans,* 149.

34. See the comprehensive source book by Eugeniusz Misiło, *Repatriacja czy deportacja: Przesiedlenie Ukraińców z Polski do USRR 1944–1946,* 2 vols. (Warsaw, 1996).

35. See RGASPI, Font 17, op. 121, Tekhsekratariat Org. Buro, SK VKP (b), Delo 545, 47–51.

36. Quoted and translated from Maria Wanatowicz, *Ludność napływowa na Górnym Śląsku w latach 1922–1939* (Katowice, 1982), 345. On Silesian collective memory, see Andrew Demshuk, "Reinscribing Schlesien as Śląsk: Memory and Mythology in a Postwar German-Polish Borderland," *History & Memory* 24 (2012): 39–86.

37. On the ethnic cleansing of Hungarians from Slovakia to Hungary and the border regions, see Štefan Šutaj, "Zwangsaustausch bzw: Aussiedlung der Magyaren aus der Slowakei—Pläne und Wirklichkeit," in Brandes et al., *Erzwungene Trennung,* 266–72.

38. Many Germans workers were also kept there. See Tomáš Dvořák, "Těžba uranu versus "očista" pohraničí: Německé pracovní síly v Jáchymovských dolech na přelomu čtyřicátých a padesátých let 20. století," *Soudobe Dějiny* 12, nos. 3–4 (2005): 626–71. This volume of the journal also contains other interesting articles on the postwar development of the Czech borderlands.

39. On Czech population policy, see Andreas Wiedemann, *"Komm mit uns das Grenzland aufbauen!" Ansiedlung und neue Strukturen in den ehemaligen Sudetengebieten* (Essen, 2007). (On the "buffer" concept and individual examples of criminals, see 41 and 99–100).

40. Ibid., 258.

41. See Ther, *Deutsche und Polnische Vertriebene,* 123–26.
42. See Gregor Thum, *Die fremde Stadt: Breslau 1945* (Munich, 2003), 142. (An English translation of Thum's book has been published by Princeton University Press. See the annotated bibliography).
43. See Ther, *Deutsche und Polnische Vertriebene,* 272–75.
44. See the comparisons between Wrocław and old Polish industrial towns in Padraic Kenney, *Rebuilding Poland: Workers and Communists, 1945–1950* (Ithaca, NY, 1997).
45. See Ahonen et al., *People on the Move,* 71.
46. On this and the migratory movements, see Şandru, *Mişcări de populaţie,* 195–99.
47. See the relevant quote from a conversation between Stalin and the general secretary of the Romanian Communist Party, Gheorghe Gheorghiu-Dej, in *Vostochnaja Evropa v dokumentakh rossijskikh archivov 1944–1953,* vol. 1, *1944–1948* (Moscow, 1997), 582.
48. On these deportations, see Ewa Ochman, "Population Displacement and Regional Reconstruction in Postwar Poland: The Case of Upper Silesia," in *Warlands: Population Resettlement and State Reconstruction in the Soviet-East European Borderlands, 1945–50,* ed. Peter Gatrell and Nick Baron (Basingstoke, UK, 2009), 216–17. The estimate cited by Ochman of 90,000 people includes other categories of forced laborers.
49. As former enemies in the war, Hungarians were systematically deported and subjected to particularly harsh reprisals. These deportations were, however, stopped at a fairly early stage. See Ahonen et al., *People on the Move,* 77.
50. See Pavel Polian, "'Das Staatskomitee für Verteidigung verfügt …': Die Deportationen deutscher Zivilpersonen aus Ost- und Südeuropa und aus dem Hinterland der Front 1944/45 in die Sowjetunion," in Melville et al., *Zwangsmigrationen,* 370. The figures are based on the death rates of deportees of various nationalities.
51. See Portmann, *Die kommunistische Revolution,* 268. This would suggest that the numbers given by Tamáš Stark in Ahonen et al., *People on the Move,* 79, are exaggerated.
52. Quotes translated from Portmann, *Die kommunistische Revolution,* 275.
53. Portmann, *Die kommunistische Revolution,* 274.
54. See Benjamin Liebermann, *Terrible Fate: Ethnic Cleansing in the Making of Modern Europe* (Chicago, 2006).
55. See Timothy Snyder, *Bloodlands: Europe between Hitler and Stalin* (New York, 2010), 313–338.
56. Ahonen et al., *People on the Move,* 104.
57. On *foibe,* see Paul Ropo, *Il lungo esodo: Istria: le persecuzioni, le foibe, l'esilio* (Milan, 2005).
58. On this number, see Marina Cattaruzza, "Der 'istrische Exodus': Fragen der Interpretation," in Brandes et al., *Erzwungene Trennung,* 295–322.
59. On the "exodus" of the Italians from Istria and Dalmatia, see the interesting publication (especially with respect to methodology and terminology) by Marina Cattaruzza, *L'Italia e il confine orientale 1866–2006* (Bologna, 2007); see also the regional study by Piero Purini, *Metamorfosi etniche: I cambiamenti di populazione a Trieste, Gorizia, Fiume e in Istria, 1914–1975* (Udine, 2010).
60. See the original citation in Cattaruzza, "Der 'Istrische Exodus,'" 305.
61. See John Koliopoulos, *Plundered Loyalties: Axis Occupation and Civil Strife in Greek West Macedonia, 1941–1949* (London, 2000), 270.
62. See Koliopoulos, *Plundered Loyalties,* 284.
63. See Brandes, Sundhaussen, and Troebst, *Lexikon der Vertreibungen,* 412–14.
64. See the informative entries by Ulf Brunnbauer in Brandes, Sundhaussen, and Troebst, *Lexikon der Vertreibungen,* 662–67. See also Iskra Baeva, Evgenia Kalinova, "Bulgar-

ian Turks during the Transition Period," in *Bulgaria and Europe. Shifting Identities*, ed. Stefanos Katsikas (London 2010), 63–78 und 218–221.

65. On the German-Danish conflict over Sleswick and its settlement in the postwar period, see Karl Christian Lammers, "Konflikte und Konfliktlösungen in der dänisch-deutschen Nationalitätenfrage seit 1840: Der Fall Schleswig," in Ther and Sundhaussen, *Nationalitätenkonflikte*, 203–18. To compare Sleswick with Upper Silesia, see Wiesław Lesiuk, *Dunsko-niemieckie doświadczenie w rozwiązywaniu problemów etniczno-narodowościowych na pograniczu z perspektiwy polskiej* (Opole, 1994).

66. On the collapse of the constitutional Czechoslovak state and the transition to collective punishment, see Benjamin Frommer, *Retribution against Nazi Collaborators in Postwar Czechoslovakia* (Cambridge, 2005).

67. On transfer history and the original French term *transferts culturels*, see Michel Espagne, Michael Werner, "La construction d'une référence culturelle allemande en France - Génèse et Histoire (1750-1914)," in: *Annales E.S.C.* (juillet-aout 1987), 969–992.

68. This assessment is concealed in a quote by Walter Lippmann, but obviously shared by the author. See Wm. Roger Louis, *Ends of British Imperialism: The Scramble for Empire, Suez and Decolonization: Collected Essays* (London, 2006), 410.

69. Stanley Wolpert, *Shameful Flight: The Last Years of the British Empire in India* (New York, 2006); Shahid Hamid, *Disastrous Twilight: A Personal Record of the Partition of India* (London, 1986).

70. See Anita Inder Singh, *The Origins of Partition: India 1936-1947* (Oxford, 1987), 1. This work was republished in Mushirul Hasan, ed., *The Partition Omnibus* (New Delhi, 2002).

71. See Wolpert, *Shameful Flight*, 44–45 and 68.

72. See Ian Copland, "The Further Shores of Partition: Ethnic Cleansing in Rajasthan 1947," *Past and Present* 160 (August 1998): 232. This study also analyzes local dynamics of conflict.

73. On Direct Action Day, the subsequent riots, and numbers of victims, see Wolpert, *Shameful Flight*, 118–26.

74. See Khan, *The Great Partition*, 138.

75. Ibid., 124.

76. On Mountbatten's policies, see the devastating (and well-founded) character study by Wolpert, *Shameful Flight*.

77. Quoted by Wolpert, *Shameful Flight*, 138–40.

78. Quoted by Khan, *The Great Partition*, 100.

79. Wolpert, *Shameful Flight*, 103, 177. On Trieste, see Wolpert, *Shameful Flight*, 132. On Indian references to Lausanne, see also Yıldırım, *Diplomacy*, 13.

80. Khan, *The Great Partition*, 114 and 120.

81. On the drawing of the border and Mountbatten's and Radcliffe's ignorance, see Khan, *The Great Partition*, 122–27; Wolpert, *Shameful Flight*, 157–69.

82. On the statistics, see Khan, *The Great Partition*, 156; see also Ian Talbot, "The 1947 Partition of India and Migration: A Comparative Study of Punjab and Bengal," in Bessel and Haake, *Removing Peoples*, 325.

83. Talbot, *The 1947 Partition*, 324.

84. Ibid. Singh, *The Partition of India*, 101.

85. See Talbot, *The 1947 Partition*, 339.

86. See Ian Copland, *The Further Shores of Partition*.

87. See Urwashi Butalia, *The Other Side of Silence: Voices from the Partition of India* (New Delhi, 1998) (Butalia is the most prominent author representing the recent trend toward remembrance literature). For an academic perspective, see Gyanendra

Pandey, *Remembering Partition, Violence, Nationalism and History in India* (Cambridge, 2002).

88. The commission's wording ran: "A precedent is afforded by the exchange effected between the Greek and Turkish populations on the morrow of the Greco-Turkish War of 1922. ... so vigorously and effectively was the task accomplished that within about eighteen months from the spring of 1923 the whole exchange was completed. The courage of the Greek and Turkish statesmen concerned has been justified by the result. Before the operation the Greek and Turkish minorities had been a constant irritant. Now Greco-Turkish relations are friendlier than they have ever been before." Quoted from the Report of the Palestine Royal Commission, presented by the Secretary of State for the Colonies to the United Kingdom Parliament by Command of His Britannic Majesty (July 1937), at http://www.jewishvirtuallibrary.org/jsource/History/peel1.html (accessed 21 February 2011).

89. See Ilan Pappé, *The Ethnic Cleansing of Palestine* (Oxford, 2006).

90. On the Bukovina Compromise and other attempts at conflict mediation on a regional level, see Gerald Stourzh, *Die Gleichberechtigung der Nationalitäten in der Verfassung und Verwaltung Österreichs 1848–1918* (Vienna, 1985), 213–29.

91. See Nur Masalha, *Expulsion of the Palestinians: The Concept of "Transfer" in Zionist Political Thought, 1882–1948* (Washington DC, 1992); Ilan Pappé, *The Ethnic Cleansing*.

92. Pappé, *The Ethnic Cleansing*, 23. For more reference material, see also Benny Morris, *1948: A History of the First Arab-Israeli War* (New Haven, CT, 2008), 18.

93. On the consensus among Zionists and the King of Jordan, see Avi Shlaim, *The Politics of Partition: King Abdullah, the Zionists and Palestine 1921–1951* (Oxford, 1998). Eventually, Britain shared this view, hoping to build Jordan into a postcolonial satellite state. See Shlaim, *The Politics*, 11.

94. See Pappé, *The Ethnic Cleansing*, 40.

95. See Louis, *Ends of British Imperialism*, 442.

96. See Morris, *1948*; Pappé, *The Ethnic Cleansing*.

97. Quoted by Pappé, *The Ethnic Cleansing*, 49.

98. The British Foreign Ministry, at least, made this connection. The principle of transfer for Palestine was discussed in reference to the example of Czechoslovakia at the highest levels of government. See Frank, *Expelling the Germans*, 78.

99. Quoted by Pappé, *The Ethnic Cleansing*, 82.

100. This denotes a purification process. On this operation, see Morris, *1948*, 140–47.

101. Morris limits his account, as usual, to the military side of the conflict and does not address the internal Jewish differences at all (see Morris, *1948*, 139). His terse appraisal, "Arab Tiberias was no more," does not do justice to the fact that the houses and livelihoods of many Jews had also been destroyed. See the inquiry by Palestinian historian Mustafa Abbasi, "The War on the Mixed Cities: The Deportation of Arab Tiberias and the Destruction of its Old, 'Sacred' City (1948–49)," *Holy Land Studies: A Multidisciplinary Journal* 7, no. 1 (May 2008): 45–80.

102. On this order, see Pappé, *The Ethnic Cleansing*, 88.

103. See Morris, *1948*, 269.

104. On the Transfer Committee, see ibid., 300.

105. Quoted from ibid., 346.

106. See Michael Mann, *The Dark Side of Democracy: Explaining Ethnic Cleansing* (Cambridge, 2005).

107. See Hayden White, *Metahistory: The Historical Imagination in Nineteenth Century Europe* (Baltimore, 1973).

108. See Robert Conquest, *Stalin: Breaker of Nations* (London, 1991); Snyder, *Bloodlands*.

109. See Brandes, *Der Weg.*
110. See Mann, *Democracy and Ethnic Cleansing.* This book focuses almost exclusively on authoritarian systems and dictatorships.
111. On ethnic cleansings from a global perspective, see Stephane Rosière, *Le nettoyage ethnique: Terreur et peuplement* (Paris, 2006).

CHAPTER 5

GHOSTS OF THE PAST

THE FORMER YUGOSLAVIA AND THE CAUCASUS
1991–99

⁓◦§§◦⁓

Although the ethnic cleansings in the former Yugoslavia in the 1990s affected far smaller areas and groups than those of earlier periods, they must be included in any survey of the phenomenon. This was when the term "ethnic cleansing" (*etničko čišćenje* in Serbo-Croat) was picked up by the Western media and disseminated to a broad public as well as to academic research. The International Court of Justice in The Hague was set up to prosecute the human rights violations and war crimes committed in the former Yugoslavia. Records of these trials provide important insight into the motives of the perpetrators and the dynamic of violence. Yet despite a surge of social science publications on these events in the 1990s, the conflict in the former Yugoslavia is only now beginning to be confronted by historians. This marks it out from the previous three, well-researched periods of ethnic cleansing. Important files in Serbia, Croatia, and Bosnia and Herzegovina, which would enable the planning and unfolding of these events to be more closely analyzed, remain inaccessible.

The world was shocked by what happened in the former Yugoslavia in the 1990s. The international community's unanimous condemnation of the mass forced migrations placed them in a very different context from those in the period after World War II. Without the support of the great powers and the neighboring states, the ethnic cleansing remained limited in scale. After the Dayton Accords, refugees were even able to return. This indicates that the ethnic cleansings in the former Yugoslavia were closely linked to the course of the war and should be analyzed in this context. Yet the international community's opposition to population removals—in contrast to its endorsement of them in the first three phases of ethnic cleansing—had less of a decisive influence on events. In view of this, and the fact that a large majority of society in the former Yugoslavia also disapproved of such brutal measures, the question arises of why radical nationalists were able to enforce ethnic cleansing on a still profound scale. The same question can also be applied to the former Soviet Union, where a relatively small number of radical nationalist activists caused masses to flee.

On account of the unanimous international condemnation of ethnic cleansing, the limited availability of archival material, and the global trend toward victim narratives, literature on the former Yugoslavia has hitherto taken a predominantly normative and strongly politicized victim perspective. But the recent revision of the war mortality rate, initially commissioned by the Bosnian government and later carried out by a reputable nongovernmental organization backed by the Norwegian government, shows how shaky a foundation this is based on. The independent research and documentation center in Sarajevo (Istraživačko dokumentacioni centar, IDC) found the widely circulated figure of 200,000 to 250,000 war casualties in Bosnia and Herzegovina to be about double the actual sum of less than 100,000 provable cases.[1] This reduces above all the number of casualties among the Muslim Bosniaks, who suffered by far the most civilian losses but were not the sole victims.

Serbs, who constituted about one-third of the population when the conflict erupted, made up about one-quarter of all the war casualties in Bosnia and Herzegovina. In contrast to the Bosniaks, however, the Serb victims were predominantly (80 percent) soldiers. This fact throws more light on the nature of the hostilities and the asymmetry of power at play than any assignments of guilt. The Serbian military effectively defended its own civilian population, but mainly by attacking the enemy civilian population.

The revised statistics do not necessarily promote a revisionist view of history, but they indirectly call the victim narratives of the 1990s into question. These must also be reappraised from a historical perspective, since they were a product of the war. Certainly the claim by the normative school associated with Sabrina Ramet that one side were victims and the other side exclusively perpetrators does not hold. The term genocide, which the Bosnian government used to make the international community sit up and listen, should also be approached with caution. Taking the earlier phases and cases analyzed in the previous chapters as a yardstick, the mass flight and expulsion—no contractually arranged forced resettlements took place—of Bosniaks, Serbs, and Croats should be classified as ethnic cleansing. Another factor supporting this is the proportion of casualties to refugees: 100,000 to 2.2 million. The former figure includes 50,000 soldiers killed in action.

But why did the mass murder of 7,000 Bosnian men in Srebrenica happen? The causes of this genocidal massacre, which marked the end of the war in Bosnia and Herzegovina, will be elucidated in detail below. The fact that the death toll of the war has been revised does not imply that the individual atrocities committed should be seen in relative terms. The brutality of paramilitary brigades and official army units, the concentration camps that existed at the beginning of the war in northern Bosnia, and the massacres in the supposed UN-protected enclaves remain symbols of a breach of civilization, at odds with the peace prevailing in Europe since 1945. This is also symbolized by the very term "ethnic cleansing," which, unlike the technocratic terms "population exchange," "transfer," and "resettlement," inherently implies disapproval.

Even if one is inclined to criticize ex post facto the international community's various negotiations and deals with the Serbian leader Slobodan Milošević as well as its hesitant and sometimes contradictory policies,[2] it managed to prevent ethnic cleansing spreading across Yugoslavia and to the neighboring states. The same is true of the former Soviet Union, a detailed consideration of which would go beyond the scope of this book. Here, ethnic cleansing was also confined to smaller regions such as Abkhazia, South Ossetia, and Nagorno-Karabakh. The conflict in the former Yugoslavia in the years 1991–95 did not spread beyond two former constituent republics—that is, specific regions of Croatia, Bosnia and Herzegovina, and, a few years later, Kosovo. While international diplomacy frequently contributed to extending ethnic cleansings until 1948, its role in the 1990s was far more constructive.

The Breakup of Yugoslavia

To explain the ethnic cleansing in the former Yugoslavia, one must first consider the political collapse of the state separately from the mass violence attending it. The economic crisis of the 1980s and mounting international debts left the Socialist Federal Republic of Yugoslavia de facto bankrupt by 1990. Extensive financial transfers between the constituent republics as well as to the central government in Belgrade would have been necessary to keep the state functioning. But the failure of regional authorities to agree on economic reforms made the country's breakup inevitable. Yugoslavia had already introduced a federal system following the constitutional reform of 1974, which caused the constituent republics to drift ever further apart in terms of politics, economy, and society. Differing views of history were conveyed in education in the different republics. The three ideological pillars of the Communist state—partisan mythology, antifascism, and the brotherhood of Communist nations—were gradually displaced by memories of the wars within the war in 1941–45 and contemporary political conflicts. Eventually the general secretary of the Serbian Communist Party, Slobodan Milošević, tried to overcome the economic and political crisis by means of recentralization. While this served to stabilize Serbia, where he revoked the autonomy of Kosovo and Vojvodina in a coup d'état scenario, it intensified Slovenia's and Croatia's secessionist tendencies.

Nationalism only started to play a crucial role at this point, when all the parties in the conflict tried to rally the population to their cause by means of nationalist propaganda and symbolism. The start signal was given by Milošević's speech at the Kosovo Polje, the mythological site of a medieval battle against the Ottoman Empire, in 1989. Milošević portrayed the Serbs as a humiliated and threatened nation. He was not the only one to propagate this view. In the mid-1980s, the Serbian Orthodox patriarch in Belgrade and the Serbian Academy of Sciences had expressed similar opinions, even making the incendiary claim that Serbs had been the subject of genocide in a notorious declaration of 1986.

In Croatia, Franjo Tudjman (*Tuđman*) countered this purportedly defensive but de facto highly aggressive Serb nationalism. A former brigadier general of the Yugoslav National Army (YNA) who had been incarcerated for two years for publishing nationalist writings during the Croatian spring of 1971, Tudjman reintroduced the currency of the Ustasha era and the red and white checks in the middle of the Croatian flag. He also made light of the genocidal crimes committed during World War II. The reappearance of earlier Croatian nationalist symbols alarmed the Serbian minority, whose fears had already been roused by Milošević and the accounts of older generations. In Croatia's declaration of independence, moreover, Tudjman made no concessions to minority rights.

Why the conflict escalated into a bloody civil war in 1991–92 is another question. In 1990, the collapsing state of Yugoslavia could have reorganized in one of two possible ways: the secessionist constituent republics could have declared independence on the basis of the existing borders, or the state could have reorganized along ethnic lines of separation. Slovenia, Croatia, and the initially hesitant Bosnia and Herzegovina were in favor of the former option and declared their independence, but the Serbian elites were resolutely opposed to it.

The rhetorical escalation was accompanied by a buildup of arms, which was completely unequal from the outset. While Serbia and the Serbian minority in Croatia and Bosnia had access to most of the YNA's arms, the Croatian and Bosnian governments were dependent on arms supplies from abroad, especially from the national diaspora. Another fatal legacy of the Yugoslav army was that it had actively prepared the population for guerilla warfare, putting arms into circulation on a huge scale and training regional and local societies to defend themselves in the event of another major conflict or world war.

The nationalist rhetoric of Milošević, Tudjman, and their followers often conveyed the impression that the populations of the former Yugoslavia stood as united fronts behind these nationalist causes. But when civil war was looming in summer 1991, the opposite proved to be the case. In Serbia especially, many reservists and recruits tried to evade conscription. Political scientist Chip Gagnon convincingly claims that the nationalist rhetoric and violence was mainly intended to stifle the popular demands for political and economic reforms, intimidate the population, and preserve the power of the old elites.[3] It was not ethnic conflict—an issue that dominated the media and academia in the 1990s—or the often-cited "ethnic hatreds" that led to war in Yugoslavia, but a politically engineered process. This opinion is shared by leading German experts such as Holm Sundhaussen.[4]

An unintentional side effect of the popular reluctance to fight was the deployment of mercenaries in the war. In Croatia in late 1991 and Bosnia in spring 1992, Milošević and the leadership of the YNA fell back on paramilitary units such as the notorious Arkan Tigers (named after warlord Željko Ražnatović) to achieve their objective of a Greater Serbia encompassing all Serb-inhabited regions in the former Yugoslavia. Combat units consisting mostly of unemployed criminals were responsible for the worst war crimes.[5] A few thousand of these fighters were enough to terrorize several million people.

Croatia and Bosnia and Herzegovina

The conflict in the former Yugoslavia developed in a number of distinct phases. The YNA's failure to prevent Slovenia's independence in June

1991 spelled Yugoslavia's final breakup and presaged armed struggle. While Milošević let Slovenia leave the common state, the Serbian elites in Belgrade and the leaders of the Serbian minority in Croatia announced their resistance to independence. Some 600,000 Serbs lived in Croatia, most of them in Slavonia, and the rural Krajina region, that had been the site of mass violence during World War II. The radical nationalist leaders of the Serbian minority disarmed the Croatian police, occupied strategic positions, and had members of the Croatian elites and supporters of a multiethnic Yugoslavia killed. Vukovar in eastern Slavonia, which was razed to the ground by the YNA's heavy artillery, came to symbolize the devastating impact of the Serbo-Croatian war. After the Serbian invasion, paramilitary units terrorized the population, even opening fire on defenseless hospital patients.[6] The extreme violence of summer and fall 1991 was intended to drive rifts into the still multiethnic society, bring national deviants into line, and induce the remaining Croats to emigrate. Within three months, the Serbian units succeeded in occupying about one-third of Croatia and putting a large part of the local Croatian population to flight.

Encouraged by their advance in Croatia, the Serbian nationalists proceeded in a similar manner in Bosnia. Before the constituent republic of Bosnia and Herzegovina could declare independence following a Serbian-boycotted plebiscite, civil war broke out here, too. Together with assorted paramilitary units, the YNA brought almost all of eastern and northern Bosnia under Serbian control within a few months. Symbolic violence, including public executions, rape in the presence of victims' family members, and the violation of corpses, was inflicted to induce the non-Serbian population to flee. How this was done is conveyed by a personal account of a woman from Drina valley in eastern Bosnian:

> I live in the village Stović near Foča, a small town on the border between Bosnia and Herzegovina and Serbia. 60% of the population in our village are Muslims. The rest are Serbs who were armed by the Yugoslav Federal Army back in 1991. Since then, they have been harassing and threatening Muslims. Our troubles began on April 10, 1991, when Serbs from our village started to shoot our houses by automatic fire. On April 11, we were told that we cannot live here anymore, and that we must leave the village. My husband, two kids and myself got packed and left the village by car. The kids are 8 and 6. 1 kilometer outside the village all the Muslims who were leaving the village were stopped by armed Serbs who were giving us a hard time. That was on April 11, 1992. April 12, I intended to go to the village to take some more clothes for the kids. On the same spot we were stopped by the Serbs, who kept my husband and let me go. When I returned I saw those Serbs gathered around our car. When I approached it, I saw that the car was drilled by bullets. My husband was lying down dead. [...] They chased me away, telling me never

to come back or they would kill me too. I was hiding for about four days to pick up the dead body of my husband and bury him, for they did not let me take him. It was in the fourth night that I took him out and buried him. His body was massacred. His eyes were taken out. A wooden cross was tied to his back. They took all the money we had, namely 5500 DM and 18000 Austrian shillings [...] After the burial, I joined the refugee column that was going towards Goražde. For four days we were hiding in the woods and going on foot. We slept in the open. There were many children with us. On our way we went through a Muslim village Pirni Dol where my aunt and uncle live. I found them dead in front of their burned house. They tied wooden crosses on them too, and their bodies were drilled with bullets. All Muslim houses in the village were burned."[7]

The West protested against the extreme violence but, apart from some half-hearted economic sanctions, imposed only an arms embargo on truncated Yugoslavia. This embargo, intended to prevent the fighting from escalating further, only served to cement the military imbalance.

In summer 1992, Milošević and his regional allies in Croatia and Bosnia appeared to be the certain victors of a short war. This is one reason why the ethnic cleansings in this first phase did not cover wider areas and were not total. Certain regions, such as Bihać in northwest Bosnia, which was controlled by a local Muslim entrepreneur, were exempted. Another reason is that Milošević was more concerned with gaining political and military control of the Greater Serbia he sought to build than with changing the composition of the population on ideological grounds. In Serbia proper and its ethnically mixed regions of Vojvodina and Kosovo as well as in the Muslim-dominated Sandžak, relatively little physical violence was applied, since these regions were already under Milošević's political control. A Belgrade master plan to expel all minorities from the occupied territories has not been discovered and most probably never will be. This was shown in the International Criminal Tribunal for the former Yugoslavia (ICTY) trial against the former chief of staff of the Yugoslav National Army, Momčilo Perišić, who was acquitted in 2013.[8]

Belgrade's regional allies in Croatian Krajina and Bosnia increasingly evaded Milošević's control and pursued a more radical course. The state and army leadership of the Serbian Republic of Bosnia and Herzegovina proclaimed in 1992 (later renamed *Republika Srpska*) proceeded with the clear aim of expelling all Bosniaks and Croats. Their secessionism was based on an ethnically exclusive nationalism that diverged from Milošević's regional imperialism. Nevertheless, the YNA and the Serbian State Security Service (SDB) supported Radovan Karadžić, who was elected the first president of Republika Sprska. Support from Belgrade was also pivotal for building up the Bosnian Serb Army (*Voj-*

ske Republike Srpske, VRS). The YNA supplied tanks and light and heavy arms, which were used locally against the enemy and the civilian populations.

What were the motives behind the extraordinary brutality shown by many members of the "territorial defense" (*Teritorijalna Obrana*), the police, and the VRS toward Bosniaks and Croats as well as any reconciliatory Serbs? Soldiers and the paramilitary were galvanized into action by exaggerations of the threat they faced and the call to protect their immediate homeland and families. To the simple soldier, the willful and excessive violence toward the Bosniaks confirmed the nationalist propaganda in a perversely self-justifying way, since the brutality of their own actions seemed to verify the severity of the threat they were fighting.[9] Moreover, the Serbian propaganda effectively picked up on the enduring trauma of World War II. The flash points of excessive violence in the 1990s corresponded with those in the 1940s. These were in Croatian and Bosnian Krajina, the Drina Valley in eastern Bosnia, and in northern Bosnia—all regions in which the crimes of the Ustasha had claimed an especially high toll two generations previously. In total, this first phase of the war and the ethnic cleansings it involved claimed the most civilian lives.

In summer 1992, the Serbs found themselves confronted by a surprisingly strong resistance, which defended the capital of Sarajevo against the superior might of the VRS. In the second half of the year and early 1993, the Army of Bosnia and Herzegovina (ABiH) even succeeded in liberating parts of eastern Bosnia in the Srebrenica area by means of the guerilla warfare learned from the YNA. Small units under the command of Captain Naser Orić worked their way behind the Serbian front, where they carried out attacks and seized control of substantial areas.

These counterattacks, the strong defense of the regions held by the Bosnian government, and the mounting Bosniak-Croatian conflict mark the second phase of the war and ethnic cleansing. In the context of intensifying warfare, the Bosniak and Croatian civilian populations remaining in the Republika Sprska were expelled almost without exception in 1993.[10] The military rationale behind this measure was to cut off reinforcements to guerilla units and to gain control of the occupied territory. The lost territories in the Srebrenica area were recaptured, the last villages still held by Muslims in the mountainous region of eastern Bosnia captured, and the three remaining Muslim enclaves, Žepa, Goražde, and Srebrenica, drastically reduced.[11] The ethnic cleansings arranged by the VRS in 1993 affected less people than those in 1992 but caused greater trauma. The Bosniaks remaining in the Serbian sphere of control often had to flee chaotically in several stages and were willfully shot at as they tried to escape on foot. The history of ethnic cleansing in Bosnia and Herzegovina shows how a couple of ten-thousand or even less dedicated radical nationalists, who often had a record of childhood abuse, failed careers and criminal activities in Socialist Yugoslavia, could devastate an entire country.[12] The VRS' war against the civilian population also included the shelling and bombing of Sarajevo and the enclaves still under the control of the central government.

The Serbs in Bosnia achieved a series of military successes in the second year of the conflict but lost the war on another, equally crucial front: in international politics and the media. News of the conflict was publicized by newspapers and television stations all over the world. Images were regularly transmitted of Sarajevo under siege, where dozens of civilians were dying weekly, sometimes even daily, in cowardly artillery attacks on food markets and water fountains. Of the 5,600 civilian victims in Sarajevo, 1,133 were Serbs—the highest number of civilian Serb casualties in any Bosnian town or village.[13] Although the involvement of the international media did not redress the imbalance between the military and the civilian population, it shook the general public out of its indifference toward ethnic cleansing. Serbia and its allies were identified as the aggressors and politically isolated. The United Nations declared a large part of the regions still under Bosnian control United Nations Safe Areas. Creating a fait accompli such as Milošević had planned in 1991–92 was no longer possible in this changed international situation.

Yet the UN's efforts to stabilize Bosnia and Herzegovina on the basis of the territorial status quo could not prevent the emergence of a second front. The first skirmishes between Bosnian government troops and Croatian units occurred in late 1992 over mixed regions in central Bosnia. The fighting had been sparked by negotiations over reorganizing Bosnia and Herzegovina along cantonal lines. The UN-commissioned Vance Owen Plan proposed dividing the country into ten territorial units.[14] Acquiring land became strategically imperative for the conflicting sides to influence these veiled partition plans, which were repeatedly revised to keep up with the changing balance of power in Bosnia and Herzegovina. Moreover, since the postwar distribution of land was to be based on population statistics before and during the war, further ethnic cleansings were incorporated into the conflicting sides' strategy.

In April 1993, the Bosniak-Croatian conflict that had been smoldering in the central Bosnian Lašva valley for some time started to rage uncontrollably. It was during the course of this conflict that the old bridge in Mostar was blown up. The advancing Croatian troops committed atrocities such as the massacre of Ahmići. Units of the Croatian Defense Council (HVO), the main military arm of the Croats in Bosnia and Herzegovina, went from house to house, killing the remaining inhabitants, before they razed the entire village.[15] From June 1993, however, the HVO suffered a series of unexpected defeats, indirectly caused by the disastrous refugee crisis. Tens of thousands of young Bosniak men had been rendered homeless, practically driving them into the arms of the government-loyal Bosnian army, the ABiH. There were two-and-a-half times more Bosniaks than Croats in Bosnia and Herzegovina; they also outnumbered the Serbs by a considerable margin. This difference in "manpower," as the Central Intelligence Agency's (CIA) analysts put it in *Balkan Battlegrounds*,[16] compensated to a degree for the ABiH's lack of arms. At this stage, the Croatians no longer held a significant enough advantage over the Bosniaks to create a fait accompli. The United States took the opportunity to forge a lasting alliance between Zagreb and Sarajevo in order to rearm the ABiH and force the VRS onto the defensive.

The continuing influx of refugees created a new social dynamic. The hundreds of thousands of newcomers in need of accommodation put considerable pressure on the remaining minorities. Sixty thousand Croats fled the ABiH's counteroffensive in central Bosnia,[17] partly because—responding to the war propaganda—they did not want to live in an "Islamic state." Bosnia and Herzegovina collapsed into a number of ethnically consolidated subregions.

In 1995, the war and related ethnic cleansings entered their final phase. The Croatian and Bosnian Serbs were weakened by a number of factors, including their international isolation, for which Milošević was partly responsible, and above all a military problem of very long and overstretched front lines. The Bosnian Serbs made up only one-third of the population of Bosnia and Herzegovina, but occupied more than two-thirds of the country. The demographic ratio was even less balanced in Croatia. Although the situation behind the front lines seemed to have been brought under control by the ethnic cleansings of 1993–94, the fronts in the contested regions were too long and geographically complex to be safeguarded permanently. Contrary to the stereotypical image of hypernationalist Serbs, the Republika Sprska had considerable problems mobilizing new recruits and maintaining the strength of its troops. The military balance consequently began to tip in Herzegovina and Croatian Krajina. In 1995, the only chance the Bosnian Serbs had to strengthen their military basis and consolidate their position in the approaching peace talks was to break up the three eastern Bosnian enclaves, Srebrenica, Žepa, and Goražde.

Thus the third, distinctly genocidal phase of ethnic cleansing in the former Yugoslavia began. In July 1995, VRS troops overran the enclave of Srebrenica, a symbol of Bosniak resistance by its very existence since the counteroffensive in winter 1992–93. The ensuing military action has been well documented and does not need to be recounted in detail here.[18] At least three-quarters of the roughly 25,000 inhabitants of the enclave were refugees from other Bosnian towns and villages. Theoretically, they were guaranteed protection by the UN, but the reality was that there were only a few, lightly armed peacekeeping soldiers on the ground. NATO, meanwhile, still wavered on whether to intervene. While the women and children were taken out of Srebrenica in convoys to central Bosnia, the VRS executed 6,975 able-bodied men and youths of sixteen and older and cast their corpses into mass graves.[19] A few thousand men who had evaded capture escaped through the woods. But the areas held by the ABiH were around 70 kilometers away, and the Bosniaks suffered many casualties en route.

Although women and children were spared, this was nevertheless the worst crime against humanity in Europe since World War II. The state and army leadership of the Bosnian Serbs achieved four short-term goals by this mass murder: the occupation of all of eastern Bosnia (except Goražde); revenge for the defeats of 1992–93 and later attacks proceeding from the enclave; a military victory releasing forces to fight on other fronts without driving new recruits to the Bosnian army; and, not least, the humiliation of the UN. The cold-blooded murder and the mass expulsion of another 30,000 people from Srebrenica and Žepa were not, then, prompted by blind hatred, which at most played a role in inciting the men to act, but were rationally calculated maneuvers. Did the VRS under General Ratko Mladić secure any long-term goals in this way? At the Dayton Accords, the Bosnian Serbs were indeed awarded nearly all of eastern Bosnia which they had claimed for the Republika Srpska, including Srebrenica.

But just a few weeks after Srebrenica, the champions of an ethnically pure Greater Serbia failed to avert the loss of extensive areas in Croatian Krajina. Some 180,000 Croatian Serbs were forced to flee during Operation Storm (*Operacija Oluja*) carried out by the army of neighboring Croatia.[20] Again the question arises of why the international community was not able to prevent such foreseeable retaliation from being inflicted on the civilian population. In 1991–92, the West might have been taken by surprise by the criminal actions of the Croatian and Bosnian Serbs and their allies in Belgrade. Halting the advance of the VRS and the subsequent ethnic cleansings at short notice would certainly have proved difficult and would only have been possible by the massive deployment of ground forces. The shifting coalitions and lines of conflict—Tudjman and Milošević had even negotiated dividing Bosnia and Herzegovina—made the political situation confusingly complex.[21] It was difficult, then, to gauge the effect an intervention would have. In 1995, however, the situation was less complex. By this time, an observable pattern of ethnic cleansing had emerged to suggest that there might be more to come. Croatia, its regular army and the HVO were indirectly dependent on the West and its arms supplies. Moreover, Croatia was not in a position to take any UN Safe Areas hostage like the VRS had between 1993 and 1995. Yet the expulsion of and attacks against the remaining Serbs in Croatian Krajina were condemned only in a low voice by the international media and politics. It took many years to capture the main commander of the Croatian army in the area, General Ante Gotovina, and to bring him to trial at the International Court of Justice in The Hague. In 2004, he was sentenced for war crimes and crimes against humanity, among them forced displacement. But in 2011 he was acquitted, thus exonerating the entire Croatian conduct of war.[22]

The empathy and humanitarian aid from the West did not alter the fact that little had been done to stop the ethnic cleansing and other serious violations of human rights. Spectacular relief actions such as the Sarajevo airlift and the planes dropping food supplies on the eastern Bosnian enclaves reacted to the consequences of ethnic cleansing but did not prevent it from occurring—although reports by the UN and various NGOs, which are accessible in the Open Society Archive in Budapest,[23] had urgently warned of the humanitarian disaster as early as summer 1992. In his first report of 28 August 1992, Tadeusz Mazowiecki, the UN's special rapporteur, called for immediate and concerted action, including the neutralization of heavy arms and the disarming of paramilitary units.[24]

A plethora of literature exists on the failure of international politics in the former Yugoslavia. It tends to focus on the European Union's (EU) weakness and the disagreements between the EU and the United States, as well as between individual EU states. Britain and France, in particular, feared the reestablishment of World War II's Berlin-Vienna-Zagreb axis, proving that irrational, conflict-ridden memories were not confined to the Balkans. Most of this literature concludes that the West should have intervened earlier, more resolutely, and not only by means of aerial attacks from a great height. But international pressure on Belgrade and the Republika Srpska achieved at least one thing: the two most notorious concentration camps in northern Bosnia, Omarska and Trnopolje, were closed in August 1992. Norman Cigar criticizes above all the arms embargo, which destroyed the Bosniaks' and, for a time, the Croats' chances of defending themselves against the superior might of the Serbs.[25] Indeed, with hindsight, it emerges that the Bosniaks were victimized on two levels: first, by the ethnic cleansings committed by radical nationalist Serbs and, second, by the Western media and international politics.[26] It would have been more helpful to recognize the Bosniaks as one of the warring parties and to support the legitimate government in Sarajevo with armaments. Like in earlier cases of ethnic cleansing, not all refugees were only victims. The ABiH committed human rights violations in 1993 and 1995 in the conflict with the HVO and when recapturing Serb-occupied regions. Torture and mass shootings occurred then, too, albeit on a far smaller scale than on the Serbian and Croatian sides. Sarajevo was the only party in the conflict to clearly defend a multiethnic state. This fact could have justified the West providing military support to the Bosnian government at an earlier stage against the attacks from the VRS and the HVO. The international community has been painstakingly trying to rebuild just such a state ever since the Dayton Accords. In the final analysis, human rights policies and humanitarian relief actions are sometimes just as poor a substitute for power politics as victim narratives are an alternative to critical historical analyses.

The outcome of the war and ethnic cleansing in the former Yugoslavia remains alarming despite the IDC's revision of the death toll. The number of refugees has not been revised. According to international and regional estimates, in 1991–92 at least half a million people in Croatia fled, and a million people in Bosnia and Herzegovina were put to flight in spring 1992 alone—almost exclusively Bosniaks and Croats. By 1995, the number of refugees in and from Bosnia and Herzegovina had risen to 2.2 million. Toward the end of the war, mostly Serbs were displaced, including 300,000 just from Croatia.[27]

The speed, scale, and, from 1993, totality of these ethnic cleansings confirm the theory that they were carried out with increasing efficiency as the twentieth century progressed. The total of 2.2 million people uprooted—1 million were put up in makeshift accommodation in the country, 1.2 million went abroad—equals more than half of the prewar population of 4.35 million. This was unprecedented in European history. As well as obvious factors such as Greater Serbian nationalism, developments of European modernity also contributed to this. The registry of residents and the use of modern transport systems such as buses and trains—all accessories of an efficient modern state—facilitated these mass population removals. Conversely, internationally organized food donations, transport convoys, and airlifts helped the civilian population in Bosnia and Herzegovina to survive three severe wartime winters. At least, the number of civilian victims was limited to 40,000, which is relatively few for a conventional war on the ground with guerilla operations and deliberately planned expulsions. Today, the residents' registry serves as the basis for the IDC project documenting the place, time, and cause of death of every individual victim of the war. Individualizing events in this way not only underlines the horror and senselessness of the war that also claimed the lives of 57,000 soldiers, but can perhaps also clear a path toward reconciliation.

The war in the former Yugoslavia marks a turnaround in the history of ethnic cleansing in another respect. Although the VRS and paramilitary units like the "Arkan Tigers" were able to occupy two thirds of the territory of Bosnia and Herzegovina and commit horrible crimes against humanity, the international community prevented a military fait accompli. The Serbian plan to simply remove a population group from its home and appropriate its land was frustrated. This failure might act as an equally effective deterrent as the sentences passed by the International Court of Justice in The Hague. Moreover, it was the first time in the history of ethnic cleansing that such a complex and comprehensive return program was resolved, also providing for the restitution of real estate. In principle, all refugees were to return to their hometowns or villages and, providing they were still standing, their houses.[28] But many were now skeptical of life in a multiethnic society, or as part of a minority. Following the withdrawal of the VRS in fall 1995, there was a Serbian exodus from the suburbs of Sarajevo. To many returning refugees, the old homeland did not feel like home anymore, whether because of personally experienced trauma, the changed surroundings, or a lack of confidence in the future locally. The return of property, insofar as it was not destroyed during the war, took time and met with the resistance of the new residents. Due to the global hegemony of neoliberalism in the 1990s, the international community was overly focused on property. But many people had rented their apartments in former Yugoslavia, and their leases were hardly renewed.[29]

Areas where expulsions had occurred were plunged into a deep economic crisis, analogous to the situation in 1923 in western Asia Minor and after 1945 in the Bohemian borderlands. Bosnia and Herzegovina has hardly recovered from the consequences of the war to this day; the situation in Krajina, the Drina Valley, and other ethnically cleansed regions is even worse. For these reasons, only about half a million refugees returned permanently to their homes; the others did not even try, or moved away again once they had sold their property. The reestablishment of a multiethnic society as resolved in Dayton might prove to be just as utopian a venture as the pursuit of ethnic homogeneity.

Kosovo

The peace treaty of 1995 left one more post-Yugoslav question unanswered: the conflict in Kosovo between the Serbs and the two million

Kosovar Albanians. Initially, Milošević, one of the signatories of the Dayton Accords, had almost free rein in the region. Under the informal leadership of writer Ibrahim Rugova, the Kosovar Albanians fought to regain the autonomy they had lost in 1989 by a strategy of nonviolent resistance in parallel with promoting Albanian culture and society. But the authorities in Belgrade had no intention of conceding Rugova's demands. Thus, fighting eventually broke out in Kosovo in 1996, five years after the breakup of Communist Yugoslavia. The Kosovo Liberation Army (*Ushtria Çlirimtare e Kosovës*, UČK) carried out attacks on Serbian police, officials, and collaborators. The authorities in Belgrade responded with ever more drastic reprisals. In 1998, the spiraling conflict turned into outright civil war in which first the UČK and then the Serbian security forces and paramilitary units held the advantage. In this first phase of the war some 300,000 people fled, about 30,000 of them abroad.

The West reacted to the mounting deployment of Serbian troops and increasing human rights violations with massive sanctions against Yugoslavia and secret arms supplies to the Kosovo underground army. Following a NATO ultimatum and the failure of peace talks, Serbia and all its subregions were targeted by heavy aerial attacks from March to June 1999. As threatened, Belgrade retaliated with even more ethnic cleansing. However, the "horseshoe plan" publicized by the international media, aiming to hedge the Kosovar Albanians in on three sides before driving them out to Albania, is probably a fake.[30] NATO air raids in spring 1999 were designed to weaken Milošević's troops and the police in Kosovo and prompt a handover of power in Belgrade, but did not help to protect the civilian Albanian population.

Any moral justification this unprecedented and legally controversial intervention against ethnic cleansing might have had was undermined by the fact that it exposed the Serbian minority in Kosovo to willful reprisals. The West was not able to prevent the exodus of a large part of the remaining Serbian population in 1999 or the anti-Serb pogroms of 2004. A multiethnic society was not, then, reestablished here anymore than in Croatian Krajina. Refugees cannot be forced to return to their former homes.

Conflicts in the Caucasus Compared

The ethnic cleansings in the former Soviet Union took place in very different regions, at different points in time, and had different causes and consequences. The complex history of the post-Soviet cases of the

1990s is, then, characterized by a high level of diversity and has hitherto been little researched. In overall terms, the collapse of the last multinational empire in Europe occurred remarkably peacefully in comparison to Yugoslavia. While special units of the Ministry of the Interior and the Committee for State Security (KGB) tried to violently suppress the independence movement in the Baltic states and Georgia in 1990, this was an isolated episode. After the failed putsch of 1991, the collapse of the Soviet Union gained increasing momentum. All the former Soviet Socialist Republics soon declared independence, including Ukraine with its capital, Kyiv, which is widely considered to be the cradle of Russian and Orthodox culture. On account of the large Russian minorities in the Soviet Union's successor states, some observers feared events mirroring those in Yugoslavia.[31] But there was no agitator here akin to Milošević, challenging the borders of the republics or promoting the myth of national victimization.

The Caucasus was the only region of the former Soviet Union where several violent conflicts broke out. These can be divided into categories of "classic" territorial conflicts between neighboring republics and conflicts within newly independent states. The conflict surrounding the predominantly Armenian-populated enclave Nagorno-Karabakh in Azerbaijan falls into the former category. Over the course of the four-year war between Armenia and Azerbaijan (1988–92), both sides resorted to ethnic cleansing to achieve short-term strategic and long-term political goals. Armenian troops and paramilitary units were most active in the disputed region itself and along the roads leading to the Armenian heartland. In Azerbaijan, in contrast, there were pogroms primarily in larger towns. These launched a major wave of migration in which at least 300,000 Armenians and between 800,000 and a million Azeri fled.[32] A solution for lasting peace that is acceptable to both sides has still not been found in the dispute over Nagorno-Karabakh.

All the other conflicts in the Caucasus were not initially disputes over entry into an external nation-state but over autonomy within a state. Georgia was the site of many conflicts in 1992, at first in Abkhazia, which had been a Soviet republic from 1921 to 1931, then in South Ossetia and the region bordering Turkey. The nearly 100,000 Abkhazi resisted submitting to the central power in Tbilisi after Georgia gained independence. The government, led by nationalist writer Swiad Gamsachurdia, sent in troops, which were repelled. In 1992–93 about 230,000 Georgians were forced out of Abkhazia.[33] As in Bosnia and Herzegovina, the extent of ethnic cleansing varied greatly. While southeastern Abkhazia even retained a Georgian majority, the number of Georgians in the capital of Sukhumi sank from over 40 to 4 percent.[34] These differences point to the influence of local warlords, who also played a major role in Bosnia and Herzegovina.

In contrast to the former Yugoslavia, the conflicting sides in Abkhazia were primarily concerned with the distribution of power rather than with creating ethnic homogeneity. Ten years after the fighting, just over 20 percent Armenians, almost 20 percent Georgians, 10 percent Russians, and a number of smaller groups lived in the region by the Black Sea, along with 43 percent Abkhazi. Georgians and Abkhazi had, then, traded places in the population statistics. This took place in the context of a significant drop in the overall population, which fell from over half a million in 1989 to 215,000 in 2003.

The constellation was similar in South Ossetia in the early 1990s. Unwilling to bow to the authority in Tbilisi, the Iranian-speaking Ossetian elites took up arms. Expulsions on both sides followed. Since the disputed region was only about the size of a county in the United States, the numbers affected were less significant than in Abkhazia. Nevertheless, Georgia and Russia fought a short war over South Ossetia in 2008, which launched renewed refugee movements but has not yet been the focus of historical research.

Another disputed region in the European part of the former Soviet Union is Transnistria. Here, the weak central government of a newly independent former Soviet republic struggled for power with the regional elites. As in Abkhazia, the separatists succeeded in gaining a military advantage and forced the members of the titular nation to flee in spring 1992. About 130,000 Moldavians fled, most of them from the disputed towns of Tighina and Dubasări. As in Sukhumi, however, this was only a local and partial ethnic cleansing, as the proportion of Romanian-speaking Moldavians in the total population of Transnistria only fell by one-fifth, from 40 percent to 32 percent. The rationale behind this borderline case of ethnic cleansing lay in the ideology of prominent Transnistrian actors. As Stefan Troebst has shown, the self-proclaimed president of Transnistria, Igor Smirnov, claimed that the nation-state of Moldavia had been founded on the basis of a Fascist conspiracy, which he sought to counter with his own Soviet-style antinationalism.[35] Whatever the truth of this propaganda, the establishment of ethnic purity was not one of the goals of this regional elite.

This again refutes the paradigm of "Soviet ethnic cleansing." As comparison with the former Yugoslavia shows, the ethnic cleansings in parts of Europe with a longer tradition of nation-state ideology were much more extensive than in the post-Soviet sphere. This does not imply that the Soviet Union was an ideally tolerant multinational empire. All the conflicts considered here that broke out in the early 1990s can be

traced back to the deportations and settlement programs of the Stalinist period. The Soviet Union was a breeding ground for ethnopolitical
conflicts, but these cannot be equated with ethnic cleansing. A third
conclusion can be drawn from the timing of the violent conflicts. With
the exception of Nagorno-Karabakh, violence broke out *after* the former
Soviet republics gained independence and in consequence to disputes
over the internal distribution of power. This confirms the theory that
it was not the collapse of empires but the building of nation-states that
caused most of the violence.

Conclusion

Although the ethnic cleansings of the 1990s took place across much
smaller areas than those of earlier periods, they devastated large parts
of the former Yugoslavia and the Caucasus. The number of refugees
in this fourth phase of ethnic cleansing totaled at least 5 million. This
sum is calculated from the following geographically ordered cases: Croatia, 600,000 (1991–92 and 1995); Bosnia and Herzegovina, 2.2 million
(1992–95); Kosovo, including Serbian refugees, 1 million; Armenia and
Azerbaijan, at least 1.15 million (1990–94); South and North Ossetia,
100,000 (1989–2008); and Transnistria (a borderline case), 130,000 (1992).
The total of 5 million excludes a number of mass flight movements, such
as that in Chechnya, and should therefore be regarded as a minimum.

In contrast to the period after World War II, in nearly all these cases,
the international community supported the remigration of refugees
and devised complex return programs to this end. The success of these
programs depended on the individual political context in each of the
regions concerned. In places where conflicts remained unresolved, such
as Nagorno-Karabakh, only a few refugees were able to return to their
former homes. The resettlement of refugees in Croatian Slavonia and
parts of Bosnia, in contrast, was relatively successful. One-quarter of
the population that was uprooted returned to live in those places as a
minority. In view of the devastation caused by the war, this is a positive
signal. Finally, the revision of earlier ethnic cleansings in the former Soviet Union must be considered, such as that of the Crimean Tatars, who
returned to their previous areas of settlement from 1988 after forty-four
years in exile. This case and the peaceful remigration and integration
of several million ethnic Russians from Central Asia prove that nonviolent solutions predominated in the former Soviet Union. Refugees
from Kosovo were able to return on a massive scale after the balance of
power had changed. Almost all the Albanians who had fled in 1998–99

were able to move back into their houses and apartments, albeit at the expense of the Serbs, Roma, and other groups who in turn emigrated from Kosovo or were forced out. The case of Kosovo shows that military intervention—in this case by NATO—can help stop ethnic cleansing but still fail to rebuild a multiethnic society.

Indeed, for many former refugees, the prospect of return was not appealing. The exodus of hundreds of thousands of Serbs from Croatia and Bosnia in 1995 and from Kosovo in 1999 was not only prompted by the fear of reprisals but also by an unwillingness to live as a minority in a non-Serbian-dominated state or region. Moreover, the international community's neoliberal fixation on returning property was shortsighted and unhelpful to many refugees who had lived in rented Socialist housing. They could not return to their apartments because they had been leased to others in the meantime. Yet at least one-third of the five million refugees of the periods 1991–95 and 1998–99 returned to their old homelands. Thus, the fourth phase of ethnic cleansing reversed the political verdicts of the first phase. Neuilly and Lausanne stood for extending the scope of ethnic cleansing; Dayton was an attempt to contain it and, where possible, to revise it.

The conflicts in the 1990s caused a drastic drop in the population in all the areas concerned. Bosnia and Herzegovina had a population of 3,237,000 in early 1998—one-quarter less than before the war. The population of Abkhazia was reduced by half. The material losses were equally immense: in Bosnia and Herzegovina alone, 1,239 sacred buildings were destroyed, including over 1,000 mosques.[36] The skirmishes between Armenian and Azerbaijani units, which continue to flare up, show that ethnic cleansing cannot guarantee stability after a conflict has ended. While the Cold War constellation and *Pax Sovietica* created a measure of stability in East Central Europe and the Soviet sphere of influence, violent conflict repeatedly broke out in the flash points of the 1940s. Paradoxically, this was due to the lack of contractual arrangements on resettlement. As long as there is no international agreement on ethnic cleansings that have already been carried out, using force to revise them remains a political option. For this reason, too, the integration of the refugees in the countries of reception is only just beginning. In Bosnia and Herzegovina, peace could only be secured in the context of an international protectorate.

But this is not the place to go into conflict mediation. Sociologist Peter Waldmann has demonstrated by the example of Northern Ireland how difficult it is to contain violence and integrate the agents of conflict in democratic processes and civilian working life.[37] Revising ethnic cleansing and guaranteeing nonviolent coexistence poses an even greater challenge. Beyond Europe, the chances of it being accomplished are even slimmer. In Darfur, for example, millions of people have been driven into exile in recent years in full view of the public without any acute consequences for the Sudanese authorities. The unanimous international disapproval of contractually arranged forced resettlements has double-edged consequences for refugees. Return is only possible in exceptional cases. But as long as this prospect exists, no reception state will seek to integrate the newcomers. History has shown that refugees whose status is not recognized often do not settle in their new home, but remain metaphorically poised to move on. The example of the Palestinians shows that having little or no hope of returning, insecure prospects in one's reception country, and no active government support aiding integration is the worst possible scenario.

Notes

1. Documentation was available on the IDC's website at http://www.idc.org.ba/index.php, last accessed 20 February 2011. After a financial scandal, the IDC closed and the site is no longer available as of this printing.
2. See Susan Woodward, *Balkan Tragedy: Chaos and Dissolution after the Cold War* (Washington DC, 1995). Woodward's book is a very early yet conclusive product of the political realist school.
3. See Valère P. Gagnon, *The Myth of Ethnic War: Serbia and Croatia in the 1990s* (Ithaca, NY, 2004).
4. See the seminal book by Holm Sundhaussen, *Jugoslawien und seine Nachfolgestaaten, 1943–2011* (Vienna, 2012).
5. On the social profile of these fighters, see Marie-Janine Calic, *Krieg und Frieden in Bosnien-Hercegovina: Erweiterte Neuausgabe* (Frankfurt, 1995), 141–48.
6. See the "Vukovar Hospital" trial in The Hague at http://www.icty.org/case/mrksic/4 (accessed 14 August 2010).
7. Quoted from Open Society Archive (OSA), HU OSA, 304-0-3, Box 2, Sheet 659. Report by Zuhra Džuderia on May 30, 1992. See more accounts of the violation of corpses and etching nationalist symbols on prisoners in the personal records collected by the NGO "Save The Humanity" in the spring and summer of 1992. See Open Society Archive (OSA), HU OSA, 304-0-3, Box 2, Sheets 667 and 669.
8. The main reason for his acquittal on appeal was that a direct chain of command could not be proven. See the court ruling at http://www.icty.org/x/cases/perisic/acjug/en/130228_judgement.pdf (accessed 12 April 2013).
9. On the motivations for going to war, especially on the ground in the disputed areas of Bosnia and Herzegovina, see Tomislav Dulic, "Yugoslavs in Arms: Guerrilla Tradition, Total Defence and the Ethnic Security Dilemma." *Europe-Asia Studies* 62, no. 7 (2010): 1051–72.
10. On the fate of the Bosniaks still remaining in Republika Srpska, see the excellent case study by *Armina Galijaš, Eine bosnische Stadt im Zeichen des Krieges: Ethnopolitik und Alltag in Banja Luka (1990–1995)* (München, 2011).
11. On the course of the war in eastern Bosnia, see the CIA analysis *Balkan Battlegrounds: A Military History of the Yugoslav Conflict, 1990-1995.* vol. 1, By the Office

of Russian and European Analysis, Central Intelligence Agency (Washington: 2002), 184–86.

12. The individual cases of perpetrators presented by Sundhaussen, *Jugoslawien und seine Nachfolgestaaten,* 381–96.

13. The statistics on victims in Sarajevo are accessible on the website of the IDC. See http://www.idc.org.ba/index.php?option=com_content&view=section&id=35&Itemi d=126&lang=bs (accessed 2 August 2010).

14. On the Vance Owen Plan and its many variations, see Steven L. Burg and Paul S. Shoup, *The War in Bosnia-Hercegovina: Ethnic Conflict and International Intervention* (Armonk, 1999), 189–262.

15. CIA, *Balkan Battlegrounds,* 192. Details of this and other war crimes were dealt with in the ICTY trials against members of a special unit of the HVO. See http://www.icty .org/case/bralo/4 (accessed 17 August 2010). See also the proceedings against HVO general Tihomir Blaškić at http://www.icty.org/case/blaskic/4 (accessed 17 August 2010). On the conflict as a whole, see Željko Ivanković and Dunja Melčić, "Der bosniakisch-kroatische 'Krieg im Kriege,'" in *Der Jugoslawien-Krieg: Handbuch zu Vorgeschichte, Verlauf und Konsequenzen,* ed. Dunja Melčić (Opladen, 1999), 423–45.

16. See *Balkan Battlegrounds.*

17. Ibid., 194–95.

18. On Srebrenica, as well as Dutch publications (e.g., the very detailed account in Ger Duijzings, *Geschiedenis en herinnering in Oost-Bosnië: De achtergonden von de val van Srebrenica* [Amsterdam, 2002]), see also the ICTY proceedings against VRS general and some-time commander of the Drina Corps, Radislav Krstić, at http://www .icty.org/case/krstic/4 (accessed 17 August 2010).

19. All the statistics on casualties given here are accessible on the website of the IDC in Sarajevo. See http://www.idc.org.ba/index.php?option=com_content&view=section &id=35&Itemid=126&lang=bs (accessed 2 August 2010).

20. On the course of this ethnic cleansing, see the case records against the Croatian general and commander-in-chief of Operation Storm, Ante Gotovina, and the two co-accused persons at http://www.icty.org/case/gotovina/4 (accessed 18 August 2010). On the number of refugees, see Matthias Vetter and Dunja Melčić, "Synopse zu Opfern, Schäden und Flüchtlingen," in Melčić, *Der Jugoslawien-Krieg,* 527.

21. These plans were discussed in March 1991 at a secret meeting in Karadjordje. Recently, further documents showing the cooperation between Serbia and Croatia have come to light, including the war diary of the head of the VRS, Ratko Mladić. See the newspaper *Süddeutsche Zeitung,* no. 130, 10 June 2010.

22. On his indictment, see http://www.icty.org/x/cases/gotovina_old/ind/en/got-ai040224e .htm. On his acquittal, see http://www.icty.org/cases/party/691/4 (accessed 16 October 2013).

23. See the holdings HU OSA, 304-0-2 (International Human Rights Law Institute, Interim and Supplementary Reports of the UN Special Rapporteur). See also HU OSA 304-0-6 (International Human Rights Law Institute, Materials on Ethnic Cleansing); HU OSA 304-0-4 (International Human Rights Law Institute, United Nations, International Red Cross Committee, International Court of Justice).

24. See the report on the human rights situation in the territory of the former Yugoslavia submitted by Mr. Tadeusz Mazowiecki, Special Rapporteur of the Commission on Human Rights, UN Document E/CN.4/1992/S-1/9. All Mazowiecki's reports are accessible on the website of the High Commissioner for Human Rights at http:// www.unhchr.ch/Huridocda/Huridoca.nsf/73f0f4bfad30544b80256633004b698c/ 42b34825c70b136c802566330057676b?OpenDocument&Start=73.2.14&Count=30 &Expand=73.2. (accessed 18 August 2010).

25. See Norman Cigar, *Genocide in Bosnia: The Policy of "Ethnic Cleansing"* (College Station, TX, 1995), 174–77. A critique of Cigar's terminology or other aspects of his book would go beyond the scope of this book. On how the ABiH finally managed to become armed and stop the ethnic cleansings, see Marko A. Hoare, *How Bosnia Armed: The Birth and Rise of the Bosnian Army* (London, 2004).

26. On the media involvement, see the comprehensive press documentation in HU OSA 304-0-12 (International Human Rights Law Institute, Press Reports on War in Bosnia).

27. On all refugee statistics given here and in the following paragraph, see Vetter and Melčić, "Synopse."

28. On the return of refugees, see Gerard Toal and Carl T. Dahlman, *Bosnia Remade: Ethnic Cleansing and its Reversal* (New York, 2011).

29. See Caroline Leutloff-Grandits, *Claiming Ownership in Post-War Croatia: The Dynamics of Property Relations and Ethnic Conflict in the Knin Region* (Münster, 2006).

30. On the course of ethnic cleansings in Kosovo, see Brandes, Sundhaussen, and Troebst, *Lexikon der Vertreibungen,* 356–57.

31. On the collapse of the Soviet Union, see Roman Szporluk, *Russia, Ukraine and the Breakup of the Soviet Union* (Palo Alto, CA, 2000).

32. In the mid-1990s, 340,000 refugees from abroad were registered in Armenia. See Brandes, Sundhaussen, and Troebst, *Lexikon der Vertreibungen,* 50–51 and 58–59.

33. On Abkhazia, see Brandes, Sundhaussen, and Troebst, *Lexikon der Vertreibungen,* 266–67.

34. The statistics from censuses in Abkhazia from 1886 to 2003 are accessible at http:// www.ethno-kavkaz.narod.ru/rnabkhazia.html (accessed 27 August 2010). They are from the Russian State Archive for Economy (РГАЭ) and Abkhazi sources (for 2003).

35. See Stefan Troebst, "Separatistischer Regionalismus als Besitzstandswahrungsstrategie (post-)sowjetischer Eliten: Transnistrien 1989–2002," in Ther and Sundhaussen, *Regionalismen,* 185–214.

36. On the former Yugoslavia, see Vetter and Melčić, "Synopse," 524–25. On Abkhazia, see Brandes, Sundhaussen, and Troebst, *Lexikon der Vertreibungen,* 266.

37. See Peter Waldmann, "Konfliktkontinuität versus Friedensdynamik in Nordirland," in Ther and Sundhaussen, *Nationalitätenkonflikt,* 219–38.

CONCLUSION AND HISTORICAL TYPOLOGY

⌘₰₰—

The Four Phases of Ethnic Cleansing

The history of ethnic cleansing adds further shading to Mark Mazower's metaphor of the "dark continent," blackening points with the gloom of mourning and loss. At least thirty million people in Europe alone were forced to permanently leave their homelands over the course of all four phases of ethnic cleansing. This number should be seen in relation to the total of twenty-five million recognized minority members in Europe after World War I estimated at the Paris Peace Conference of 1919. Moreover, majority populations were also affected by border changes and subsequent population removals. Even mixed marriages and people with no clear national identity were persecuted in many countries. Although most European countries still have at least one officially accepted national minority (the postwar labor migrants or *Gastarbeiter* were never accepted as such), these statistics show how far the entire continent was homogenized.

The number of refugees rose almost exponentially over the course of the twentieth century, from 2.8 million in the first period (1912 until the mid-1920s), to 6.4 million under German occupation and hegemony and within the Soviet Union (1938–44), to 16 million as a consequence of postwar territorial reorganization (1944–49). Taking the lands formerly under British rule in India and Palestine into account, another 12.8 million people must be added to the list. In the 1990s, about 5 million people were uprooted in Europe and the Caucasus, which belongs as much as Asia Minor in any broad consideration of European history.

These forty-three million are only the officially registered refugees and therefore constitute a minimum number. Including borderline cases such as those deported during World War I, those temporarily deported to perform forced labor during World War II, and the millions of ethnic migrants after 1919, the number is far higher. Moreover, millions of ethnic Germans and other remaining minorities emigrated from Eastern European states in the postwar period as an indirect consequence of previous ethnic cleansings. All in all, the sum of those affected far exceeds the number of immigrant workers moving around the continent after 1945, which is often overlooked in migration history. However, the aim here is not to present sensational or symbolically charged statistics, but to highlight the dynamics of these inhuman processes.

Ever larger-scale plans and increasingly comprehensive targeting caused a drastic rise in ethnic cleansings in the first half of the twentieth century. In the first organized forced resettlements affecting Macedonia, Thrace, and Alsace, Greece, Bulgaria, and France removed around one-third of their respective minorities in these regions. Even the allies of Nazi Germany did not remove larger shares of their minority populations. The ethnic cleansings of 1944–48, however, were virtually total. Only a small proportion of each affected minority was able to remain in their homeland. This spatial and demographic escalation cannot be attributed to hate or other emotions. The decision to remove specific population groups from their homes and way of life was typically made on the basis of political considerations and diplomatic negotiations.

The course ethnic cleansings were to take was set in the international arena. The sequence of the Paris Peace Treaties gives an early indication of a tendency away from protecting and toward eliminating minorities in the first phase of ethnic cleansing. In terms of both international law regulations and the practical execution of "population exchange," the Treaty of Neuilly set a precedent, not the Treaty of Lausanne, which is often cited in this context. Neuilly provided for the minority populations on either side of the Greek-Bulgarian border to change places. Because they did not volunteer to emigrate, the principles of voluntariness and reciprocity written into the Treaty of Neuilly were revoked. This policy change took place against the background of the Greco-Turkish War, when the Greek government settled the majority of refugees from Asia Minor in the disputed regions bordering on Bulgaria, thus destroying the local social balance. Here, as in many later cases, ethnic homogenization by means of forced emigration was coupled with demographic transformation by means of purposeful settlement.

Later, the Treaty of Lausanne marked a turning point by lifting the constraints on the geographic range of ethnic cleansing. Neuilly "only" affected the border region in northern Macedonia; Lausanne concerned an area more than ten times that size. With one regional exception on each side (Istanbul and western Thrace), it provided for the ethnic cleansing of two entire nation-states. But the first signs of such an almost total "solution" being accepted were already discernible in earlier diplomatic talks between Greece and the Ottoman Empire and in the Treaty of Sèvres. The fateful legacy of Neuilly and Lausanne was that they were regarded as models for solving domestic and international conflicts.

In East Central Europe, no ethnic cleansings took place on a comparative scale after 1918. France, however, set a negative example for dealing with minorities in Alsace and Lorraine, in opposition to the Paris Peace Treaties' regulations on protecting minorities. The Geneva Convention on Upper Silesia of 1922 also effected a drastic reduction of the minorities on both sides, German and Polish. Minorities rather than the nation-state order created in 1918–20 were increasingly regarded as the cause of the problems erupting throughout Europe.

The Munich Agreement of 1938, the beginning of the second phase of ethnic cleansing, marked an even more significant change. The four signatory states abandoned the minority protection provided for by the Paris Peace Treaties in favor of rearranging the borders of Europe along ethnic lines. The new borders were to be consolidated by mass population removals, in most cases on both sides. The continuation of this program in the First and Second Vienna Awards served to engender further strife between the countries and societies affected. While the Munich Agreement and its successor treaties betray elements of continuity with the first phase of ethnic cleansing, the one-sided expulsions under German occupation and the chain of ethnic cleansings linking several countries in Nazi-ruled Europe were unprecedented.

Ultimately, the German Reich was not able to put more than a fraction of its megalomaniac plans into practice, since invading the Soviet Union and destroying the European Jews consumed all its available resources. Yet under Germany's influence, the German-allied revisionist states Hungary, Romania, and Bulgaria also took purposeful action against the minorities in their recaptured border territories. While their purgative form of nationalism should not be equated with Nazi racism, the latter was a significant motive prompting them to hand over their Jewish minorities to the Germans, which can also be regarded as a form of ethnic cleansing. This should be distinguished from cases of internal genocide, such as that of the Romanian Jews under the Antonescu regime in 1941–43 and that of the Jews, Roma, and Serbs by the Ustasha in Croatia. The industrial mass destruction of the Holocaust, however, remains an exceptional crime against humanity in European history.

The Western powers, of course, disassociated themselves from Europe's reorganization under Nazi supremacy. Nevertheless, attitudes to minorities were characterized by continuity. This is especially strikingly illustrated by Great Britain's revocation of the Munich Agreement in 1942, which symbolized a turn away from appeasement and promised to restore the integrity of Czechoslovakia. But at the same time, the British government agreed to the "transfer" of a large part of the German minority in Czechoslovakia and thus to an ethnic border, as in 1938. Where the eastern border of Poland was concerned, the Allies adhered to the Molotov-Ribbentrop Pact and the Nazi-Soviet repatriation agreement of 1940. The Treaty of Craiova between Romania and Bulgaria was also silently retained. Moreover, the Allies adopted the strategy of forging a chain of ethnic cleansings by shifting Poland westward.

In contrast to the discussions and treaties after World War I, which focused on the concept of population *exchange,* in the periods 1938–44 and until 1949, population *transfer,* that is, one-sided forced migrations, became the key idea. Transfers did not require two parties to agree, and thus marked a paradigm shift in terms of both a limitation and a removal of restraints. On the one hand, transfers could only affect one nation but, on the other, they could be carried out in a number of directions. The concept of transfer stems from British discourse; it was advanced by the Peel Commission in 1937 and the Foreign Research and Press Service, made up of distinguished Oxford professors, and later the British government.

In the event, one-sided population transfers were only enforced on Germany, the aggressor and main loser of World War II. The only similar case was that of the Finns from Karelia. But they, in contrast to the Germans, had a responsible government, which evacuated all civilians before the Red Army's invasion. All other cross-border ethnic cleansings between 1944 and 1948, the third phase of ethnic cleansing, were reciprocal, at least on paper.

The consensus on population transfers started to slip as soon as the Allies were confronted with the consequences of their resolutions: millions of homeless, sick and malnourished refugees in their zones of occupation in postwar Germany. The subsequent bilateral agreements, drawn up between several Central and Southeast European countries in 1946–47, show the international community reverting to the idea of population exchange and the example of Lausanne. In the context of the postwar period, this return to the policy of population exchange limited the extent of population removals. It is possible to conclude, then, that the German war of aggression and occupation terror provoked a particularly drastic counterreaction: Germans were removed from all neighboring countries where they might be the cause of future trouble. Hence, the German case took on unique dimensions not only on account of retrospective score settling but equally because of the victors' forward-looking plans.

These plans went far beyond the removal of the German minorities from Poland and Czechoslovakia. After World War II, the victorious powers were determined to create homogenous nation-states in the entire larger region of East Central Europe. For this reason, in addition to twelve million Germans, millions of Poles and many Ukrainians, Byelorussians, and Hungarians were shifted around Europe like Churchill's matches on the conference table in Tehran. But when the Allies were confronted with the results of their decisions in postwar Germany, they began to doubt the usefulness of ethnic cleansing and became worried about its side-effects. In the case of the Germans, further treaties were concluded in the winter of 1946 in order to better organize their "transfer".

In the Danube basin, the removal of minority populations was halted or restricted, and in some cases even reversed. The Soviet Union played a pivotal role in this change. In 1945, it allowed the return of most Hungarian refugees to Transylvania, and gave Czechoslovakia a clear signal to interrupt the expulsion of its Hungarian minority. The reason for limiting and eventually halting ethnic cleansing in the southern part of East Central Europe was power politics. It was harder to stabilize the peoples' democracies and, in the mid term, establish Communist regimes when there were millions of uprooted people in the streets. Stalin also aimed to increase his influence on Hungary, and therefore refrained from penalizing this most loyal ally of the Nazis in the same way he had collectively punished the Germans. Moreover, Stalin and the native Communists of Romania and Yugoslavia defined these two largest countries of Southeastern Europe as multiethnic states, withdrawing the ideological basis for further population removals. Stalin did not, however, take this as an opportunity to advance an alternative model to the nation-state, either on an international level or within his sphere of influence.

The Soviet show of restraint, which was most instrumental in developing Allied policy, was paralleled by doubts about the utility of ethnic cleansing and, subsequently, by normative debates in the British and American public. Media reports from postwar Germany and its eastern neighbors showed the plight of the refugees, which had been largely ignored during the spring and summer of 1945. The criticism of the ensuing humanitarian disaster fed well into the human rights discourse that was intensifying as a result of the emerging Cold War constellation. This might explain why the Paris Peace Treaties in 1947 were the last international agreements based on the earlier consensus on ethnic cleansing. When India and Palestine descended into mass violence and war over the postcolonial order in 1947–48, the great powers did not arrange international conferences like in Potsdam in 1945 or in Lausanne in 1923 to organize and regulate mass-scale ethnic cleansing.

As shown in the chapter above, in India and Palestine, the British government provided political and logistic support for reshuffling populations, e.g. by evacuating and transporting refugees, but no longer acted as masterminds of ethnic cleansing. The Israeli government recognized the waning consensus for population shifts and acted with reticence. Neither David Ben Gurion nor his cabinet members proudly announced the transfer of the Arab population as the postwar Polish and Czechoslovak governments had propagated the transfer of the Germans. The governments of India and Pakistan soon became aware of the economic disaster triggered by the mass exodus of their Muslim and Hindu minorities. In 1948, they took steps to halt the violence and even concluded a treaty to stop and reverse some of the ethnic cleansing in 1950. Thus, the third phase of ethnic cleansing petered out in the second half of the 1940s and finally ended when the Cold War constellation concretized.

In the postwar period, the international context was changed by the widespread rejection of ethnic cleansing. The prominence of the human rights discourse and the increasing experience and appreciation of societal diversity precluded public approval of large-scale population removals. The international community was truly shocked about the violence and ethnic cleansing in Yugoslavia. This shock might serve as a more benign explanation, besides inner conflicts and political inertia, why the European Union and the international community remained inactive for such a long time.

Nevertheless, the influence of the international community helped to contain ethnic cleansings in the 1990s, the fourth phase of ethnic cleansing. It remained limited to three federal republics of the former Yugoslavia and certain regions of the Caucasus. There was no ethnic cleansing in parts of Europe where it had occurred before. The Soviet Union was dissolved with very little violence except in the Caucasus. In the first half of the twentieth century, similar circumstances of a crumbling empire, subsequent power vacuum and a new order of nation-states being established in ethnically mixed areas had resulted in much worse and larger-scale ethnic cleansing.

Yet despite the international community's explicit disapproval of population removals, radical nationalists in the former Yugoslavia and the Caucasus put millions of people to flight within the space of a few months. Once again, achievements of European modernity played a key role here. Population statistics, modern infrastructure, transportation, and logistics allowed ethnic cleansings to be drastically extended. Modern weaponry compounded the asymmetry between perpetrators and civilians targeted for removal. But achievements of the modern age also made humanitarian relief actions possible. The airlift enabled the inhabitants of Sarajevo to survive the over three-year siege of the city, convoys of trucks with food supplies fed hundreds of thousands of refugees in Bosnia and Herzegovina. For this reason, the loss of life among the refugees remained lower than in previous periods of ethnic cleansing.

As in comparable, earlier conflicts, the most civilian lives in Bosnia and Herzegovina were claimed in the first phase of the war, when the invading army units overran local populations, treating them as combatants. Moreover, the Bosniaks were humiliated by means of mass rape and similar atrocities. Ultimately the Serbs lost the war precisely because they relied entirely on the use of violence. A contractual settlement accepting part of the Serbian fait accompli was put on the agenda several times in 1992–93, but large-scale ethnic cleansing did not find international approval. The Dayton Accord ending the war in Bosnia and Herzegovina tried to reverse ethnic cleansing and organize the return of the refugees. Most of them did not return for a variety of reasons shown in chapter 5, above all fear of further persecution and a lack of economic prospects. Nevertheless, the Dayton Accord marks an endpoint in the long history of ethnic cleansing in Europe.

The escalation of the Kosovo-conflict in 1998/99 needs to be mentioned in this summary since it was directly related to the Dayton Accord. The NATO intervened in the Kosovo conflict in order to prevent a repetition of the Bosnian scenario in 1992 with a Serbian military, paramilitary units and police expelling hundreds of thousands of people. Eventually, the West got a scenario like in the Croatian region of Krajina in 1995: the Serbs were driven out of their homes and left to fend for themselves. As in other constellations, the ethnic homogenization continued when the war had ended.

Ethnic Cleansing during Wars and after Wars

The typology of ethnic cleansing presented here is not based on the kind of theoretical models used in social sciences, but on empirical findings derived from the study of all four major phases of ethnic cleansing. The character of ethnic cleansing depended on five major variables, the first being whether it occurred during or after wars. This also influenced the kind of violence which was applied. A closely related distinguishing factor to the two above is that between contractual ethnic cleansing and ethnic cleansing unregulated by treaty. Since most cases of ethnic cleansing were covered by international contracts, this helps draw a line between this inhumane practice and genocide—the fourth distinction discussed in this final chapter. Last, but not least, one can distinguish retrospective from forward-looking ethnic cleansing. These distinctions might appear moot at first glance, but they often determined between life and death, and the level of traumatization of the refugees.

Ethnic cleansings occurring in the context of armed conflict generally claimed the highest toll in all four phases. Refugees became caught in the cross fire and were typically only able to flee to safety in a number of stages, during which they were exposed to sniper fire and targeted like the military. It was mostly in this context that entire villages were burned down along with their remaining inhabitants. These extreme cases were committed either as revenge for previous acts of violence or to intimidate populations. The death toll rose accordingly. Ethnic cleansings during war claimed the lives of up to 10 percent of all refugees. Examples for this especially costly variant of ethnic cleansing occurred in Volhynia and parts of eastern Galicia and in the most contested parts of the eastern German territories, such as East Prussia and Silesia on the right bank of the Oder. The proportion of Greeks who died during the Greco-Turkish War in Asia Minor was probably larger but can no longer be verified.

The mortality rates and general trauma suffered during population shifts regulated by international treaties contrast strikingly with this. In some cases, such as the Nazi *Heim ins Reich* resettlement campaign and the Bulgarian-Romanian population exchange under the Treaty of Craiova, virtually no rise in the mortality rate was recorded, although the aged and very young among the migrants would certainly not have taken their "transplantation" with ease. The Sudeten Germans were at greater risk, suffering a number of massacres in spring 1945 (including during the Prague uprising, at Postoloprty and Ustí). Yet the death toll in relation to the total number of refugees from Czechoslovakia was still only 1 percent at most, indicating that the rate was even lower after the Potsdam Agreement.[1]

The situation in postwar Poland was worse for a number of reasons, not only for the remaining Germans but also for the ethnic Poles sent to settle the region. The frequent conflicts between the Red Army and the Polish administration, interior conflicts in the Polish government and the large scale destructions in the last phase of World War II all contributed to a situation of general chaos, insecurity and food shortage. In the former eastern Polish territories, in contrast, the supply situation began to improve in summer 1945, not least because the evacuations to the west ran more smoothly. Lower mortality rates also suggest there was less disease and physical abuse. Finally, the fate of refugees depended to a degree on whether they were able to retain any possessions. Fleeing in a rush from the advancing front or local aggressors, just escaping with one's life, or having time to pack a few bags with food and clothing made a huge difference for the postwar lives of the refugees.

The ethnic cleansing in Croatia and Bosnia and Herzegovina does not fit the pattern of cases occurring during and after a war, since the atrocities all took place during armed conflict. However, there were areas, where almost no fighting took place, while the mass violence in other regions echoed the events of World War II. The formal conclusion of a peace treaty or one side's capitulation rarely marked a clear turning point in any case of ethnic cleansing; a more crucial factor was how long active armed conflict continued in regional contexts.

Conversely, a war could last longer in the minds of the population than it did on paper. The conduct of the Polish and Czechoslovakian armies and administrations in spring and summer 1945 shows that they were to a large extent still mentally at war. Their treatment of the remaining Germans improved after the Potsdam Agreement, when the Allies decided to completely remove the German minority from East Central Europe. This was partly in response to the wishes of the governments in Warsaw and Prague, which had come to the realization that systematic abuse ultimately slowed the progress of the "transfer." The hate propaganda abated and violent criminals no longer had the same scope for action as in May or June 1945.

It is especially important to differentiate between flight, expulsion, and forced resettlement in the case of the Germans because they had very different repercussions for the people affected. Many Nazi functionaries were able to escape to the West with considerable assets, even very late in the war. They started a new life in relative comfort, often without being subjected to de-Nazification, by claiming, for example, that all their personal documents had been lost during expulsion. It was the "ordinary folk" who typically got entangled in the advancing front and lost all their possessions and frequently also their health or even their lives. These differences become blurred if all the groups and individuals affected by ethnic cleansing are placed in the same category of victims.

It should, moreover, be remembered that many refugees had previously taken sides in persistent conflicts, such as the long-standing chairperson of the Sudeten German Expellee Association, Lodgman von

Auen, who had demanded the mass resettlement of Czechs even before the war. Sometimes refugees became the agents of new conflicts and intensified them. Some examples are the Balkan Muslims following their arrival in eastern Thrace, the Greeks from Asia Minor in Macedonia, and the Punjabis in Delhi. Reception places were often so overcrowded that local minorities were displaced to accommodate the refugees.

Forms of Violence

The last point in the subchapter above relates to the topos of violence and its various forms. Acts of direct revenge were rare, since there was little opportunity for them in circumstances when the fortunes of war and front lines were changing quickly. Retributive violence was mostly instigated by political leaders who wanted to drum up popular support by fueling the hatred of former or actual enemies of war. Acts of violence were often committed with the intention to intimidate, including public beatings and executions and the violation of corpses. In his book about the former Yugoslavia, Holm Sundhaussen has presented some biographies of perpetrators. His portrayal and the documented cases at the ICTY used for this book show that quite often the perpetrators had a criminal record or descended from families with a tradition of abuse and violence.[2] Traumatization by previous ethnic cleansing or experiences of war also played a significant role.

But it is remarkable how swiftly mass violence could be halted once the military or state authorities gave the order. Plundering, physical abuse or shootings often ended as quickly as they had started. This was especially noticeable in Czechoslovakia and Poland in the spring and summer of 1945. The concentration camps in northern Bosnia, where Bosniaks experienced the worst abuses in 1992, were also closed when the international community became aware of them and threatened sanctions. The changing behavior of medium and even low level agents of ethnic cleansing shows that a lot depended on the tolerance or even support of extreme violence given by the respective authorities.

There is another, more organized and lasting form of violence, which is illustrated by the example of the Czech borderlands and the former eastern territories of Germany in 1945. The public beatings and killings here mostly stopped in the summer of 1945. After the Potsdam agreement, the vanquished enemy was exposed to a rationalized kind of violence. Now, the defeated Germans were exploited by being made to perform a maximum amount of work in return for minimum provisions. Experiencing the complete transformation of their familiar environment, these Germans were longing to leave what they often described as a kind of hell.

This change in forms of violence can to a certain extent be applied to the twentieth century in general. From a *longue durée* perspective, violence was increasingly rationalized and brought under state control. Though the regulation of ethnic cleansing brought mortality rates down and thus distinguished it from genocide, it made this inhumane practice possible on an unprecedented scale. In terms of iconography, ethnic cleansings are often typified by treks of walking refugees, but cattle trucks or goods trains would actually be more appropriate symbols. The rationalization of violence minimized death tolls but resulted in dehumanizing all those involved.

Unregulated and Contractual Ethnic Cleansing

Levels and forms of violence also depended on a third major distinction to be made in this typology: contractual ethnic cleansing and ethnic cleansing unregulated by treaty. The most and by far the most extensive ethnic cleansings in Europe were carried out pursuant to international arrangements. However, population shifts that were entirely contractually arranged were rare, occurring above all in Nazi-ruled Europe. Cases in point are the ethnic cleansings following the First and Second Vienna Awards, the Treaty of Craiova, and the Nazis' *Heim ins Reich* resettlement program, as well as the population exchange under the Treaty of Neuilly twenty years previously.

Most treaties were concluded subsequent to mass violence and a phase of flight. It was therefore often claimed ex post facto that they merely confirmed the status quo, justifying the ethnic cleansings they provided for. This can be empirically refuted by a number of arguments. First, the Treaty of Lausanne was the only example in the twentieth century in which the same number of people actually fled during the war (some 500,000 or, according to other sources, 750,000) as were subsequently contractually resettled (approximately 750,000).[3] In all other cases, the number of those contractually forcibly resettled far exceeded the number of refugees and deportees. Second, mass flight can be halted or reversed even in unfavorable conditions. This is demonstrated by the example of Transylvania in 1945, the history of Bengal in the early 1950s, and the partial return of refugees in the former Yugoslavia from 1995. Third, many refugees—whose personal motivations are often overlooked—attempted to return to their old homeland on their own initiative and even at considerable risk to their lives. Examples are the roughly one million Silesians who returned to their old homeland in spring 1945 from the Sudetenland and other temporary places of refuge. But the Potsdam Agreement then ordered the transfer of the entire German population, which implied the prohibition of their return.

The contractual arrangement of ethnic cleansing led to the extension of this inhuman practice. The treaties concerned could at most be justified by the fact that they prevented worse violations of human rights and humanitarian disasters, although this was always a secondary objective. The 1990s were the only phase of ethnic cleansing in which no international treaties on population exchanges or transfers were concluded. On the contrary, the international community now supported the repatriation of refugees. It is questionable whether this was primarily motivated by humanitarian considerations. Relieving the potential reception countries in the West and their welfare systems of the burden of permanently accommodating the refugees from Bosnia or the Caucasus was certainly an equally pressing concern.

Whether the provisions of contracts on ethnic cleansing were actually observed is another story. In general, this was more likely to be the case if representatives of the nationality to be removed were involved in negotiations and could at least partially influence the course of ethnic cleansing. The bilateral Polish-Soviet treaties of 1944 and all other treaties of 1946-47 enabled the weaker side to intervene against the grossest violations of human rights. A controlling device of this kind was missing in the case of the "transfer" of the Germans. They were forcibly resettled on the basis of the Potsdam Agreement, a multilateral treaty made without the involvement of their national government but subject to the intervention of the occupying powers. Moreover, the Potsdam Agreement did not contain any concrete resolutions on the transport of luggage or supply of provisions. Nevertheless, if one compares the forced resettlement under the Potsdam Agreement with the non-contractual expulsion of the Germans from Yugoslavia, the positive effect of contractual arrangements on the course and immediate aftermath of ethnic cleansing is clear. The loss of life among the Danube Swabians was several times higher than among the Sudeten Germans and the Lower Silesians.

Still, the provisions of contracts were by no means carved in stone. There was a huge discrepancy between the terms of even the most detailed agreements, such as the Polish-Soviet evacuation treaties of 1944, which provided for those affected taking much of their mobile assets and livestock, and how they were actually implemented. The forcibly resettled were rarely treated fairly, let alone considerately. Physical abuse and the pillaging of migrants' last remaining possessions were common occurrences. The transports themselves posed a certain risk to the migrants' lives and health, varying in severity according to the time of year. The mere fact that most refugees were transported in cattle trucks says much about attitudes toward them. But journeys in specially provided train carriages or organized treks were easier to endure than spontaneous flight or expulsion. Although the death toll of only very few cases of ethnic cleansing can be precisely determined, such as the most recent ones in the 1990s, it was certainly up to ten times higher in cases of flight or expulsion than of contractually arranged population shifts. The forms of violence used also varied: public executions, physical abuse, and rape typically attended the former two but were rarely committed during contractually arranged resettlements. Striking differences such as these can be observed not only between specific cases of ethnic cleansing but also to an extent between the different phases of many cases of ethnic cleansing. In Czechoslovakia, for example, almost all of the (maximum) 30,000 deaths among the Sudeten Germans occurred before the Potsdam Agreement in the summer of 1945. While there are no precise statistics on Poland, it would certainly be unrealistic to claim that the mass murder committed during Nazi occupation was paid back in kind after the war. One should therefore refrain from pointing a finger at "the Poles" or "the Czechs" in such a collectivizing manner or to equate these cases with genocide, as the German expellee associations attempted on many occasions.

Ethnic Cleansing and Genocide

Mortality rates provide evidence of a clear difference between ethnic cleansing and genocide. While the contrast is especially striking in relation to the Holocaust, when 90 percent of the Jewish population of Poland was murdered, there are also other examples. In Srebrenica, the site of the only crime against humanity in the former Yugoslavia that is regarded as genocide under international law, Bosnian Serbs killed one-third of the town's Bosniaks, all the men of fighting age. The ethnic cleansings in the rest of the country, no matter how inhumanly or murderously they were enforced in some places, did not cause a comparable loss of life. In the other cases classified in this book as genocides (the persecution of Serbs in the Ustasha Croatian state, 1941–44; the deportation of Jews from Bessarabia to Transnistria, 1941–42), the number of those murdered was higher than those who survived expulsion or deportation.

Distinguishing ethnic cleansing from genocide by measuring the loss of life is of course only one method of classification and does not correspond with Raphael Lemkin's original definition of genocide. He placed

the attempted destruction of an ethnic group and the basis of its liveli-
hood within the parameters of genocide.[4] The UN Genocide Convention
of 1948 subsequently narrowed the concept down, not least in order to
prevent the Potsdam Agreement and postwar order of states from being
retrospectively delegitimized. Following Lemkin and the rising field of
genocide studies, nearly all the cases of ethnic cleansing considered here
could be defined as genocide. Although applying as inclusive a definition
of genocide as possible may be tempting for research purposes, generalizing on this scale risks relativizing the Holocaust and other genocides.
Moreover, the *dolus specialis*—the primary intent to kill and destroy as
an end in itself—remains a specific feature of genocides.

It was on the basis of this legal principle that the International Court
of Justice differentiated between genocide and serious crimes against
humanity in the former Yugoslavia. Consequently, though the long
prison terms (up to forty years) or life sentences of several condemned
Serb functionaries from northern and eastern Bosnia were not com-
muted, the charges of genocide were dropped in appeal proceedings.[5] The
planned mass murder in Srebrenica was the only crime to be punished
as genocide. Yet even here, at the climax of the war in the former Yugoslavia, women and children were spared—in contrast to Lidice, Oradour,
Marzabotto, and countless places in Eastern Europe where the German
army and the SS committed genocidal massacres. The Ustasha in Croatia and the Antonescu regime in Romania ordered comparable acts of
terror. The genocide of Srebrenica was perceived as particularly deplorable because such extreme acts of violence had become exceptional in
the second half of the twentieth century, at least in Europe. Hence the
outcry by the international community and the West's delayed military
intervention, if only by aerial means to avoid sustaining Western losses.
From a cynical point of view, Western lives seemed to be more highly
valued than those of Bosnian civilians, who could have been more effectively protected by troops on the ground.

Genocides are never committed with the approval of a government or
other institution representing the persecuted group. Contractual genocide never occurred—it would be a contradiction in terms. In contrast,
most—and the most extensive—ethnic cleansings were enforced on the
basis of bilateral or international agreements. In view of these basic,
empirically documented differences, there seems little justification for
defining ethnic cleansing as a subcategory of genocide. They are closely
related but clearly distinguishable phenomena. Moreover, exaggerating
the nature of crimes committed, and thereby in effect misrepresenting
them, does not do justice to the trauma of those affected. Various crimes
against humanity were committed in the twentieth century with differ-

ent causes and outcomes, and they should not be lumped together in one gory landscape of blood.

The internal deportations within the Soviet Union have more commonalities with genocide. Devised as a form of collective punishment, they were resolved without any contractual basis and of course with the consent of representatives of those affected. The Stalinist deportations also claimed a death toll of up to 25 percent (in the worst case, that of the Chechens). Yet to categorically define the Soviet deportations of 1941–44 as genocide would be to convey a distorted impression of the Stalinist regime's goals. It did not aim to eliminate the Tatars, Chechen, or other nationalities per se. The intent to destroy the kulaks was more pronounced. They fell victim to a "sociocide" in which the main cause of death was hunger, the cold and lack of provisions and medical care. Hunger was also a major cause of death in India, where two to three million people died during the great famine in Bengal in 1943, probably ten times more than during the ethnic cleansing of 1947–48.

Rather than following the premise of "Soviet ethnic cleansing," it is more elucidating to ask why the utopia of social homogeneity led to the rejection of ethnic diversity in the Soviet Union. Obviously there is a dynamic connection between various kinds of societal leveling. As soon as class diversity had been leveled, the Stalinist regime directed its instruments of terror against national "deviants." In contrast to the abduction of the kulaks, the deportations during World War II were no longer concerned with pursuing the utopia of a society of equals or creating a new Soviet man, but with collectively punishing those targeted for their alleged disloyalty during the war.

Retrospective and Forward-Looking Ethnic Cleansing

The Soviet reprisals relate to a fifth distinction: retrospective as opposed to forward-looking ethnic cleansing. In the second half of the 1930s, the Soviet Union deported nationalities with an external nation-state to avert certain scenarios in the future. Stalin had a paranoid fear of invasion and sought to remove all potential risk factors. But from 1941, Stalin's preventative cleansings mutated into retrospective punishment. In contrast to the reeducation the kulaks were subjected to, these deportations failed to change or destroy the identity of the deportees. On the contrary, the collective experience of deportation indirectly consolidated the sense of a common identity among the affected groups. These typically returned to their old homelands, united, as soon as de-Stalinization allowed it.

Some nation-states also carried out ethnic cleansing in response to past conflicts, a form of retrospective ethnic cleansing. The Greeks were expelled from Asia Minor to pay for earlier defeats and territorial losses on the Balkan Peninsula and in the Caucasus. On an individual level, especially, the trauma this caused probably had a deeper impact than the Young Turks' propaganda promoting a purely Turanist Anatolia, which can hardly have reached the millions of illiterate people in the region. The policies of the nation-states allied to the German Reich also stemmed from the memory of past conflicts. In 1941–44, Hungary, Bulgaria, and Romania persecuted the political and social elites of the nation-states created or expanded after World War I first. Even the Independent State of Croatia, which was Nazi Germany's closest ally in terms of ideology, initially pursued a political selection of its persecuted minorities. The Hungarian government spoke of "redressing injustices" in Transylvania caused under Romanian rule, alluding to the land reform of 1921 and the subsequent settlement of Romanian peasants. Independent Slovakia renounced its common history with the Czechs in interwar Czechoslovakia and cited alleged negative experiences to justify the ousting of most of the Czechs who had settled there. Verifiable facts played a secondary role in these nationalist views of the past.

Crucially, all the nation-states analyzed here combined retrospective score settling with the pursuit of forward-looking utopias of homogeneity. The significance of the latter soon superseded the former as a motivating factor. For this reason, not only former functionaries of enemy states were persecuted, but also future minorities. Thus, the premise of kin liability was frequently cited to justify the expulsion or forcible resettlement not only of the nationalist head of a family but also of his children or extended family. This radical form of ethnocracy, which cannot be equated with democracy, as Michael Mann seems to suggest,[6] depopulated a number of border regions. The perpetrators hoped to transform contested regions in this way to their advantage in future conflicts and peace talks.

Nazi Germany's responses to the past and designs for the future were unparalleled. The conception of a racially pure *Lebensraum* and the planned expulsion of ten million Poles (from the annexed regions alone), half a million Slovenes, and millions of other people belonging to nations considered inferior were utterly utopian. This became apparent when the German Reich—the only state in the twentieth century to carry out ethnic cleansings not only in nearby border regions but also far away areas of future settlement—tried to put these plans into practice. Operation Zamość, carried out shortly before Germany's defeat at Stalingrad, gave an indication of the dimensions of the Nazis' Germanization plans for Eastern Europe. But when the projected ethnic reshuffle proved difficult to realize, it was relegated in favor of prioritizing the war economy and the destruction of the Jews. From spring 1941, Nazi nationality policy largely abandoned ethnic cleansing, opting instead for forced assimilation and the maximum exploitation of the subjugated nations by means of forced labor.

Ethnic cleansing was most effective and extensive when it combined retrospective score settling with concrete plans for the future. Examples are the removal of all Christians from Asia Minor, even from regions that were nearly a thousand miles from the actual war zone, and the almost complete ethnic cleansing of Poland after World War II. In countries that were not striving to establish an ethnically pure nation-state, such as Romania, Yugoslavia, and India, ethnic cleansing stalled in the early stages or was confined to specific regions.

A combination of retroactive and future-oriented motivations can also be observed in Allied policies after World War II. The Germans were to be severely punished for their belligerence and occupation terror. Stalin was especially merciless in this respect. For this reason, in Yalta and Potsdam, the Allies resolved not only the removal of Hitler's (alleged) "fifth column" from the Third Reich's eastern neighboring states but also the forced resettlement of all Germans from the eastern territories lost in 1945. In addition, the catalog of reprisals included collective punishments such as forced labor.

Britain and the United States had a less pronounced desire for retribution, having not suffered directly from German occupation. The Western powers supported ethnic cleansing mainly as a peacemaking strategy for Europe's future. All sides agreed that Germany should never be in a position to start a war again. Punishing Germany therefore became an integral part of Europe's postwar order. Winston Churchill, especially, citing Lausanne, held the opinion that Europe and its individual states could only be stabilized if the "endless trouble" caused by minorities was ended. Interestingly, in his key speech on the future of Poland in December 1944, Churchill also referred to the example of Alsace.[7] At this point, however, France pursued a far more conciliatory policy than after World War I, and avoided mass evictions.

The "British Track"

Churchill's words and similar, earlier statements by Lord Curzon and many other members of the British political and intellectual elite illustrate Britain's major role in ethnic cleansing. The "British track" is

evidenced by a long list of international treaties resolving and regulating ethnic cleansing in the first half of the twentieth century in which
London was a key player. It starts with Neuilly (1919) and is followed by
Sèvres (1920, though never ratified by the Ottoman Empire), Lausanne
(1923), Palestine (1937, aborted), Munich (1938, nullified but continued in a reverse manner in 1942), Tehran (1943), Yalta (1945), Potsdam
(1945), Paris (1947), and Trieste (1947), and ends with the partition of
India (1947) and the partition of Palestine (1947, proposed by the UN
but following the plan proposed by the British in 1937). If one extends
the temporal radius, Bengal (1905) could be added as a precursor, marking the first time that the partition of a disputed territory was proposed,
and Cyprus (1974) included as a late case with British involvement.

How did this "British track" come about? Why was a Western democracy involved in so many cases of ethnic cleansing? It espoused the
concept of partition in the belief that conflicts between nations and nationalities could be resolved by assigning each of them specific territories. And partition inevitably involved the migration and removal of
populations that lived on the "wrong side" of the new border. Although
partitions were only implemented in colonies or parts of Europe that
were regarded as backward (Macedonia, Galicia, etc.), the principle of
the binary and dialectical distribution of power is rooted in British (and
American) democracy. While majority rule and "the winner takes all"
principle may function well in a system with a strong tradition of checks
and balances, it cannot work in areas where there is fierce national or
ethnic rivalry over power. Yet the British government universally applied the principle of a binary division of society and politics to colonial
societies, separating Jews from Arabs (on the basis of language, ignoring other religious distinctions) and, in India, Hindus from Muslims
(based on religion, ignoring linguistic and other distinctions). While
"binarism" was only one outcome of the maxim divide et impera, as an
organizing principle it exacerbated and ethnicized conflicts in many areas under British rule. The utopian confidence in rational and technical
"solutions" also had a profound influence on political thought, leading
many—not only British—statesmen to believe that population removals
could be carried out to stabilize individual countries and the international order. As Matthew Frank has shown, any doubts they had about
ethnic cleansing were of a more practical than moral nature.[8] The mass
removal of populations was not significantly questioned until it resulted
in chaos and catastrophe, such as in postwar Germany. Hence, one-sided
population *transfers* were halted, but reciprocal population *exchanges*
were still supported by London in 1946–47.

The point of this argument about the "British track" is not to lay the blame on a specific country or on individual statesmen but to stress that ethnic cleansing was a distinct characteristic of democracies or semi-democratic regimes like the postwar peoples' democracies, not dictatorships. Totalitarian regimes such as the Stalinist Soviet Union or Nazi Germany used other, even more destructive means to achieve their aims of reshuffling societies and territories. Ethnic cleansing was also clearly a feature of European modernity, which is evidenced by the fact that most and the most extensive cases happened in Europe or in colonial areas ruled by the most advanced European empire, Great Britain.

After the Potsdam Conference, the experiences of the past and projected future scenarios paled in comparison with the challenges of the present. Faced with an acute refugee crisis in Germany, the United States and Britain criticized the manner in which the Soviet Union and its allies implemented the Potsdam resolutions. They did not, however, disassociate themselves from the postwar order, instead discreetly reminding West Germany that the border settlement and the population removals according to the Potsdam Agreement were permanent whenever Chancellor Adenauer began to echo the rhetoric of the German exiles' associations too vocally.[9]

Lessons Learnt?

For many years, the stability of the postwar borders and the enduring period of peace in Europe were seen as indications that the ethnic cleansing between 1944 and 1948 had ultimately served its purpose. This argument can be found in international specialist literature until the mid-1960s, including Joseph Schechtman's book on population transfers.[10] Dimitri Pentzopoulos expressed a similarly positive opinion of Neuilly and Lausanne[11]; in Poland and Czechoslovakia, approval of the "transfer" of the Germans and the supposed solution of all minority problems was part of state doctrine. This consensus between Western scholars and Communist countries may appear surprising, but it was built upon the same modernist thinking that was also the basis for the "British Track" outlined above.

Postwar "cleansed" Europe can also be evaluated through the lens of counterfactual considerations. Although the ethnic borders drawn in 1945 remained stable, they were deeply controversial. The German exiles' associations and, influenced by them, West German governments until the mid-1960s supported a dual revisionism, demanding the possibility of return for expellees as well as the revision of the eastern border of Germany. The political consequences of this revisionism were kept in check by Germany's division. The Socialist Unity Party of Germany (SED) stifled all debates on the Oder-Neisse border precisely because large sections of society in the Soviet zone of occupation and later the German Democratic Republic and, for a time, the East German Christian Democratic Union (CDU) called for its revision.[12] The former inhabitants of the eastern Polish territories, in contrast, had little hope of the eastern border imposed by Stalin being revised or of being able to return to their old homeland. Similar to the "resettlers" in the GDR, the Polish "repatriates" were not permitted to organize lobbies for or publicly speak out in favor of regaining the eastern territories. Yet despite this strict censorship, the "packed bags" syndrome was prevalent. In the first years after World War II, some eastern Poles even hoped for a third world war or an attack on the Soviet Union by the Western powers. The trauma of Trianon remains politically relevant in Hungary to this day. In view of this open or subtle resistance to the postwar order, it seems highly questionable whether the ethnic cleansing resolved in 1945 actually has stabilized East Central Europe or Europe as a whole.

There was no repeat of the revisionism of the interwar period mainly because the ethnic borders along the Iron Curtain and in East Central Europe became cemented due to the presence of the Red Army. The *Pax Sovietica* was the primary reason for the postwar stabilization of borders in central and eastern Europe; in the West and the South the rapprochement between former enemy countries caused greater permanence. Furthermore, West Germany eventually made a decisive break with its imperial and Nazi past. Due to the political paradigms introduced by the 1968 generation, and the Social Democrats' policy of reconciliation with the Eastern Bloc, attitudes toward the "expulsions" and Germany's neighbors to the east began to change.

In recent years, conservatives, but also quite a few liberals and former Marxists in Germany have claimed that the expulsion of the Germans was thus made a taboo subject. But since West Germany was a democratic country with constitutional freedom of speech, how could such a taboo have been imposed and upheld? Even during the détente years, when the German Expellee Association lost much of its earlier influence on the government, it continued to play a prominent public role, organizing conventions and rallying political support for the Conservative parties. Dozens of books appeared every year, dealing with the expellees, their fate in 1945–48 and their postwar integration in Germany.[13] Hence, the claim that the subject was a taboo is certainly grossly exaggerated, if not false. The fact that the territorial losses of 1945 and the removal of the Germans from East Central Europe ceased to rouse revisionist demands marked a major achievement of history politics in the "old" Federal Republic of Germany.

Ethnic migrations of a not distinctly compulsory nature, such as the departure of ethnic Turks from Southeastern Europe and Germans from East Central and Eastern Europe, contributed to easing tensions in postwar Europe. The projected ethnic homogenization of many countries progressed further after the main periods of ethnic cleansing, although it had not been explicitly intended or resolved in either Lausanne or Potsdam. In conclusion, it is possible to claim that the second postwar order, which emerged in 1948 from the East-West conflict and the Soviet dominance over eastern Europe, did more to promote Europe's stabilization than the first postwar order, arranged in 1945 and involving extensive ethnic cleansing. The Greco-Turkish conflicts after 1945 (the *Septembrianá* in 1955 and Cyprus in 1974–75), the wars in the former Palestine and between India and Pakistan, and the violent breakup of Yugoslavia all indicate that ethnic cleansing tended to generate further conflicts in the mid and long term. The German-Polish tensions arising since 2001 show that the problems in East Central Europe have not been completely overcome.

Doubts as to the expediency of ethnic cleansing even attended the implementation of the Treaties of Lausanne and Potsdam. In India, the idea of population exchange was abandoned on account of the negative repercussions of the mass flight and expulsion of 1947–48. The Nehru-Liaquat Agreement of 1950 provided for the return of refugees to Bengal and the coexistence of Muslims and Hindus on both sides of the border. A few years later, the Soviet Union reversed the Stalinist deportations and enabled the deportees (with the exception of the Germans and the Crimean Tatars) to return to their old homelands.

A discourse on human rights began in Great Britain and the United States in response to the Cold War that was disseminated to a broad public and anchored in society via the student protest movement of 1968. The value of social homogeneity began to be questioned and the model of the "salad bowl society" promoted as an alternative to the "melting pot." A paradigm shift also took place in the Communist states. During the Prague Spring, reformist Communists and dissidents in Czechoslovakia criticized the course of the "transfer" of the Sudeten Germans. In Poland, supporters of *Solidarność* went even further, challenging the entire construct of eternal enmity with (West) Germany. Against this changed international background, the Cyprus conflict in 1974–75 marked the last case of an internationally sanctioned territorial partition and a contractually arranged population exchange across a newly created border.[14]

The atrocities committed during the war in Bosnia and Herzegovina finally led to an international consensus against ethnic cleansing. Correspondingly, the Dayton Accords aimed to reverse previous expulsions and allow the refugees to return to their homelands as far as possible. NATO intervened in the Kosovo conflict in 1999 to stop ethnic cleansing. This marked a controversial turning point, since it was the first time that preventing ethnic cleansing was given precedence over the sovereignty of an independent state.

In view of this development, there is reason to assume that ethnic cleansing is indeed a historical phenomenon, at least in Europe. Yet the interventions of the international community in the former Yugoslavia were morally devalued by the fact that they did not prevent the retaliation against and expulsion of the Serbian minorities in Croatia and Kosovo. Moreover, a potential consequence of the international consensus against ethnic cleansing is that unwanted minorities are no longer deported to neighboring states but in extreme cases killed on the spot. Conflicts in African trouble spots such as Darfur seem to indicate a trend in this direction. The century of ethnic cleansing could, then, be succeeded by an age of genocide in global terms.

Notes

1. In the Federal Republic of Germany, the number of deaths was exaggerated to a staggering 200,000–250,000 until the mid-1990s. This figure was derived from a misinterpretation of census results in the Soviet zone of occupation and, moreover, counted among the dead all those missing and those who changed nationality.
2. See Sundhaussen, *Jugoslawien und seine Nachfolgestaaten,* 381–96.
3. See the figures in Psomiades, *Fridtjof Nansen,* 295 and 314.
4. See Martin Shaw, *What is Genocide?* (Cambridge, 2007). The distinction between ethnic cleansing and genocide attempted here is based partly on discussions with Dirk Moses of the European University Institute, to whom I am indebted for his suggestions. His publications include the recently published reference work, Donald Bloxham and A. Dirk Moses, eds., *The Oxford Handbook on Genocide Studies* (Oxford, 2010).
5. See two key proceedings concerning the events in northern Bosnia, where many human rights violations were committed in 1992. Despite severe sentences for the accused, the charges of genocide were dropped in all appeal proceedings. See the ICTY website at http://www.icty.org/x/cases/stakic/cis/en/cis_stakic.pdf and http://www.icty.org/x/cases/jelisic/cis/en/cis_jelisic.pdf (accessed 18 October 2010).
6. See Mann, *The Dark Side of Democracy.*
7. See Churchill, *His Complete Speeches,* 7069.
8. See Frank, *Expelling the Germans.*

9. See Pertti Ahonen, *After the Expulsion: West Germany and Eastern Europe 1945–1990* (New York, 2003), 110–15 and 273.

10. See Joseph Schechtman, *Postwar population transfers in Europe. 1945–1955* (Philadelphia PA, 1962).

11. Pentzopoulos's book was republished in 2002 without any critical foreword or editor's comment. It seems that his ideas still enjoy some support in Greece. See Pentzopoulos, *The Balkan Exchange.*

12. See Ther, *Deutsche und Polnische Vertriebene,* 262–64 and 343–46.

13. See Krallert-Sattler, *Kommentierte Bibliographie.*

14. Stefan Troebst, "Vom Bevölkerungstransfer zum Vertreibungsverbot: Eine europäische Erfolgsgeschichte?," *Transit, Europäische Revue* 36 (Winter 2008–9): 158–82.

ACKNOWLEDGMENTS

In a globalizing world of academia, translations into English are increasingly important for enhancing scholarly exchange, avoiding self-referentiality within academic cultures, and spreading the findings of research from various parts of the world. I would like to thank the institutions and persons who have made this translation possible. The German Booktrade Organisation (Börsenverein des Deutschen Buchhandels) provided a generous translation grant, my original German publisher Vandenhoeck & Ruprecht helped to get this grant, and Marion Berghahn's publishing house is functioning once more as a transmitter in this globalizing academic world. Besides being the series editor, Dirk Moses has also been a great partner for discussion and controversies. I would also like to thank Omer Bartov for inspiring exchanges in Providence and Paris. Last but not least, I would like to praise the translator, Charlotte Hughes-Kreutzmüller, who has done a great job in translating a history book from the complicated German language.

However, this book is more than just a translation. It has been a work in progress inspired by many debates with colleagues in the United States and in Europe. I am very grateful to Charles Maier (Harvard University), Mark Mazower (Columbia University), and Mark von Hagen (now Arizona State University), who gave me the opportunity to present some concepts and chapters of this book at an early stage. I am indebted to Norman Naimark (Stanford University), who has encouraged my research and writing in many ways for the last fifteen years. Martin Schulze-Wessel (Ludwig-Maximilians-Universität Munich), Jürgen Kocka (Free University Berlin), Holm Sundhaussen (Free University Berlin), Manfred Hildermeier (University of Göttingen), Karl Kaser (University of Graz), Hannes Grandits (Graz and Humboldt University Berlin), Klaus Nellen, and Janos Kovacs (IWM, Vienna) have provided great fora for discussion in Austria and Germany. Stefan Troebst (University of Leipzig) offered essential advice on many chapters of this book, Caroline Leutloff-Grandits (Graz and Berlin) on former Yugoslavia and Marina Cattaruzza on Italy. Menachem Klein, Sandy Kedar, and Yfaat Weiss taught me a lot about Palestine and Israel; the Goethe-Institut in Kolkata introduced me to the Indian discussion.

Furthermore, I would like to thank my numerous colleagues in the Czech Republic and in Poland, who have discussed the sad topic of this book on countless academic and private occasions in the past twenty-five years. Of those in Prague, I would like to personally thank Jaroslav Kučera (Charles University Prague), Jiří Pešek (Prague), and Miloš Havelka (Czech Academy of Sciences); in Poland, Krzysztof Ruchniewicz (University of Wrocław) and Włodzimierz Borodziej. Without his advice and our working vacations in Masuria, this book would not have been possible. The Polish edition of my book that appeared in 2012 under Krzysztof's patronage was also an important step toward the English language version.

Most of this book was written during my tenure at the European University Institute in Florence. The EUI was the ideal environment for writing a book with European and global dimensions. Sebastian Conrad (now Free University Berlin) enhanced my interest in connections between Europe and its former colonies, Kiran Patel (now Maastricht) was an ideal partner to discuss European history with, Heinz-Gerhard Haupt taught me a lot about violence, and Maria Todorova (University of Illinois) made important comments on style and Southeastern Europe.

Former students and wonderful colleagues have informed me about countries and regions about which my knowledge was previously limited. Ostap Sereda (L'viv and CEU Budapest) gave me additional insight into Ukrainian research; Iris Engemann (Berlin) provided information on Slovakia, Claudiu Oancea (EUI) on Romania, Michael Esch and Christiane Kohser Spohn on France. Jannis Panagiotidis (now Imre Kertesz Kolleg Jena) contributed excellent summaries of the Greek literature, shared his knowledge of the Soviet Union, and gave numerous hints on small but important details. Last but not least, I would like to thank my wife, Martina Steer, for being a wonderful intellectual partner and giving me every freedom to pursue my research interests in spite of the demands of four children growing up around us.

ANNOTATED BIBLIOGRAPHY

⊂ऽ∫ऽ∽

$\mathbf{A}$ comprehensive list of the literature on all cases of ethnic cleansing, the international and domestic contexts in which they took place, and their specific regional and local characteristics would fill several volumes. The bibliography below therefore makes a selection of the available literature. Overviews of the history of ethnic cleansing are listed first, followed by publications from current fields of research and, last, the major international and national studies on each country affected. Publications on some historical states that no longer exist are listed under their contemporary successor states, e.g. literature on the Ottoman Empire can be found in the section on Turkey. A number of recently published source documentations are also mentioned as valuable reference works. In this way, the bibliography supplements the case studies in the main section of this book. In contrast to many study books published today in the United States and Great Britain, this bibliography also attempts to cover the most important books published in languages other than English. It is intended to facilitate extended research by its readers, whether they are undergraduate or postgraduate students, representatives of refugee organizations, or any other specialist, or general readers. Since ethnic cleansing is increasingly the object of academic research and often included in courses of genocide studies, it may also provide an aid to study in this field. Book titles are listed in order of mention, not in alphabetical order. As outlined above, this bibliography makes no claim to be exhaustive, but is intended as an introduction to the major publications in the field.

Comprehensive Histories of Ethnic Cleansing

Since the 1990s, when ethnic cleansings gained renewed relevance, a broad field of research has emerged on the subject. Norman Naimark takes the credit for writing the first overview of the history of ethnic cleansing. His book, published in the United States in 2001, deals with the genocide of the Armenians, the ethnic cleansing of the Greeks, the Nazi persecution of the German Jews until 1941, and the "expulsion" of the Germans from Poland and Czechoslovakia, as well as the events in the former Yugoslavia. His choice of case studies can be regarded (and in detail, criticized) as the result of necessary reduction, though it simultaneously broadens the book's perspective toward genocide. Naimark must also be credited for his pioneering work elucidating the persecution specifically of women and thus a gender aspect of the subject. Benjamin Lieberman's book, which stretches back to the nineteenth century, provides a useful supplement to Naimark's study. The anthology by Richard Bessel and Claudia Haake *Removing Peoples: Forced Removal in the Modern World* sets the parameters even wider apart. Taking a global perspective, it includes the persecution of indigenous peoples in the settler colonies, which differed from the ethnic cleansings in Europe both in terms of motivation and implementation. The French-language study by Stéphane Rosière also takes a global perspective and develops a sociological typology of ethnic cleansings. Although Joseph Schechtman's survey was written three generations ago and, in the spirit of the day, regards population transfers as a legitimate means of international policy, it marks a major academic achievement and is still worth reading. In 2008, Pertti Ahonen and a team of six European historians published an excellent book on forced migrations in Europe during World War II and in the early postwar period. It contains several previously little-researched case studies, elucidates the international context, and shows how productive academic teamwork can be. A further outstanding publication is the *Lexikon der Vertreibungen* (Encyclopedia of Expulsion), comprising entries from over 120 international authors. It is an ideal reference work and point of departure for further reading. The same is true of the 2008 anthology on forced migrations in Eastern Europe between 1938 and 1950 edited by the German and Czech historians Ralph Melville, Jiří Pešek and Claus Scharf. This comprehensive study covers a number of individual cases of ethnic cleansing, never before analyzed in a Western language. An anthology from 1999 on behalf of the German-Czech and German-Slovak historical commission by Detlef Brandes, Edita Ivaničková and Jiří Pešek can be read as a complementary work. Finally, the reader's attention must be drawn to a Polish-language atlas that contains a great selection of maps with excellent accompanying texts. The title of this book is *Wysiedlenia, wypędzenia i ucieczki 1939–1959: Atlas ziem Polski* (Resettlements, Expulsions and Flight 1939–1959: Atlas of the Polish Lands).

Naimark, Norman M. *Fires of Hatred: Ethnic Cleansing in Twentieth-Century Europe.* Cambridge: Harvard University Press, 2001.
Lieberman, Benjamin. *Terrible Fate: Ethnic Cleansing in the Making of Modern Europe.* Chicago: Ivan Dee, 2006.
Bessel, Richard, and Claudia B. Haake, eds. *Removing Peoples: Forced Removal in the Modern World.* Oxford: Oxford University Press, 2009.
Rosière, Stéphane. *Le nettoyage ethnique: Terreur et peuplement.* Paris: Ellipses, 2006.
Schechtman, Joseph. *European Population Transfers 1939–1945.* New York: Oxford University Press, 1946.
Ahonen, Pertti, Gustavo Corni, Jerzy Kochanowski, Rainer Schulze, Tamás Stark, and Barbara Stelzl-Marx. *People on the Move: Forced Population Movements in Europe in the Second World War and its Aftermath.* Oxford: Berg, 2008.
Brandes, Detlef, Holm Sundhaussen, and Stefan Troebst, eds. *Lexikon der Vertreibungen: Deportation, Zwangsaussiedlung und ethnische Säuberung im Europa des 20. Jahrhunderts.* Vienna: Böhlau, 2010.
Melville, Ralph, Jiří Pešek, and Claus Scharf, eds. *Zwangsmigrationen im mittleren und östlichen Europa: Völkerrecht—Konzeptionen—Praxis (1938-1950).* Mainz: Zabern, 2008.
Brandes, Detlef, Edita Ivaničková, and Jiří Pešek, eds. *Erzwungene Trennung: Vertreibungen und Aussiedlungen in und aus der Tschechoslowakei 1938–1947 im Vergleich mit Polen, Ungarn und Jugoslawien.* Essen: Klartext, 1999.
Hryciuk, Grzegorz, Małgorzata Ruchniewicz, Bożena Szaynok, and Andrzej Żbikowski. *Wysiedlenia, wypędzenia i ucieczki 1939–1959: Atlas ziem Polski.* Warsaw: Demart, 2008. (German edition: *Atlas Zwangsumsiedlung, Flucht, Vertreibung: Ostmitteleuropa 1939–1959.* Warsaw: Demart, 2009.)

Literature on the Resettlement of Ethnically Cleansed Regions

The ambit of most of the literature on flight, expulsion, and other forms of ethnic cleansing extends only to the moment when victims are forced from their homes, implicitly suggesting that the history of the affected countries and regions ended there. Most of the older literature, moreover, concentrates on one specific victim group. However, as this book has shown, the primary goal of ethnonational homogenization and border consolidation was typically coupled with a purposeful settlement policy. Consideration of the history of these regions *after* ethnic cleansing overcomes both the limits of national history and distinct temporal phases. Today, literature is available on the history of a wide number of countries, regions, and towns that were completely transformed by the removal and settlement of their population.

In Poland and Czechoslovakia, the national settlement and reconstruction in the regions that had belonged to the German Reich until 1945 formed an integral part of Communist founding mythologies. But as far back as the 1970s, Polish sociologists and the historian Krystyna Kersten conducted research that circumvented the regime's requirement to concentrate on the pioneers of "re-Polonization" and the success of integration in postwar society. Czesław Osękowski compiled these older studies in his 1994 book on society in northern and western Poland and described how painstaking the process of resettlement actually was and the social conflicts it generated. Andreas Hofmann's dissertation on Silesia in 1945–48 is one of the few works to give equal consideration to deportations, forced resettlement, and initial settlement. The local study of Wrocław (formerly Breslau) by Gregor Thum is recommended for its innovative cultural history approach and dense portrayal. Similarly, Oliver Loew und Jan Musekamp have written informative books about Danzig and Stettin. The 2006 publication by the *Nordost-Archiv* deals with the incorporation of history into many other East Central European towns. The anthology by John Czaplicka, Nida Gelazis and Blair Ruble also contains excellent case studies of major cities that underwent ethnic cleansing.

Regional history did not evolve to the same extent in Poland's neighboring countries, where research in the field was just beginning in 1989. Czech studies of the 1990s were taken up by Andreas Wiedemann and extended in his monograph. Eagle Glassheim has paid attention to the specific but important aspect of environmental changes and devastation resulting from ethnic cleansing and the Communist settlement policy in the Czech borderlands. The anthology by Adrian von Arburg and Martin Schulze-Wessel deals with newly settled regions in Poland, Czechoslovakia, Hungary, Yugoslavia, and the Soviet Union.

While the issue of resettlement is especially relevant to the establishment of Communist societies and economic systems in East Central Europe, it also had considerable repercussions in Western-oriented states affected by ethnic cleansings. The state dirigism of Turkey, Greece, and Israel until the 1980s was based not least on the fact that these states had acquired large stretches of land by means of ethnic cleansing. Furthermore, integrating conational refugees posed an enormous challenge and demanded huge efforts by the states affected (see for references the section on Greece, Turkey and Israel).

Osękowski, Czesław. *Społeczeństwo Polski zachodniej i północnej w latach 1945–1956: Procesy integracji i dezintegracji.* Zielona Góra: WSP, 1994.
Hofmann, Andreas. *Die Nachkriegszeit in Schlesien: Gesellschafts- und Bevölkerungspolitik in den polnischen Siedlungsgebieten 1945–1948.* Cologne: Böhlau, 2000.

Thum, Gregor. *Uprooted: How Breslau became Wroclaw.* Princeton, NJ: Princeton University Press, 2011.

Loew, Peter Oliver. *Danzig und seine Vergangenheit 1793–1997: Die Geschichtskultur einer Stadt zwischen Deutschland und Polen.* Osnabrück: Fibre, 2003.

"Die Aneignung fremder Vergangenheiten in Nordosteuropa am Beispiel plurikultureller Städte (20. Jahrhundert)." Special issue, *Nordost-Archiv: Zeitschrift für Regionalgeschichte* 15 (2006).

Musekamp, Jan. *Zwischen Stettin und Szczecin: Metamorphosen einer Stadt von 1945 bis 2005.* Wiesbaden: Harrassowitz, 2010.

Czaplicka, John, Nida Gelazis, and Blair Ruble, eds. *Cities After the Fall of Communism: Reshaping Cultural Landscapes and European Identity.* Baltimore: Johns Hopkins University Press, 2009.

Wiedemann, Andreas. *"Komm mit uns das Grenzland aufbauen!" Ansiedlung und neue Strukturen in den ehemaligen Sudetengebieten.* Essen: Klartext, 2007.

Glassheim, Eagle. "Ethnic Cleansing, Communism and Environmental Devastation in Czechoslovakia's Borderlands." *The Journal of Modern History* 78 (2006): 65–92.

von Arburg, Adrian, and Martin Schulze-Wessel, eds. *Zwangsumsiedlung und neue Gesellschaft in Ostmitteleuropa nach 1945.* Munich: Oldenbourg, 2010.

Literature on Remembrance and Collective Memory

Separating history from memory, as Pierre Nora has attempted in a recent essay, is widely regarded as outdated today. The study of history is always influenced by current affairs and, by extension, public memory. Historiography, in turn, creates memories and identities, which is partly why it was once closely affiliated with the state in most countries. One of the main differences between *historia* and *memoria* and most studies on collective memory is the temporal horizon. The specialists in this rising field of research tend to concentrate on contemporary or very recent memories (see, for example, H. Welzer, and for a counter-example, Jay Winter's multivolume work on the remembrance of World War I). Studies on remembrance also have the drawback that they often deal only with the collective memory of one nation. The various *lieux des mémoire* projects—the first of this kind was published by Pierre Nora in the 1980s and followed by comparable projects in many European countries—operated within the framework of national history. (These are not listed below due to space limitations.)

Another theoretical problem of studies on memory and remembrance is their frequent combination of the two incompatible-seeming elements of a Freud-based psychological orientation toward trauma and its cure and Maurice Halbwachs's sociological approach. The most prominent German specialist on collective memory, Aleida Assmann, was criticized for blending Freud and Halbwachs by Lutz Niethammer. He analyzed this and other theoretical problems of studies on collective memory in his book on the term identity, which was never translated into English probably due to its extensive length, but is a German academic book in the very best sense.

The fixation on trauma has also been very strong in the US and has been advocated by Jay Winter, who seems to be unfamiliar with Lutz Niethammer's theoretical considerations. The exclusive focus on the suffering of refugees is one of the reasons why measures to integrate refugees and the opportunities they had for social advancement, which can be proven to have existed in a number of cases, have been largely disregarded. The old press maxim "only bad news is good news" continues to influence the role of the media, which emphasizes trauma and conflict with an eye to maximizing circulation. Politics also plays a part in shaping historical memories, primarily by initiating festivals and commemoration days and inaugurating memorial sites. The topic is therefore best approached in an interdisciplinary manner. Here, the task of historical science is to promote critical, historical memory research.

On the subject of the history of remembrance of the German postwar refugees, Christian Lotz's book is outstanding. The question of why in certain cases memories of conflict were nurtured, such as in German-Polish relations, while in other cases the political leadership fostered a process of forgetting, such as in Franco-German relations, has been little researched. Memory in Germany and other European countries differed according to region, generation, social environment, and status, as well as a number of other factors, which are rarely touched upon. An interesting object of research would be the question of why some memories of conflict (e.g., between Germany and France) faded while in other circumstances (e.g., from 2001 in German-Polish relations) old patterns of conflict were reconfigured. It should be noted that memories are not only formed in the national public realm but also in transnational communication spaces, which are analyzed theoretically and empirically in three excellent recent publications by Michael Rothberg, Martin Aust (et alia) and Moritz Csáky.

Nora, Pierre. "Gedächtniskonjunktur.", *Transit Europäische Revue* 22 (Winter 2001–2002):, 18–31. (An English version of the article has been published by the journal *Eurozine* at, http://www.eurozine.com/articles/2002-04-19-nora-en.html, [accessed 1 March 2013].)

Welzer, Harald. *Das kommunikative Gedächtnis: Eine Theorie der Erinnerung.* Munich: C. H. Beck, 2002.

Winter, Jay. *Remembering War: The Great War Between History and Memory in the Twentieth Century.* New Haven: Yale UP, 2006.

Nora, Pierre. *Les Lieux de mémoire,* 3 vols. Paris: Gallimard, 1984–92.

Halbwachs, Maurice. *On collective memory.* Chicago: The University of Chicago Press, 1992.

Assmann, Aleida. *Der lange Schatten der Vergangenheit: Erinnerungskultur und Geschichtspolitik.* Munich: C. H. Beck, 2006. (English edition: Aleida Assmann. *The Long Shadow of the Past: Cultures of Memory and the Politics of History.* New York: Fordham University Press, forthcoming.)

Niethammer, Lutz. *Kollektive Identität: Heimliche Quellen einer unheimlichen Konjunktur.* Hamburg: Rowohlt, 2000.

Winter, Jay. "The Generation of Memory: Reflections on the 'Memory Boom' in Contemporary Historical Studies." *Bulletin of the German Historical Institute* 27 (Fall 2000): 69–92.

Lotz, Christian. *Die Deutung des Verlusts: Erinnerungspolitische Kontroversen im geteilten Deutschland um Flucht, Vertreibung und die Ostgebiete (1948–1972).* Cologne: Böhlau, 2007.

Rothberg, Michael. *Multidirectional Memory: Remembering the Holocaust in the Age of Decolonization.* Palo Alto, CA: Stanford University Press, 2009.

Aust, Martin, Krzysztof Ruchniewicz, and Stefan Troebst, eds. *Verflochtene Erinnerungen: Polen und seine Nachbarn im 19. und 20. Jahrhundert.* Cologne: Böhlau, 2009.

Csáky, Moritz. *Das Gedächtnis der Städte: Kulturelle Verflechtungen—Wien und die urbanen Milieus in Zentraleuropa.* Vienna: Böhlau, 2010.

Literature on Individual Countries

Germany

As mentioned above, several anthologies on ethnic cleansing have appeared in recent years in Germany. With respect to the flight, expulsion, and forced resettlement of Germans, most of the impetus came from Germany's neighboring countries to the east. The most significant new publication in the field is the documentation collection by Włodzimierz Borodziej and Hans Lemberg on the Germans in Poland in 1945–50. Arranged into regions, it impressively conveys the considerable variations in the course of expulsion and forced resettlement in different parts of present-day Poland. The study by Ray Douglas does not draw on the same depth of research, but the reports by Western aid organizations and government representatives that form the book's main source provide an additional perspective on the widespread misery and suffering in the former German eastern territories. One of Borodziej's and Lemberg's important findings is that the remaining Germans became alienated from their "old homeland." Czech historian Tomáš Staněk has dealt with the treatment of the Germans in Czechoslovakia in several volumes (see the section on Czechoslovakia). The state of research on the Kaliningrad region (the northern part of the former East Prussia) and other areas of German settlement further east or south is far less advanced. Detlef Brandes elucidates the Allies' decision-making processes and the role of the East Central European states in his comprehensive book. Timothy Snyder addresses the ethnic cleansing of Germans in a chapter in his recent book *Bloodlands,* but it relies heavily on a narrative of (Soviet) revenge and bloodshed, while the later phase after the Potsdam Agreement in the summer of 1945 receives much less attention.

The wealth of German-language literature from the postwar period on flight, expulsion, and forced resettlement should not be passed over. In spite of its ideological foundations and express mission to record only the cruelest treatment of Germans, Theodor Schieder's collection of documentation on expulsion is nevertheless of interest. Other, more in-depth ego-documents are listed in Krallert-Sattler's bibliography. The state of research on ethnic cleansings caused by Germans and especially by later refugees, such as in Nazi-occupied Poland and Slovenia, is far less advanced. This can perhaps be accounted for by the fact that the Nazis' ethnic cleansing (*ethnische Flurbereinigung* in Nazi terminology) was perceived as secondary in relation to their other crimes. While the German (and recent American) literature focused on the suffering of the German refugees, their entanglement in Nazism was not seriously researched until a very recent publication by Michael Schwartz, who has shown that two-thirds of the thirteen members of the executive committee of the West German expellee organization (*Bund der Vertriebenen*) were severely tainted, and only two were not members of the Nazi Party. The expellees' integration into postwar Germany is a field of inquiry in its own right. Space precludes listing more than the summarizing survey by Andreas Kossert, with the apt title *Kalte Heimat* (Cold Homeland). Pertti Ahonen has highlighted the conflicts in domestic and foreign policy arising from the Federal Republic of Germany's policy on the German expellees.

Borodziej, Włodzimierz, and Hans Lemberg, eds. *Niemcy w Polsce 1945–1950: Wybór Dokumentów.* 4 vols. Warsaw: Neriton, 2000–2. (German edition: Hans Lemberg and Włodzimierz Borodziej, eds. *Die Deutschen östlich von Oder und Neiße 1945–1950: Dokumente aus polnischen Archiven.* 4 vols. Marburg: Herder Institut, 2000–3.)

Douglas, Ray M. Orderly and. *Humane: The Expulsion of the Germans after the Second World War.* New Haven: Yale University Press, 2012.

Brandes, Detlef. *Der Weg zur Vertreibung: Pläne und Entscheidungen zum "Transfer" der Deutschen aus der Tschechoslowakei und aus Polen.* Munich: Oldenbourg, 2005 (second edition).

Snyder, Timothy. *Bloodlands: Europe between Hitler and Stalin.* New York: Basic Books, 2010.

Schieder, Theodor et alia, eds. *Dokumentation der Vertreibung der Deutschen aus Ost-Mitteleuropa.* 5 vols. Bonn: Bundesministerium für Vertriebene, Flüchtlinge und Kriegsgeschädigte, Bonn: 1953–61.

Krallert-Sattler, Gertrud. *Kommentierte Bibliographie zum Flüchtlings- und Vertriebenen problem in der Bundesrepublik Deutschland, in Österreich und in der Schweiz.* Vienna: Braumüller, 1989.

Schwartz, Michael. *Funktionäre mit Vergangenheit: Das Gründungspräsidium des Bundesverbandes der Vertriebenen und das "Dritte Reich."* Munich: Oldenbourg, 2013.

Kossert, Andreas. *Kalte Heimat: Die Geschichte der deutschen Vertriebenen nach 1945.*
    Berlin: Siedler, 2008.
Ahonen, Pertti. *After the Expulsion: West Germany and Eastern Europe 1945–1990.* New
    York: Oxford University Press, 2003.

Poland

No other European country in the twentieth century was as deeply affected by ethnic cleansing (and genocide) as Poland. The various territorial and ethnic dislocations play a major role in Włodzimierz Borodziej's
history of Poland in the twentieth century, which still awaits translation into English. During Communist rule, the forced resettlement of
the Poles from the *kresy* (the eastern Polish territories) could only be
addressed within the context of the official paradigm of "repatriation."
It took some years for this gap in research to be filled. Succeeding my
own comparative study on German and Polish expellees, an extensive
source documentation was published in 1999 by Stanisław Ciesielski
dealing with the "resettlers" from the former Polish eastern territories.
Although Polish authors before 1989 were in a better position to criti-
cally discuss the contractual resettlement, a comprehensive account of
the history of eastern Poles before and after Poland's shift westward is
yet to appear.

Ciesielski has also coedited a book on the Soviet deportations during
World War II, which includes investigations of the fate of the eastern
Poles deported to Siberia and Central Asia. The Polish historian Maria
Rutowska published a monograph on the expulsion and deportation of
Poles from the Nazi-occupied Warthegau in 2003, which was followed
by Phillip Rutherford's volume some years later. In addition, the Polish historian Piotr Madajczyk has published a European-scale survey,
which deals with nationalistically and sociopolitically motivated cleansings in parallel.

Since 1989, a wide field of research into ethnic cleansing from Poland
to Germany and Ukraine has emerged. For information on Germans, see
the documentation collection by Borodziej and Lemberg (mentioned in
the section on Germany). With respect to the expulsion, forced resettlement, and deportation of Ukrainians, Grzegorz Motyka's book provides
valuable insight, as does the two-volume source collection by Eugeniusz
Misyło. The KARTA documentation center has compiled interesting
ego-documents by Polish (and other) expellees, deportees, and forcibly
resettled persons, some of which have been published in the journal of
the same name. The journal and some of the documents are accessible
on the KARTA website (http://www.karta.org.pl/).

Borodziej, Włodzimierz. *Geschichte Polens im 20. Jahrhundert.* Munich: Beck, 2010.

Ther, Philipp. *Deutsche und polnische Vertriebene: Gesellschaft und Vertriebenenpolitik in der SBZ/DDR und in Polen 1945–1956.* Göttingen: Vandenhoeck und Ruprecht, 1998.

Ciesielski, Stanisław, ed. *Przesiedlenie ludności polskiej z kresów wschodnich do Polski 1944–1947.* Warsaw: Neriton, 1999. (German edition: Stanislaw Ciesielski, ed. *Umsiedlung der Polen aus den ehemaligen polnischen Ostgebieten nach Polen in den Jahren 1944–1947.* Marburg: Herder-Institut, 2006.)

Ciesielski, Stanisław, Grzegorz Hryciuk, and Aleksander Srebrakowski, eds., *Masowe deportacje radzieckie w okresie II wojny światowej.* Wrocław: Instytut Historyczny Uniwersytetu Wrocławskiego, 1994.

Rutowska, Maria. *Wysiedlenie ludności polskiej z Kraju Warty do Generalnego Gubernatorstwa 1939–1941.* Poznań: Instytut Zachodni, 2003.

Rutherford, Phillip T. *Prelude to the Final Solution: The Nazi Program for Deporting Ethnic Poles, 1939–1941.* Lawrence: University Press of Kansas, 2007.

KARTA. http://www.karta.org.pl/

Madajczyk, Piotr. *Czystki etniczne i klasowe w Europie w XX wieku: Szkice do problem.* Warsaw: ISP PAN, 2010.

Motyka, Grzegorz. *Tak było w Bieszczadach: Walki polsko-ukraińskie 1943–1848.* Warsaw: Oficyna Wydawnicza Volumen, 1999.

Misyło, Eugeniusz, ed. *Repatriacja czy deportacja: Przesedlenie Ukraincow z Polski do USSR 1944–1946: Dokumenty.* 2 vols. Warsaw: Oficyna Wydawnicza "Archiwum Ukrainskie," 1996–99.

Ukraine

In the first years after independence in 1991, much of the Polish and Ukrainian literature on the ethnic cleansings these countries enforced on each other was characterized by nationally biased viewpoints. Many historians dealing with the Polish-Ukrainian conflict had been adversaries and in some ways still acted as such, but the same applies to much of the national literature reviewed here. It is unrealistic to expect authors who were directly affected to approach their subject in a purely scientific and objective manner.

Later, the closer Poland and Ukraine cooperated politically, the more recognition historians promoting reconciliation, such as Grzegorz Motyka (see the section on Poland), gained. On the Ukrainian side, the Lemberg historian Iurii Slyvka edited a documentation series based on secret service documents and interviews with eyewitnesses in the early 1990s. The next entry titled *Pol'shcha ta Ukraina* [...] is a documentation based on secret service archives. Publications by a new generation of historians, including a dissertation on foreign policy aspects of ethnic cleansings (Kozlovs'kyi) and regional studies (Tkachov) are also valuable. A few years ago, a special edition of the journal *Ï* (published in L'viv) discussed current trends in the debate on the massacres in Volhynia. A 2003 anthology edited by Iaroslav Isaievych brings together articles by Ukrainian, Polish, and international authors on the same subject. Timothy Snyder offers a good English-language survey in his earlier book on Poland's relations with its eastern neighbors (see esp. 158–78). He also deals with the civil war between Poles and Ukrainians in his most recent and better-known book, *Bloodlands* (see the section on Germany).

Slyvka, Iurii, ed. *Deportatsii: Zakhidni zemli Ukrainy kintsia 30-kh—pochatku 50-kh rr: Dokumenty, materialy, spohady*. 3 vols. L'viv: NAN, 1996–2002.

Pol'shcha ta Ukraina u trydtsiatykh-sorokovykh rokakh XX stolittia:. Nevidomi dokumenty z arkhiviv spetsial'nykh sluzhb. Tom 2 (vol. 2,). *Pereselennia poliakiv ta ukraintsiv 1944–1946*. Warszawa-KyivWarsaw: Arkhiv Ministerstva vnutrishnikh sprav i administratsii Respubliky Pol'shchi; Kiev: Derzhavnyi Arkhiv Sluzhby Bezpeky Ukrainy, 2000.

Kozlovs'kyi, Ivan. *Vstanovlennia ukrains'ko-pol's'koho kordonu 1941–1951 rr.* L'viv: Kameniar, 1998.

Tkachov, Serhii. *Pol's'ko-ukrains'kyi transfer naselennia 1944–1946 rr: Vyselennia poliakiv z Ternopillia*. Ternopil: Pidruchnyky i posibnyky, 1997.

"Volyn' 1943: Borot'ba za zemliu." Special issue, *Ï: Nezalezhnii kul'turologychnyi chasopys*, no. 28 (2003). See more volumes on www.ji-magazine.lviv.ua

Isaievych, Iaroslav. *Volyn' i Kholmshchyna 1938–1947: Pol's'ko-Ukrains'ke protystoiannia ta ioho vidlunnia: Doslidzhennia, dokumenty, spohady*. L'viv: NAN, 2003.

Snyder, Timothy. *The Reconstruction of Nations: Poland, Ukraine, Lithuania, Belarus: 1569–1999*. New Haven, CT: Yale Univerity Press, 2003.

The Former Soviet Union

After the collapse of the Soviet Union, the relations between its nationalities and its policy toward them were among the most intensively researched subjects of Eastern European history. The focus was initially placed on *korenizatsiya*, that is, Soviet attempts to make communism take root in society by fostering national ambitions. Later, Stalin's U-turn on nationality policy and "Soviet ethnic cleansing" were investigated. The author most often cited in this field is Terry Martin, who has published the leading anthology on the subject (together with R. G. Suny) as well as a number of studies. The study by Peter Holquist in this anthology and a later article published in the journal *Kritika* are especially interesting for dealing with lines of continuity from the later years of the tsarist empire to the Stalinist era. The book by Antonio Ferrara and Niccolò Pianciola combines the study of imperial Russia and the Soviet Union and discusses the (dis)continuities between the two states. Otto Pohl's monograph on ethnic cleansings in the Soviet Union provides a brief overview of the many deportations and contains a lot of data and statistics, but does not go into great detail. Pavel Polian's Russian-language book on the subject has since been translated into

English. Nikolai Bugai has published several books on deported nationalities (Baltic nations, Caucasian and Crimean nations, Poles, Koreans)
in Russian, which are all worth reading. An English-language summary
of his earlier research has also been published. The individual studies
on all the larger nationalities affected by ethnic cleansing are referenced
in the main section of this book and not listed again here due to space
limitations. Since these ethnic cleansings can only be understood in the
context of Stalinist terror and the preceding class-specific cleansings,
the monograph by Jörg Baberowski on this subject provides useful information. Similar to Timothy Snyder (see the section on Germany), he
stresses the mass killing more than the mass removal of populations,
which recalls older readings such as Robert Conquest's. Norman Naimark's book (see the initial section in this chapter) provides a sound
overview of the case of the Chechens and the Crimean Tatars, which is
a useful reading assignment for BA or MA classes.

Suny, Ronald Grigor, and Terry Martin, eds. *A State of Nations: Empire and Nation Making in the Age of Lenin and Stalin*. Oxford: Oxford University Press, 2001.
Martin, Terry. "The Origins of Soviet Ethnic Cleansing." *The Journal of Modern History*
70 (1998): 813–61.
Holquist, Peter. "Violent Russia, Deadly Marxism: Russia in the Epoch of Violence."
Kritika: Explorations in Russian and Eurasian History 4, no. 3 (Summer 2003):
627–52.
Ferrara, Antonio, and Niccolò Pianciola. *L'età delle migrazioni forzate: Esodi e deporta-
zioni in Europa (1853–1953)*. Bologna: Il Mulino, 2012.
Pohl, J. Otto. *Ethnic Cleansing in the USSR, 1937–1949*. Westport, CT: Greenwood Press,
1999.
Polian, Pavel. *Against Their Will: The History and Geography of Forced Migrations in the
USSR*. Budapest: CEU Press, 2004.
Bugai, Nikolai F. *The deportation of peoples in the Soviet Union*. New York: Nova Science
Publishers, 1996.
Baberowski, Jörg. *Der rote Terror: Die Geschichte des Stalinismus*. Munich: DVA, 2003.
Conquest, Robert. *The Nation Killers: The Soviet Deportation of Nationalities*. London:
Macmillan, 1970.

The Czech Republic and Slovakia

The ethnic cleansing of co-nationals was never as prominent an issue
in the Czech Republic as in its neighboring countries because of the
comparatively low number of Czech refugees. The most extensive ethnic cleansing of Czechs occurred after the Sudetenland was annexed
by Nazi Germany. The subsequent emigration of 190,000 Czechs is
dealt with by Jan Gebhart in the above-mentioned anthology by Detlef
Brandes, Edita Ivaničková, and Jiří Pešek (see the section on compere-
hensive histories of ethnic cleansing). Some interesting local studies

such as the one by Paul Mähner are also available. After the breakup of Czechoslovakia, the ethnic cleansing of Czechs from Slovakia, which was silenced for many years, was viewed as expulsion by Valerián Bystrický. It is discussed, together with all other attempts at ethnic homogenization, in a recent dissertation on the Slovakization of Bratislava by Iris Engemann.

The delay in confronting the Czecho-Slovak conflict was partly due to the greater importance attached to the expulsion and forced resettlement of the Sudeten Germans and the strain this placed on German-Czech relations. Czech historian Tomáš Staněk has refuted the official view that the "transfer" went off in accordance with the Potsdam regulations in his studies on the course of the expulsions and the systematic abuse of migrants in labor camps (only those of his books that have been translated into German are listed here, there are more in Czech). This and the retribution against collaborators, which tended to be eclipsed by the Czech-German conflict, are discussed in an English-language publication by Benjamin Frommer. Eagle Glassheim has drawn attention to the connection between ethnic cleansing and environmental devastation. Adrian von Arburg and Tomáš Staněk have published the first parts of an eight-volume documentation collection that analyzes the ethnic cleansing and the Czech settlement of the border regions from 1945. The Slovakian-Hungarian conflict and the consequent ethnic cleansings have been analyzed by Štefan Šutaj.

Gebhart, Jan. "Migrationsbewegungen der tschechischen Bevölkerung in den Jahren 1938-39, Forschungsstand und offene Fragen." In *Erzwungene Trennung: Vertreibungen und Aussiedlungen in und aus der Tschechoslowakei 1938–1947 im Vergleich mit Polen, Ungarn und Jugoslawien*, ed. Detlef Brandes, Edita Ivaničková, and Jiří Pešek, 11–22. Essen: Klartext, 1999.

Mähner, Paul. "Gnadlersdorf (Hnanice)—ein südmährisches Dorf an der Grenze." In *Bevölkerungstransfer und Systemwandel, Ostmitteleuropäische Grenzen nach dem Zweiten Weltkrieg*, ed. Helga Schulz, 163–210. Berlin: Berliner Wissenschaftsverlag, 1998.

Bystrický, Valerián. "Vyst'ahovanie českých štátnych zaměstnancov zo Slovenska v rokoch 1938–1939." *Historický Časopis* 45 (1997): 596–611.

Engemann, Iris. *Die Slowakisierung Bratislavas 1918–1948: Der Prozess nationaler Aneignung aus institutionsgeschichtlicher Perspektive*. Wiesbaden: Harrassowitz, 2012.

Staněk, Tomáš. *Internierung und Zwangsarbeit: Das Lagersystem in den böhmischen Ländern 1945–1948*. Munich: Oldenbourg, 2007.

Staněk, Tomáš. *Verfolgung 1945: Die Stellung der Deutschen in Böhmen, Mähren und Schlesien (außerhalb der Lager und Gefängnisse)*. Vienna: Böhlau, 2002.

Frommer, Benjamin. *Retribution against Nazi Collaborators in Postwar Czechoslovakia*. Cambridge: Cambridge University Press, 2005.

Glassheim, Eagle. "Ethnic Cleansing, Communism, and Environmental Devastation in Czechoslovakia's. Borderlands, 1945-1989." *Journal of Modern History* 78 (2006): 65–92.

Arburg, Adrian von, and Tomáš Staněk, eds. *Vysídlení Němců a proměny českého pohraničí 1945–1951: Dokumenty z českých archive.* Středodukly: Susa, 2010. (A translation of these volumes into German is in progress.)

Šutaj, Štefan. *Maďarská menšina na Slovensku v rokoch 1945–1948.* Bratislava: Veda, 1993.

Šutaj, Štefan. *Nútené presídlenie Maďarov zo Slovenska do Čiech: Deportácie obyvateľstva maďarskej národnosti zo Slovenska do Čiech po druhej svetovej vojne.* Prešov: Universum, 2005.

Hungary and Romania

Holly Case's book on Transylvania and the Nazi reorganization of Europe is indispensable for understanding the conflict between Hungary and Romania over the disputed region of Transylvania. But Romanians were also affected by other population removals, which are summarized by Vladimir Solonari. Despite its nationalist leaning, Dumitru Şandru's survey of migrations in Romania in 1940–48 is a valuable source of factual information. The same is true for the collective volume edited by Sorina Bolovan et alia. Typically, Romanian and Hungarian research focuses more on the ethnic cleansings suffered by its own nation than on those it caused. Agnes Toth has well advanced the state of research on the forced resettlement of the Danube Swabians after the Potsdam Agreement and the broader context of Hungarian minority policy. The extent and nature of ethnic cleansings in northern Transylvania in the years 1941–44 is the subject of greater controversy. Ottmar Traşcă und Rudolf Gräf have published a good summarizing article and coedited a useful conference publication. Mariana Hausleitner and two more German colleagues have published an excellent volume on the deportations of Jews from Bessarabia and northern Bukovina. While the state of research on the Romanian Jews and Holocaust is relatively good today, there are still large gaps to be filled with respect to the history of the persecution of Roma. Viorel Achim is one author who has addressed both subjects; his book on Roma has also been published in English.

Case, Holly. *Between States: The Transylvanian Question and the European Idea during World War II.* Palo Alto, CA: Stanford University Press, 2009.

Solonari, Vladimir. *Purifying the Nation: Population Exchange and Ethnic Cleansing in Nazi-Allied Romania.* Baltimore: Johns Hopkins University Press, 2010.

Şandru, Dumitru. *Mişcări de populaţie în România (1940–1948).* Bucharest: Editura Enciclopedică, 2003.

Bolovan, Sorina Paula, Ioan Bolovan, Rudolf Gräf, and Corneliu Pădurean, eds. *Mişcări de populaţie şi aspecte demografice în România în prima jumătate a secolului XX: Lucrările conferinţei internaţionale "Mişcări de populaţie în Transilvania în timpul celor două războaie mondiale," Cluj-Napoca, 24–27 mai 2006.* Cluj: Presa Universitară Clujeană, 2007.

Tóth, Ágnes. *National and Ethnic Minorities in Hungary, 1920–2001.* Boulder, CO: East European Monographs, 2006.

Traşcă, Ottmar, and Rudolf Gräf. "Rumänien, Ungarn und die Minderheitenfrage zwischen Juli 1940 und August 1944." In *Zwangsmigrationen im mittleren und östlichen Europa: Völkerrecht—Konzeptionen—Praxis (1938–1950),* ed. Ralph Melville, Jiří Pešek, and Claus Scharf, 259–308. Mainz: Zabern, 2008.

Hausleitner, Mariana, Brigitte Mihok, and Juliane Wetzel, eds. *Rumänien und der Holocaust: Zu den Massenverbrechen in Transnistrien 1941–1944.* Berlin: Metropol, 2000.

Achim, Viorel. *The Roma in Romanian History.* Budapest: CEU Press, 2004.

The Former Yugoslavia

The many books on the former Yugoslavia tend to represent one of two main trends: a normative (and typically anti-Serb) school, led by Sabrina Ramet, and a school of political realism, which focuses on the balance of power in the region and the international context. The former emerged from contemporary indignation at the ethnic cleansings and uses the term genocide for the crimes against the Bosniaks as the ultimate condemnation. The literature representing the second school is more useful for analyzing the ethnic cleansings in Croatia and Bosnia and Herzegovina and their causes. The study by Burg and Shoup is a good example. Since the troubles can only be understood in the context of the collapse of the former Yugoslavia, this is also an important field to consider. Susan Woodward describes the international context, including the West's mistakes at the outbreak of the war. Political scientist Valère Gagnon's book prompted much debate. It refutes the label of "ethnic conflict" and highlights the considerable problems the Yugoslav army had mobilizing recruits, which ultimately led to the deployment of mercenaries and the further escalation of violence. A very detailed and useful military history of the conflict was published by the CIA.

There is also a strong tradition of German-language research on the former Yugoslavia. Holm Sundhaussen has written another seminal book dealing with Tito's state, the successor states of Yugoslavia, and the many conflicts and wars of the 1990s. Marie-Janine Calic's earlier book remains relevant despite being written in the immediate aftermath of the war. The handbook on the war in Yugoslavia by Dunja Melčić is another standard work on the subject. The background to Greater Serbian ideology and expansionism in the 1990s is elucidated in Holm Sundhaussen's history of Serbia. Armina Galijaš has written an excellent local study about Bosnian Serb nationalism and the persecution of minorities in Banja Luka. Alexander Korb has published a prize-winning monograph on the Ustasha and violence in wartime Croatia, a topic also dealt with by Sweden-based historian Tomislav Dulic, who refutes the myth of evil neighbors being responsible for much of the killing in his recent publications. A *Historikerstreit* has broken out over the reappraisal of the conflict in Bosnia and Herzegovina. While the state Institute for Research of Crimes Against Humanity and International Law still gives the number of murdered Bosniaks as 250,000 (see the book by Smail Čekić), the nongovernmental Istraživačko dokumentacioni centar (IDC) in Sarajevo has revised the number of fatalities, bringing it down to less than 100,000. The relevant inquiries are accessible on the website of the IDC. Caroline Leutloff-Grandits elucidates the difficulties facing returning refugees by the example of various local studies. Gerard Toal and Carl T. Dahlman also deal with attempts to reverse ethnic cleansing.

Ramet, Sabrina. *Balkan Babel: The Disintegration of Yugoslavia from the Death of Tito to the War for Kosovo.* Boulder, CO: Westview Press, 1999.

Burg, Steven L., and Paul S. Shoup. *The War in Bosnia-Hercegovina: Ethnic Conflict and International Intervention.* Armonk: M. E. Sharpe, 1999.

Woodward, Susan L. *Balkan Tragedy: Chaos and Dissolution after the Cold War.* Washington: The Brookings Institution, 1995.

Gagnon, Valère P. *The Myth of Ethnic War: Serbia and Croatia in the 1990s.* Ithaca, NY: Cornell University Press, 2004.

Balkan Battlegrounds: A Military History of the Yugoslav Conflict, 1990- 1995. Vol. 1. By the Office of Russian and European Analysis, Central Intelligence Agency. Washington: GPO, 2002.

Melčić, Dunja, ed. *Der Jugoslawien-Krieg: Handbuch zu Vorgeschichte, Verlauf und Konsequenzen.* Oplaten: Westdeutscher Verlag, 1999.

Sundhaussen, Holm. *Geschichte Serbiens: 19.–21. Jahrhundert.* Vienna: Böhlau, 2007.

Sundhaussen, Holm. *Jugoslawien und seine Nachfolgestaaten 1943–2011.* Vienna: Böhlau, 2012.

Galijaš, Armina. *Eine bosnische Stadt im Zeichen des Krieges: Ethnopolitik und Alltag in Banja Luka (1990–1995).* München: Oldenbourg, 2011.

Calic, Marie-Janine. *Krieg und Frieden in Bosnien-Herzegovina: Erweiterte Neuausgabe.* Frankfurt: Suhrkamp, 1995.

Korb, Alexander. *Im Schatten des Weltkriegs: Massengewalt der Ustaša gegen Serben, Juden und Roma in Kroatien.* Hamburg: Hamburger Editionen, 2013.

Dulic, Tomislav. "Yugoslavs in Arms: Guerrilla Tradition, Total Defence and the Ethnic Security Dilemma." *Europe-Asia Studies* 62, no. 7 (2010): 1051–72.

Istraživačko dokumentacioni centar (IDC). http://www.idc.org.ba/index.php

Čekić, Smail. *Aggression against the Republic of Bosnia and Hercegovina: Planning, preparation, execution.* 2 vols. Sarajevo: Institute for Research of Crimes Against Humanity and International Law, 2004.

Leutloff-Grandits, Caroline. *Claiming Ownership in Post-War Croatia: The Dynamics of Property Relations and Ethnic Conflict in the Knin Region.* Münster: LIT, 2006.

Toal, Gerard, and Carl T. Dahlman. *Bosnia Remade: Ethnic Cleansing and its Reversal.* New York: Oxford University Press, 2011.

Greece and Turkey

Greek literature in the field reveals a change in attitudes toward ethnic cleansing in the postwar period. While Dimitri Pentzopoulos explicitly approves of the national homogenization of Greece in his standard work that was first published in 1962, more recent authors emphasize the negative consequences of ethnic cleansing. This change was prompted in part by Renée Hirschon's study, which described the humanitarian disaster resulting from the reception of refugees from Asia Minor, took a skeptical view of integration, and highlighted the instability of Greek society after 1922. Elisabeth Kontogiorgi has shown how the refugees from Asia Minor were used to consolidate the border in northern Greece, antagonizing the local Bulgarian minority. Michaēlidēs's study, which is unfortunately only available in Greek, deals with this minority and state nationality policy in greater detail.

Turkish historians have also taken new paths in recent years. Onur Yıldırım has published a basic reference work on the Treaty of Lausanne and the positions of the participatory states. Netherlands-based author Uğur Ümit Üngör has investigated the founding of the nation-state and Turkish nationality policy in eastern Anatolia. His book considers Armenian Kurds, Arabs, and Aramaeans as well as the titular nation. Alexander Toumarkine provides a useful overview of the Muslims' ousting from the Balkans between 1876 and 1913. For a long durée account of violence and homogenization in Southeastern Europe, see the book by Marc Biondich. A recent edited volume is specifically dedicated to the Balkan Wars and their consequences. With respect to the Caucasus, Fikret Adanir and Bernd Bonwetsch have shown how productive the cooperation between historians specializing in Eastern Europe and experts on the Ottoman Empire can be.

Pentzopoulos, Dimitri. *The Balkan Exchange of Minorities and its Impact upon Greece.* London: Hurst, 2002 (second edition).

Hirschon, Renée. *Heirs of the Greek Catastrophe: The Social Life of Asia Minor Refugees in Piraeus.* Oxford: Clarendon Press, 1989.

Kontogiorgi, Elisabeth. *Population Exchange in Greek Macedonia: The Rural Settlement of Refugees, 1922–1930.* New York: Oxford University Press, 2006.

Michaēlidēs, Iakōbos. *Metakinēsis Slavophōnōn Plēthysmōn (1912–1930): O polemos tōn Statistikōn.* Athens: *Kentro Ereynōn Meionotikōn Omadōn,* 2003.

Yıldırım, Onur. *Diplomacy and Displacement: Reconsidering the Turco-Greek Exchange of Populations, 1922–1934.* New York: Routledge, 2006.

Üngör, Uğur Ümit. *The Making of Modern Turkey: Nation and State in Eastern Anatolia, 1913–50.* New York: Oxford University Press, 2011.

Toumarkine, Alexandre. *Les migrations des populations musulmanes balkaniques en Anatolie 1876–1913.* Istanbul: Isis, 1995.

Biondich, Mark. *The Balkans: Revolution, War, and Political Violence since 1878.* Oxford: Oxford University Press, 2011.

Blumi, Isa, Hakan Yavuz and Edward J. Erickson, eds. *War and Nationalism: The Balkan Wars, 1912-1913, and Their Sociopolitical Implications.* Utah: University of Utah Press, 2013.

Adanır, Fikret, and Bernd Bonwetsch, eds. *Osmanismus, Nationalismus und der Kaukasus.* Wiesbaden: Reichert, 2005.

Britain, France, and Italy

Superficially, it may seem absurd to include the former two countries in this bibliography, since ethnic cleansings were not implemented at all in Britain and only for a limited time in France, in Alsace and Lorraine. But recent English-language research has provided impressive evidence of the crucial consensus on mass population shifts in British politics and the British public. Matthew Frank's book is an indispensable contribution to the subject of ethnic cleansing precisely for this reason. The introductory section deals with the British position after World War I and various conflicts in Southeastern Europe, East Central Europe, and Palestine in the late 1930s. The empirical main section analyzes the planning of population transfers during World War II, the increasing doubts about the practice in view of the refugee crisis in occupied Germany, and the beginnings of human rights policy.

A comparable book on France has not yet appeared, although the country was also a major international actor with respect to ethnic cleansing. Most of the research on the *triage* (selection) and expulsion of about 150,000 German nationals from Alsace and Lorraine was conducted by historians outside France. Christiane Kohser-Spohn's inquiry is especially impressive; David Allen Harvey has published an article in English. The mechanisms of forgetting after World War II have been less researched here, as in Germany. French research on ethnic cleansing and genocide on a theoretical level (Rosière [see the section on comprehensive literature], Semelin) is, in contrast, very advanced.

On Italy, Swiss-based historian Marina Cattaruzza has conducted key research and published a standard reference work on the eastern Italian border and all the conflicts and population movements related to it. Several regional studies are available on Trieste; the two books by Piero Purini and Raul Pupo are listed here.

Frank, Matthew. *Expelling the Germans: British Opinion and Post-1945 Population Transfer in Context.* Oxford: Oxford University Press, 2007.
Kohser-Spohn, Christiane. "Staatliche Gewalt und der Zwang zur Eindeutigkeit: Die Politik Frankreichs in Elsass-Lothringen nach dem Ersten Weltkrieg." In *Nationalitätenkonflikte im 20. Jahrhundert: Ursachen von inter-ethnischer Gewalt im Vergleich,* ed. Philipp Ther and Holm Sundhaussen, 183–202. Wiesbaden: Harrassowitz, 2001.
Kohser-Spohn, Christiane. "Die Vertreibung der 'Altdeutschen' aus dem Elsass 1918–1920." In *Die "Volksdeutschen" in Polen, Frankreich, Ungarn und der Tschechoslowakei: Mythos und Realität,* ed. Jerzy Kochanowski and Maike Sach, 79–94. Osnabrück: Fibre, 2006.
Harvey, David Allen. "Lost Children or Enemy Aliens? Classifying the Population of Alsace after the First World War." *Journal of Contemporary History* 34 (1999): 537–54.
Semelin, Jaques. *Purifier et détruire: Usages politiques des massacres et genocides.* Paris: Le Seuil, 2005.
Cattaruzza, Marina. *L'Italia e il confine orientale 1866–2006.* Bologna: Mulino, 2007.

Pupo, Raul. *Il lungo esodo: Istria: Le persecuzioni, le foibe, l´esilio.* Milano: Rizzoli 2005.
Purini, Piero. *Metamorfosi etniche: I cambiamenti di populazione a Trieste, Gorizia, Fiume e in Istria: 1914–1975.* Udine: Kappa Vu, 2010.

Global Perspectives: India and Palestine

In India and Pakistan, explaining the traumatic partition of the subcontinent took precedence over addressing the ethnic cleansing it involved for many years. Now, the *Partition Omnibus* compendium, containing the major works of the postwar era on this issue, provides valuable information on the prehistory of partition and the violence it unleashed. US historian Stanley Wolpert deals with the escalation of violence, emphasizing the destructive role of the British colonial power and especially the last viceroy, Mountbatten. Ian Talbot has analyzed the ethnic cleansings in various regions of India and their causes, providing a showcase of the usefulness of historical comparisons in the process. Ian Copland's study on the local dynamics of violence is another instructive work. Since the late 1990s, a trend toward ego-documents and memory research focusing on gender aspects has emerged in India, represented here by Urwashi Butalia.

In the late 1980s, the "new history" movement in Israel began investigating the violence against the civilian Palestinian population in 1947–49, thereby deconstructing the heroic, defensive image of the state's founding. In 2004–5, disagreement broke out among the protagonists of the "new history" movement, giving rise to interestingly divergent approaches to this field of history. While Benny Morris attempts to explain—and thus ex post facto rationalize—the military principles behind the violent actions against the civilian Arab population in 1948–49, Ilan Pappé interprets the same events as a morally deplorable case of ethnic cleansing. Although the apologetic undertone of Benny Morris's book may irritate some readers, in terms of source research it is the more accomplished. A recent local study on Haifa by Yfaat Weiss addresses not only local processes of ethnic cleansing but also their long-term effects on the urban spaces and culture in the former Arab quarter and local tensions within Israeli society.

Hasan, Mushirul, ed. *The Partition Omnibus.* New Delhi: Oxford University Press, 2002.
Wolpert, Stanley. *Shameful Flight: The Last Years of the British Empire in India.* New York: Oxford University Press, 2006.
Talbot, Ian. "The 1947 Partition of India and Migration: A Comparative Study of Punjab and Bengal." In *Removing Peoples: Forced Removal in the Modern World,* ed. Richard Bessel and Claudia B. Haake, 321–48. Oxford: Oxford University Press, 2009.
Copland, Ian. "The Further Shores of Partition: Ethnic Cleansing in Rajasthan 1947." *Past and Present* 160 (August 1998): 203–39.
Butalia, Urwashi. *The Other Side of Silence: Voices from the Partition of India.* New Delhi: Penguin, 1998.

Morris, Benny. *1948: A History of the First Arab-Israeli War.* New Haven, CT: Yale University Press, 2008.

Ilan Pappé. *The Ethnic Cleansing of Palestine.* Oxford: Oneworld, 2006.

Weiss, Yfaat. *A Confiscated Memory: Wadi Salib and Haifa's Lost Heritage.* New York: Columbia University Press, 2011.

INDEX